THE RISE OF
ATHENS

THE RISE OF
ATHENS

---

*The Story of the
World's Greatest Civilization*

ANTHONY EVERITT

RANDOM HOUSE
New York

Illustration Credits: "Athens Acropolis/Reconstruction": akg-images/Peter Connolly;
"Achilles and Patroclus," "Plato," "Hetairas": Bibi Saint Pol; "Parthenon," "Athena
Relief": Harrieta 171; "Athena Parthenos": Dean Dixon; "Themistocles," "Foundry":
Sailko; "Pericles," "Athenian Hoplite," "Discus Thrower": Marie-Lan Nguyen;
"Demosthenes": Gunnar Bach Pedersen; "Greek and Persian Soldiers": Alexikoua;
"Helmet of Miltiades": William Neuheisel; "Lion of Chaeronea": Philipp Pilhofer;
"Socrates": Yair Haklkai; "Aristotle," "Sacrificed Boar," "Symposium": Jastrow;
"Baby and Mother": Marsyas.

LIBRARY OF CONGRESS CATALOGING-IN-PUBLICATION DATA
Names: Everitt, Anthony, author.
Title: The rise of Athens: the story of the world's greatest civilization /
Anthony Everitt.
Description: First edition. | New York: Random House, 2016. |
Includes bibliographical references and index.
Identifiers: LCCN 2016014843| ISBN 9780812984989 |
ISBN 9780812994599 (ebook)
Subjects: LCSH: Athens (Greece)—History.
Classification: LCC DF285 .E94 2016 | DDC 938/.5—dc23
LC record available at https://lccn.loc.gov/2016014843

Printed in the United States of America on acid-free paper

randomhousebooks.com

2 4 6 8 9 7 5 3 1

For John Brunel Cohen,
my ever-loyal stepfather

—from Salamis to D-Day—

PREFACE

As a small child I devoured a Victorian storybook that told tales of Greek and Roman mythology. I read every word, except for the sickly sweet poems that were scattered across its pages.

My paternal grandmother noticed my interest in the ancient world and bought me three Penguin Classics, then a new publishing enterprise. She chose E. V. Rieu's versions of Homer's *Iliad* and *Odyssey* and a translation of Plato's *Symposium*. A farmer's wife, she was no classicist, and the last of these books came a little early for a prepubertal child, who was mystified by the references to Hellenic homosexuality. But I could not have been given a better sense, smell, flavor, of Greek civilization. Homer and Plato introduced me to a world that was new and ravishing, which, for all the tragedy and the bloodshed, radiated the sunlight and luminous skies of free thought.

For a span of two hundred years in the fifth and fourth centuries B.C., the ancient Athenians pioneered astonishing advances in almost every field of human endeavor. They invented the only real or complete democracy (the word itself is Greek) that has ever existed outside the classical age. Whereas we merely elect representatives to act on our behalf, citizens then met in assembly and took every important decision themselves. (I need to enter a reservation here: the franchise was limited to adult males and so excluded two large social groups—women and slaves.)

The Athenians believed in reason, and its power to solve the mysteries of the human condition and of nature. They established the concepts and language of philosophy, and raised issues with which today's thinkers still wrestle. They pioneered the arts of tragedy and comedy, architecture and sculpture. They invented history as the accurate narration and interpretation of past events. With their fellow-Greeks they developed mathematics and the natural sciences.

We must beware of exaggeration. The Athenians were part of a general Hellenic advance and borrowed ideas and technologies from their non-Greek neighbors—for example, the Egyptians and the Persians—in spite of their vaunted scorn for "barbarians." If only we knew as much about other societies in and around the Eastern Mediterranean in classical times as we do about them, they might not look to be quite so exceptional. We would probably have to make a lesser claim.

Nevertheless, even if the Athenians were not unique, that takes nothing away from the fact of what they did achieve. The greatness of Socrates will not be compromised by the discovery of a mute, inglorious counterpart.

Although Athenians were indeed rationalists, they were also deeply religious. Worship of the Olympian gods was integrated into every corner of daily life. Most of them believed these anthropomorphic divinities to be players in the great game of history quite as much as human beings.

We in the West complacently note that a fully independent Athenian democracy lasted only two hundred years or so. It is well to remember that our own democracies, in their complete form, have yet to last that long.

The mechanics of the Athenian democratic system are relevant to today's electronic world: the arrival of the computer means that should we so wish we could move back from representative to direct democracy. As in the heyday of classical Athens the people would genuinely be able to take all important decisions. Each citizen would, in effect, be a member of the government. Are we brave enough to take such a rational step?

For all the wonders of ancient Athens, or rather because of them, I faced a fundamental question. How was it that this tiny community of 200,000 souls or so (in other words, no more populous than, say, York in England or Little Rock in Arkansas) managed to give birth to towering geniuses across the range of human endeavor and to create one of the greatest civilizations in history? Indeed, it laid the foundations of our own contemporary intellectual universe.

In my account of the city's rise and fall I seek to answer this question—or at least to point towards an answer.

If we were able to travel back more than two millennia and walk the streets and alleys of ancient Athens, we might very well come across the master playwrights Aeschylus, Sophocles, and Euripides; the sculptor Pheidias; the comedian Aristophanes; and the bad boy of Athenian politics, Alcibiades. Perhaps we overhear a class in ethics that Socrates is giving in a shoe shop on the edge of the *agora* and meet two of his students, Plato and Xenophon. At a citizens' assembly we listen to a speech by that greatest of statesmen, Pericles.

This is the Athens I evoke, beginning with its early centuries of kings, tyrants, and aristocrats, moving on to the invention of democracy and the city's political and cultural heyday, and concluding with its decline into a pleasant "university town."

The story is much less well known than that of Rome, but it had just as great an influence on posterity, on today's Western civilization, in a word, on us. The Athenians laid the foundations of the house in which we live today. We ought to remember and celebrate what they built. And what a story it is—crammed with adventure and astounding reversals of fortune.

On the game board of Eastern Mediterranean politics from the sixth to the fourth century B.C., there were three main players.

The first of these was Athens. It was a maritime rather than a land power and encouraged trade throughout the known world. Its fleets came to dominate the Aegean Sea. Its citizens bought and sold goods and services, were devoted to culture and the arts, and were inquisitive and open-minded.

Sparta was different in every way, one of the strangest societies in the history of the world. A city-state in the Peloponnese, the peninsula that makes up southern Greece, it was highly disciplined and dedicated to warfare. It was widely recognized as the leading Greek power. Male citizens lived collectively and spent much of their lives in communal messes. Called Spartiates or (to deny them their individuality) Equals, they were forbidden to farm or trade, and were brought up to be professional soldiers. They conquered much of the Peloponnese and enslaved its population as serfs, or *helots*. These *helots* served their masters by working their estates for them; they were regularly humiliated and could be put to death at will.

Young Spartiates were trained brutally to be brutal. The aim was to turn them into pitiless fighters, to abjure personal wealth, and to be silent, modest, and polite. Theirs was a self-sufficient community—closed, dour, and totalitarian—with little interest in the outside world.

The third player was the vast Persian Empire on the far side of the Aegean Sea. In the mid-sixth century an Iranian nobleman, Cyrus the Great, conquered and annexed all the great kingdoms of the Middle East. Ultimately Cyrus's domains stretched from the Balkans to the Indus, from Central Asia to Egypt. He was an absolute monarch.

The prosperous Greek cities along the littoral of Asia Minor fell under his sway. This was a standing insult to the entire Greek world, which saw foreigners as barbarians—that is, *barbaroi* or people who make noises sounding like "bar bar" instead of speaking proper Greek. Here the tectonic rock layers of two cultures met and ground against each other.

Conflict was inevitable. As in a complicated ballet, these dancers would entwine their bodies, exchanging friends and enemies, moving in turn from war to peace and to war again.

The three great powers enjoyed golden zeniths, but all three ended up facing defeat and disaster. Their progress conveys all the thrills of a historical roller-coaster ride.

I write narrative history. I never reveal future outcomes or endings during the telling, for I want readers to have no better idea of what is to happen next than those who lived through the events I describe. If they are unfamiliar with ancient history, they are in for a lively time.

Some of the stories in the ancient sources have a suspiciously fictional ring, or so picky scholars claim. Solon's encounter with King Croesus of Lydia (see page 69) is a good example. We cannot always say at this distance of time whether they are true or false. But, like the myths and legends, they are good stories and even if some of them have been embellished they cast a bright light on how Greeks saw themselves. So I happily retell them.

I do my best to sketch the Athenian record in the fields of philosophy and the arts, but a sketch is all I have space for. Aeschylus, Sophocles, and Euripides are represented by masterpieces, including *The Oresteia, Antigone,* and *The Trojan Women,* and the ideas of Plato and Aristotle are only adumbrated. *Lysistrata* speaks up for Aristophanes. But I hope to have done enough to illustrate their greatness.

Ancient historians are very variable in quality, with part of the fifth century being much more fully covered than the fourth. The work of many writers has been wholly or partly lost thanks to the corrosive passage of time. Thucydides is the greatest writer of history in history. In fact, he is so good that we are trapped inside his version of events. Lesser authors give themselves away, offer some purchase for the modern scholar, and allow corrections and new interpretations. What Thucydides does not write about is an empty space that usually we cannot fill, and what he does write about is usually irrefutable.

There are topics that even the finest chroniclers, such as Thucydides, do not touch except tangentially—for example, economics and social life. Also we know far more about Athens than any other of the many city-states and their Mediterranean colonies that made up ancient

Greece. One way or another, we have less to say than we would like about wider developments.

There are many matters on which today's experts disagree. In general, I touch on their debates only in the Endnotes and leave the main narrative clean of scholarly controversy.

How should I spell the names of people and places? In Western Europe we were first introduced to the literature and history of ancient Greece via the Romans and their language, Latin. The convention was established of using Latinate spelling for Hellenic proper nouns. It was only in the Renaissance that most Europeans came into direct contact with Greek as a language, and by then the practice was too ingrained to change.

So most of us speak of Achilles and not Achilleus, Alcibiades and not Alkibiades, Plato and not Platon. I have decided to keep to these Roman forms because of their familiarity; readers would be puzzled and daunted by a strictly accurate transliteration from the Greek to the European alphabet. A few esoteric technical terms are exempted from this rule.

Also some very famous names have anglicized versions that most people use and I prefer—for example, Athens to Athenai (Greek) or Athenae (Latin), Corinth (English) to Korinthos (Greek) or Corinthus (Latin), and Sparta (Latin) to Sparte (Greek). I borrow the Greco-Latin versions of foreign and mostly Persian names: so I refer to Astyages, the Median king, rather than Ishtumegu. Lesser-known places in the Greek world take their original form. In sum, every rule has an exception and I have followed my taste.

In proper names ending with "e," the "e" is pronounced in the English way as "ee" (in Greek it would be "ay" as in hay); and in those ending with "es" as "ees."

It is hard to be precise about the value of money, because the relative worth of different products varies from time to time and from economy to economy. The principal units of the Athenian currency were

6 obols	=	1 drachma
100 drachmas	=	1 mina
60 minas	=	1 talent

One drachma was a day's pay for a foot soldier or a skilled worker in the fifth and fourth centuries. From 425 B.C. a juror received from the state a daily allowance of half a drachma or three obols, just enough to maintain a family of three at a basic level of subsistence. So the payment was adequate rather than extravagant. A talent was a unit of weight and equaled twenty-six kilograms; it also signified the monetary value of twenty-six kilograms of silver. The two hundred rowers who crewed a trireme during the Peloponnesian War were paid a talent for one month's worth of work.

An obol was a small silver coin. It was placed in a dead man's mouth so that he had the wherewithal to pay the ferryman Charon for passage across the river Acheron to the underworld.

I omit the term B.C. (or A.D.) with dates except in the rare cases where there might otherwise be a misunderstanding.

In many respects we can recognize the people of Athens; this is no great surprise, for they pioneered so many of the fields of knowledge that are current and alive today. But in so many ways they inhabited a different moral and technological universe. Their motto was "know yourself"; they simply would not have understood the Christian command to "love your neighbor as yourself."

If I have helped to bridge the gap between ourselves and our Hellenic forebears and conveyed a little of my enthusiasm for the founders of our civilization, I shall be well pleased.

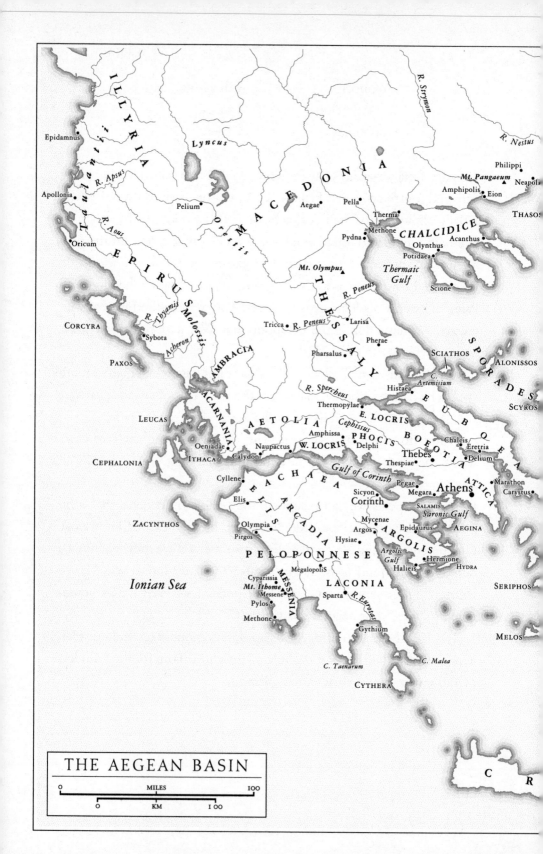

ILLYRIA

Epidamnus

Lyncus

Apollonia

R. Apsus

Pelium

Oricum

R. Aous

EPIRUS

MACEDONIA

Aegae

Pella

Therma

Methone

Pydna

Mt. Olympus

R. Peneus

THESSALY

Tricca

R. Peneus

Larisa

Pherae

Pharsalus

R. Spercheus

Thermopylae

E. LOCRIS

Histaea

Artemisium

Amphissa

Cephissus

PHOCIS

Delphi

BOEOTIA

Chalcis

Eretria

W. LOCRIS

Thebes

Delium

Thespiae

AETOLIA

Naupactus

Oeniadae

Calydon

Gulf of Corinth

Pegae

Megara

Athens

Marathon

ITHACA

Cyllene

ACHAEA

Sicyon

Corinth

SALAMIS

Saronic Gulf

Carystus

Elis

ELIS

ARCADIA

Mycenae

Epidaurus

AEGINA

Olympia

Hysiae

Argos

ARGOLIS

Pirgos

PELOPONNESE

Megalopolis

Argolic Gulf

Hermione

HYDRA

Cyparissia

MESSENIA

Haliels

Mt. Ithome

Messene

LACONIA

SERIPHOS

Pylos

Sparta

R. Eurotas

Methone

Gythium

MELOS

Ionian Sea

C. Taenarum

C. Malea

CYTHERA

CORCYRA

Sybota

Acheron

AMBRACIA

ACARNANIA

PAXOS

LEUCAS

CEPHALONIA

ZACYNTHOS

Molossis

R. Thyamis

Orestis

Taulantii

Philippi

Mt. Pangaeum

Neapoli

Amphipolis

Eion

R. Strymon

R. Nestus

THASOS

CHALCIDICE

Olynthus

Acanthus

Potidaea

Thermaic
Gulf

Scione

SCIATHOS

SPORADES

ALONISSOS

SCYROS

EUBOEA

THE AEGEAN BASIN

| 0 | | MILES | | 100 |

| 0 | | KM | | 100 |

C

R

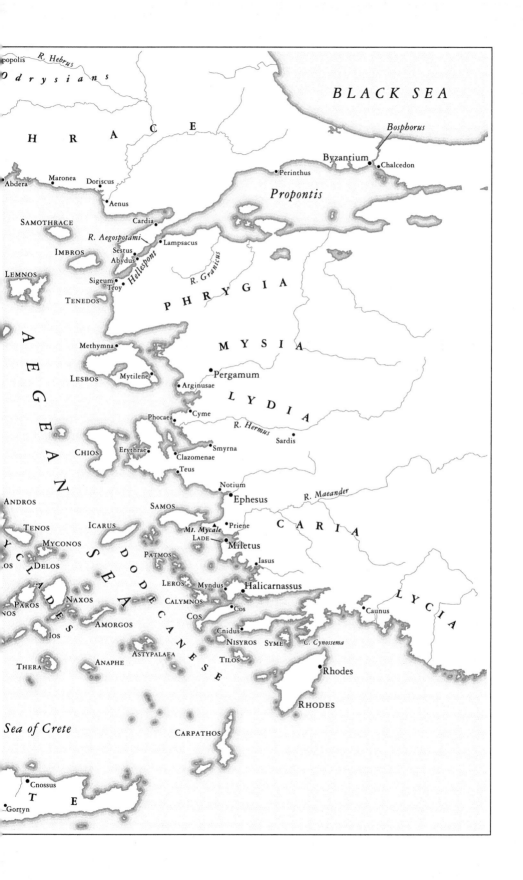

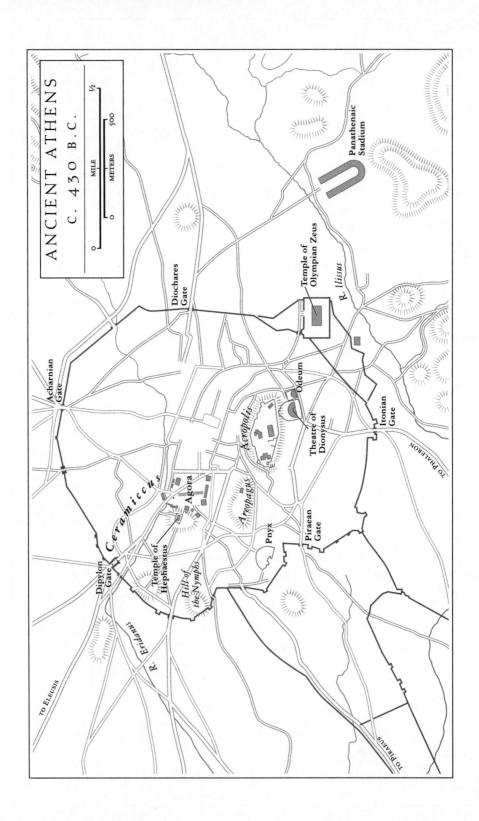

ANCIENT ATHENS
C. 430 B.C.

MILE   ½
0
METERS   500
0

Panathenaic
Stadium

Diochares
Gate

Temple of
Olympian Zeus

R. Ilissus

Acharnian
Gate

Odeum

Acropolis

Ironian
Gate

Theatre of
Dionysus

TO PHALERON

Ceramiccus

Agora

Areopagus

Pnyx

Piraean
Gate

Dipylon
Gate

Temple of
Hephaestus

Hill of
the Nymphs

R. Eridanus

TO ELEUSIS

TO PIRAEUS

CONTENTS

LIST OF MAPS

INTRODUCTION

The young king from foreign and uncivilized Macedon forced the great city of Athens into submission and enslaved the whole of Hellas, together with its quarrelsome horde of city-states. This was not because he seriously disliked the Greeks. Far from it. He was deeply impressed by their military and cultural achievements. In fact, he longed to be accepted as a full and complete member of the Hellenic club.

He was Alexander the Great, son of Philip, and it was the year 334.

But what was the nature of Greekness and how did one get hold of it? The simplest way of answering the question was to study and digest the epic poem the *Iliad*. Set in a remote past, it concerned the ten-year siege of Troy, a city in Phrygia, by a Greek army.

Every Athenian, indeed every Greek, boy learned of heroes such as Achilles and Agamemnon, Hector and Odysseus, who fought in the war, and did his best to emulate them. Their deeds embodied Greekness. Alexander cast himself as the new Achilles, as the bravest Hellene of them all.

He first encountered the *Iliad* as a child and it guided his life. He took a copy with him on his travels and when a finely made casket was presented to him that had previously belonged to the Persian Great King he asked his friends what precious object he should keep inside it. All kinds of suggestions were made, but Alexander said firmly that he would deposit his *Iliad* there for safekeeping and for splendor.

Hellenes at home will have laughed at the royal upstart's pretensions, but they were just as deeply indebted as Alexander was to the world that Homer conjured to life. It was here that they found their moral, personal, social, and political attitudes.

In fact, it was a lost world, even when the *Iliad* was composed sometime towards the end of the eighth century. The poem was a long written text, but inspired by compositions learned by heart and spoken or sung at important social occasions. Homer may or may not have existed, we simply don't know. He could have been one man, a collective, or even a woman. But anyone reading the poem will feel that he has been in the presence of a controlling mind, whatever its name and nature. (Its companion piece, the *Odyssey,* which describes the adventures of Odysseus, king of a small island off western Greece, and his ten-year journey home from Troy, may have been another author's work.)

Did the Trojan War take place? We do not know. But if it or something like it *was* a historical event, it can be dated towards the end of the second millennium B.C. This marked the high point of a Bronze Age civilization that dominated Greece and the Eastern Mediterranean. We call it Mycenaean after its main city Mycenae in the northeastern Peloponnese. It was its kings and warriors who sailed across the Aegean Sea and sacked Troy.

Not many years after this victory mysterious invaders put a violent end to the Mycenean civilization. It is uncertain who they were, but they ushered in a poorly understood period that modern scholars have called a Dark Age. Centuries of economic and social collapse followed. This meant that Homer was evoking a way of life only dimly remembered. The *Iliad* and the *Odyssey* are fictions, but in one crucial sense they embody an essential historical truth, in that they showed many generations of Greeks who they were and what values to live by.

Homer exercised an almost biblical authority. Here, in brief, is the story that he tells.

The siege of Troy lasted for a decade, but the events in the *Iliad* cover only a period of fifty-four days in the ninth year and most of the action takes place within four full days. But this close shot captures the glory and the tragedy of slaughter that seems to have no end.

Warfare in Homer is, in essence, a succession of duels between princes and kings; they ride in chariots and throw spears at their opponents. The common people mill about in the background. Achilles, a handsome, lordly, and invincible fighter, occupies the heart of the story. He is by far the best soldier among the Greeks, but he has a terrible temper. He falls out with his commander-in-chief, King Agamemnon of Mycenae, over two pretty girls. The first is Chryseis, the daughter of a local priest dedicated to the archer god Apollo, in appearance a handsome youth eternally in his late teens. Captured by the Greeks on a raid, she is donated as human booty to Agamemnon. Her father complains to the god and pleads for redress.

Then a plague strikes the expeditionary force. The soldiers are crowded into huts on a beach not far from the city of Troy a few miles inland. Their ships are drawn up on the sand beside them. Many die. A soothsayer announces that the epidemic is the god's punishment for Chryseis's capture and advises that she be returned to her father at once.

The Hellenic universe was very different from our own. Homer's men and women live simultaneously in what could be called parallel universes. In one of them things are as they seem. A plague is a plague. But in the second the gods are in charge. On this occasion Apollo comes down in fury on the camp. His arrows clanged in their quiver.

"His descent was like nightfall," says the poet. "He sat down opposite the ships and shot an arrow, with a dreadful twang from his silver bow. He attacked the mules and the nimble dogs. Then he aimed sharp arrows at the men, and struck again and again. Day and night innumerable fires consumed the dead."

So through one door of perception an event has a rational explanation, through another, supernatural. The Greeks believed that both are true at one and the same time.

. . .

The chief deities in the Hellenic pantheon are a squabbling family of anthropomorphic immortals. They live in a palace on the peak of Mount Olympus in northern Greece. They enjoy tricks and practical jokes and their "unquenchable laughter" echoes around the mountaintops. Their loves and hates make an entertaining soap opera, but, as we have seen, they are not funny at all when they turn their attention to human beings.

Head of the family is Zeus, the Thunderer and Cloud Compeller— and a henpecked husband. His wife, Hera, is always plotting to obstruct his plans. Then there is the warrior Athena, protectress of Athens. She is the goddess of wisdom and patron of the arts and crafts. She calls her father "an obstinate old sinner, always interfering with my plans." Both goddesses loathe the Trojans and work tirelessly for their downfall.

This is because they and the goddess of love, Aphrodite, competed long ago for a golden apple, which was to be awarded to the most beautiful of the three. A young Trojan prince, Paris, was the judge and he gave the prize to Aphrodite. If he chose her, she promised him the most beautiful woman in the world for his paramour.

Her name is Helen and, inconveniently, she is already spoken for. She is the wife of King Menelaus of Sparta in southern Greece. Paris pays her a visit and they elope to Troy. It is this offense that sets off the war.

These gods are not models of virtue and do not expect invariable virtue from their worshippers; rather, each of them stands for emotions or principles or skills that reflect and magnify those of human beings.

The Greeks were deeply religious, not so much to learn the rules of morality as to keep on the good side of the gods and to find out what their intentions were. They achieved this by sacrificing animals in their honor and reading their entrails, and by consulting soothsayers, prophecy books, and oracles before any important decision was taken. They held festivals and conducted ceremonies in their honor. They peppered the countryside with temples, shrines, groves, and sacred caves in honor of one deity or another. They did not trouble themselves over theological dogma. Religion was about ritual rather than belief.

Agamemnon calls a general assembly of the army and his fellow-kings and princes. He agrees to return Chryseis to her father and Apollo stops shooting. The plague ends. The king then makes a bad mistake. To make up his loss, he confiscates Briseis, another attractive female captive, who has been allocated to Achilles. Enraged, the warrior withdraws from the war and sulks in his hut.

He broods over his fate. At his birth destiny gave him the alternatives of a short but glorious life on the field of battle or a long but undistinguished one at home. It is no choice. Since his birth, his mother, a sea goddess called Thetis, has tried every trick to save him from an early death. When he was a boy, she dressed him in girl's clothes and had him brought up among girls. But the unexpected pregnancy of a fellow-pupil revealed his true gender.

Like most Greeks, the adult Achilles recognizes the brevity of life and, while he believes that death is not the end, has few hopes of happiness in the underworld where the spirits of human beings pass a dim and futile eternity.

On his long return journey home after the war is over, the crafty Odysseus is given the rare privilege of visiting the underworld while still alive. He encounters the ghost of Achilles, who is as angry as he used to be in the light of the sun. He complains about the afterlife:

> Put me on earth again, and I would rather be a serf in the house of some landless man, with little enough for himself to live on, than king of all these dead men that have done with life. But enough.

A few years earlier, as the still-living Achilles sits idly on the beach in front of Troy, he is aware of what lies in store for him. He is supremely competitive, a characteristic he shares with future generations of Greeks who will be as contentious as he is. Homer expresses the general attitude concisely, when he puts these words in the mouth of a warrior: "Let your motto be, *I lead*. Strive to be best." However, for the time being Achilles is letting his aggression rust.

The Trojans, led by Prince Hector, the king of Troy's eldest son and their match for Achilles, begin to gain the upper hand in battles on the plain that lies between the city and the sea. The Greeks (or Achaeans, as they were called in the poem) build a great defensive wall to protect their ships and the encampment on the beach. Homer describes the fighting in great, gory detail. He achieves two simultaneous and contradictory effects. War is glorious and, at the same time, a great evil.

A ferocious Greek warrior called Aias runs amok. Homer, who has a wonderful talent for comparing the high deeds of kings and princes to the low experiences of ordinary life, compares Aias to a "donkey who gets the better of the boys in charge of him; he turns into a field they are passing and helps himself to the standing crop." He adds that the animal pays no attention to the sticks that are broken on his back until he has eaten his fill.

In another telling image, the goddess Athena implants in the breast of King Menelaus "the daring of a fly, which is so fond of human blood that it returns to the attack however often a man may brush it from his face."

But for every winner in war there is a loser. The poet gives each of the unnumbered fallen a touching epitaph. To select one killing from many, an archer fires an arrow into the chest of a young Trojan. In a moving, pitch-perfect simile, Homer writes: "Weighed down by his helmet, Gorgythion's head dropped to one side, like the lolling head of a garden poppy, weighed down by its seed and the showers of spring."

Zeus sits on a nearby mountaintop, thundering balefully and sending down flashes of lightning, as he surveys the scene. He never shifts his "bright eyes" from the fighting.

. . .

Things are looking so bad for the Greeks that Patroclus, who is Achilles' best friend (and, according to some, older lover), begs him to let him join the fighting and save the day. Achilles reluctantly agrees and lends Patroclus his famous armor.

There is something almost psychopathic in the nature of Achilles. Talking with his friend, he imagines them alone, alive and triumphant over all the world. "How happy I should be if not a single Trojan got away alive, not one, and not a Greek either; and if we two survived the massacre how happy I would be to pull down Troy's holy diadem of towers single-handed!"

When Patroclus enters the battle everyone mistakes him for Achilles, because of the armor he is wearing. He dispatches many of the enemy, but he does not know when to stop. He comes up against Hector, a better fighter, who kills him and strips him of Achilles' armor. After a fierce struggle, the Greeks rescue his corpse.

Achilles is devastated. Heroes in Homer express their feelings, and he cannot stop crying. One night he dreams of Patroclus and holds out his arms to embrace him. In vain. The vision

> vanished like a wisp of smoke and went gibbering underground.
> Achilles leapt up in amazement. He beat his hands together and
> in his desolation cried: "Ah then, it is true that something of us
> does survive . . . but with no intellect at all, only the ghost and
> semblance of a man."

Determined on revenge, Achilles makes up his quarrel with Agamemnon and goes out once more to fight the Trojans. He chases after Hector, who loses his nerve and runs away. Eventually the breathless Trojan halts and faces his unforgiving foe.

The gods watch in silence. Zeus confesses to a fondness for Hector and asks the others to agree to spare his life. "What are you saying?" Athena bursts out, adding that his doom has long been settled. "But do as you please. Only don't expect the rest of us to applaud." Zeus yields the point.

Achilles dispatches Hector. He then maltreats his body, which he intends to throw to his dogs. But a proper burial is an essential passport to the underworld and after military defeats Greeks invariably negotiate burial rights for their fallen.

Zeus insists on dignity for the dead man. He has a message sent to the brutal victor: Hector is to be given his full funeral rites. The old king of Troy, Priam, secretly travels across the windy plain and presents himself to Achilles, to whom he offers rich presents. For once the Greek warrior behaves nobly. He recognizes Priam's grief for his son as being of the same depth and character as his own father's love and misery for himself, seeing that he will not return home for burial.

The two mourners share supper. This is important, for it signifies that Achilles has recognized Priam as his guest, a sacrosanct relationship sealed with gifts. In return for those he brought, the king has received Hector's body. They weep together in shared grief. Achilles says: "We men are wretched things, and the gods, who have no cares themselves, have woven sorrow into the very pattern of our lives." Alongside their ruthless rivalries, their sociopathically sunny egoism, Greeks understand very well the tragedy of the human condition. Life is ephemeral and filled with pain.

Homer writes elsewhere, in justly famous lines:

Men in their generations are like the leaves of the trees. The wind blows and one year's leaves are scattered on the ground, but the trees burst into bud and put on fresh ones when the spring comes round. In the same way one generation flourishes and another nears its end.

After a night's sleep, Priam and Achilles part and go their ways. Both know what destiny has in store for them. The king buries his son. Here the *Iliad* comes to an end, but what has been predicted comes to pass. Soon Achilles is shot dead by an arrow from Paris's bow. He does not live to take part in the fall of Troy, which is brought about by cunning rather than courage.

The Greeks pretend to abandon the siege and sail away. They leave behind a huge wooden horse, as an offering to the gods. The foolish Trojans drag it inside the city and celebrate the end of the war. But, of course, the horse contains a body of armed men. In the middle of the night they emerge and let the Greek army into the city. Troy falls and is destroyed. Priam is slaughtered by the son of Achilles.

Helen goes back to Sparta.

Homer hints broadly that the Trojan War achieved little. Too many brave men have died. And the argumentative family on Olympus moves on to other topics. Deities who took different sides of the argument, the sea god Poseidon and Apollo, decide to destroy the great defensive wall the Greeks erected around their ships. It had been built without the mandate of heaven.

Now that Troy has gone and "all the best of the Trojans were dead, and many of the Greeks too, though some were left," all that remains is this massive fortification. The gods turn against it the united waters of all the rivers in the area. Zeus the sky god lends a hand by raining continuously. After nine days the wall and its foundations have been washed out to sea. Poseidon then covers the wide beach again with sand and turns the rivers back to their old courses.

It is as if nothing had ever happened on that bloodstained shore. Had Helen been worth it? What had Hector, Achilles, and all the others really died for? To most Greeks the answer was obvious. Whatever their pointless ostensible purpose, brave deeds conferred glory in and for themselves. No other rationale was needed. From a vantage point in the underworld valor brought no practical benefits.

Virtue was its own regard, one might say.

So now through the fog of time we discern the shape of Greekness. The very fact of an expedition journeying a long distance by water is evidence of the importance of seafaring to a people inhabiting a rocky landscape with few roads. Hellenes shared a language, with mutually intelligible dialects, and gods. They believed profoundly in honor or personal status (*timē*). They were committed to fairness and the rule of law. They saw the cruelty and waste of war, but celebrated bravery. They recognized the harm done by rashness, but felt at the same time that there was something splendid about it.

We cannot call a society headed by impulsive rulers such as Agamemnon or Achilles democratic, but these were no despots. They had to consult public opinion and called regular mass meetings to advise on matters of importance, a tradition maintained in later centuries.

They were religious without doctrine; their family of unpredictable deities felt the same "human" passions as they did. What we see as myths and legends were real to the Greeks; their gods truly existed and heroes from the remote past were historical figures.

There was no sacred code handed down for mortals to follow. They could only hope to control the Olympians through prayer and sacrifice. There was a limit, though, to what could be done, for the course of men's and women's lives was foredoomed by the Fates, three old crones who spun the future from the threads of human lives.

The competitive pursuit of excellence was an essential attribute of a fine man. But, as Homer shows, this disputatious rivalry had its dark side and in later centuries was reflected in poisonous quarrels that disfigured the many independent city-states that made up Hellas. The Greeks made a point of disagreeing with their neighbors, a habit that led ultimately to their downfall.

Despite the flow of blood that is shed in the pages of the *Iliad,* the underlying atmosphere is optimistic. This is partly due to Homer's sense of humor; as we shall see, comedy and laughter are to infuse Athenian, if not Greek, culture. Also, in the *Iliad,* man-made objects— ships or tools or furniture—are always found to be *well* made. When mentioning by name one of his characters, Homer likes to add a descriptive phrase or adjective. So Paris is "godlike" even when he is being cowardly. These epithets describe a man's true character, especially when he is not living up to it.

If Hellenes were united on anything it was the abiding enmity between them and the successors of Troy. From about the middle of the sixth century these were the Great Kings who founded and maintained the Persian Empire, stretching at its greatest extent from Egypt and Anatolia to the frontier of India. These decadent orientals, as they regarded them, were the bogeymen of the Hellenic world.

In a word, Greece was not a place, as today's nation-state in the Balkans is, but an idea. And wherever he lived a Greek was someone who spoke the same tongue—and knew his Homer.

Although the great philosopher Aristotle tutored him in the latest thinking about the world, Alexander the Great felt himself to be a throwback. He was a Homeric warrior, a latter-day Achilles, a man of action rather than of intellect. It is ironic that this lover of all things Greek brought to a violent end the liberties of the civilization he so admired and halted the great democratic experiment that the city of Athens had pioneered.

It is the extraordinary story of that experiment which the following pages tell. First of all, we must meet the three leading powers in the Eastern Mediterranean, Athens itself, Sparta, and the empire of Persia, for it was their interwoven rivalries and opposing values that led, one after another, to their triumphs—and to their ruin.

THREE'S
COMPANY

1

National Hero

The geography of their homeland helped mold the collective character of the ancient Athenians and of all the other sporadic communities that shared the Greek peninsula. Rocky, bare mountains are interspersed with numerous, small, fertile plains. But much of the soil is dry and stony, and more suitable for olive trees than fields of wheat. Travel by land between the meager centers of habitation was laborious.

Athens was the chief city of Attica, a triangular tract of level ground about nine hundred square miles in extent. This plain is punctuated by hills and surrounded by mountains on two sides and on a third by the sea. Mount Hymettus was famous for its honey, and still is, and Pentelicon for its honey-colored marble, from which it built its temples to the gods. Rich lead and silver deposits at Laurium in the southeast were found and mined. Summers are hot and dry and heavy outbursts of rain mark the fall.

The poverty of the land of Greece brought with it three consequences. It bred a fierce individualism, a cantankerous refusal to agree with those living on the other side of mountains; states were many and tiny and Athens was one of the largest. Unable to feed their growing

numbers, the Athenians became seafarers, although sailing was dangerous in the windy winters. Around the eighth century they joined other
Greek statelets in exporting surplus citizens to new settlements around
the Mediterranean littoral and importing grain from the Black Sea and
elsewhere in growing quantities.

The citadel of Athens was the Acropolis, or "high city," an almost
impregnable outcrop that rises one hundred and fifty meters above sea
level. There is evidence of human occupation as early as 5,000 B.C., but
we hear little of the place during the age of the Mycenaean monarchs.

The Athenians held that they belonged to an ethnic group called the
Ionians, who had always lived in Greece (the word derives from Ion, a
legendary king of Athens). Not long after the traditional date of the
fall of Troy towards the end of the second millennium, another group
called the Dorians, Greek speakers but with their own cultural customs
and dialect, came down from the north and settled in Greece. Under
pressure from these newcomers, some Ionians emigrated to Asia Minor
where they settled and prospered. Athens argued that she was "the eldest land of Ionia" and felt some ongoing responsibility for her cousins overseas.

How many of these beliefs are true cannot now be told and we have
no choice but to open our narrative with instructive fiction rather than
irretrievable fact.

The future of Athens was determined by a goddess, Pallas Athena, and
by a king called Theseus, whose legendary character traits express, for
good or ill, Athenian identity.

It was as well not to cross Athena's path. From the moment of her
birth she emanated power. Her father, Zeus, had sex with Metis, the
divine personification of Wisdom, but then had second thoughts. Fearing that their child would grow up to be more intelligent than he was
himself, he opened his mouth wide and swallowed Metis up. Nine
months later he experienced a raging—literally, it would turn out, a
splitting—migraine. He ordered his son Hephaestus, god of metal-

work, to strike his head with an ax, hoping that this would relieve the pain. The divine blacksmith obeyed and out jumped Athena from the crack in his skull, adult and fully armed.

She was a perpetual virgin and tomboy. As goddess of war, she could vanquish in combat her half brother Ares (the Roman Mars), lord of battles who delighted in the slaughter of men and the sack of towns. However, Athena took no pleasure in fighting and preferred to settle disputes by discussion and mediation. She patronized crafts and the making of clothes.

She is unique among the Olympians in having a city named after her. She regarded Athens as hers following a quarrel with the sea god and brother of Zeus, Poseidon. As a mark of possession, he thrust his trident into the Acropolis and a spring of seawater sprang out from the rock (it still flows today). Later, Athena laid her own claim in a more peaceful manner, by planting the first olive tree alongside the spring. A furious Poseidon challenged her to a duel, but Zeus insisted on peaceful arbitration. A court of Olympian gods awarded the prize to Athena. Poseidon resentfully sent a tsunami to flood Attica, so she took up residence in the city and kept it under watchful guard.

From early times the Athenians welcomed the goddess with open arms. She was foster mother to one of the first kings, the semi-divine Erechtheus. From his vantage point in the eighth century, Homer celebrated

the Athenians from their splendid citadel in the realm of the magnanimous Erechtheus, a child of the fruitful Earth who was brought up by Athena Daughter of Zeus and established by her in her own rich shrine, where bulls and rams are offered to him yearly in due season by Athenian youths.

The Athenians learned from their tutelary goddess that military force was an invaluable arm of policy, but that it should be tempered by *metis,* wisdom or, in its less complete sense, ingenuity and craftiness.

. . .

Aegeus, legendary king of Athens during the Mycenaean age, was childless, but on his travels he enjoyed a one-night stand with an attractive princess. He suspected, or perhaps just hoped, that he had made her pregnant, so he hid a sword and a pair of sandals under a rock. Before leaving, he told the woman that if she gave birth to a son she should show him where they were when he grew up, and tell him to take them with him to Athens.

A baby duly arrived, whom she named Theseus. When a young adult he learned about the tokens from his mother, who gave him Aegeus's message. He did as he was told and lifted up the rock with ease. He refused to take ship to Athens, although it was the safest method of travel. Instead, looking for adventure, he set off by land to Athens. En route he sought out and destroyed a number of dangerous opponents. The first of them wielded a large club, which Theseus carried about with him ever afterwards, rather as Heracles, whom he greatly admired, invariably wore the skin of a lion he had killed. Next came Sinis the Pine-bender, who tied travelers to two pines he had bent down to the ground; he then let them go, tearing the victims apart.

Feeling randy, Theseus chased after Sinis's pretty little daughter, who had very sensibly run away. Plutarch reports that he

> looked for her high and low, but she had disappeared into a place which was overgrown with shrubs and rushes and wild asparagus. The girl in her childish innocence was imploring the plants to hide her; and promising that if they saved her, she would never trample them down or burn them. Theseus called her and gave her his word that he would not harm her but treat her with respect—and she came out.

Once he had caught her, he took her to his bed. After she had borne him a son, he married her off to some nonentity. Throughout his life Theseus was a sexual predator.

After this diversion he resumed his Heraclean labors. Next on his list was the terrifying Crommyonian sow; some said she was not a pig but a depraved murderess who was "nicknamed the Sow because of her life and habits." Either way, Theseus killed her. He then dispatched the robber Sciron. His modus operandi had been to stick out his feet to passersby on a narrow cliff path and to insist they wash them. While they were doing so he tipped them into the sea. Of other challengers the most alarming was Procrustes, who forced travelers to fit onto his iron bed; if they were too tall he cut off their legs and if too short stretched them as on a rack until they were the right size.

At long last Theseus made it to Athens. He was unknown to anyone there. His tunic was unusually long and touched his feet. His hair was plaited and, according to an ancient commentator, "nice-looking." He passed a temple construction site and the builders jeered at him. What, they bantered, was a marriageable girl doing wandering about on her own? Theseus said nothing, but took the oxen from the men's cart and flung them over the temple's half-built roof. He was not a man to suffer fools gladly.

Strangers in ancient Greece were routinely given a hospitable welcome and the king offered Theseus a meal in his palace on the Acropolis. His wife, the celebrated witch Medea—back from the Black Sea with the Argonauts—knew who Theseus was. Fearful that her position would be threatened by the arrival of a son, she persuaded the aged and infirm Aegeus to have this potentially troublesome foreign guest poisoned at dinner.

For his part the young man thought it best to reveal his identity to his father tactfully; when the meat was served he drew his sword as if to cut off a piece, hoping that the king would recognize it. Aegeus saw the weapon and immediately acknowledged his son's identity. We may assume that the food was removed. After beating off some competitors for the succession to the throne, Theseus became heir apparent. Medea left town.

. . .

Not long afterwards collectors of human tribute arrived from Crete. Largest of the Greek islands, it was the center of a great maritime civilization that flourished from about 2,700 to the fifteenth century. Modern archaeologists have called it Minoan after the mythical king of Crete, Minos.

His son died a mysterious but violent death while on a visit to Athens, possibly at the hands of Aegeus. Minos was enraged with grief. He fought and won a war of revenge against Athens and in compensation for his loss demanded the handover every nine years of seven young men and seven young women, chosen by lot. They were sent to Crete and imprisoned in a labyrinth where a monster half man and half bull lived, called the Minotaur. He was the product of an extramarital liaison between Minos's wife, Pasiphae, and a white bull with whom she had become infatuated. He killed all the captives.

Athenian public opinion was highly critical of Theseus. Here was the heir to the throne, a bastard and a foreigner, coming off scot-free, while ordinary people's legitimate children were being sent to a dreadful fate. Theseus took the point and volunteered to be a member of the tribute group and destroy the Minotaur.

Being of a tricky frame of mind, he swapped two of the girls for a couple of pretty (but manly) boys; he softened their skins by warm baths, kept them out of the sun, got them to use makeup, gave them frocks, and trained them to walk in a feminine manner (we shall see later that this was not the only time a Greek used drag as a deadly ruse).

On previous occasions the ship carrying the captives had shown a black sail, as a sign of mourning. But Theseus promised that he would give the captain another sail, a white one, for him to hoist on the return voyage as a sign that he had killed the Minotaur.

Minos's daughter Ariadne fell in love with Theseus and showed him how to master the intricacies of the labyrinth. She gave him a ball of string, which he unwound as he walked along, thus enabling him to find his way back. As he had vowed, he put the Minotaur to death and cut off its head.

Theseus and the other boys and girls escaped from Crete. The now pregnant Ariadne and her sister came along with them, but they were dumped on the island of Naxos. Ariadne hanged herself in despair (or, according to another account, married on the rebound the wine god Dionysus, who was passing by).

As they approached Attica, Theseus and the ship's captain forgot to change the sails. When Aegeus saw the boat come into harbor sporting its black flag, he committed suicide by flinging himself off the Acropolis.

As we have seen, Theseus had a cheating, sometimes violent way with women. He and his best friend, a Thessalian called Pirithous, kidnapped Helen, later to be "of Troy." He was fifty years old and she a prepubescent girl; he said he meant to keep her until she was old enough to marry and have sex with. But she was rescued and the plan failed.

Theseus joined in a war with the Amazons, a race of aggressive women who forswore men. Their queen, Hippolyta, was tricked into boarding Theseus's ship; he took her back to Athens where he married her. However, he soon put her away in favor of Ariadne's little sister, Phaedra.

Pirithous had the not-so-clever idea of going down into the underworld and kidnapping the Queen of the Dead, Persephone. He took Theseus along with him and the pair wandered around the outskirts of Tartarus, a deep abyss where the wicked are endlessly tortured. They were caught and led away to eternal punishment by the Furies, ancient goddesses of vengeance, who had snakes in their hair and whips in their hands. Both men were placed on the Chair of Amnesia; they grew into it and were held fast by coiled serpents. Here they were to live or partly live forever.

By a stroke of luck Heracles happened to be visiting. He was engaged on the last of his Labors, the capture of Cerberus, the three-headed dog that guarded the entrance to the underworld. He persuaded Persephone to let bygones be bygones and Theseus was restored to the upper air. His comrade remained unforgiven and, for all we know, is still suffering.

On his return to Athens, the family atmosphere in the palace on the Acropolis became strained when Phaedra fell incestuously in love with Hippolytus, Theseus's son by Hippolyta. He rejected her advances. False evidence from Phaedra led the angry king to cause his son's death at the hands of the sea god Poseidon. She then killed herself out of guilt.

The Athenians were sure that Theseus was a historical figure. A thirty-oared galley, said to be the ship on which he had sailed to and from Crete, was preserved and was still on public display in the fourth century. Its old timbers were replaced with new wood as they rotted away. This gave philosophers a handy conundrum for their pupils. When all the timbers had been exchanged, was the ship the same ship or a different one?

In fact, of course, Theseus was fictional and probably originated as a local divinity in northern Attica. However, there was one aspect of his achievement that did actually take place, even if the date is unknown and the personal credit must go to some other leader (or leaders) whose names have been lost. It was the first step that Athens took towards greatness.

Athens with its near-impregnable citadel was the largest of numerous independent small towns and villages in Attica. Plutarch reports that Theseus

> conceived a wonderful and far-reaching plan, which was nothing less than to concentrate the inhabitants of Attica into a single urban area. In this way he transformed them into one community belonging to one city; until then they had been scattered about, so that it was difficult to bring them together in the common interest.

He campaigned vigorously village by village and won the support of the poor. To the more influential classes, he proposed that a limited form of democracy should be established. All citizens were to be on an equal footing, although the government and the conduct of religious rites would be placed (or remain) in the hands of the landed aristocracy. Many went to live in Athens, leaving it every day to work in the fields.

This process was called synoecism, or a "bringing together into one home." Attica was now a unitary polity with central control exercised by Athens. In other words, it became a city-state, or (to use the Greek word) a *polis*. Its national hero, Theseus, stood as the symbol of this groundbreaking development.

Similar reforms unfolded elsewhere in Greece, not always with complete success. In Boeotia, for instance, the lands lying to the north of Attica, the largest city, Thebes, never managed to secure more than a fractious federation. Throughout its history it was always having to use force to maintain its authority over its constituent parts.

Theseus was regarded as the first people's ruler of Athens. He laid aside his royal power, reserving to himself only the supreme command in war and guardianship of the law. In practice, of course, this meant that he was still in charge, a benevolent autocrat. Plutarch's overall verdict is that he "founded a commonwealth, so to speak, of all sorts and conditions of citizen. However, he did not let his democracy become confused and disordered by multitudes of immigrants."

These stories about Theseus reflect the attitudes of those who made them up—namely, Athenians in search of a founding myth. Banditry and violence were common in the classical world and here we have a hero ready and able to put down criminal behavior wherever he found it. What is more, his deeds are clearly constructed on the model of the celebrated Labors of Heracles, seemingly impossible tasks that the strongman completed with ease. Athens wanted its own personalized Heracles-alternative.

A believer in the rule of law, this fictional Theseus was only too happy to break it when it suited him. Careless, sexist, and a little sociopathic, intelligent and attractive, willing to thumb his nose at the gods and capable of taking punishment for his impertinence, Theseus was the kind of man Athenians liked to be like. We will meet his type time and again as we proceed through the city's history.

The "Dark Age" that followed the mysterious collapse of the Mycenean civilization lasted for about three centuries. Monarchs like Theseus became a rarity and some time before 800, when the Greeks emerged into the light, Athens became a republic governed by a group of noble families, an aristocracy. Combative and unruly, they were a collective of Theseuses.

By contrast, the Spartans, who are our second protagonist, were conservative and kept their kings. In fact, they could not have been more different from the Athenians in almost every way. The two states got on together very badly. A candid friend from the city of Corinth told the Spartans how little they had in common with the Athenians. "They are innovators, quick thinkers and swift at putting their plans into action, while you like to hold on to what you have, come up with no new ideas and when you do take action never achieve as much as you should have done."

Where the Athenians were open-minded and excited by change, Sparta feared and resisted it, as we shall now see.

2

A State of War

The Spartan boy was terrified, but absolutely determined. He must not let himself down, or his comrades. They were under strict instructions by their official trainers to steal wherever and whatever they could. Their only crime was to be found out.

The others with him in his age group had stolen a tame young fox and given it to him to look after. When its owners came in search of it, the teenager was holding the fox under his cloak. The frightened animal struggled to escape; it began biting through his side and lacerated his intestines. The teenager did not move or make a noise, to avoid being found out.

The owners left and the boy's friends realized what had happened. They told him off for his stupidity. Far better to let the animal be found than lose his life. "No!" he replied, though mortally wounded. "Better to die without giving in to the pain than to save a life and live ever after in disgrace."

This famous parable was an object lesson for young Spartans.

The origins of Sparta, or Lacedaemon, its official name, are obscured by ancient myth. Its citizens numbered themselves among the Dorian "invaders" of Greece in opposition to the "native" Ionians. By the end of the eighth century, it had become one of the great city-states of Greece. You would not think it, though, if you were to judge by appearances.

Sparta, the Lacedaemonian capital, lay in a fertile river valley in the southern Peloponnese. The land was called Laconia and the river the Eurotas. The Peloponnese was, like the rest of mainland Greece, rocky and barren with only a few pockets of farmland. The mountains were still wooded, but the process of deforestation was proceeding apace. To the west, but cut off from Sparta by the high barrier of the Taygetos range, lay the rich, flat, alluvial, and tempting plain of Messenia.

As for Sparta itself, it could scarcely be called a town, let alone a city. It looked very much like what it was—a haphazard collection of four villages. There were some visually unimpressive shrines, altars, and temples, and soldiers' barracks. It had a sort of a citadel, which, as one visitor described it, was "not so high as to be a landmark." Thucydides, the Athenian historian, was struck by the contrast between Sparta's position as a major power and the dismal appearance of its chief city. He noted politely: "There would be an impression of inadequacy."

Also, unusually for an urban settlement in an age of endless wars, Sparta had no defensive walls, a fact of which the Spartans were counterintuitively proud. When someone asked a Spartan king why there were no fortifications, he simply pointed at some Spartan soldiers. "These are our walls!" There was truth in this, but Sparta was also protected by near-impassable mountains.

This then was where a young Spartan was brought up. Children were held to be the property of the state, not of their parents. On their birth a committee of elders examined the infant to decide whether or not he or she should be allowed to live. The life of the epileptic, the sickly, and the disabled infant was "of no advantage to itself or to the state," so it was taken to a ravine called Apothetae, which translates as a "place reserved for special occasions." The euphemistical special occasion was the baby's exposure to the elements (not to mention wild animals) and death.

Those allowed to live were reared without traditional swaddling clothes, leaving their limbs and physiques to develop naturally. Their nurses taught them to be happy and contented, to eat up their food and not be afraid of the dark or of being left alone. Tantrums and tears were discouraged.

At the age of seven, boys were taken on by the state and divided up into companies or troops. From this early age they were trained in the art of war. Their education—or, as it was called, *agogē*—was designed to make them "obey orders, cope with stress and win battles." They were taught to read and write—but "no more than was necessary." They lived together, rather as in a Victorian boarding school. They went about barefoot, had their hair cropped, and usually played naked. They never wore a tunic, and were given only one cloak a year. They slept together in dormitories on rush-filled pallet beds. Older men came to watch their competitions and disputes, and identified the most aggressive and fearless.

When little Spartans reached the age of twelve they were allocated "lovers" from among young men of good character. The purpose was not meant to be sexual (at least in theory), but to provide role models.

A state official, the Inspector of Boys, employed a team of men with whips to administer punishments. He supervised the companies and appointed commanders for each of them from men in their early twenties. They ordered the bigger boys to fetch and carry, to find firewood and food. The idea was that, like the boy with the fox, they stole all these things from gardens and the messes for adult Spartans, and became adept at pouncing on sleepers or catching people off their guard. According to Plutarch,

> any boy who is caught is beaten and has to go hungry. For their meals are meager, so they have to take into their own hands the

fight against hunger. In this way, they are forced into daring and villainy.

Adolescents took part in a fearsome rite of passage in honor of Artemis Orthia (Artemis was the twin sister of Apollo, goddess of the hunt and childbirth; she was identified with Orthia, a local Peloponnesian divinity), held at the goddess's sanctuary on the bank of the Eurotas. Cheeses were piled on an altar and guarded by men with whips. Competitors had to snatch as many cheeses as they could while running a gauntlet of flagellators. Blood stained the altar.

The Athenian writer and soldier Xenophon, who lived through Sparta's heyday in the fifth and fourth centuries, was an admirer of the system. He observed: "All this education was planned in order to make the boys more resourceful at feeding themselves, and better fighting men."

That is true as far as it goes, but is not completely right. A good Spartan was expected to embody apparently contradictory qualities. Criminal guile, aggression, and tolerance of pain cohabited with obedience, deference, and modesty. A boy was taught to keep his hands inside his cloak, to walk in silence, and to fix his eyes firmly on the ground.

There were a few acceptable pleasures. Food at the Spartan dinner table may have been terrible, as can be guessed from its most famous delicacy, "black broth," which was made from pig's blood and vinegar; but alcohol was permitted, although not to excess. An admiring Athenian poet noted:

> *The Spartan youths drink just enough*
> *To bring each mind to pleasant thoughts*
> *. . . and moderate laughter.*

Festivals allowed an opportunity for dancing and singing. The Gymnopaideia, the Festival of Naked Boys, was one of the state's most solemn celebrations during which young Spartans danced in the nude in the main square (also referred to as the Dancing Floor). Three choirs would perform. Old men would begin, singing "We once were valiant young men"; then men in their prime would respond: "That is what we are now: look and learn"; and, finally, teenagers chanted: "One day we will be better men than all of you."

The poems of a patriotic general called Tyrtaeus were learned by heart and used as marching songs. They called for valor in the field, as these typical lines make clear.

For a good man to die in the vanguard is a fine thing
Doing battle on behalf of his native land.
But to leave his city and rich fields,
To go begging is the most miserable of fates.

Spartans did not enjoy gossip and could not stand having to listen to long speeches. They were men of few words—hence our "laconic." Fellow-Greeks loved collecting specimens of their down-to-earth brevity, as when a Spartan king was asked what type of training was most practiced at Sparta. He replied: "Knowing how to take orders. And how to give orders."

Adult male citizens—the Spartiates or "Equals"—joined a military mess, a *syssitia* (literally, a "common meal"). It had about fifteen members, who spent most of their time together and shared everything in common.

Around the age of eighteen a trainee entered the army reserve and two years later was eligible for election to a *syssitiai* by its members. He had finished the *agogē*, but went on living with his comrades. At the age of thirty he became a full citizen, but only if he was a member of a *syssitia*—not necessarily a simple matter, for one vote was enough to blackball a candidate.

An Equal owned farming land, which was tilled by *helots,* or serfs.

Its produce enabled him to make a contribution to the costs of the *syssitia*. Apparently, this would include for every month seventy-four liters of barley, thirty-six liters of wine (not too bad a ration), about two kilograms of cheese, one of figs, and a small sum of money for cheap "relishes" (namely, flesh or fowl). In this way he was freed from working for his own living and enabled to spend his active life as a soldier, in training or on campaign. If he could not afford the contribution, he was dismissed from the mess.

All contributions were equal and the same standard of living was intended for all. Young Spartans were not to be tempted to make money. They were forbidden to engage in business or to own silver or gold. Gold and silver coins were not struck, and instead only iron bars were used. These were given a very low financial value, so that a substantial sum of money was inconveniently heavy and large to transport easily or to store. There was little point in receiving cash in this form as a gift or a bribe or in stealing it.

Cowardice was punished by social ostracism. Mothers and wives would tell their menfolk to return home victorious or dead: "Come back with your shield or on it." In fact, on the rare occasions that an army lost a battle the Spartan soldier was better advised to give his life than save it. If he was injured, it was essential that his wounds were on the front of his body. Cowards could not hold public office, were expelled from their mess, had to wear a cloak with colored patches, and were not allowed to marry.

Women in ancient Greece spent much of their lives in discreet seclusion, and above all were banned from taking part in public sports, riding, or hunting. In Sparta it was quite the opposite. Girls were brought up like their brothers to excel physically.

They were made to harden their bodies through exercise. They ran, wrestled, threw the discus, and hurled the javelin, just as the boys did. Motherhood was to be their main purpose in life and the theory was that in this way they would be able to manage the pangs of childbirth and give birth to healthy and strong sons.

Although this was shocking to other Greeks, who expected the opposite sex to be modestly clothed, Spartan girls wore only a scanty tunic or even went about naked. Makeup, long hair, or gold ornaments were barred. Women were not shy at coming forward and enjoyed engaging in hostile banter with men, but, if there was no prudery in Sparta, flirtatious and conventionally feminine behavior was discouraged.

Marriage was handled in a typically unappealing manner. Men were fined if they failed to marry. The would-be husband, who had to be at least thirty years old, carried off his intended by force. A bridesmaid shaved her head and dressed her in a man's cloak and sandals. She was then made to lie down on a rush mattress, alone and in the dark. After dining with his comrades in the mess, the groom slipped away surreptitiously and carried his bride to the marriage bed. He spent a little time with her and then went back to his barracks as if nothing of any consequence had taken place.

And this was how he continued to act. He spent his days with his comrades, and slept with them at night, visiting his wife briefly, secretly and after dark, full of dread that they would be found out. Plutarch writes:

> and they did not carry on like this for a short time only, but long enough for some of them to become fathers before they had seen their own wives in the light of day.

Married couples were to be neither jealous nor unduly amorous.

Brothers were allowed to share their wives. The techniques of animal breeding were applied; husbands could give another man permission to sleep with his wife, if he believed he "would fill her with noble sperm." He would happily adopt the consequential offspring and bring them up as if they were his own. Once they had their own families, women were expected to manage their households when their husbands were away at war, as they often were.

The name of one independent-minded great lady has come down

to us. This was Cynisca, sister of a Spartan king (for more on the monarchy see below on page 26). Born about 440, she was an expert horsewoman and, being royal, had plenty of money. She was the first woman to score a victory at the ancient Olympic Games. The games were almost entirely a men-only affair and women were only allowed to compete in equestrian events—not directly but by owning, breeding, and training horses.

Cynisca won the four-horse chariot race, but she would not have witnessed her victory for only men were allowed to be spectators. She was very proud of her achievement and commissioned a statue of herself, which stood in the Temple of Zeus at Olympia. The inscription on its stone base reads:

> I, Cynisca, victorious with a chariot of swift-footed horses,
> Have erected this statue. I declare myself the only woman
> In all Hellas to have won this crown.

A grove sacred to Zeus stood in a pleasant, grassy, and wooded plain in the northwest of the Peloponnese. Here at Olympia in the summer of the year 756 an international athletic competition was held for the first time in honor of the god. These were the Olympic Games and they were staged every four years through the next millennium. They were soon joined by others, which were also quadrennial, and filled in the empty years—the Pythian Games at Delphi, the Isthmian Games at Corinth, and the Games at Nemea between Argos and Corinth. These were genuinely Panhellenic events and attracted crowds of visitors from across the Greek world.

So that competitors and audiences could reach Olympia safely a sacred truce was declared for one month (later extended to two and then three months). Heralds called *spondophoroi* or truce-bearers, wearing olive wreaths and carrying staffs, were sent out to every Greek state to announce the date of the festival and proclaim the truce. States taking part in the Games were forbidden to wage war, to enter into legal disputes, or to put anyone to death.

Women were allowed to participate neither as athletes nor as spectators (although apparently virgins were not refused admission to the games, perhaps because of their ritual purity). They had their own four-yearly Games of Hera, at which competitors took part in three foot races for different age groups.

The Olympic Games lasted for five days. There were various foot races, including one in armor. Other sports featured were throwing the discus and the javelin, the long jump, wrestling, and boxing. The most extreme event was the *pancration*. This was a combination of boxing and wrestling, with almost no rules except that gouging and biting were banned (although in practice contestants sometimes tried to get away with both). It was not unknown for competitors to lose their lives. The pentathlon challenged all-around athletes with five tests—discus, jumping, javelin, running, and wrestling. Only those with the deepest pockets, such as Cynisca, could afford to enter teams for the chariot races.

To win at the Games was to be favored by the gods. The prizes at Olympia were only crowns of olives, but a victor was a celebrity for life. His *polis* showered him with honors, among them free board and lodging at the city hall and best seats at the theater. A poet such as Pindar wrote odes in his honor and sometimes he was commemorated by a life-size statue of him in bronze or marble.

In sum, then, a Spartan's life was spartan. It was much admired by contemporaries for its purity, its elective poverty, its military efficiency, and, in a wider culture where personal willfulness had a certain allure (remember Theseus), its self-control. It was not for nothing that a leading Greek poet called Sparta "man-taming," for it broke its boys in as if they were colts.

Citizens lived austere lives and were formidable on the battlefield. Like bees in a hive everyone worked obediently and efficiently for the common good; there were no drones.

But it is hard not to detect a sense of strain. From today's perspective the Spartan system is extremely odd—even, perhaps, a little deranged. Moral standardization and the suppression of ordinary, more generous, patterns of human behavior required a fierce act of will. This could only be achieved by isolating Spartans from other Greek city-states. Would their right little, tight little world survive exposure to other, more relaxed and individualistic communities?

To understand their mindset we need to find out why the Spartans decided to create their enclosed, eccentric, militaristic society in the first place.

In the 700s many Greek communities felt the need to acquire more fertile land, probably because of a rise in their populations. There were too many wildernesses and too few productive acres. Most of them exported surplus citizens by sending them out to found "colonies" here and there on the coast of the Mediterranean. There they sat, wrote the famous Athenian philosopher Plato, "like frogs around a pond" (for more on this diaspora see page 32).

Sparta in those days was (so far as we know) a city-state like any other, but it decided on a different solution to the challenge. It would expand its borders *locally* in the Peloponnese. It began a process of conquest and assimilation of its neighbors. First, it created up to thirty dependent settlements in the Laconian plain, whose inhabitants were called *perioeci*, "people who live round about." They were responsible for all the manufacturing and other services that Sparta needed. They were also liable to be called up into the army, but they did not have the prestige of the full Spartan citizen-in-arms.

The next step was to move south along the river Eurotas, through marshes and down to the sea. Here a second group of dependents was formed, the *helots* (probably so-called after the village of Helos, or "Marsh"). These were members of a vanquished population and as such the property of the Spartan state. They were instructed where to live and given specific duties. However, they were not owned by individual Spartans. *Helots* worked in the fields and could be conscripted (although their loyalty was suspect and they were deployed with caution).

The great prize lay over the mountains to the west, the wide and productive plain of Messenia. If only that could be annexed, Sparta's economic problems would be over; there would be sufficient food for hungry mouths, and a rise in the standard of living. In fact, on the restricted Greek stage it would gain the stature of a great power.

Few details have survived, but between about 730 and 710 Sparta fought and won a long, hard war against the Messenians. Tyrtaeus crowed:

> ... *we captured Messene of the broad plain*
> *Messene good to plow, good to plant.*
> *They fought for it for nineteen full years*
>   *Relentlessly unceasing and always stout of heart.*

In the twentieth year, the story was told, the enemy abandoned its last redoubt, a near-impregnable stronghold on Mount Ithome, the highest of twin peaks that rise from the plain to about eight hundred meters. Many Messenians fled their homeland for good to the safety of Arcadia in the northern Peloponnese.

It was a decisive victory, but the Spartans realized that they had consumed more than they could easily digest. How could they keep their prize in the face of bitter opposition from the remaining Messenians? The question was given a sharp relevance when fifty years or so later the Messenians took advantage of a Spartan defeat at the hands of Argos, a north Peloponnesian power, and domestic discontent in Laconia. They rose in revolt, but once again they were defeated.

The Spartans decided that they would have to transform themselves into a fully militarized society if they were to have a chance of keeping their subject peoples under their permanent control. A series of radical reforms were introduced. The credit is traditionally given to a leader called Lycurgus, but he is probably a legendary figure.

We are told that the reforms were based on a consultation with the famous oracle at Delphi in central Greece. "The Lord of the Silver Bow, Far-shooting Apollo, the Golden-haired spoke from his rich shrine," wrote Tyrtaeus. On this occasion, the god did not initiate a plague as he had among the Greeks in front of Troy. He gave helpful advice and a proclamation, the Great Rhetra, which reflected his ideas, was issued.

The basic proposition was to give full citizenship to several thousand (perhaps nine thousand at the outset) Spartan males and, as we have seen, to free them from the business of earning a living from farming or manufacturing. They would be trained to be the best soldiers in Greece. The Messenians were all "helotized," or turned into public serfs. Their task was to farm the allotments allocated to Spartan male citizens. According to Tyrtaeus, they were

Just like donkeys weighed down with heavy burdens
Bringing to their masters from cruel necessity
Half of all the produce their land bears.

The state's political institutions were reorganized. At its base was a citizen assembly, or *ecclesia,* which passed laws, elected officials, and decided policy. But in practice its powers were limited; it could not initiate or amend legislation. Votes at elections were measured in a most peculiar way (presumably it was designed to counter vote rigging). Some specially selected judges were shut up in a nearby building; candidates for office were silently presented to the assembly, which shouted its endorsements. The judges assessed the volume of the shouts, without knowing which candidates they were for. Those who attracted the loudest applause were declared elected.

The assembly was guided by a council of elders or *gerousia* and Sparta's two kings. These elders were all more than sixty years old and were members for life. They were "ballast for the ship of state," as Plutarch put it, and a force for conservatism, although they could fall under the influence from time to time of a particularly able king. The *gerousia's* main power was to prepare the agenda for the assembly and it was empowered to set aside any popular decision of which it disapproved.

Executive authority lay in the hands of five *ephors*. Appointed by the assembly, they held office for one year and could not be reelected. They wielded great (and somewhat sinister) powers, and played a role not altogether unlike that of the political commissars who accompanied officers in the Red Army. They had a judicial function, and could levy instant fines. They could depose, imprison, and bring to trial any official, including a king (in which latter case they sat in judgment alongside the other king and the council of elders). They also negotiated with foreign embassies and expelled unwelcome foreigners. They chaired the assembly and implemented its decisions. When a king led an army abroad, two *ephors* accompanied him to oversee his behavior. Once a year they formally declared war on the *helots,* so that killing them would not be illegal and a religious pollution.

The Spartans were terrified that their helots would rise again against them and believed that the most efficacious means of preventing this was through wholesale oppression. A secret police called the *crypteia* (literally "hidden things") was tasked with ensuring peace and quiet in Messenia. Its members were recruited from the brightest and best of the younger generation, and only those willing to serve were likely to obtain senior public posts in later life. According to Plutarch, the *ephors* from time to time sent out into the countryside young Spartiates in the *crypteia,* equipped only with daggers and basic rations. "In the daytime they scattered into obscure and out of the way places, where they lay low and rested. At night they came down into the roads and murdered every helot they came across." Often they even went into the fields where *helots* were working and cut down the strongest and best of them.

On one occasion in the fifth century it is reported that the *helots* were invited to volunteer names of those who had shown bravery on the battlefield and deserved to be given their freedom. Two thousand *helots* were singled out, crowned with wreaths, and ushered in procession around the sanctuaries of the gods. But then a little while later they all disappeared and were secretly liquidated. No one ever found out how they had met their ends.

At the head of Spartan society stood two kings from separate royal families, the Agiad and the Eurypontid, who reigned simultaneously. This was a unique arrangement in Greece and its purpose is unclear, although the existence of an alternative may have constrained an autocratically minded monarch from stepping out of line. Over time the kings saw their powers diminish. As a rule they could not initiate policy, although a man with a talent for politics could win over the *gerousia* and the assembly to his way of thinking. As noted, executive authority became the prerogative of the *ephors*.

In military affairs, however, the kings remained supreme. One or other of them led the Spartan army and wielded absolute power on the battlefield. They were accompanied by a bodyguard of one hundred horsemen and could summarily execute any soldier for cowardice or treason. However, they were liable to prosecution for mishandling campaigns and a number of kings were convicted of bribery.

A king had another equally weighty and demanding duty. As religious leaders, he and his colleague were responsible for relations with the gods. They often consulted the oracle at Delphi and conducted frequent ceremonies on behalf of the state. Before setting out on a military campaign a king sacrificed to the gods to make sure that the enterprise had their approval. He did so again when crossing Sparta's frontier, and sacrificed daily while on campaign and before a battle.

These matters were taken very seriously. A commander would not advance against an enemy if the omens were unfavorable—for example, unusual signs on an animal's liver. The king might have to sacrifice again and again before getting the right result; in the meantime his men were forced to stand idly by. An earthquake or an eclipse was enough to send a Spartan army marching home.

In peacetime kings had comparatively little to do—except for enjoying their wealth. They owned large estates and were the only Spartans who were permitted to be rich; they were the first to be served at public banquets and were given double portions. They were entitled to decide whom heiresses should marry—a profitable occupation, we may surmise—and adoption ceremonies had to take place in their presence.

The takeover of Messenia made Sparta the most powerful of the Greek city-states and its opponents thought twice before meeting their army in the field. But it was not naturally predatory or expansionist. Its primary concern was to control the Peloponnese and, above all, to ensure that the *helots* were broken in and docile. So far as the wider Hellenic world was concerned it had no particular ambitions, except that it expected—and received—a general acknowledgment of its superiority. Its formidable army could repel all comers and its constitution seemed to many outside observers to be a fine example of *eunomia,* or "good order and stability under just laws."

Sparta would have liked nothing better than to be left alone, but its interests were to be challenged in future years by its polar opposite and rival, the changeable and creative city of Athens.

3

The Persian Mule

Even today Delphi is an astounding place. The town is a series of headlong terraces perched dangerously on the limestone slopes of Mount Parnassus in central Greece. In classical times, it was almost inaccessible. Pausanias, the author of a guidebook to ancient Greece, who wrote in the second century A.D., walked along the craggy path that was the only way into the town. He found it hard going. He observed: "The highroad to Delphi gets more precipitous and becomes difficult even for an active man."

It was here that the classical world's leading oracle was located. Oracles were shrines where mortals could consult the immortals who warned, guided, and rewarded their worshippers. There were at least eight on the Greek mainland and many more around the Eastern Mediterranean. They were popular with foreigners, or "barbarians," as well as true Hellenes.

Once the visitor was inside the town he found himself on the Holy Way, a street that wound its course uphill towards the great temple of Apollo. He passed numerous Treasuries: these were stone buildings, looking like tiny temples, with columns and pediments, where grateful states stored votive gifts to the god, often one tenth of the spoils of a military victory—gold or silver artifacts, tripods, and bullion. They were decorated with brightly painted sculpture and with metal ornaments, as was typical of Greek architecture. Everywhere stood statues of prizewinning athletes in their hundreds. Paintings celebrated antique myths and great historical events.

The temple itself was a fine marble structure, partly resting on bedrock and partly on a specially built platform. On its walls three inscriptions were carved, which summed up basic principles of the good and fulfilled life. They were "know yourself," "nothing in excess," and, somewhat cynical advice to steer clear of rash pledges, "make a promise and ruin follows."

We are told that beneath the *cella* or inner room was a small secret chamber, the *adyton* (Greek for "inaccessible"), where the *omphalos* stood, a stone object that represented the center or "navel" of the earth. Its surface was covered with the carving of a knotted net and it had a hollow center widening towards the bottom.

The temple was managed by a priest who was recruited from Delphi's ruling elite. He served for life. The position was one of high prestige, but the incumbent was not expected to live a particularly virtuous life. He was assisted by five *hosioi* (or holy ones), and one or more *prophetae,* who may have had some role in interpreting or explaining the god's messages.

The key figure in the oracular process was the Pythia, the priestess or prophetess. She was an ordinary local woman, not of high birth, and she too served for life. She was past childbearing age when appointed, but on duty she wore the costume of an unmarried girl—a sacred sheep dressed as lamb. She was expected to be chaste.

Apollo was supposed to live at Delphi for nine months of the year, and the oracle appears to have been available for consultation only for one day in each of these months. It is not clear whether the god was willing to open up shop in cases of emergency; when a city-state like

Athens needed advice we do not hear of them having to wait for Apollo's convenience. As to inquirers, priority was given to the city of Delphi and its citizens, to states with "most favored nation" status, and to specially honored individuals. In general, states took preference over individuals.

In front of the temple stood a large altar. Here a preliminary sacrifice was conducted on behalf of all the day's inquirers. If this went well—that is, the animal reacted to a sprinkling of water by appearing to nod in acceptance of its fate—it was duly slaughtered.

An inquirer was led inside the temple and performed a second sacrifice, depositing the victim or parts of it on a table at the door to the *adyton,* the sunken room where the *omphalos* stood and where the Pythia was awaiting him. He was shown into a place from which he could hear but not see her.

The priestess had prepared for the consultation by purifying herself at the Castalian Spring in a ravine (two fountains fed by the spring still flow). At an altar inside the temple she burned laurel leaves and barley meal. Crowned with laurel she sat on a tripod and became possessed by the god. She then delivered her prophecy.

While we know broadly how consultations were managed, there are important aspects of the Delphi process about which we are in the dark. First of all, how was the Pythia's prophetic trance induced? We can be sure that she did not chew some kind of hallucinogenic leaf. No ancient source mentions this, and if she did do so, she would probably have chosen leaves of bay or laurel, both plants sacred to Apollo. The former would have produced no effect at all, and the latter are poisonous.

The author Plutarch, a local man and a priest of Apollo who knew the oracle from the inside, writes in the first century A.D. of a sweet smell emanating from the Pythia's consulting room. Was there a vent from which subterranean fumes rose? No trace of it could be found when archaeologists excavated the temple of Apollo in the twentieth century.

However, recent geological research suggests that the temple was built over the confluence of two fault lines and that gases including ethylene, which is both explosive and anesthetic, did come up from them. But the oracle functioned for a thousand years and it is hard to believe that the production of gas did not fluctuate. Even if the gases, when flowing, were of assistance to the Pythia it seems very probable that mostly her trances were self-induced.

The second problem concerns the presentation of the prophecies. Ancient historians such as Herodotus quote well-turned verses, rich in meaning and often carefully ambiguous. It is hardly plausible that the Pythia would have been able to improvise them, so one possibility is that her "ravings" were not altogether articulate and were later translated into poetry by the *prophetae* or some other persons.

We do not know whether the oracle was notified in advance of questions to be put. If it was, both officials and the Pythia would have had time to consider her response; even if not, the content of inquiries submitted by governments could often be guessed. Thoughtfulness does not necessarily mean that fraud was involved. That said, Apollo could be bribed; on one known occasion, for example, the Athenians paid money to have the Pythia influence the Spartans. But we do not know if the oracle was easily corrupted or if this was a frequent occurrence.

In this context, how "political" was the oracle? States frequently consulted Delphi and it is hard to believe that the officials at the oracle did not take care to monitor contemporary events and perhaps develop views or even policies that colored the prophecies. But we have no hard evidence.

Croesus, the king of Lydia in western Asia Minor, was wealthy, famous, and counted himself the luckiest of men. But in 547 he was also a worried man. Obscure and frightening changes were upsetting the balance of power in the Middle East. Although Croesus was not a Greek, he made himself into an honorary one. His donations to the god at Delphi were extraordinarily generous. They included the statue of a lion made from refined gold, two huge bowls, one of silver and the other of gold, and a large quantity of gold ingots. He urgently needed guidance from the oracle about his enemies and their prospects of success.

Lydia was a fertile territory. The nearby coastline was occupied by a multiplicity of noisy Ionian Greek city-states. They were the interface between the Hellenic world and the kingdoms of the east. Croesus had uneasy relations with them. He had brought most of them under his control and although they resented this, they recognized that he was a lover of all things Hellenic and provided protection from other potential threats in the region.

The Ionian settlements were originally founded by colonists sent out from mainland Greece. As we have seen, tradition had it that they were refugees from an invasion by newcomers, called Dorians, who arrived towards the end of the second millennium and made their home mainly in the Peloponnese. For many of them their departure point was Athens, which in later centuries claimed to be their mother-city. Ionians such as the Athenians spoke their own dialect of Greek, the other main ones being Dorian, spoken by the Spartans among others, and Aeolian, spoken mainly in Thessaly, Boeotia, and Lesbos.

The Ionians were the forerunners of an extraordinary, mostly peaceful diaspora throughout the Mediterranean between 734 and about 580 B.C. Nowhere in Greece is far from the sea, and mainland states sent out teams of citizens interested in sailing away and starting a new life. They founded city-states on the coasts of Spain and southern France. They even reached Tartessus, the Tarshish of the Bible, a port beyond the Pillars of Hercules (today's Gibraltar), which became a source for rare metals such as tin, and silver from northwest Spain. They peppered Sicily and southern Italy with new foundations; so substantial was the Hellenic presence that the region was nicknamed Greater Greece.

Athens was unable to produce enough food for its population and depended on Greek settlers in the Black Sea for importing grain from their hinterland (in today's Ukraine and the Crimea) and sending it on by ship.

Links between the mother-city (the original meaning of "metropolis") and her colonies were usually warm, but once they had established themselves the offspring were completely independent. Occasionally bad blood flowed: Corinth and its colony, Corcyra (today's island of Corfu), were on famously unfriendly terms.

Colonies facilitated the development of trade throughout the Mediterranean. They imported goods, such as bronze, silver and gold vessels, olive oil, wine, and textiles, from mainland Greece and elsewhere in the Mediterranean or manufactured them themselves, and then exchanged them with local communities—from the west, grain and slaves, from Thrace, silver, hides, timber, and slaves, and from the Black Sea, corn, dried fish, and (once more) slaves.

Greeks also set up trading posts, or *emporia,* which had no civic sponsor and attracted citizens from all kinds of different states: an important example was Naucratis on the Nile Delta.

It is hardly an exaggeration to say that by 580 practically every suitable spare spot for colonization on the Mediterranean coastline had been taken up. There were, of course, non-Greek colonizers, most especially the Phoenicians, who founded the great trading city of Carthage in North Africa. But the Hellenic achievement was remarkable all the same.

Not only did it create a far-flung Greek "world," but it also threw light on the early development of a corporate Hellenic "personality"— flexible, international, inquiring, and opportunistic.

Croesus's neighbors to the east were the kingdoms of Babylon and of Media, which had joined forces to destroy the old Assyrian Empire and sack its capital, Nineveh, in 612. Babylon was one of the great cities of the world. Once free of the Assyrians, its king built high, impregnable walls enclosing about one thousand acres and with eight gates. The most spectacular of these was the Ishtar Gate, faced with glazed blue bricks on which were bas reliefs of various animals, including lions and aurochs. The gate opened onto a grand processional way that led into the heart of the city.

To the northwest of Babylon and south of the Caspian Sea lay Media, a vigorous and newly centralized state. In the first half of the seventh century a founding king, Deiokes, built a great capital on a hill, Ecbatana. If the Greek historian Herodotus is to be trusted, its fortifications were as remarkable as those of Babylon. Looking very much like a ziggurat, they consisted of a series of massive concentric walls, each out-topped by the one within it. Inside the innermost and tallest wall stood the royal palace and the treasury.

> The parapets of the first circle are white, of the next black, of the third scarlet, of the fourth blue, of the fifth orange; all these colors being painted. The last two have their battlements coated respectively with silver and gold.

The rulers of the three states were on reasonably good terms, and had intermarried.

Eastwards in the southwestern part of Iran, roughly coextensive with the modern region of Fārs, there was the small dependent kingdom of Persis. Its new king was the youthful, hook-nosed Cyrus (in Old Persian, Kūruš), an ambitious and energetic ruler. He assembled the Persian tribes in 550 and persuaded them to approve his plan to revolt from his Median overlord. The campaign met with total success, as a Babylonian priest recorded.

> King Ishtumegu (Astyages) [of Media] called up his troops and marched against Cyrus, king of Anshan (a city under Persian rule), in order to me[et him in battle]. The army of Ishtumegu revolted against him and they de[livered] him in fetters to Cyrus. Cyrus [marched] against the country Agamtanu (Ecbatana); the royal residence [he seized]; he took as booty silver, gold, (other)

valuables ... of the country Agamtanu and brought [them] to Anshan.

It was this disaster that captured Croesus's full attention. He decided that he needed to act rather than wait, like a tethered goat, for Cyrus's next step, which would very probably be an invasion of Lydia.

However, before making any definite move, he consulted Apollo's oracle at Delphi.

Croesus wanted to be sure that Delphi and other well-known oracles were all they were cracked up to be, or so writes Herodotus. As a first step he sent delegates to the oracle, instructing them to consult the Pythia on the hundredth day after they had left Sardis, the Lydian capital. They were to ask what the king was doing at that very moment. This they did, and in the versified response the prophetess claimed that she could smell

hard-shelled tortoise
Boiling in bronze with the meat of lamb,
Laid upon bronze below, covered with bronze on top

Croesus was most impressed, for at the relevant time he had chopped up a tortoise and a lamb, and boiled them together in a bronze cauldron with a bronze lid. It was now that the king began to deluge the shrine at Delphi with generous gifts. The god looked after patrons like Croesus, generous and trusting. The king was given priority consultation rights, exemption from fees, and the best seats at Delphi's festivals.

In due course a second delegation raised a more substantive issue. This was the king's question: "Croesus, king of the Lydians and other peoples, in the belief that yours is the only true oracle in the whole world, gives you gifts worthy of your prophetic insight, and asks whether he should wage war against the Persians and whether he should seek to add any military force to his own as an ally."

The god replied that if Croesus were to cross the Halys River, the boundary of his empire, and wage war on the Persians, he would destroy a mighty empire. So victory was guaranteed. The Lydian envoys asked a third question. Would his reign be a long one?

The Pythia answered in cryptic verse:

Wait till a mule becomes king of the Medes,
Then, tender-footed Lydian, run away to the pebbly River Hermus.
And hurry, hurry, don't feel ashamed of being a coward.

More good news, thought Croesus. He had never heard of a mule ruling a kingdom and he could safely look forward to many years on the throne.

He mobilized his army and led it northeastwards. He found Cyrus in Paphlagonia and an indecisive battle ensued. He attributed his lack of success to his army being much smaller than that of Cyrus. He decided to return to the safety of Sardis and disband his troops, who were all mercenaries. Winter was approaching, when wars were not usually fought, and he would spend the interval before spring seeking allies and reinforcements. He concluded a military alliance with the Bab;ylonians, who could imagine themselves being next on Cyrus's imperial shopping list if Lydia fell. Apparently he also sent embassies to Egypt, which might regard the emergence of a new and aggressive power in the Middle East with alarm, and to the Spartans, who had no obvious locus in the conflict and were not interested.

Cyrus liked to fight a war of movement, and saw the Lydian withdrawal and demobilization as an opportunity. He followed hot on Croesus's heels and, much to the king's dismay, soon appeared outside Sardis. A new army was swiftly raised and Croesus led it out against the Persians. Cyrus unexpectedly used camels as cavalry. They frightened the Lydian horses, which turned around and fled as soon as they caught the camels' scent. The Lydian infantry fought on bravely, but the day belonged to Cyrus, who now placed Sardis under siege.

Nothing happened for a time. Then one day a Lydian guard on the city's citadel accidentally dropped his helmet down a cliffside, so precipitous that it had not been fortified. The man scrambled down the slope, retrieved his helmet, and climbed back up without difficulty. A Persian happened to be watching and realized he had witnessed a way into the city. He passed the word to Cyrus.

In this period siege machines and artillery were incapable of destroying strongly built walls, but once a few men had managed by trickery, treachery, or clever observation to bypass the defenses, a city's fate was usually sealed. Cyrus made good use of the intelligence he had received and Sardis fell.

A legend grew that Cyrus intended to burn Croesus alive, but that a timely rainstorm doused the flames. Perhaps it was the doing of Apollo, feeling a little guilty at having so comprehensively hoodwinked a loyal admirer. What happened to him in truth is unknown. He may have become an adviser at the Persian court. But the Babylonians told a different story.

> Cyrus, king of Persia, called up his army and crossed the Tigris. . . . In the month of Aiaru (May/June) he marched against the country of Lydia . . . killed its king, took his possessions, put there a garrison of his own.

But of one thing there could be no doubt. Croesus had allowed himself to be misled by Apollo's crooked words. A mule is a cross between a horse and a donkey; in the oracle this signified Cyrus himself, also a mongrel, for his mother was a Mede and his father a Persian. And the empire Croesus had destroyed was his own.

What was to be the fate of the Ionian city-states now? Cyrus had invited them to join him in the conquest of Lydia, but they had declined. Instead, they sided with their ruler, Croesus, for they could not believe that he would be totally overthrown and feared his vengeance once the Persians had gone away. After the debacle they put out feelers to Cyrus, but he was still irritated at having been snubbed and did not respond (although he agreed to a treaty with the great mercantile city of Miletus, which had been neutral).

At this point the Ionians would have been wise to unite and plan a common resistance to the Persians, who would surely launch an invasion. The greatest philosopher of the age, Thales of Miletus, intervened. He rejected religious and mythological explanations of the universe and applied reason to the question.

Turning to political matters, Thales argued that the Ionians should unite into a single political entity and set up a governing council on the island of Teos. As a more extreme variation on this idea it was further suggested that all the Ionians should emigrate to Sardinia and found an integrated state there, far beyond the Great King's reach.

The Ionians met together at their general assembly, the Pan-Ionium, but agreed on little except to make a general appeal for assistance to the international Hellenic community. The Spartans sent a herald to Cyrus, telling him not to attack the Ionians, "for the Spartans will not tolerate it." A bemused Cyrus asked his officials: "Who are the Spartans? And how many of them are there?" Having received an answer, the Great King dismissed the herald with the comment that he was not afraid of anyone who had a marketplace in the center of his city where people swore false oaths and cheated each other.

Having failed to hang together, the Ionians were, of course, hanged separately. Cyrus took on each *polis* one by one and reduced them all. They now had a new master.

A clay cylinder has been found, inscribed in Babylonian cuneiform (one of the earliest known systems of writing, consisting of wedge-shaped marks on clay tablets), which gives Cyrus's own account of his next victory, now that he had disposed of the Lydians. This was nothing less than the conquest of the ancient city of Babylon in 539. It took some years to accomplish, but the king presented his victory as a walkover, almost as if his invasion had not simply been peaceable but the result of an invitation by the people. He entered the city "without fighting or battle" and the ruling elite welcomed him. "Their faces shone."

Cyrus saw himself as the inheritor of the "perpetual seed of kingship," as if it were in his genes, and did not allow himself to be knowingly undersold:

I am Cyrus, king of the universe, the great king, the powerful king, king of Babylon, king of Sumer and Akkad (ancient territories under Babylonian rule), king of the four quarters of the world, son of Cambyses, the great king, king of the city of Anshan, grandson of Cyrus, the great king, ki[ng of the ci]ty of Anshan, descendant of Teispes, the great king, king of the city of Anshan.

The Persians under Cyrus now controlled a large empire stretching from the Ionian Greek city-states on the western seaboard of Asia Minor to Persia. At some stage (we do not know exactly when) Cyrus also conquered Central Asia. It was an extraordinary rise. At its fullest extent and for the first time in the history of the Middle East, countries from the river Indus to the Balkans, from Central Asia to Upper Egypt were incorporated into a single political system.

Cyrus the Great, as he came to be known, did not have many years to enjoy his achievements. He continued aggressively campaigning in the east of his domains. In 539 he fought with an Iranian nomadic confederation, the Massagetae, who probably roamed lands south of the Caspian Sea and who were then ruled by a queen. The Persians captured her son, who felt so shamed that he killed himself at the first opportunity.

His enraged mother assembled all her forces and defeated the Persians in a great battle during which Cyrus lost his life. She found his corpse on the battlefield and stuffed its head into a wineskin filled with blood. "I said I would make you have your fill of blood."

His tomb, set in a park, was a modest stone building with a gabled roof and two small stone doors, standing on a stepped platform. The monument survives, although the body and grave goods are long gone. Apparently it once contained a golden bed, a table with drinking cups on it, a golden coffin, and various ornaments studded with jewels. There was also an inscription on the tomb. According to the first-century B.C. geographer Strabo, this read:

> O man, I am Cyrus. I won an empire for the Persians, and was
>   king of Asia.
> So do not grudge me this monument.

How was this enormous empire run? It is a hard question to answer, for the Persians left behind them no books of political theory, nor descriptions of their system of government, nor even a history of their times. However, there is no question but that the Achaemenid dynasty (so-called after its founder, Achaemenes, an early king of Persia) that Cyrus founded was autocratic. The Great King, as he was called, lived in splendid and solemn state. He was divinely appointed and divinely accountable.

Distances from the imperial capitals of Susa and Persepolis to the farthest provinces were so great that it was essential to make communications as speedy as possible. A highway, called the Royal Road, was created that ran from Sardis, Croesus's old base, to Susa. At intervals all along the way, more than one hundred posthouses were established where royal messengers and public officials could obtain a change of horses, food, and rooms for the night. Sometimes this express service operated around the clock; night messengers succeeded day messengers in relays. "Nothing prevents these couriers," comments Herodotus, "from completing their allotted course in the quickest possible time—neither snow, rain, heat or darkness." Even so travel was painfully slow, for nothing could go faster than a horse. According to the indefatigably curious historian, "the distance from Sardis to what is called the Palace of Memnon [at Susa] will be 13,500 furlongs. Thus those travelling at a rate of 150 furlongs a day, will take just ninety days to make the journey."

Clay tablets have been unearthed at Persepolis that record officials' traveling expenses. As this typical example shows, the Persians ran an efficient bureaucracy: "1:5 [?] quarts of flour supplied by Bakadusda. Muska received, as a fast messenger. He went from the King to Zissawis. He carried a sealed document of the King. In the tenth month."

However hard he might try, the Great King was not able to respond quickly enough to events as they arose in the more remote corners of his dominions. He established a network of provincial governors, called satraps, whose main duty was to collect taxes and remit them to the central authority in Persia (in some places local kings were employed rather than satraps). The precise details are unclear, but, according to Xenophon, there was also a network of military garrisons and commanders who looked after security but were not to meddle with anything else. This division of powers was obviously intended to guard against plots and insurrections. However, it seems that on occasion one man controlled both the army and civilian affairs. Such satraps ran small wars and were known to fight with one another and even to rise up against the Great King himself.

Until now this had been a world without coinage. It is said that Croesus invented coins and the Persian government picked up on the idea, less as a means of day-to-day exchange than of making bulk payments with gold and silver currency. Most of the Great King's subjects did not use coins and restricted themselves to barter: they would have been hard put to recognize them or know what they were for. Satraps minted their own coinages, but they only did so in extraordinary military circumstances when armies needed to be paid. The golden *daric* of the Persians and the silver *siglos* did not merely have practical uses, they were symbols of the wealth, grandeur, and stability of the empire.

The Great King seldom went on progresses throughout his realms and spent most of his time in his palaces in Persia, but he needed to check on the performance of his satraps and generals. Every year (again according to Xenophon) a government inspector at the head of an army went out on a provincial tour. An advance announcement would be made: "the King's son is coming down," or "the King's brother," or, more anonymous and sinister, "the King's eye," but one never knew whether he would actually turn up, for at any moment the Great King might recall him. It was an economical way of keeping people alert to their duties.

The Persian system of government was hardly ideal. As we shall see, satraps often misbehaved and acted in their own rather than their employer's interest. Palace politics could be lethal and the transition from one ruler to his successor fraught and murderous. But the Great King understood that the majority of his subjects were at their most productive and governable if they were left alone to live their own lives. It was a sound and civilized imperial principle.

Cyrus wanted to be regarded as a just ruler and sought the moral approval of his subjects; in the Cyrus Cylinder he speaks of the blessings of his kingship and boasts: "I have enabled all the lands to live in peace." Political and economic stability was indeed the chief benefit that the empire could confer. It also promoted religious and linguistic diversity. Communities were expected to speak in their own tongues and to practice their own faiths. The empire tried not to intrude.

It was annoying to have to pay tribute, but there was a return on the investment. In his book *The Education of Cyrus,* Xenophon has the Great King say of tribute: "It is no more than fair, for if any danger comes it is we who have to fend it off." And peace fostered the main source of most people's solvency—mainly agricultural production, but also, especially in cities, manufacturing (pottery, tools, weapons, and luxury goods).

We are not sure of the religious faith of Cyrus the Great, for there is no direct reference to it in his surviving inscriptions, and the same applies to his son Cambyses. But he is polite about other peoples' gods.

He even gave financial assistance for the building or rebuilding of temples dedicated to foreign faiths. It was forbidden to disturb the cult of Ahura Mazda or any other religion. In the Cyrus Cylinder the Great King pays his respects to the Babylonian deity, Marduk, and in the Bible receives the honorific title of Messiah. According to Isaiah, he was the anointed of Jehovah (this was a thank-you for repatriating the Jews exiled to Babylon).

Thereafter the Achaemenid kings speak of themselves as worshippers of Ahura Mazda (literally Being and Mind). He was a perfectly good, benevolent uncreated spirit who created the universe. His worship often took place in the open air in walled gardens (in Greek, *paradeisos,* whence our word "paradise") or even mountaintops. Except for Cyrus. Great Kings were buried in tombs built into a high cliff-face not far from the imperial city of Persepolis.

Against Ahura Mazda stood a destructive spirit, Ahri-man. As in Zoroastrianism (a religion, to which that of the Achaemenids seems to be related, founded by the prophet Zarathustra or, as the Greeks called him, Zoroaster, who may have lived around the year 1000), the essential struggle in the universe was that between the "Truth" and the "Lie." So far as the Achaemenid kings were concerned, the Lie referred to the ever-present dangers that threatened Persia and its empire. By contrast, they believed that "the man who has respect for that law which Ahura Mazda has established and worships Ahura Mazda and Arta [one of the other gods in the divine pantheon] reverently, he becomes happy while living, and blessed when dead."

The Achaemenids were expansionist. Cyrus's son Cambyses succeeded him and in 525 launched an attack on the Egypt of the pharaohs, a civilization that had already lasted for millennia. He defeated the Egyptians at the Battle of Pelusium, the fortress town that is the gateway into the kingdom from the east. He made himself pharaoh, assuming the ruler's official titles, regalia, and uniform.

Then in 522 something happened that made him rush back to Persia. His long absences in Egypt and his despotic style of government had led to unrest back home. Cambyses had a younger brother or half brother, Bardiya (the Greeks called him Smerdis), who revolted and set himself up as Great King. He was extremely popular in Persia and Media, the heartland of the empire. The challenge had to be addressed, but en route from Egypt, Cambyses died childless in disputed circumstances.

There are different versions of what happened. Herodotus says that in March 522, the scabbard of Cambyses' sword fell off and he accidentally stabbed himself. The wound went gangrenous and in eleven days he was dead. Another account by his lance-bearer, a nobleman called Darius, has it that the Great King "died his own death"—a gnomic phrase that some have taken to mean that he committed suicide.

Whatever precisely happened, this death left Bardiya still on the imperial throne, but only for seven months. Darius, who was a member of the imperial family and the son of a satrap, joined six other nobles in a successful conspiracy to assassinate the pretender. Darius was then appointed his successor.

He himself promoted a different version of events, according to a large inscription carved on a mountainside in Persia. He claimed that Cambyses had his brother Bardiya killed, before he himself died. Darius wrote: "When Cambyses slew Bardiya, it was not known unto the people that Bardiya was slain." Then a *magus,* or priest from Media, called Gaumata, seeing the unpopularity of the government, impersonated Bardiya and hijacked the throne.

Darius continued: "The people feared him exceedingly, for he slew many who had known the real Bardiya. For this reason did he slay them, 'that they may not know that I am not Bardiya, the son of Cyrus.' There was none who dared to act against Gaumata, the Magian, until I came."

Darius put Gaumata to death, but had a hard time maintaining his authority. In his first year in office he claims to have fought nineteen battles and captured nine kings. He punished them with horrifying severity; he writes of one rebel, proudly:

Phraortes, seized, was led to me. I cut off his nose and ears and tongue, and put out one eye; he was kept bound at my palace entrance, all the people saw him. Afterward I impaled him at Ecbatana; and the men who were his foremost followers, those at Ecbatana within the fortress, I flayed and hung out [that is, their hides, stuffed with straw].

So what are we to believe? There was not much passing trade to read Darius's mountaintop inscription, although copies were distributed through the empire. He intended his narrative to last forever and to be read by posterity. However, there are inherent improbabilities in his account.

How likely is it that a senior member of the imperial family could be put to death on the order of Cambyses without anyone noticing? And surely many people knew Prince Bardiya by sight and would not have been taken in by a Median *magus*. And they could hardly all have been put to death. Nothing can be proved, but it is probable that it was Darius who was the usurper, who, Cambyses having died, murdered a real Great King and with barefaced effrontery replaced him. This could never be acknowledged, but the cover story he concocted is so thin as to insult the intelligence. One wonders what Ahura Mazda was supposed to make of this Great Lie.

Darius turned out to be a strong and effective ruler who earned his sobriquet "the Great," as he came to be called, but the method of his accession exposed the chief weakness of the Persian state. At the center of affairs lay not so much a government as a palace. Intrigues were de rigueur, and maneuvers for the succession frequently fraught and bloody.

Compared with statelets like Athens and Sparta, the empire of Persia suffered from elephantiasis and good Hellenes thoroughly disapproved. For them, whether on the mainland, or in the many Greek colonies in Italy, Sicily, or Ionia, the best constitutional arrangement was the *polis*— that is to say, a small self-governing city that had all the competences of an independent state. Its citizens were potent stakeholders. They felt themselves to be superior to other peoples governed by despots. So far as Greeks were concerned, the man who was not politically active did not deserve to be a citizen, a *politēs*.

The philosopher, sociologist, and political theorist Aristotle, writing in the fourth century, claimed that "man is by nature a creature of the *polis*." Anyone who "by nature and not by chance" is without a *polis* is either a bad man or a supernatural being. He is like the "outlaw, without a tribe or a hearth," whom Homer condemns in the *Iliad*. Such a person is necessarily by nature a lover of war.

A city should not be too small to be incapable of being self-sufficient or too large to govern effectively. In Aristotle's opinion, it should be possible to see all its citizens when gathered together in one place in assembly. (It must be remembered that women, slaves, and foreign residents—*metics*—were excluded from the franchise.) The philosopher Plato was even more specific. He proposed a citizen body of about five thousand men.

The issue of population size was important for one very good reason. The Greeks had no notion of representative democracy. When rule by the people was introduced in Athens in the sixth century (see chapter 7), decisions were taken directly by citizens meeting in public. In the middle of the sixth century, a poet called Phocylides wrote:

> . . . *a little* polis *living in good order*
> *In a high place is greater than block-headed Nineveh*

Not all *poleis* (the plural of *polis*) were democracies. Among the Ionians the Great King liked to insist on one-man rule or oligarchies. But they maintained citizen assemblies, even if their powers were limited or only a few citizens were allowed to vote.

Despite the recommendations of Plato and Aristotle, the city-state was prone to fierce, sometimes murderous quarreling between two factions, democrats and oligarchs. Civil war was common. Oppositions were invariably disloyal and, if not liquidated, were driven into exile, where they plotted their return and the expulsion or execution of those presently in power.

Nevertheless, unless a Hellene was free and lived in a *polis,* his condition was felt to be shameful. He was the next best thing to a barbarian—not simply foreign, but the shadow of a man, cowardly, effete, slavish, murderous, susceptible to luxury and comfort.

The Persian Empire had not finished expanding. To secure its northwestern edge, Darius led a campaign in 513 to conquer Macedonia and Thrace, home of untamed tribal groups (today, southeastern Bulgaria, northeastern Greece, and the European part of Turkey). There was a lesson here for mainland Greeks who could foresee a day when the Great King might cast a greedy eye in their direction.

Persia already controlled the myriad city-states along the Asian seaboard, having taken them over with Lydia from Croesus. Like all Hellenes, the Ionians were passionate for their liberties and resented foreign control. They were tired of Persian rule. The seeds of revolt against the Great King were sown in the port of Miletus near the mouth of the Maeander River in the satrapy of Caria.

Its leader, a certain Aristagoras, who was deputy governor for the Persians, turned coat, and persuaded the city-states as well as Caria and Cyprus to form an anti-Persian alliance. He crossed over into Greece to win more support. He told the Spartan king Cleomenes: "It is a disgrace that the Ionians are slaves rather than free men." But he failed to win him over, for in his view the Persian Empire was much too far away to be of concern.

Aristagoras did better at Athens where he won over the assembly by promising that the war would be a walkover. Twenty warships were voted to help the Ionians. It was not the most generous of commitments, but it infuriated Darius when he came to hear of it. Herodotus famously commented: "These ships turned out to be the beginning of evils for both Hellenes and barbarians."

In 499 the rebels, Athenians among them, marched north from Miletus and then Ephesus. They turned inland and arrived at Sardis, which put up no resistance. But although they had taken the city, they were unable to plunder it. Many of its houses were made of reeds and after a soldier had set fire to one of them flames swept through Sardis. A sanctuary dedicated to the greatly respected mother goddess, Cybele, was burned to the ground. This was sacrilege, and the Persians were shocked, for, as we have seen, their policy was to privilege and protect all religions. Another ground for dismay was that the Lydian kingdom was technologically very advanced and Sardis was its industrial center. Its products included the making and dyeing of fine woolen cloth and carpets. The river Pactolus flowed through the city's marketplace carrying gold dust in its mud. It was during Croesus's reign that the secret of separating gold from silver was discovered, thereby producing both metals of a purity never before known.

At this point the Athenians withdrew from the war and sailed back to Athens. We are not told why, but it is possible that they came to a view that the revolt was bound to fail. This was because it would be won and lost at sea. Most of the states taking part were maritime powers, but the Persian fleet bristled with state-of-the-art Phoenician warships and employed well-trained crews. In any battle at sea the odds were against the rebels.

As time passed, the Ionian confederation began to fall apart. Its members may have been allies, but they simply could not bear to act in unison for any length of time. In 494 an Ionian commander, Dionysius of Phocaea, a Greek city-state on the Asian coast, was dismayed by the state of the fleet that had gathered at the little island of Lade not far from beleaguered Miletus. In theory it was a powerful force with more than 350 warships, but it was ill disciplined and morale was low. Dionysius attempted but failed to introduce rigorous training to prepare the fleet for battle with the Persians.

The result was predictable. Some contingents from the Aegean islands sailed away and the Persians won a decisive victory. Seeing that all was lost, the Greek admiral made good his escape. He did not return to Phocaea, his homeland, guessing at the vengeance the victorious Persians would wreak against his fellow-citizens. He sailed south and attacked the Phoenician merchant fleet. Having captured valuable booty, he set a course for Sicily where he made a living as a pirate who preyed on Carthaginian and Etruscan shipping. He had done his best for the Ionians, but he knew when he was beaten. Beaten, that is, not by the enemy but by his fractious Ionian allies.

Miletus fell and was sacked. Most of its men were killed and the women and children were sold into slavery. It was a bitter blow to Ionian pride. Modern archaeologists have found evidence of the destruction and abandonment of parts of the city.

There was a lesson in the failure of the uprising for all Greeks. Until they learned to cooperate with one another, they would never beat the Persians with their vast reserves of wealth and human capital.

The Athenians were dismayed. It was scandalous that civilized communities had lost their liberty to a barbarian monarchy. A popular dramatist, Phrynichus, staged a play on the subject of the fall of Miletus. It was a hit and spectators wept at the moving reenactment. This did not do Phrynichus any good. He had laid bare their emotions and people were furious. They made him pay a heavy fine for reminding them of a real-life tragedy with which they were only too painfully familiar. They decreed that no drama on this subject should ever be presented again.

Darius brooded over the fiery fate of Sardis. He had a justifiable reputation for religious toleration. A letter of his to an official survives, whose discouraging opening sentence reads: "I understand that you are not completely obedient to my commands." We can imagine the panic with which the recipient of this missive read on. The Great King explains his anger. "You have levied tribute on the sacred gardeners of Apollo and you have ordered them to till profane land, disregarding the will of my ancestors towards the god." He added that through his oracle at Delphi Apollo had always spoken truth to the Persians.

History does not record the official's reply, nor what happened to him. But we have other evidence that Darius was not a merciful man. Ionia had passed back under his yoke, but so far the Athenians had gotten off scot-free despite their part in the firing of the Lydian capital and the destruction of the Great Mother's sanctuary. In his eyes they were not in the least civilized, as they liked to claim; they were no better than the pirates or sea raiders who until the peace of the Great King had infested the Eastern Mediterranean. One day, he promised himself, flames would consume *their* gods.

He began to lay plans for the invasion of Greece.

THE INVENTION
OF DEMOCRACY

———————

4

The Shaking-Off

I t was the greatest moment of his life.

The young Athenian nobleman had won the *diaulos* at the Olympic Games of 640. He was Cylon and the *diaulos,* literally a "double flute" in Greek, was the name given to a foot race of about 400 meters. The competitors, stripped to the buff, ran the length of the stadium, which in those days was not much more than a dirt track (later it was remodeled with raised banks for spectators), and back again.

Cylon was crowned with a wreath of olive leaves, an inexpensive honor, but, as we have seen, the real prize was glory. The great poet Pindar, writing more than a century later, was a specialist in composing praise hymns for winners, and in one of them he summed up what was important about victory at the games. Life was filled with pain and ended in the defeat of death, but the triumph of an athlete in bloom offered a kind of immortality.

Man's life is a day! What is he?
What is he not? A dream of a shadow

Is our mortal being. But when there comes to men
A gleam of splendour given by heaven,
Shining life is on earth
And life is sweet as honey.

Cylon intended to add to his glory another great deed. In 632 he led a plot to overthrow the constitution and set himself up as tyrant, or sole ruler, of Athens. He knew something about tyranny as a form of government, for he was married to a daughter of the tyrant of Megara, Theagenes. This was a small city-state just north of the Isthmus of Corinth with a claim on the strategic island of Salamis, which Athens fiercely contested. Theagenes' approach to the business of power was simple and direct. He won and kept the approval of the poor by slaughtering the cattle of the rich, which were grazing on other people's well-watered land. He understood that he needed the confidence of the people and, as the clear-eyed philosopher Aristotle put it, the "confidence of the people [depended] on hostility to the rich."

At this time Athens was ruled by an aristocracy, the so-called Eupatridae (literally, "men with good fathers"). Although an aristocrat himself, Cylon knew his peers had no interest in supporting him. He would need popular backing, and he must have had some evidence that this was forthcoming.

He took sensible precautions. He consulted the oracle at Delphi, which advised him to seize the Acropolis, the city's citadel, during the "greatest festival of Zeus," so he made his attempt during that year's Olympic Games. This surely was Greece's "greatest" celebration. His father-in-law supplied him with troops.

When he presented himself to the people, his careful preparations went for nothing. He seized the Acropolis, but not the city. Ordinary Athenians failed to cheer him along. In fact, when they realized what was going on they came in from the countryside where they were working in their fields and placed Cylon under siege.

It turned out he had gotten the oracle wrong too. Apollo had not meant the Olympic Games, but the Diasia, a great Athenian festival that was held outside the city walls and was attended by all citizens. With the city itself deserted, Cylon and his men would have met with little or no opposition.

The only remaining business to be decided was what to do with the failed revolutionaries. Cylon himself and his brother managed to slip away unseen, but the remainder sought sanctuary in the old temple of Athena on the Acropolis. The protection of the goddess was absolute for so long as the suppliants chose to remain.

However, the ruling aristocrats wanted to teach the traitors a lesson, while sticking to the letter of the law. The chief official of that year, or Eponymous Archon (for more on Archons see page 60), was Megacles, a very grand man indeed, who was a leading member of the Alcmeonidae, a fabulously wealthy clan with influential international connections.

He persuaded Cylon's men, who were short of food, to come down and stand trial. They would technically remain in sanctuary because they would all have their hands on a long thread tied to the cult statue of the goddess inside the temple. Megacles solemnly promised they would not be harmed.

They walked past the Areopagus hill and the shrine of the Erinyes. These were the Furies, unforgiving and ferocious punishers of the forsworn oath. Ancient deities older than Zeus and the Olympians, they were usually imagined as disgusting hags; they were variously described as having coal black bodies, bat's wings, snakes in place of hair, and dog's heads. They wielded cruel brass-studded scourges. By a malign coincidence, it was just at this point that the thread broke—and so did the oath of Megacles.

He and his fellow-Archons were delighted by the convenient accident. The goddess had clearly withdrawn her gift of sanctuary. This was justification, he claimed, for his next move. Those outside sacred precincts were stoned to death and even those who sat down at the altars of the "august goddesses" (as the Furies were politely called) in a vain attempt to save their lives were butchered. Some who begged for mercy from the wives of the Archons were spared.

If Cylon had miscalculated, it was as nothing to Megacles' hasty error of judgment. He had soiled himself by his own trickery. Nothing was more important than a man's purity when he entered into relation with the divine. Homer writes: "In no way can [he] pray to Zeus spattered with blood and filth." Hands had to be washed and clean, sometimes white clothes were worn at sacrifices. When entering a sanctuary a suppliant would sprinkle himself with water in a font. Sexual intercourse, birth, death, and, especially, murder defiled all those involved.

Athens had been preserved from a despot, but in the process had incurred the gravest of pollutions. The murder of anyone under the guardianship of the gods was an insult to the gods themselves. The Olympians were not mocked.

So how could the city purify itself?

Cylon, his brother, and their descendants were condemned to perpetual banishment. But Megacles and the entire clan of the Alcmaeonids were tried and found guilty of sacrilege. They too were all exiled in perpetuity and even those who died between the date of the offense and the passing of the sentence were exhumed and their remains thrown out. The point was not so much to punish those convicted as to remove the threat of divine displeasure.

A curious shaman-like figure, Epimedes, who was a Cretan seer, philosopher, and poet, was brought in to purify the city itself. He was said to have fallen asleep for fifty-seven years in a cave sacred to Zeus and died at an extreme old age. Tattoos were found on his corpse and his skin was preserved in the *ephors'* court at Sparta, for whom he had prophesied on military matters.

The seer accepted the Athenian commission and conducted the necessary rituals. He only charged for his services an olive branch and an alliance of friendship between the now cleansed city and Knossos, the capital of his homeland.

. . .

In the seventh century we at last enter an era of something looking like history. In the Mycenaean world, as we have seen, most states were monarchies, but by the time the "Dark Age" was over and light again suffused the scene, hereditary rulers like Theseus had mostly vanished.

In the place of kings, there was almost continuous civic strife between dominant aristocracies and impoverished peasants. Cylon's story is evidence of something unsettled in the Athenian polity, and much the same was the case in other Greek city-states, or *poleis*. There was a shift from animal husbandry to arable farming and migration from the country to the city. Between 1000 and 800 the Hellenic population seems to have remained more or less constant, but then, alongside a general economic and social revival, came rapid population growth, a major destabilizing factor. To have too many citizens was a problem that could only be partially alleviated by sending out citizen colonies. It inevitably contributed to unrest at home over land ownership and food production.

The nobility hijacked the Greek word for good, *agathos,* which came to mean of high birth. In Athens, these Eupatridae were connected with each other by intermarriage and ties of kinship. They forged international links, often traveling around Greece and the Mediterranean and giving each other generous hospitality and gifts. They were fiercely proud of their genealogies and fiercely competitive with one another. They looked back with regret to the obsolete heroes of old.

Unsurprisingly, men of this cast of mind strongly objected to new money and resisted upwards social mobility on the part of wealthy parvenus. The worst thing was to marry rich girls with no background. A poet, Theognis, a Greek from Megara who flourished in the middle of the sixth century, noted sourly: "Wealth has mixed up the race."

The lords and ladies of Homer's epics were the model for later aristocratic lifestyles. Theognis put the conservative case against social change in tones that have been repeated through the ages by defenders of privilege:

This city is still a city, but the people are not the same.
Once they knew nothing of justice nor laws,
But wore old goatskins
And lived outside the city like deer.
And now they are "noble" . . . while those
Who used to be noble are worthless.

The Eupatridae were satisfied with the way things were. The peasantry took a different view. For them the status quo had become unacceptable. Aristotle summed up their situation:

> The poor were enslaved to the rich—themselves and their children and their wives. The poor were called dependents and "sixth-parters," since it was for the payment of a sixth of what they produced that they worked the fields of the rich. All the land was in the hands of a few, and if the poor failed to pay their rents both they and their children were liable to seizure. All loans were made on the security of the person.

Many of the common people were in debt. They pledged their persons and could be seized by their creditors. Some of them became slaves at home, and others were sold into foreign countries.

Just as important as the problem of indebtedness, perhaps even more important, was the rising anger of ordinary Athenians at their subordinate relationship to the rich, their dependence on them as clients. They simply wanted to be free of their masters.

During the seventh and sixth centuries two ways were found of resolving this conflict between the classes. The first was to install one-man rule—in other words, a tyranny. The second was to invite an experienced politician to recommend radical constitutional reform—in other words to hand over the problem to a wise, all-knowing lawgiver.

A tyrant, or *turannos,* was a despot who depended on the backing of the people. Aristotle writes:

The tyrant is set up from among the people and the mob against the notables, so that the people may suffer no wrong from them. This is clear from the facts of history.

Charismatic and ruthless, he was usually a dissident nobleman, who seized power by coup d'état. Tyrannies tended to last for two or three generations, but seldom for longer. Of the main Greek states only Sparta and the island of Aegina appear to have escaped periods of tyranny. The word "tyrant" did not acquire a pejorative connotation before the fifth century. Many of these rulers were no worse than the aristocrats who had preceded them, and some were a distinct improvement. Above all, what they did was to quash the class war by the use of force.

The Cylon affair only exacerbated social and political tensions in Athens. It was clear that tyranny would not attract support, so a trusted lawgiver called Dracon was appointed in 622 or 621 to prepare a legal code and for the first time in the history of Athens to put it in writing. Perhaps it was meant to address, among other things, the fallout from the Alcmaeonid prosecutions. Little of the code survives, but it reflected the world of the blood feud and the rituals of purification. The legislator won a reputation for harshness. Apparently, the death penalty was applied to people convicted of idleness, and indeed for almost every offense. According to Demades, an Athenian orator and politician in the fourth century, Dracon "wrote his laws in blood, not ink."

The criticism seems to be unfair, for the only laws of his to come down to us are sensible and humane rulings on manslaughter. Involuntary homicide was punished by exile, and relatives of the dead man were entitled to give the offender a pardon. If a person defended himself against "someone unjustly plundering him by force" (that is, a burglar) and killed him, "that man shall die without a penalty being enforced."

Whatever the truth about Dracon's work, a review of Athenian legislation did little to calm the atmosphere of political rancor.

• • •

Solon was born into a good family in about 638, although it had fallen on hard times. It claimed descent from Codrus, last of the semimythical kings of Athens who flourished towards the end of the second millennium.

Those were the distant days of the Dorian invasions of mainland Greece. The Athenians were determined to resist the newcomers. They boasted proudly that they were autochthonous. They had not come from anywhere and they were going nowhere.

The oracle at Delphi prognosticated that a Dorian attack on Attica would only succeed if its king was unharmed. So Codrus decided to give his life for his country. He disguised himself as a peasant and made his way to the Dorian encampment, where he provoked a quarrel with some soldiers and led them on to killing him. Once the Dorians realized what had happened, they piously withdrew from Attica and left the Athenians in peace.

Some time after Codrus's death, the monarchy was abolished and replaced by three annually elected officials. The Basileus (or king) retained the old title, but was restricted to important religious duties. The Eponymous Archon (so-called because he gave his name to the year in which he held office) was, as we have seen, the civilian head of state and government; and the polemarch (or "war-ruler") was the army's commander-in-chief. These officials with executive powers were later supported by six others, making a total of nine Archons. Archons were appointed on the basis of birth and wealth. According to Aristotle, at first they held office for life, although this was apparently reduced later to ten years and by the seventh century to one year.

Solon's father, one Execestides, maintained a long-standing tradition of public service and, if we are to believe Plutarch, got himself into financial difficulties by excessive charitable giving. After his death, his son was too proud to approach his friends for loans; his family was accustomed to *giving* help, he told himself, not receiving it.

Short of funds and despite the fact that aristocrats did not approve of going into trade, Solon entered on a commercial career. It required a great deal of travel and the young merchant was able to see many different kinds of Greek governance. Once he had made his fortune, he gave himself over to a life of pleasure. However, he insisted: "I am not prepared to become rich unjustly, for retribution is certain."

Solon was a copious poet. Unlike his great contemporary Sappho from the island of Lesbos, who wrote the most passionate love lyrics, he wrote verse chiefly because there was no prose literature at that time and he had no other option. It was not for a century or so that authors such as the "father of history," Herodotus, took to prose as a matter of course.

A good deal of Solon's work survives. To begin with, he wrote with no particular end in view, but over time he used verse to communicate his political views. Paradoxically, as he rebuilt his family's fortune, he grew increasingly sympathetic to the poor. He once compared the differing fortunes of two men. One of them "owns much silver/And gold, and wide fields" and another has only enough to feed and clothe his family. But the latter also has a "child and a blooming wife . . . wealth enough for mortals."

While Solon was setting himself up in his writing as a defender of the poor, the political situation at Athens deteriorated. It appears that law and order broke down. Aristotle quotes from an important poem about Athens, the original Ionian territory, which Solon wrote at this time.

I know, and the pain lies in my heart,
When I look on the eldest land of Ionia
Tottering.

Solon built a reputation as a reconciler and at the request of all the city's political factions he was elected Eponymous Archon in 594/93. He was given sweeping powers to reform the state. It was agreed that whatever he recommended would be implemented. Solon claims to have accepted the commission reluctantly, but behind the scenes he gave assurances in advance to the parties.

This got him into a lot of trouble. He incautiously confided in some unreliable friends that he would not be confiscating land, but had made up his mind to cancel debts. Anticipating his decree, they immediately borrowed large sums of money and bought up estates; after Solon announced the cancellation, as he had assured them, they declined to pay their creditors. His embarrassment was only alleviated when, according to the terms of his legislation, he forgave large debts he himself was owed.

The new lawgiver moved fast. An Archon usually opened his term with a routine proclamation that he would protect property rights; but Solon evidently recognized that his reforms would attract strong opposition. He needed to build momentum from the outset if he was to stay the course and hustle the public into acquiescence.

He declared that all mortgages and debts which pledged the debtor's person in the event of default were annulled. Everyone who had become a slave because he could not repay what he owed was now a free man again. Those who had been sold abroad would be bought back at the state's expense and returned to Athens with their citizenship restored. This seismic event was nicknamed the *seisachtheia,* or the "shaking off of burdens."

Solon passed a law forbidding debt bondage in the future and fixed a maximum amount of land that an individual could own. However, as already mentioned, he refused to confiscate and redistribute the large estates. As a result he pleased nobody and there was widespread grumbling. Rich creditors were annoyed to lose what they were owed. The poor had been looking forward to owning the freehold of their allotments, but were disappointed to find that they still had to pay rent. Criticized on all sides, he was a wolf at bay encircled by attack dogs.

Solon's underlying sympathies lay with the poor, as he made clear in his poetry. In fact, he presented himself, unembarrassedly if inaccurately, as one of them. He wrote:

Many evil men are rich, and many good men poor;
But we will not exchange our virtue
for their wealth, since virtue lasts forever.
Whereas wealth belongs now to one man, now to another

However, the role of the lawgiver was to be an arbiter between con-
flicting interests and Solon convinced his fellow-citizens that he would
be evenhanded, as indeed he was. Although he had started out as a
radical, he ended as a moderate.

Solon was no democrat; he simply wanted all classes to be of good
standing in the state. This was how he put it:

I have given the masses as much privilege as is enough
neither taking away nor adding to their honor.
As for those who had power and were envied for their wealth,
for them I took care they should suffer no slight.
I stood holding my valiant shield over both sides,
and I did not allow either of them to triumph unjustly.

However, his political reforms took a giant step from aristocratic government in the direction of democracy, even if Solon did not perceive
it at the time.

His first priority was to create a new kind of aristocracy—an aristocracy of wealth rather than the existing one of birth. He divided the
population of Attica into four economic groups, measured according
to the annual yield of landed property in the form of grain, wine, or oil.

The richest were the *pentacosiomedimni;* these were landowners
whose income reached five hundred *medimni,* or bushels of grain, either grain alone or in combination with equivalent measures of oil and
wine. Only these men were eligible for the Archonship and the important financial post of Treasurer of Athena. Of course, many noblemen
were rich enough to be *pentacosiomedimni,* but the point was that now it

was to be only their money that qualified them for high office, not their parentage. There were wealthy "commoners" more than ready to compete with them.

Next came the *hippeis,* whose property produced less than five hundred and more than three hundred bushels. Their name means "horsemen," for they were judged rich enough to afford the upkeep of a horse and so could act as cavalry in time of war. The third class were the *zeugitai* (able to keep a team or *zeugos* of oxen), who needed to produce two hundred *medimni.* Various official jobs were open to both these classes.

Finally, at the bottom of the heap were the *thetes* (serfs), who were manual laborers with property worth less than 150 *medimni.* They could not hold any public office and in wartime served as light-armed infantry or oarsmen in the fleet.

Citizens in a *polis* like Athens attended meetings of a general assembly or *ecclesia.* Its authority and its membership varied according to the kind of regime in power at the time. At a minimum it decided on war and peace and formally elected magistrates. The poor were often excluded or at best not expected to play an active part in proceedings. In any case, they had little free time to attend meetings. In a groundbreaking move, Solon opened the assembly to the *thetes* as full participants.

He also created a new council, or *boulē,* of four hundred members drawn from the four tribes, which met regularly and prepared business for the assembly. A preexisting all-purpose body, the council of the Areopagus (a hill near the Acropolis named after Ares, god of war, where it met), had been dominated by the nobility and its powers were now limited to guardianship of the constitution and to criminal trials.

Solon was still not convinced that he had prized the fingers of the aristocracy from the levers of power. So he introduced a remarkable innovation into the election of the nine Archons. This was the principle of randomness. Each of Athens's four tribes (or subdivisions of the citizen body) elected ten men for the Archonship, forty in total. The successful nine were then chosen from the forty by lot.

The use of lot (the technical term is sortition) was a typically imaginative Greek device. It had two purposes—one religious and the other political. First, it was a respectful invitation to the gods to play their part in an election and, so to speak, leave them with the last word. Then, it ensured equality of opportunity and prevented the corruption that can mar elections. So far as Solon was concerned, it was a mechanism for weakening the influence of over-mighty factions. The nobility would find it harder to monopolize the Archonship.

To the modern mind, random selection is absurd. But sortition took the sting out of electoral contests. Perhaps most significantly, it encouraged citizens (at least, the better-off ones) to keep up-to-date with the issues of the day, for there was a reasonable chance that at some point they might have to play an active part in public life. Vetting and the preliminary long list went some way to preventing totally unsuitable or incapable appointees.

One of Solon's most curious measures underlines the seriousness with which he meant Athenians to take politics. He ruled that in times of faction and great policy debates a citizen who held back and did not involve himself or take sides should lose his civic rights and have no share in the city's governance.

Solon had not finished. As a successful businessman, he understood the value of economic growth to social harmony and the alleviation of poverty. Too much was being exported for higher prices than in the domestic market. So the Archon forbade the export of agricultural products, except for olive oil, of which there was probably a surplus. To encourage manufacturing, citizenship was granted to craftsmen (for example, in metalwork and ceramics) who settled in Athens with their families. Fathers were obliged to teach their sons a trade, if they were to enjoy support in their old age. The rapid rise in the production and dissemination of decorated Attic pottery at about this time is probably no coincidence.

Domestic ceramics were popular throughout Hellas. Corinthian ware was widely exported and featured black figures in silhouette on a red ground. The style was copied in Athens where it achieved very high levels of artistry from about 570. By about 530 Athenian potters developed a new, more realistic technique, with black backgrounds and human figures drawn by brush in red. Modern scholars have identified, on stylistic principles, more than one thousand ceramic artists.

Vases, cups, and plates depict a wide range of social activity—athletes training in the gymnasium, wining and dining at drinking parties or *symposia,* battle scenes, ships at sea, religious ceremonies, attractive young men (often accompanied by a fond toast—"Here's to the lovely Alexias" or whomever), mythological scenes (sometimes ghoulish, as when Medea is shown killing her children), people having sex, a reveler with a prostitute, women making music at home, and many, many more. Small vases (called *lecythoi*) show figures on a white ground; they held olive oil used for anointing the corpses of young unmarried men. Athenian pottery is not only aesthetically pleasing, but it also goes a long way to making up for the lack of literary accounts of everyday life.

For the first time Athens began minting its own coinage. Until then it had used the money of its nearby commercial rival, the island of Aegina. The object of the exercise was to assert the city's arrival as a serious economic force.

As well as his social and economic policies and his constitutional changes, Solon tackled the legal system of Athens and repealed Dracon's legal code except for his homicide laws.

He brought in two radical legal measures. In Athens there was no police or prosecution service. When a crime was committed it was for the victim in person to prosecute the alleged offender; but few poor men had the education or the audacity to take a nobleman to court. Solon ruled that any citizen, not simply the person affected, could bring a prosecution. An experienced orator was now able to speak for the injured party, thus improving the odds on a conviction.

The most far-reaching of all Solon's measures was the creation of a jury court of appeal against decisions taken by elected officials, particularly the Archons. This was the *heliaea.* Anyone could qualify to be a juror, even the impoverished *thetes.* This supreme court may indeed have been the *ecclesia* itself, in legal session.

In later times the annual jury list consisted of six thousand citizens over thirty years of age, chosen by lot. These sometimes met in full session and, as required, could be subdivided (also by lot) into panels some hundreds strong and served in various different courts. Cases were heard in the open air in a marked-off area of the *agora.* The large number of jurors not only encouraged citizens' participation in public affairs, but made bribery less likely. As we shall see, the judicial powers of the Archons were eventually taken over by the *heliaea,* and they merely prepared cases to be heard by it.

Whether or not Solon understood the full consequences of what he was doing, the establishment of his jury courts was the foundation of Athenian democracy, because they gave the citizens control over the executive arm of government.

Solon's settlement was inscribed on four sides of wooden tablets that were set in rotating frames, so they could be consulted easily. These tablets were still in existence in the third century and fragments survived to the lifetime of Plutarch in the first century A.D. They were in an antiquated and more or less incomprehensible script and were written "as the ox plows"—that is, in alternating lines from left to right and then right to left. But they were a treasure from Athens's time-honored past.

Once Solon had finished his work, what was he to do? And, despite all the assurances, how could he be certain that his reforms were properly carried out? The city appears to have been in turmoil; there is little detail but, in the light of the fact that the lawgiver lost an eye, we may suppose a forceful reaction, even riots. Also he faced endless advice on improvements to what he had written and inquiries about the exact meaning of one law or another.

Solon could have established himself as a tyrant and governed by decree. But this would have gone against everything he stood for—the rule of law, constitutional government, and social reconciliation. He would never be a Cylon. He wrote:

And if I spared my homeland,
And refused to set my hand to tyranny
And brute force, staining and disgracing my good name,
I am not ashamed. For I think in this way I will outdo
All other men.

Tyranny, he once remarked, was a delightful place, but there was no way out of it.

So, instead, he recalled his days as a trader and set off on his travels again. He obtained a leave of absence for ten years and advised his fellow-citizens simply to do what he had written and make no changes. He himself had no regrets, confessing contentedly: "I grow old, forever learning many things."

Apparently he visited Egypt, where he met the pharaoh, Amasis II, a man of lowly origins who seized the throne during an army revolt. He spent time studying with priests. From them he heard the story of the lost island of Atlantis (later taken up by Plato), which offended the gods and was swallowed up by the Atlantic Ocean. Solon is then said to have sailed to Cyprus, an island of numerous small kingdoms, where one of its mini-monarchs was a friend of his and was said to have named a new town in his honor, Soli.

At some point many years later, Solon, who had become an international celebrity as a wise man, went to Lydia, or so legend has it. There, at the capital, Sardis, he met King Croesus, then at the height of his power. Plutarch, who was the lawgiver's biographer, doubts the tale; the dates are difficult (albeit just about feasible), for Solon's Archonship was in 594 and Croesus only acceded to his throne in 560. But Plutarch can never resist a good story. He observed: "It so accurately fits Solon's character that I do not propose to reject it for reasons of chronology."

Solon was dismayed by the vulgarity of the Lydian court, but tried to keep his feelings to himself. Croesus asked him who he judged to be the happiest of men, confidently expecting the sage to name him. Solon was not prepared to flatter the king and nominated an Athenian who had died gloriously in battle.

Then who was the second most happy man? said the king, crossly. The unforgiving Solon said that Cleobis and Biton were his next choice. These two young men collapsed and died after hauling a wagon with their mother in it for five miles so that she could attend a religious festival. The sage's point was that life was uncertain and no one should be counted happy till the day of his death.

After Croesus's defeat by the Persians, the story that Cyrus the Great had intended to burn the Lydian king to death until a timely tempest doused the pyre was further enriched. As the flames licked upwards to him, Croesus groaned the word "Solon" three times. When asked to explain whom he was talking about, he replied: "A man to whom I would pay a fortune if only he could talk to all tyrants."

He then spoke of his encounter with Solon. Herodotus writes:

Cyrus learned through interpreters what Croesus had said. He reflected that he, too, was human, and changed his mind about committing a living man to the fire, a fellow human being who had been blessed with happiness no less than he. Moreover, he began to fear retribution, and to contemplate the fact that nothing is really secure and certain for human beings.

Cyrus pardoned Croesus for opposing him, spared his life, and appointed him as an adviser on high policy.

The anecdote is an elaborate fiction, but all the same it expresses a profound truth about the Hellenic mind. It embodies Apollo's maxims at Delphi—"nothing in excess" and "know yourself"—and was a bleak reminder that the fate of human beings lay not in themselves, but (as Homer put it) "on the knees of the gods." The Lydian king had offended them by his presumption. So he paid the price.

. . .

Was Solon a success or a failure? He himself knew that what he had achieved was imperfect. Someone once asked him: "Have you enacted the best possible laws for the Athenians?" "The best they would accept," came his undeceived reply.

His social, legal, and economic reforms brought undoubted benefits. Thanks to him Athens became an increasingly prosperous, progressive, and well-administered state with an emphasis on social justice. But the attempt to lower the political temperature failed. The Eupatridae were furious that they had lost so much wealth, prestige, and power. They were going to fight with all their might for a return to the old world of aristocratic privilege.

Within five years of Solon's Archonship, law and order broke down. In one year no Archons at all were elected, and in 582 an Eponymous Archon called Damasias tried to make his post permanent and in effect founded a tyranny: he lasted two years before being expelled.

Party strife broke out and three mutually hostile factions emerged. The party of the Coast was led by the Alcmaeonid Megacles (Solon had organized an amnesty for the exiled clan) and promoted moderate policies, while the men of the Plain advocated a return of the dismantled aristocratic system. The men "beyond the Hills" promoted the cause of the unprivileged. For the unpalatable fact remained that, in spite of the "shaking off of burdens" the poor were still poor, and angry. There were many more of them than noblemen. They were led by an ambitious young politician called Pisistratus, who could see an opportunity when it presented itself.

He was eager for power, and was determined to avoid Cylon's mistakes.

5

Friend of the Poor

The island of Salamis, hilly and dry, lies less than two miles off the coast of Attica. With nine thousand hectares of land, it is a rocky, inlet-rich crescent with few fertile acres. Unproductive though it was, its dark, rugged outline could be seen from the Acropolis and stood as a threat to freedom of passage for the merchant ships of Athens.

The export trade in olive oil, with Solon's encouragement, was thriving and the city was undoubtedly prospering. But until the Athenians controlled the island they faced the ever-present threat of a blockade. In the sixth century, Salamis was owned by Megara, the small but energetic and not always friendly *polis* on the mainland just west of the island.

In the days of the tyranny of Theagenes, Cylon's father-in-law, Megara was too troublesome a problem to solve. The Athenian assembly passed a law forbidding anyone to lay before it a proposal to annex the island by force on pain of death. At some point in the 560s the aged Solon decided to circumvent this prohibition.

He chose a bizarre means of doing so, if we are to believe Plutarch.

His family let it be known that he had become demented. In the privacy of his home, he secretly wrote a poem of a hundred lines about Salamis. When he had learned it by heart, he ran out of doors into the marketplace and recited it. He began:

> *I have come as a herald from lovely Salamis*
> *With a beautifully written song, not a political speech.*

Solon's point, a technical one to put it mildly, was that his verses did not qualify as a formal proposition. But his message could hardly have been plainer.

> *Let us go to Salamis to fight for a beautiful island*
> *And clear away bitter disgrace.*

In what must have been a preplanned move, Solon's friends, and in particular the leader of the peasant faction, Pisistratus, praised the poem to the skies and advised the people to act on his words. The law was repealed and war was declared against Megara. Solon took command of an expeditionary force and set off with Pisistratus on his staff to conquer the island.

They sailed past a headland on the southern coast of Attica and saw a large number of Athenian women sacrificing to the harvest goddess Demeter. A man who made himself out to be a deserter was dispatched to the Megarians. He told them that if they hurried they would be able to capture the wives and daughters of many leading Athenian families. The Megarians fell into the trap and sent a party of men to kidnap them. Meanwhile the women were sent away and replaced by attractive young men in dresses who did not yet need to shave. They caught the Megarians completely by surprise and killed them all.

Greeks much admired tricks of this sort. Guile was seen as a virtue and its "patron saint" was Odysseus, who devised the wooden horse at Troy and whose foxiness got him out of trouble more than once on his way home after the city's fall.

The ambush did not win the war, which carried on bloodily for some time. The two parties were so exhausted by the fighting that they agreed to submit the quarrel to the Spartans, who were the acknowledged if informal leaders of the Greek world. Apparently Solon thought of yet another device to help their cause. In the sixth century there was no agreed text of the Homeric epics. The revered lawgiver slipped two lines into the famous catalogue of the ships that the Greeks sent across the Aegean Sea to Troy. They referred to the flotilla of Ajax, king of Salamis.

Ajax brought twelve warships from Salamis
And beached them close to the Athenian army.

The couplet helpfully emphasized the close relationship between the islanders and Athens. And so it was to Athens that, after careful consideration, the Spartans awarded Salamis.

Solon and Pisistratus were very fond of one another. We are told they entered into a love affair when Pisistratus was a good-looking lad in his teens. Despite a wide gap of thirty years between them, this is not implausible. Solon was highly sexed, if we may judge from his poetry, where he writes of the delights of falling in love "with a boy in the lovely flower of youth,/Desiring his thighs and sweet mouth."

However, it would be wrong to believe that either man was necessarily, in our modern sense, gay. This is because from the eighth century onwards the Greek upper classes established and maintained a system of pederasty as a form of higher education. A fully grown adult male, usually in his twenties, would look out for a boy in his mid-teens and become his protector and guide. His task was to see him through from adolescence into adulthood and to act as a kind of moral tutor.

Sex was not compulsory, but it was under certain strictly defined conditions allowed. The older man was the active lover/partner or *erastes* and the teenager was the loved one, or *eromenos*. Buggery was absolutely out of bounds and brought shame on any boy who allowed it to be done to him. It could have the most serious consequences, as the fate of Periander showed. This famous tyrant of Corinth in the seventh century unwisely teased his *eromenos* in the presence of other people with the question: "Aren't you pregnant yet?" The boy was so upset by the insult that he killed Periander.

A popular and acceptable technique for achieving orgasm was intercrural sex: both participants stood up and the *erastes* inserted his erect penis between the thighs of the *eromenos* and rubbed it to and fro. The youth was not meant to enjoy his lover's attentions or show signs of arousal; rather, he was making a disinterested gift of himself to someone he admired.

The great Athenian writer of tragic dramas, Aeschylus, wrote a play about the love between the two Greek heroes, Achilles and Patroclus. It was called *The Myrmidons,* after the warriors whom Achilles commanded during the Trojan War. Achilles is presented as the *erastes,* and reproaches his lover, in rather roundabout terms, for declining an intercrural proposition.

> *And you rejected my holy reverence for your thighs,*
> *Spurned our many kisses.*

These same-sex unions were perfectly respectable provided that the conventions were observed, and that the teenager developed into a good man without disgracing his *erastes,* and so had been worth the trouble. Fathers would give couples their blessing. Just to the north of Attica in neighboring Boeotia, man and boy lived together as if they were married. In time of war lovers might fight alongside each other. A memorial stone found in the countryside outside Athens survives, in which an *eromenos* sadly records his lover's death.

> *Here a man solemnly swore for love of a boy*
> *To take part in strife and tearful war.*
> *I [i.e., the memorial stone] am sacred to Gnathios, who lost his life in battle.*

The romantic phase of a pederastic relationship did not last long, and once an *eromenos* had started to shave, sexual relations were felt to be improper.

The gods gave pederasty their blessing. They routinely had affairs with attractive young human beings and quite often their eyes lighted on pretty boys. Theognis, a lyric poet from Megara who flourished in the sixth century, argued that the king of the gods set his seal of approval on same-sex love by having numerous affairs with handsome youths.

In fact, he was not averse to committing rape, as the case of Ganymede goes to show. He was a Trojan shepherd whom Zeus fell for. Turning himself into an eagle, the god swooped down, grabbed him, and flew him off to his palace on Mount Olympus, where he appointed him his cup-bearer—in effect, chief sommelier.

> *There is a certain pleasure in loving a boy, for even Zeus,*
> *The son of Cronus, king of the immortals, fell in love with Ganymede,*
> *And snatching him up took him to Olympus, and made him*
> *A god, keeping forever the lovely bloom of youth.*

Couples were expected to graduate to marriage and children, those without a gay orientation doubtless heaving a sigh of relief. In fact, most of them will have been heterosexual and not much wanted sex with one another. These pederastic relationships were essentially adopted for cultural reasons. They often evolved into a lifelong friendship and, like marriages, were a useful means by which families could form connections and alliances.

There was, of course, a routine spread of homosexuals throughout the population, and evidence has survived of energetic sexual activity that seems to have had little association with the *erastes/eromenos* ideology.

High up a rocky promontory on the volcanic island of Thera in the southern Aegean Sea some curious inscriptions have survived, probably dating to the early or mid-seventh century. They were carved into the mountainside in large, deeply scored letters. The spot appears to have been a rendezvous for archaic sex. The messages evoke a distant erotic past with touching immediacy. One of them reads: "I swear by Apollo of Delphi, right here Krimon fucked [So-and-So . . . the name is missing], the son of Bathykles." Another boy praises his partner: "Barbax dances well and he gave me pleasure."

Greeks would not understand the language of modern psychology. So far as sex was concerned they thought in terms of a man's acts not of his essence, of what he did rather than what he was. He might have sex with another man, but that did not make him a homosexual, for neither the concept nor the word had been invented. However, to have sex only with someone of the same gender aroused stern comment. One was expected to spread one's favors.

Particular disapproval was reserved for effeminacy, and there was a name for it. A *cinaedus* was a man-woman, soft, degenerate, and depraved. He allowed himself to be penetrated and, worse, enjoyed it. He was regarded as not far off from being a male prostitute.

Solon and Pisistratus cherished the memory of their love, long after the passion had died. This was fortunate, for they came to disagree sharply on political issues. It was evident that Solon's reforms had not quelled the regular disruptions of daily life in Athens, and intelligent minds turned to the desirability of a tyranny. Pisistratus, with his successes in the war with Megara behind him and as leader of a major political movement, believed he was the man for the job.

He presented himself as a "great friend of the poor" and the *thetes,* the lowest and most numerous of Solon's four classes, saw in him a savior. One day he drove into the *agora* in a chariot, apparently wounded as if he had just escaped an assassination attempt and complaining of a plot against him because of his policies to help the underprivileged. However, the aged Solon arrived on the scene and claimed that the whole affair was a trick. He accused the people of being empty-headed: "You listen to the words of a crafty man, but not to what he does."

The matter was raised at the *ecclesia*.

The meeting was packed with supporters of the Hills faction. They paid no attention to Solon's objections and decided that Pisistratus should be allowed a bodyguard of fifty men armed with clubs. With their assistance the would-be tyrant then seized the Acropolis and made himself master of the city.

He took no steps to silence the ever-vociferous Solon; their common, loving past presumably protected the old man. The lawgiver had kept his integrity, but if he looked back he must have considered himself and his reforms to have failed. But he did not repine. He devoted himself to the joys of sex, wine, and the arts. He wrote up the story he had heard in Egypt about lost Atlantis. A year or so into the tyranny he died.

Megacles and his fellow-clansmen saw that the game was lost and immediately went back again into the safety of exile. Five years passed and the other two factions of the Plain and of the Coast put their differences on one side and joined forces to overpower and eject Pisistratus. The tyrant was driven from Attica. But the victors soon fell out.

The Alcmaeonids were not fools. They must have noticed that they and the other great clans lacked popular support. Without it, they would find it hard to hold on to their old monopoly of power. Their best option was to restore Pisistratus and govern through him, be his collective éminence grise. So despite the family's hostility to tyranny, another Megacles, grandson of the man who massacred the followers of Cylon, did a deal. He would help Pisistratus return to power on condition that he marry his daughter. The aspirant despot agreed, although he already had a perfectly good wife and two healthy sons, Hippias and Hipparchus.

Pisistratus understood the value of publicity and of symbolism. He staged a grand entrance into Athens. He found an unusually tall young woman from a country district. Pisistratus dressed her up in a suit of armor, taught her how to present herself convincingly as a goddess, and drove her in procession into the city. Town criers went ahead shouting: "Men of Athens, give Pisistratus a warm welcome, for Athena herself is bringing him home to her own citadel. She honours him more than all men." What better way of demonstrating that Pisistratus enjoyed divine approval and had a legitimate claim to rule?

Herodotus calls the stunt "the silliest idea I have ever heard of," and claims that some people were taken in by the impersonation. Maybe so, but in an age that saw the birth of drama, most Athenians will have recognized a theatrical spectacular when they saw one, were entertained by it—and accepted the political point that Pisistratus was making.

It was not long before Pisistratus fell from grace again. The problem was the arrangement with Megacles. He did not want to imperil the succession of his legitimate sons by new rivals, so, to avert the risks of pregnancy, he avoided ordinary sexual intercourse with his new wife and penetrated her up the anus. This was a grave insult and Megacles was furious when he found out about it. He withdrew his backing for Pisistratus and began assembling a grand alliance against him. The tyrant conceded without a fight and fled the country.

The second exile lasted ten tedious years. Pisistratus and his sons talked the matter over and agreed that they would work to regain power at Athens, however long it took. They went to Thrace, a large territory lying between Greece and the Hellespont, which was inhabited rather than governed by rough, semi-barbaric peoples. Evidently he was neither short of money or international contacts—nor sheer organizational energy.

First, he settled in the northeastern shoulder of Greece off the Thermaic Gulf. The king of the notoriously wild Macedonians may have made him a grant of land. In any event he established some kind of fortified outpost or town there. This was no mean achievement, for, although full of economic promise, the area was dangerous; a quarter of a century previously an Athenian colony had been wiped out by locals. Sometime later Pisistratus moved along the coast to the mountain range of Pangaeum north of the island of Thasos, where he exploited abundant silver and gold mines.

Pisistratus became very rich and in 546/5 recruited a small mercenary army. He won support for his cause from the important city-states of Argos in the Peloponnese and of Attica's neighbor Thebes, as well as from the friendly tyrant of Naxos, the largest island of the Cyclades. Sensing that his moment had finally arrived, he moved to the town of Eretria on the island of Euboea. Attica lay just across the water. It was fairly obvious what was going to happen next and public sentiment in Athens rallied to the former tyrant. Once he was sure he would receive a warm reception, Pisistratus made his move. He sailed across the narrow strait and landed on the beach of Marathon.

Men from town and countryside flocked to meet and greet him. Herodotus commented sardonically: "These were people who found tyranny more welcome than freedom." Little is known of the government of Athens during the decade of Pisistratus's absence, but we will not go far wrong if we presume aristocratic misrule. An army of the self-defined better class of persons assembled to halt the invader.

The vicissitudes of his life had taught Pisistratus a lesson. He knew that his tyranny would not succeed by trickery, women dressed up as goddesses, the use of force, or ingenious alliances with former enemies. If he was to avoid going on his travels again he would have to rule by consent. During the coming battle he kept this very much in mind. He wanted as little blood to flow as possible.

The two sides met at a sanctuary of Athena near bee-loud Mount Hymettus. A seer gave Pisistratus a prophecy, which said:

The net has been cast, and the trap opened;
The tuna will swarm through the moonlit night.

Although obscure, the tone of the message was positive, and Pisistratus welcomed it.

He noticed that a shoal of optimistic Athenians had eaten their lunch and were either asleep or playing dice. He led his soldiers in a surprise attack, broke in on their siesta, and routed them. He sent his sons on horseback to chase after the fleeing enemy and when they had caught up with them to promise there would be no reprisals. They told them not to worry and go home.

Tyrant for the third and last time, Pisistratus wanted to show from the outset that he intended to run a tolerant and forgiving regime. Nobody need fear punishment or persecution—except perhaps for the Alcmaeonids.

6

Charioteers of the Soul

Pisistratus had a debt to pay.

Leader of the *thetes,* the unpropertied poor, he knew they had great expectations of his government. If he wanted to hold on to power, he would have to make a real difference to their lives. Fortunately, the means of doing so was to hand.

Most aristocrats had fled the country on the restoration of the tyranny and abandoned their estates. Solon had not dared, nor wished, to threaten their titles of ownership, but now the time had come for turning the screw.

If there was one group of people whom Pisistratus could not pardon it was the absent Alcmaeonids and their like. So he confiscated the vacant farming land, divided it into lots, and distributed it among those in greatest need—landless laborers in the fields and unemployed men in the city. He offered start-up loans to enable the new owners to make the most of their opportunity. Pisistratus's aim was not only to develop agriculture, but also to encourage citizens to engage in private enterprise (rather than political activism).

The state did not lose by the arrangements, for smallholders were liable to a land tax amounting to one tenth of what they produced. This tax, which may have been introduced by Pisistratus, applied to all kinds of estate and formed a substantial part of the public revenue. To this may be added the income from the silver mines at Laurium in Attica, which were more effectively worked now than they had been in the past. The silver was mainly used for coinage, and so added to the liquidity of Athenian wealth and eased trade.

Land reform was not enough by itself to heal the woes of the countryside. The regime sought to improve the efficiency of farming and, building on Solon's encouragement of olive oil exports, it planted olive trees more widely.

The creation of a class of peasant proprietors was a substantial achievement and removed in part at least the grievances of the poor that still plagued the body politic. Many Athenians found the loss of civic liberties a fair price for social reconciliation and economic development. And nobody much missed Megacles and his friends.

The heart of a *polis* was the *agora*. This was where people could shop, idle, do business deals, find out the latest news, and, above all, talk politics. A busy market square was evidence of a politically engaged citizenry, so it is more than a little surprising that Pisistratus laid out the famous *agora* of Athens.

Of course, the tyrant took all the necessary precautions to protect the regime, and employed a permanent force of mercenaries, which included Scythian archers, fierce nomad peoples from the northeast of Europe. But once he had looked after his personal security and warded off any risk of a coup d'état, he relaxed and trusted the people.

The space Pisistratus chose for the *agora* was roughly triangular. It was skirted by the main road into the city, the Panathenaic Way. Private houses were demolished, an old burial ground cleared, and wells closed. A fountain house was built and opened to the public, into which water was fed by a terra-cotta pipeline. A vestibule was entered through a colonnade and gave access to basins and running water spouts (hence the fountain house's name "The Nine Spouts").

In the southwest corner of the marketplace a substantial building rose from the ground, much larger than other Athenian homes of the period. A collection of rooms surrounded a courtyard. Modern archaeologists have found evidence of cooking, and it has been sensibly suggested that this was the residence of Pisistratus and the headquarters of the tyranny.

Establishing the *agora* could have meant no more than paying lip service to the people's rights. But in fact, as the author of *The Athenian Constitution* put it, Pisistratus was "humane, mild and forgiving to criminals" and governed "more like a citizen than like a tyrant." He left the constitution and institutions of Solon in place. Archons took office every year as usual, although the name of a family member or a reliable ally regularly appeared on the list. We are not certain that they were elected or appointed by him, but one way or another his wishes prevailed. Gradually political unrest subsided.

At some point Pisistratus or his successor, his son Hippias, was reconciled with the aristocracy. Leading noblemen returned to Athens and took part in the government. A fragment of an inscription recording annual Eponymous Archons throws light on how the tyranny organized power, making it effective without being blatant.

Onetorides
Hippias
Cleisthenes
Miltiades
Calliades
Pisistratus

Pisistratus died in 528/7 at about the age of seventy-five. Onetorides, of whom we know nothing (except he was probably the handsome youth whose name appears on painted vases in the middle of the century), was appointed while the old man was still alive. We may assume that the Hippias here was the ruler's son. The Alcmaeonids liked to claim that they lived in exile throughout the tyranny; we can see that this was not true, for Cleisthenes was a member of the clan. Miltiades belonged to the powerful and extremely rich Philaid clan. Calliades was a common name and is unidentified, but Pisistratus must have been the tyrant's grandson.

Despite officially being the tyrant's political enemy, the step-uncle of the Miltiades on the inscription, also named Miltiades, collaborated with Pisistratus on an important foreign project.

He was sitting one day on the porch of his country house beside the road from Athens to Eleusis when a group of men passed by. Their clothes looked foreign and they were carrying spears. Inquisitive, he asked them over and gave them lodging, and food and drink—a gesture no one had made until then. He learned that they were Thracian tribesmen from the Chersonese (today's Gallipoli) who were returning from Delphi. They had consulted the oracle about a war with an aggressive neighbor they were fighting and losing. The Pythia told them to appoint as their leader the first man who offered them hospitality. So Miltiades was invited to take charge of their affairs. He checked with Delphi to be sure he should accept the commission, and on receiving clearance from the oracle set off for the Chersonese.

It is a nice story; but the simple truth of the matter is that the tribe appealed to Athens to found a settlement or colony in their territory. This would strengthen their ability to defend themselves from their enemies. Always keen to support Athenian trade, Pisistratus was delighted to gain a strategic foothold on the trade route from the Black Sea. The arrangement had the secondary benefit of removing from the scene a potentially dangerous competitor for power.

Although Miltiades disapproved of the tyranny at home (while collaborating with it), he had no qualms about making himself absolute ruler of the Chersonese, which in effect became a family possession of the Philaids.

. . .

Pisistratus represented much more than a style of governing—he governed with a purpose. He wanted to turn Athens into an international religious and cultural center, and to promote the city as the motherland and moral leader of the Ionian Greeks.

The regime built and built and built. At Eleusis, a town twelve miles from Athens near the border with Megara, an annual festival was held in honor of the goddesses Demeter, patron of agriculture, and her daughter Persephone, queen of the underworld. Pisistratus had a great hall erected where initiates conducted visually spectacular but secret rites, giving them hope of a happy afterlife.

Back in Athens a new temple of Athena duly appeared on the rugged terrain of the Acropolis. Not far away in the south of the city, work started on a vast temple to Olympian Zeus. In this case, Pisistratus had overreached himself and it was many centuries before the building was completed.

The small island of Delos in the Cyclades was a center of pilgrimage for loyal Ionians. It was here that the god Apollo and his twin sister, Artemis, were born to Leto; she was one of the Titans, the generation of divinities that preceded Zeus and the Olympians. A hymn to Apollo reports that "the long-robed Ionians assemble with their wives and children" on Delos for a great annual festival with songs, dancing, and athletic games. It has Leto address the island as if it were a sentient being. She calls on it to build a temple of "far-shooting" Apollo. If they did this, she promised, "all men will bring you hecatombs and gather here, and incessant smells of rich sacrifices will always fill the air." To be sure that Delos got the point, she predicted that tourists would grow the economy, "for you have to admit that your own soil is not rich." The islanders obeyed. A temple rose from the ground and a twenty-six-foot-high marble statue of the god was erected.

Pisistratus staked his claim to the hegemony of Ionia by conducting a purification of the island. He did this by digging up all graves that were within sight of the temple and reburying the polluting dead elsewhere. Evidence of the presence of Athenian workmen suggests that he also improved in some way the shrine itself.

Pisistratus wanted Athens to become a lively tourist destination. He revamped, or perhaps founded, two great festivals. The Panathenaea was, in essence, a grand procession in which much of the population went up to the Acropolis and presented Athena with a robe woven by the hands of young virgins. Every fourth year this was accompanied by athletic and musical competitions.

The Great or City Dionysia was the consequence of a new temple which Pisistratus built on the southern slopes of the Acropolis in honor of Dionysus, god of wine and of out-of-body experiences. Here every spring festivities were held in his honor.

Choirs sang of legendary events and the leader of the performers, who was also the composer of the music and lyrics, took on the role of the protagonist in the story and exchanged dialogue with them. Some-time between 536 and 533, a man called Thespis is reputed to have added a prologue and speech to what had been a choral performance. Here were the first stirrings of Greek drama.

An able propagandist, Pisistratus called for support from the legendary king of Athens, Theseus. During the years of the tyranny his image is found on Attic pottery, often showing him as the slayer of the Cretan Minotaur. He was made to stand for the rights of the ordinary Athenian and for the permanence of the regime. As we have seen, the king had brought the villages of Attica into a single state. He was credited with founding the Panathenaea festival and opening the city to foreigners. He was well qualified to become the symbolic face of the new well-ordered Athens.

The tyrant also recruited to his cause Homer, the father of epic poetry and the matchless celebrant of Greekness. The tyrant ensured that during the Panathenaea he alone of all the poets should have his works recited. There was no authoritative text of Homer's poems, and it is said that Pisistratus set up a special commission to collect and review the differing versions which had multiplied with time. We have evidence of spurious additions inserted for political reasons (as, for instance, the allegedly invented couplet about Athens and Megara, for which Solon was supposed to have been responsible). In fact, a member of the commission was himself guilty of forgery: he was invited by Hippias to edit a collection of oracular sayings and was caught introducing into it a prophecy he had made up.

If the existence of the commission was not itself an invention, as modern scholars surmise, it was of course not the first time that the *Iliad* and the *Odyssey* had been written down. But it is plausible enough that two centuries or so after the poems were composed it was necessary to remove corrupt passages and produce clean and authoritative editions.

Wherever one turned in Athens, one came up against signs of the tyranny—well meaning, but patronizing. Throughout the city stood Herms; these were busts of Hermes, god of messages, boundaries, and transitions, which were carved in an old-fashioned style with a pointed beard. They topped squared, stone pillars, from the front of which a penis, usually erect, and testicles protruded at the appropriate level. Herms were talismans against harm and guaranteed success in undertakings.

Inscribed on many of them were little moral messages from Pisistratus's second son.

A reminder from Hipparchus—when out walking, think just
    thoughts

and

A reminder from Hipparchus—do not tell lies to a friend.

After their father's death, Hippias and Hipparchus took charge. They were men of very different character. The former was a public-spirited politician who ran the government and was intellectually well equipped to do so. Hipparchus was younger and flightier. A playboy, he liked to be amused. He spent time and energy on love affairs and was fond of the arts. He encouraged Greece's most famous poets to spend time in Athens. He sent a state warship to pick up a writer of lyric verse, Anacreon, from his homeland of Teos, a Greek city on the Ionian coast, and enticed to Athens Simonides of Ceos, a Cycladic island, with large subventions and expensive gifts.

Anacreon suited his patron, being a celebrant of sex and wine. He famously chased after boys, who were not invariably complaisant.

> *Young man with the girlish looks,*
> *I want you, but you will not listen,*
> *Unaware you are my soul's charioteer.*

Simonides must have been more to Hippias's taste; he was a public poet who was commissioned by states and whose work often appeared on memorials. He took a disenchanted view of human nature: "Any man is good when life treats him well, and bad when it treats him badly."

Even oddities like Lasus of Hermione were welcome; one of his claims to fame was the "hissless hymn." This was a poem in which the letter "s" was never used.

Aristogeiton was losing his patience. An Athenian in his twenties, he was an *erastes* in love with a handsome teenager, Harmodius. Unusually in such a case he was not an aristocrat, but came from the middle class. The affair was going well and the couple were happy. The relationship seems to have been passionate, but may not have been passionately sexual, for Aristogeiton also had a mistress called Leaena (or Lioness).

However, he had a powerful rival for his *eromenos*, who would not accept refusal and who just would not go away. This was Hipparchus. He propositioned Harmodius, who turned him down and immediately reported the conversation to his lover.

Aristogeiton was upset, but what could he do? He was afraid that the disappointed lover would use force to have his way with Harmodius. He decided to plot the undoing of the dynasty by cutting down the twin tyrants. Meanwhile Hipparchus tried again to seduce the teenager, but with no better luck. He realized that the snub was definitive.

Despite Aristogeiton's fears Hipparchus had no intention of resorting to violence. Instead he cast about for a way of insulting Harmodius without revealing his motives for doing so. He arranged for the boy's sister to be invited to carry a basket in a civic procession; when she arrived she was told to go home on the grounds that she was unfit to take part in the ceremony. The innuendo was that she was not a virgin. Harmodius was furious at the affront, and this made Aristogeiton even angrier.

The couple decided to go ahead with their conspiracy to assassinate Hippias and Hipparchus. The date for the attempt was the Panathenaea of 514; it was chosen because this was the one time in the year when citizens were allowed to carry weapons. To ensure secrecy they recruited only a few plotters, but hoped that once they launched their attack others would spontaneously join in. It was an extraordinarily risky plan, so likely to fail as almost to be suicidal.

Just outside the city wall and the double-arched Dipylon Gate, Hippias was organizing the Panathenaic procession. His bodyguard was in attendance. This was a great state occasion and everything had to be correct.

The lovers were present and watched for their moment. Suddenly they noticed one of their fellow-conspirators go up to Hippias and, with a smile on his face, engage him in conversation. Was the plot being betrayed? Panic-stricken, the would-be assassins rushed into the city and chanced on Hipparchus, the cause of all the trouble. They fell on him at once without thinking of the consequences and fatally wounded him. The tyrant's bodyguard killed Harmodius, but Aristogeiton managed to slip away in the general confusion. He was picked up later and, Thucydides notes, "died no easy death."

A tradition has it that he was tortured under the personal direction of Hippias, who wanted the names of fellow-conspirators. Aristogeiton appears to have had a somewhat acid sense of humor, for he only identified men he knew to be among the tyrant's supporters. He promised to provide further names and asked for Hippias's handshake as a pledge of safety. When the tyrant took his hand, Aristogeiton jeered at him for taking the hand of his brother's murderer. Hippias lost his temper and killed the prisoner with his own hand.

The main consequence of the affair was that the regime became cruel. This was understandable, but ill-advised. After his brother's death Hippias executed known and potential enemies of the tyranny. He had Leaena tortured to death for the crime of being Aristogeiton's mistress.

The mood in the city darkened. Hippias could see that he was losing the consent of the people. It was a mistake his father had never made, but he could not help himself. He saw treachery everywhere and he began to lay plans for a bolt-hole in case he were ever driven from Athens. But where could he go and be safe? The empire of Persia, perhaps? Four years after his brother's death he fortified a hill at Piraeus on the coast called Munychia. If the worst came to the worst he could escape there, catch a waiting ship and sail away.

Meanwhile the inevitable Alcmaeonids, in exile once more, launched attempt after attempt to unseat the tyrant. When one recalls that Pisistratus had confiscated their estates in Attica years previously, their continuing wealth is something of a mystery. But even in the days of Homer, Greek aristocrats cultivated their counterparts in other states and kingdoms. Political instability was endemic and we must assume that many nobles exported their resources; the record of Pisistratus in Thrace and Miltiades in the Chersonese indicates how investment in undeveloped territories could be extremely profitable. And Solon is unlikely to have been the only man of his class to dirty his hands with trade.

The Alcmaeonids built their own fortress at Lipsydrium, a spur of the densely forested mountain range of Parnes to the north of Athens. But Hippias besieged the place and drove the rebels out. They refused to be cowed. In a drinking song about the defeat they were undaunted. Their fallen comrades were, they chanted,

Fine warriors and from good families,
Who proved then what stock they were made of.

The insurrection failed to make progress not because Hippias was a capable military commander, but for a more fundamental reason. The average Athenian saw no advantage in removing the tyranny simply to reinstall a discredited nobility. How could this obstacle be circumvented?

The Alcmaeonids were not beaten. They had a secret weapon—the oracle at Delphi. The temple of Apollo there had burned down in 548, perhaps the result of the careless barbecuing of sacrificial victims or an explosion of exhalations from the fissure beneath the shrine (see page 31). A new temple had to be built at the huge expense of 300 talents. A Panhellenic fundraising campaign produced a quarter of the required sum and Delphi found the rest.

The initial contractors failed to complete the temple. The Alcmaeonids, who seem to have acted as a kind of multinational development corporation, took over the project, and as a gesture of goodwill built, at their own expense, a frontage of top-quality Parian marble. The new temple seems to have been splendid. According to Euripides, its twin pediments were "like eyebrows on a smiling face." Fine sculptural decorations depicted heroes killing monsters and on one of the pediments the Olympian gods were shown exterminating the race of giants.

The head of the Alcmaeonid clan at this time was Cleisthenes. He is the most remarkable of all the statesmen who populate this history, although his first entry on the scene is not to his credit. Unfortunately, his personality has vanished from the record; we know him only through his actions, but these are enough.

Cleisthenes and his clan realized that to overthrow the tyranny was too large a task for them alone, and that they would need outside help. The only Hellenic state with the prestige and the army to expel Hippias was Sparta. The Alcmaeonids were now, evidently, on very close terms with the Delphic officialdom. The new temple was "more beautiful than the plan" and, in the light of its cost, the oracle was short of money. Cleisthenes is reported to have bribed the oracle to advise the Spartans to depose Hippias. Whenever Sparta consulted the god, the priestess always replied: "First of all free Athens."

Within its limited geographical bounds, Sparta, disciplined and militant, was a great power, and as is the habit of great powers throughout history it liked to interfere in the policies and programs of other countries. About the middle of the sixth century it consolidated its hold on the Peloponnese. It defeated the *polis* of Tegea, an important religious center in Arcadia, a region in the highlands of central Peloponnese. Argos, a traditional enemy in the northeast of the peninsula, also came under its influence.

At this time one of its two kings was Cleomenes, an energetic and capable general. He was that rare thing, a Spartan genuinely interested in the outside world; his fellow-countrymen thought him unhinged.

Cleomenes was a man with a distinctive history. His father had married his niece, but she turned out to be infertile. The Spartan *ephors*, who supervised the activities of the two kings, advised him to marry again, have children by a second wife, and save the bloodline. This he did and the outcome was Cleomenes. Then to everyone's surprise the first wife gave birth to a son, Dorieus. Who should be the heir—the eldest boy or the son of the first wife? When the old king died, it was decided that Cleomenes should succeed. The hapless Dorieus left Sparta and set up as an adventurer. He planned to found a new city in Sicily, but died in battle.

Cleomenes played a leading role in consolidating Sparta's dominance of the Peloponnese, and wanted his country to be acknowledged beyond doubt as the leading power in Greece. But he knew his limits:

he was tempted to come to the assistance of the Ionians when they rose against the Persian king. However, on learning that it took three months to journey inland from the sea to the Great King's capital, he decided not to help, even though the incautious Athenians sent twenty warships to support the rebels.

Eventually the Spartans agreed to invade Attica and depose Hippias. It is hard to see why; the tyrants had always taken care to be on good terms with Sparta, although they also cultivated friendly relations with its rival Argos. The pressure from Delphi must have played a part, and so may the influence of the expansionist Cleomenes. Most significantly, Sparta liked doing business with aristocratic oligarchies.

Sparta's first expedition against Athens failed; the foot soldiers were overwhelmed by cavalry from Thessaly, horse-rearing country in northern Greece whose independent-minded tribesmen came to Hippias's aid. In 510 King Cleomenes was sent with a larger expedition to retrieve the situation. This time the Thessalians were beaten and went home. Hippias took refuge in the Acropolis. His prospects for holding out were quite good, for he had ample supplies of food and drink and the Spartans were not prepared or equipped for a long blockade.

At this point luck intervened. Hippias sent away his five children to a place of safety abroad, but they were captured by the enemy. This broke his spirit. On condition that they were returned to him, he agreed to gather all his possessions and leave Attica within five days. The Athenian *ecclesia* passed a law removing citizenship in perpetuity from the entire clan of Pisistratids—a sentence that was never to be rescinded. A pillar was set up on the Acropolis listing their crimes and setting down all the family's names.

Together with relatives and entourage Hippias settled in the *polis* of Sigeum on the coast of Asia Minor near Troy. Its name means "place of silence." This was probably an antiphrastic expression—namely, one that signifies the opposite of something's true characteristics. The weather in the city's neighborhood was said to be wild and stormy. The destination was a good choice, though, for Pisistratus had annexed the place in the 540s and installed an illegitimate son called Hegistratus as tyrant.

In the centuries that followed the fall of the tyranny, the contribution that Pisistratus made to the development of Athens was undervalued. Tyrants fell out of fashion and it was in nobody's interest to give him any credit. In fact, he governed well and greatly enhanced the image of Athens in the wider world. During his long reign he provided stability and calmed social discord.

Above all, he recognized the importance of winning the consent of those over whom he ruled. By sticking to Solon's reforms, ordinary, hard-pressed citizens were encouraged to believe that they had a stake in their community.

Thucydides acknowledged that for a long time both father and sons displayed "high principles and intelligence in their policy." Taxes were low, the appearance of the city greatly improved, religious sacrifices properly observed. He continued that Athens

> was still governed by the laws which had existed previously, except that [Pisistratus and Hippias] took care to see that there was always one of their own family in office.

If one had to be ruled by a tyrant, Pisistratus was clearly the man to choose. And he laid the ground for the next adventure in the history of Athens. As Herodotus noted, "Athens, which had been great in the past, now became greater still after her deliverance from the tyrants."

7

Inventing Democracy

A bright light shone on the Athenians, when Aristogeiton
And Harmodius killed Hipparchus;
The two of them made their native land equal in laws.

So reads the inscription on the marble base for a bronze statue group of the star-crossed lovers, which Cleisthenes the Alcmaeonid commissioned. It was written by that celebrated hired hand, Simonides, once in Hipparchus's employ and perfectly happy then to hail the tyranny. There they stood, proud and righteously angry, as cast by Antenor, a fashionable sculptor of the time. These were the heroes who gave back to citizens their equal rights before the law—code for destroying the tyranny.

Popular songs have survived, which young bloods chorused over their wine at dinner parties.

Darling Harmodius, we know you are not dead.
They say you are in the Islands of the Blest
Where swift-footed Achilles lives.

This is a puzzle. The assassination of Hipparchus in 514 was a botched and rather squalid business, done in a panic and lacking a truly idealistic motive. The regime survived the blow for some years and did not fall to a domestic uprising. Quite the reverse, it was a Spartan king prodded by the exiled Alcmaeonids who gave the Athenians their freedom. But this was generosity of a kind that is very hard to forgive.

Hence the less-than-historical advancement of Harmodius and Aristogeiton to the status of national heroes. Their descendants were granted perpetual freedom from taxation and, it seems, other privileges regularly bestowed on outstanding citizens, such as the right to take meals at public expense in the town hall, exemption from some religious duties, and front-row seats in the theater.

Cleisthenes and the Alcmaeonids had won. The tyranny was over and the family was back home where they ought to be. They and the other Eupatridae had every reason to believe that they could slip back into power as if Solon and the five decades of the tyranny had never taken place. However, it was not clear that the mass of the people, the *demos,* many of whom had followed the star of Pisistratus, would accept this reversion.

The situation was bound to unravel. The details are murky, but Cleisthenes expected a reward for all the expenditure and hard work he and his family had put in over so many years. He deserved to be the leading man in the *polis,* but now to his annoyance he found he had a competitor. This was Isagoras, a slippery nobleman who had spent the reigns of Pisistratus and Hippias comfortably and safely in Athens. He was in league with secret supporters of tyranny. In 508 he was elected Archon, but Cleisthenes responded by calling the poor and dispossessed out onto the streets.

In turn, the Archon summoned King Cleomenes back from Sparta, who marched into Attica with a small force, expelled seven hundred families opposed to the policies of Isagoras, and attempted to abolish the council, or *boulē,* established by Solon. Things looked bad for Cleisthenes, who briefly left Attica.

However, the infuriated populace rose in arms and blockaded the Spartans and Isagoras in the Acropolis. The king entered the temple of Athena, but received a cold welcome from the priestess, who rose from her chair and said: "Spartan stranger, go back. Do not enter the holy place." After three days, the hungry Cleomenes capitulated. He, his troops, and his protégé were allowed to leave under a truce. This inglorious affair was a blow to the king's prestige, and he meditated revenge.

Cleisthenes decided that so long as the Athenians failed to settle their domestic quarrels, they would go on risking revolution and external attack. Decisive measures were urgently required.

What should these be? No account survives of his thought processes, but we can tell from the outcome the revolutionary nature of his analysis. He realized that time could not be turned back, that the aristocratic moment had passed, and that if the Alcmaeonids and their like were to survive, let alone thrive, only the most radical solution would do.

Acting from the most self-interested of motives, Cleisthenes invented democracy.

He devised a set of extraordinarily complicated and artificial constitutional arrangements. They ought not to have worked, but the Athenians accepted them and put them into effect. They were the template for the world's first total democracy, which thrived for most of the next two centuries.

As Herodotus puts it, Cleisthenes "enlisted the people into his party of supporters." He did more than that. He recognized that the ordinary citizen would no longer put up with a top-down system of government of any kind. Although it might seem to be selling out, the best chance of saving the Alcmaeonids from oblivion was to lead the charge for people power (the word *democratia* is formed from two others—the *demos,* signifying, as we have seen, the people, and *kratos,* or power). All being well, they could then continue to play a leading role in the affairs of a grateful *polis.*

We need to be clear about what Cleisthenes and his fellow-citizens

meant by democracy. It was not the representative kind that character-
izes modern societies. Athens and the other Greek city-states had very
small populations by our standards and it was possible to assemble a
majority, or at least a large fraction, of the citizenry in one meeting
place, and debate and approve all legislation.

This was an unmediated and extreme version of the democratic
idea, but there were some important exclusions. As already noted, only
adult Athenian men were entitled to vote in the *ecclesia*. Women were
barred from the political process. There were two other substantial
groups that were also prohibited. The city attracted numerous foreigners who settled in Attica and made a good living as craftsmen and merchants; these were the resident aliens or *metics*. Also Athenians owned
slaves—captives of war or purchases on the open market—who had
no civic rights. In total, these people amounted to well over a half of
the overall population.

One of the reasons for the emergence of the people as a political force
was military. Sometime between 700 and 650, a breakthrough took
place in Hellenic warfare, which had important political consequences
for hundreds of years. It determined the balance of power in the *polis*
and put paid once and for all to aristocratic hopes of a return to undi-
luted power.

We know little of military tactics in the deep past, but it seems to
have consisted largely of bands of men with warrior leaders and ad hoc
citizen militias. If we can trust Homer, Achilles and his like would fight
duels and seek out one-to-one encounters after which general fighting
would confusedly ensue. We hear little of battlefield maneuvers, and a
great deal about courage and glory.

Mirroring the retreat of the nobles and the advance of the citizens,
new, well-trained armies of heavy-armed troops gradually replaced the
old heroes. These men were called "hoplites." They were equipped
with bronze greaves and corselets—two bronze plates connected by a
hinge, which protected the upper part of the body—and bronze hel-

mets. With their left arm they held a circular, convex wooden shield or *hoplon* (hence the name "hoplite"). They were armed with a short stabbing sword and a long stabbing spear about one and a half times the soldier's height.

All this metal reduced vulnerability, but by the same token hindered visibility and mobility. However, the hoplite never fought as a lone individual, but as part of a tight formation. This was the famous Greek phalanx. Men stood in close ranks of between four and eight men deep. So long as it stayed in line and did not break up, the phalanx was extremely difficult to beat.

The Spartan poet Tyrtaeus, who lived in the seventh century, summed up the hoplite ethos:

Let each man come to close quarters and wound his enemy
With his long spear or his sword. Also let him set foot
Beside foot, press shield against shield,
Crest upon crest, helmet on helmet
Breast against breast.

This new ethos did have two weaknesses. First, it required flat ground; otherwise soldiers would find it hard to keep together and could be picked off one by one. It is a little odd that the phalanx was invented in a land as mountainous as Greece, and one constraint on hoplite warfare was that there were few places where a battle could actually take place.

Second, a hoplite carried his shield on his left arm and so protected both himself and the right-hand side of his comrade on the left. The closer they were together the less likely they were to be wounded or killed by hostile weapons. But the men who stood at the end of the lines on the right were left partly unguarded. They would involuntarily shift to the right if they saw any danger of being outflanked by the enemy; the comrades on their left would tend to follow suit to avoid their right sides being exposed. The danger was that the line would thin and a gap would open up, which the enemy would attack and widen. Whereupon the phalanx would be either outflanked or penetrated; and the battle would be lost.

Despite these problems, the hoplite army, if well trained and led, was almost invincible. Throughout the Mediterranean world this was widely recognized and trained Greek soldiers found that they could make a good living as mercenaries if for whatever reason they left their native land. The Spartans with their commitment to lifelong military training were particularly effective on the battlefield.

One advantage of hoplite immobility was that casualties in battle tended to be low because hoplites were nervous of running after a defeated enemy and risking a loss of formation. Heavy-armed troops could not run far or fast. Victors mostly allowed the losers to make their escape unharassed, and restricted themselves to stripping the dead and erecting a victory trophy.

Cavalry played a relatively small role in Greek warfare; horses were very expensive to maintain and neither stirrups nor horseshoes had been invented. Riders were usually upper-class men, politically unreliable and of suspect loyalty to the people.

Hoplites were also citizens. Called up from civilian life when circumstance required, they were of the middling sort, affluent enough to afford to buy their own armor and weapons. They were men with a stake in the community, in the success of their *polis*. Their arrival on the scene and growing influence in the public square meant that, whatever the exact nature of the regime in power, their interests had to be taken into account. Indeed they expected to have a share in political decisions.

The counterpart of the politically active *polis* was the hoplite army.

In the *agora* near the town hall stood a grand monument. It had a marble base about sixteen meters long by two wide, and on it were set ten life-size bronze statues and at either end two metal tripods, looking like the one the priestess sat on when delivering oracles at Delphi. Around the monument a wooden railing was supported by stone posts. Here public notices of various kinds were displayed—muster rolls for the army, notices of lawsuits, draft laws, lists of young men who had come of age (*ephebi*). It must have been a busy spot with ever-changing clusters of people looking for information and instructions.

The statues depicted ten legendary heroes of Athens. They were mainly early kings, such as Theseus, and heroes or demigods, such as Heracles. Their collective title was the Eponymous Heroes because they gave their names to ten new tribes into which Cleisthenes divided the citizenry and which replaced the old quartet. These were the guardians of the city and worshipped as such.

The reformer's reason for inventing new tribes was to eliminate or at least weaken the main political factions (the Coast, the Plain, and the Hills), which were causing all the trouble, creating dissension and instability. He also wanted to reduce the power of the brotherhoods or *phratries,* which were hereditary subgroups of the old tribes. Every citizen had to belong to one of them and they may have been exploited by aristocratic clans to exert political influence.

Cleisthenes achieved his objective in a very remarkable way. Each of the ten tribes was made to draw its membership from three different regions of Attica: the coast, the interior, and the city of Athens itself. Called *trittyes* (the thirds), they were usually not contiguous. This meant that members of the same tribe came from different parts of the country. Old local and territorial loyalties were dissolved.

The basic political unit of Athens was the *demos:* this word did not only mean the whole people (as already explained), but also the village or city ward. Cleisthenes divided the territory of Attica into 139 *demes* (as they are usually referred to in English). Each *deme* was allocated to a *trittys* and so to a tribe. He understood that a democracy at state level would not succeed unless there was also democracy at home and power was devolved to localities.

The *deme* was a miniature version of the *polis.* It had its own assembly that passed decrees about local affairs, and elected officials or demarchs. It was in charge of the numerous local festivals and religious ceremonies. It took over from the *phratries* the responsibility for keeping citizen lists up-to-date and endorsing new citizens when boys came of age. In official documents men were distinguished by their *deme* rather than (as previously) by their father's name. In the first instance, a man's *deme* was where he lived; but even if he and his descendants moved away to another part of Attica, they remained forever members of the same *deme*.

It was hard work running a *deme,* but the experience was useful, for Cleisthenes demanded a great deal from the ordinary Athenian when it came to participation in national affairs.

The political life of Athens centered on the *agora*. It was here during the first years of the democracy that the general assembly, the *ecclesia,* used to meet. The market stalls were packed away and people gathered in the dusty square to take part in debate, pass laws, and levy taxes.

After ten years or so the assembly was transferred to the slopes of a rocky outcrop called the Pnyx, which overlooked the *agora,* and finally towards the end of the fifth century it moved to a specially designed shell-shaped platform on the summit of the Pnyx. This could accommodate between eight and thirteen thousand people (the platform was enlarged in the fourth century). The citizen body was numbered in the tens of thousands, so it would appear that only a minority, albeit a substantial one, was willing or available to attend regularly. Of course, at any given time many citizens would be at work in the fields or in the manufacturing industries; others would be abroad on business or serving with the army during the frequent wars that Athens waged.

The *ecclesia* was the sovereign body of the *polis* and there was no appeal against its decisions, except (if you were very lucky) to a later meeting. As Aristotle remarked, "the poor have more power than the wealthy, as there are more of them and the decision of the majority is supreme."

The assembly met on average once every nine days, although additional emergency sessions could be convened if necessary. A quorum of six thousand citizens had to be present for a meeting to be official. Attendance was not exactly compulsory, but strenuous efforts were made to ensure a full house. People brought their own food and a cushion to sit on—unsurprisingly, for meetings could last from dawn till dusk.

From the 480s, three hundred publicly owned slaves, called the Scythian Archers, formed the city's police force and on assembly days they swept through the marketplace holding a rope covered in red powder and cleared it. Any citizen found absenting himself or with red marks on his clothes could expect to be punished. Speakers addressed the citizens from a special platform or *bema*. Any citizen was entitled to intervene in debates. Voting was by a show of hands rather than secret ballot.

Not far from the Monument of the Eponymous Heroes stood a substantial building some twenty-five meters square, the Bouleuterion. It was here that the *boulē* or council met. Cleisthenes abolished Solon's council based on the old four tribes and replaced it with a new and influential body. It was five hundred strong. Each of the ten new tribes contributed fifty members, probably chosen annually by lot from a long list prepared from *deme* nominations. The outgoing council vetted those on whom the lot fell. Nobody could be appointed to the council more than twice in their lives and more than once in a decade.

Cleisthenes agreed with Solon that sortition had its uses—ensuring equality of opportunity, deterring corruption, and allowing space for the gods to have *their* say. Perhaps most significantly, sortition encouraged citizens to keep up-to-date with the political issues of the day, for there was a reasonable chance that at some point they might have to play an active part in public life.

The *boulē* was the supreme administrative authority in the state and, together with various officials, it managed all public business. Its most important task was to prepare the agenda for the *ecclesia,* which was only permitted to discuss topics that it had approved.

However, a committee of five hundred was too large to be efficient. The year (360 days with intercalated months, as and when necessary) was divided into ten parts. The fifty councillors from each tribe acted in turn as an executive subcommittee for one tenth of the year or thirty-six days and undertook the *boulē*'s routine work. They lived in a building in the *agora* called the Tholos or Roundhouse, slept there and received meals at the public expense. They worked three shifts across twenty-four hours and at least seventeen duty members were always on hand to deal with urgent business. One of their number was appointed president or chairman for the day by lot.

So far as military affairs were concerned, each tribe was required to supply a regiment of hoplites and a squadron of cavalry, which were led by a general, or *strategos*. These ten officers also acted as admirals of the fleet, as occasion called. For much of the fifth century they played a dominant role in domestic politics. The Athenians had common sense and knew that winning victories on the battlefield or at sea called for experience and talent. They avoided random selection for these posts and allowed successful generals to hold continuous command from year to year as appropriate.

It will be recalled that Solon applied sortition to the appointment of the nine Archons, who used to govern the *polis*. They included the commander-in-chief, or *polemarch* (literally, "war leader"). His executive authority declined and over the years the *strategoi* took his place as the most powerful executive authority not only in the army and navy but also in the square.

Another innovation of Cleisthenes was ostracism. The *ecclesia* voted once a year, if there was demand, on the exile for ten years of a leading politician. Citizens could propose anyone they wished. There was no question of punishment for criminality, rather a desire, in Plutarch's phrase, to "humble and cut back oppressive prestige and power." After all, Pisistratus had exploited his position as popular leader and military commander to make himself tyrant. This must be prevented from happening again.

All citizens were eligible to vote in a secret ballot at a special meeting of the *ecclesia* in the marketplace. They scratched any man's name whom they wished to see banished on a piece of broken pottery (an *ostracon,* whence "ostracism") and deposited it in an urn. A quorum of six thousand citizens was necessary for a vote to be valid. The man with the greatest number of votes against him had ten days to leave the city. If he tried to come back, the penalty was death. Otherwise, he retained all his civic and property rights and, once he had served his term, was permitted to return to Athens and, if he wished, resume his public career.

The odd thing is that ostracism was not in fact implemented for two decades. An ostracism was only held if every January or February the people in assembly decided there should be one. Year after year they voted the proposition down. It is hard to explain this delay; most probably, politicians were nervous that the procedure might backfire on them or in a later year be used against the first citizen to propose it.

Sparta was well known for preferring oligarchies as a system of government. It yielded to the temptation of intervening again in the affairs of Athens and calling a halt to the dangerous democratic experiment. Cleomenes had been humiliated once before, and the time had come for vengeance. In 506 he led a substantial army of Spartans and their allies from the Peloponnese against Athens. At the same time the Boeotians attacked from the north and a force from Chalcidice on the island of Euboea crossed the narrow channel to Attica. The prospects for the new democracy were bleak.

But one of Sparta's allies had second thoughts about the justice of the expedition and marched back to its city. Cleomenes and his fellow-king, Demaratus, quarreled. There was nothing for it but for the Spartans to swallow their pride and slink home. The Athenians then heavily defeated the Boeotians and the Chalcidians in two different battles on the same day, and were even able to annex some of the latter's territory. Altogether it was quite a result for the *demos.* Cleisthenes and his revolutionary constitution were safe.

· · ·

What is so astonishing about the reforms of Cleisthenes and the introduction of democracy to Athens is the purity of their logic, their blithe
radicalism, and their artificiality. They made no concessions and in that
sense were deeply unpolitical. There seem to have been no negotiations. They embody what a contemporary scholar has called "archaic
rationality"—that is, a capacity to confront and fundamentally rethink
a problem from scratch, and to agree on a logical solution no matter
how far-fetched.

As remarkable as the achievement of Cleisthenes was, it was
matched by the enthusiasm of the Athenians for change. His constitution lasted with few interruptions for two centuries.

Its operation required the positive commitment of every citizen. A
key principle, as Aristotle noted with unspoken disapproval, was that
"everyone is governed and governs in turn." This may not have been
too troublesome for the rich, who had time on their hands, but it demanded a great deal from those in employment and, for that matter,
the un- or underemployed poor, who might appear to have plenty of
unwanted leisure, but in fact spent most of their waking hours trying to
scrape together a living.

Some decades later, the state began to pay stipends to juries and
members of the *boulē*. This enabled those with limited resources to
play the full part in the life of the *polis* that Cleisthenes envisaged.

Direct democracy in its fullest and most elaborate form brought
with it an unforeseen consequence. One might have thought that the
effort required from everyone to make the system work would have
been exhausting and dispiriting. Counterintuitively, it seems to have energized the Athenians. There were many causes, to be sure, for the
flowering of civilization that was to ensue, but one of them was the
injection of constitutional adrenaline that Cleisthenes administered to
his native city.

In war too, the Athenian hoplites seem to have been galvanized.
Herodotus remarked that equality had a beneficial impact on every as-

pect of civic life. "Now Athens grew more powerful. And there is not only one but there are proofs everywhere that equality before the law is an excellent thing. Under the tyranny the army was no better in war than their neighbors, but once it was freed of it it became far and away the best of all." Spartans would say, correctly, that that was to overstate the case, but there can be little doubt that morale in the military was boosted.

Despite their best calculations, the Alcmaeonids profited little from the new dispensation they had brought about. Cleisthenes himself disappears immediately, altogether and without explanation. Perhaps he just died, perhaps he was obliged for some reason to quit the scene. We will never know.

Within a generation the clan was reported to be in deep disfavor. In 486 yet another relative called Megacles and two years later Xanthippus, an Alcmaeonid by marriage, were ostracized. An *ostracon* has survived inscribed with a verse couplet, recalling the family's guilt over the Cylon affair.

This potsherd says that Xanthippus, son of Arrhiphron,
Is the worst of all the Accursed Family of leaders.

Athenians refused to acknowledge Cleisthenes' contribution to the expulsion of the tyrants. This was among the reasons for the absurd over-promotion of the charming but incompetent Harmodius and Aristogeiton. Everyone seemed to be singing about them whenever Athenians came together to eat, drink, and celebrate. No wonder if Cleisthenes made his excuses and stepped out of the historical record.

However, it is hard keep a good clan down, and it was not long before the Alcmaeonids were back. As we have already observed and as Cleisthenes must have hoped, the Athenian democracy tended to confide its trust in the very aristocrats whose rule it had supplanted. This may have been due to their adaptability and also perhaps to an unspo-ken lack of self-confidence on the part of the *demos*. At any rate, on his return from banishment, Xanthippus was appointed an admiral of the fleet; and, as we shall see, two leading Athenians in the next century, one of them his son Pericles, were Alcmaeonids.

THE PERSIAN
THREAT

———

8

Eastern Raiders

The young man was tired out. A professional herald and long-distance runner, his name was Pheidippides. He had been running alone through the night with urgent news from Athens to Sparta, a distance of 140 miles over bad roads, and no roads. He brought terrible news. A Persian army had landed in Attica in force. Spartan help was urgently required, if the invaders were to be repelled and his native city saved from destruction.

It was August 5, 490, and in the hot darkness Pheidippides padded westwards past Eleusis, then Megara, and onwards to the isthmus that divided northern Greece from the Peloponnese. He had to take care not to trip and fall on the uneven shadowed ground. He skirted the great trading city of Corinth and wheeled south towards the city of Argos. He then turned right along a path that led over Mount Parthenium, or the Mountain of the Virgin, into the ancient, wooded highlands of Arcadia.

The hint of chastity was not altogether appropriate, for the place was sacred to the great god Pan, perhaps the randiest of Greek divinities (there was competition). Protector of fields, groves, and glens, he represented wilderness. He had a human torso and arms, but the legs, ears, and horns of a goat. Tortoises whose shells were suitable for making good quality harps lived on the mountain, but locals were careful to leave them alone, believing them under Pan's protection.

By now the sun was rising high in the sky and Pheidippides paused at a sanctuary dedicated to the god. And there he experienced an epiphany. Pan showed himself to the exhausted runner, whom he filled with holy terror. A modern scholar suggests that this may well have been a hallucination caused by exhaustion and lack of sleep, but that was not how Greeks regarded such events. In their eyes nature mingled with super-nature on easy terms.

The shaggy apparition spoke. "Pheidippides, kindly ask the Athenians why they pay no attention to me, in spite of my affection towards them. Not to mention the fact that I have been helpful to them in the past and will be so again."

The youth promised himself that he would pass on the message to the authorities at Athens when he returned home, and went on his way, arriving at Sparta in the evening. He had been running for two days. To complete the journey in so short a time was a remarkable athletic feat.

He found the city *en fête*. The Spartans were staging the Carneia, a festival in honor of Apollo Carneus (the epithet seems to refer to an ancient deity that looked after flocks and herds whom Apollo had subsumed into his own identity). It took place from the seventh to the fifteenth of the month of Carneus (August, roughly). During these days all military operations were forbidden.

At the heart of the celebrations was a ceremony supervised by four young bachelors, selected by lot every four years from Sparta's tribes. It began with a man wearing garlands running away. He was chased by a band of teenagers with bunches of grapes in their hands. If they caught him it was an omen of good fortune for the state.

Then nine tents, called "sunshades," were set up in the countryside. In each of them nine citizens, representing Sparta's *phratries,* or brotherhoods, and *obae,* which were population subgroups or villages, feasted together in honor of the god. Pheidippides delivered his message. According to Herodotus, he said: "Men of Sparta, the Athenians ask you to help them, and not stand by while the most ancient city of Greece is crushed and enslaved by a foreign invader."

The *ephors* were apparently moved by this appeal and replied that Sparta was willing in principle to supply troops, but not now. The Carnea prevented them, but when the festivities were over and the moon was full on August 11 to 12 they would act.

Were the *ephors* being sincere? On the one hand the Spartans were devout and made a point of obeying the wishes of the gods; on the other, they had a way of turning events into convenient obstacles. Perhaps they were not displeased at being unable to save the Athenians with all their negligent arrogance. They had humiliated the Spartans when King Cleomenes tried to intervene in the affairs of Attica. They deserved being cut down to size.

Whatever the truth, Pheidippides had no choice but to make his sad way home empty-handed. How was Athens to survive, he must have wondered, and would the old goat-god come to the rescue?

The Great King Darius had not put aside his anger with the Athenians, who had sent twenty ships to join the Ionian rebels. He could not forgive either them or a detachment from Eretria, a *polis* on the island of Euboea with a long record of maritime trading, for having torched the capital of Lydia, Croesus's old capital and a jewel in the Achaemenid crown. He took the matter personally and just in case it might slip his mind he ordered one of his household to say to him three times before dinner: "Sir, remember the Athenians."

But he was in no particular hurry. He would address the issue when he was ready. Of greater importance was, as we have seen, a strategic plan to regain control of Thrace, which the Persians had conquered in about 512.

Details are lacking, but Darius's original intention may have been to

114 / THE RISE OF ATHENS

extend his empire to the defensible frontier of the river Danube and to control, or at least influence, the unruly kingdom of Macedon. This would have the useful consequence of preventing the sale of Ukrainian grain to Greece and, more especially, to Athens, which was increasingly dependent on food imports. The campaign was tougher going than he had imagined. He found himself obliged to fight Thrace's uneasy neighbors on the far side of the Danube. Eventually he left for home, handing over the command to one of his generals, who completed the conquest.

The campaign's most striking achievement was a bridge of boats crossing the Bosphorus, over which his army marched from Asia to Europe. Long after it had been dismantled, two pillars were erected on the European side that recorded all the names of the ethnic groups which contributed contingents to the Persian host.

The engineer who designed the bridge was a certain Mandrocles, a Greek from Samos. He spent some of his fee on a painting of his remarkable feat of construction. It was displayed in a temple of Hera on his home island. An inscription read:

After bridging the fish-rich Bosphorus,
Mandrocles dedicated this to Hera
As a memorial to his bridge of boats,
Winning a crown for himself, and glory for Samos,
For his achievement gave pleasure to king Darius.

A second bridge was built to enable Darius's foray beyond the Danube.

About fifteen years later, after the quelling of the Ionians, the untameable Thracians rose up in revolt. In 492, the Great King sent Mardonius, one of his most valued officials, to reassert Persian dominance; he was a nobleman who had helped Darius win the throne and was both his nephew and son-in-law. After his confidently expected victory he was to proceed through Macedonia to Greece. There he would teach Eretria and Athens a severe and unforgettable lesson.

At the outset all went well; Thrace was brought to heel and King Alexander of Macedon made his submission, a humiliation that his successors did not forget. But then a great storm wrecked much of the Persian fleet off the dangerous promontory of Athos. Mardonius was wounded and the failure of his expedition damaged his reputation. To enable both kinds of injury to recover, the Great King relieved him of his command.

Darius was not easily put off, and determined on a new expedition against the Greeks. He was egged on by Hippias, former tyrant of Athens. He was an old man now, but still yearned for his native city. He not only wanted to be restored to power, but also to die and be buried at home. Sigeum was an uncomfortable bolt-hole, for the people of Lesbos objected to émigré Athenians in their neighborhood. So he decamped to the Persian court, where he pressed the king to hurry up and punish Athens, and reinstall his rule.

In 491 the Great King decided to test which of the mainland Greek states would side with him or, as the term went, would "medize" (that is, favor the Persians, whom the Greeks sometimes called Medes). He sent envoys demanding earth and water, a well-known token of submission. In some quarters they received dusty answers: the Athenians threw the Persians into a pit as they did to common criminals and the Spartans pushed them down a well. If they wanted earth and water that was where they could find them. These were serious breaches of international custom and practice, according to which ambassadors were sacrosanct.

This time Darius sent his fleet, with a complete army on board, straight across the Mediterranean rather than getting it to hug the northern coastline and having the soldiers march alongside it, as Mardonius had done. He announced that sacred Delos would be spared from the Great King's wrath, but, soon after the Persians had sailed past, an earthquake shook the island. Many regarded this as a portent of future woes.

. . .

The imminent threat from the east blew the flames of a local crisis, during which we meet again the ambitious, but eccentric, King Cleomenes of Sparta and witness his last hurrah.

The relations between Athens and the neighboring island of Aegina, a wealthy trading nation despite its small size and population, were and always had been chronically bad. Separated by only a few miles of water, they competed for the same trade and sooner or later one of them would have to give way. In 498 Aegina entered a state of "standing war." Her fleet sailed along the Attic coast making mischief and raided Phaleron. This was the original port of Athens, although it was more of an unprotected beach than a proper harbor, and so was easy for enemies (and the weather) to attack.

It seemed likely that the island *polis* would take the side of Persia when its fleet and army arrived. Indeed, it had not hesitated to offer earth and water to the Great King's embassy when it called. What could suit it better than the final humiliation of its old enemy?

The prestige of the Spartans was rising and they were widely recognized as an informal international ombudsman. So the Athenians filed a complaint with them that Aegina was medizing. It was willing, they claimed, to betray Hellas because of its quarrel with Athens. The islanders intended to march with the invaders.

Apparently on his own initiative, King Cleomenes went to Aegina and tried to arrest some leading Aeginetans, but was repulsed. He was not known for his approval of the Athenian democracy and people whispered he had been bribed to give way. Back in Sparta, his fellow-king Demaratus, with whom he was still on very bad terms, briefed against him.

Cleomenes put a stop to his colleague's constant sniping. A suit was launched to depose Demaratus on the grounds that he was illegitimate. The oracle at Delphi was consulted and it seems that the priestess was secretly persuaded to find against Demaratus, who fled his homeland and made his way, like Hippias before him, to the court of King Darius, who welcomed him with open arms and gave him land and cities. In effect, he was appointed as a satrap.

Meanwhile, Cleomenes was able to get hold of his hostages and ten Aeginetans were dispatched to Athens for safekeeping. However, his troubles had only begun. It leaked out that he had tampered with the Pythia at Delphi and to evade punishment he escaped to Arcadia where he encouraged dissidents to rise against Spartan rule in the Peloponnese. The authorities were frightened at the damage he might do on the loose to Spartan interests and decided that the wisest course was to forget and forgive. He was recalled and resumed his functions as king.

According to Herodotus, about 490 Cleomenes lost his mind. In modern terms, he seems to have suffered a paranoid episode. For his own and other people's safety, his family confined him to a wooden pillory, but he persuaded an unwary guard to give him a knife. He

> started to mutilate himself, beginning from his shins. Cutting his flesh lengthways, he went on to his thighs, hips and sides until he reached his belly, which he thoroughly shredded.

So died one of Sparta's larger-than-life statesmen. Cleomenes was charismatic, persuasive, and outward-looking, but also impatient and impulsive. Despite the misgivings of his countrymen, his policy was to exploit Sparta's growing prestige and give his native land an international role. If he had lived longer he might have led the resistance to Persian aggression.

Marathon was a good place for sailing craft to land and soldiers to jump out of troopships drawn up along the shelving beach. That was the advice which Hippias gave the two Persian commanders, the Great King's brother Artaphernes and Datis, an admiral from Media. The old tyrant was sailing with the fleet and hoped that his new friends would give Athens back to him.

The word "Marathon" means full of fennel plants. The flat, sickle-shaped plain, more than five miles long, will have been aflame with their yellow flowers and feathery leaves as they blossomed among clumps of trees and scrub. It lies between craggy mountains and the sea along the northeastern coastline of Attica. At its northern end a thin spit about one mile long, called Cynosura, or Dog's Tail, jutted into the sea and a marsh took up half the plain, which was bisected by a torrent that regularly flooded the whole area. A village lay a mile or so inland and upland from the plain. A road ran from a little port called Rhamnus some miles to the north, down through the plain and on-wards to Athens.

In early August 490, the Persians arrived at Marathon, which was completely undefended, after a safe journey across the Aegean. Before landing there, they had spent a week on the nearby island of Euboea, laying siege to the town of Eretria. Eventually it was betrayed by a couple of leading citizens. As Darius had instructed, the temples were torched in reprisal for Sardis and the people were enslaved. They were settled in the eastern Persian Empire not far from Susa and an oil well that was exploited for bitumen, salt, and oil (Herodotus found them years later, still speaking Greek). The expeditionary force waited for some days doing nothing; this was to give the Athenians time to con-sider their position.

It has been estimated that Datis and Artaphernes commanded an army of some 25,000 men. Their total number, including oarsmen and backup staff in charge of logistics, probably reached about 80,000 souls in all. Four hundred merchantmen were needed to transport the mili-tary. The Phoenicians, the best sailors of their day, supplied most of the Great King's warships.

During daylight hours the Persian fleet beached at a safe spot be-tween the large marsh and the Dog's Tail. They disembarked and made camp, probably across the road running down from Rhamnus where there was an abundant spring. It was a secure position with minimal access from all directions and with an easy line of retreat to the sea.

Datis and Artaphernes had every reason for feeling pleased with themselves. They had not only met their first objective, the destruction of Eretria, but were well on their way to achieving their second. They had established themselves in strength on the soil of Attica. Their next

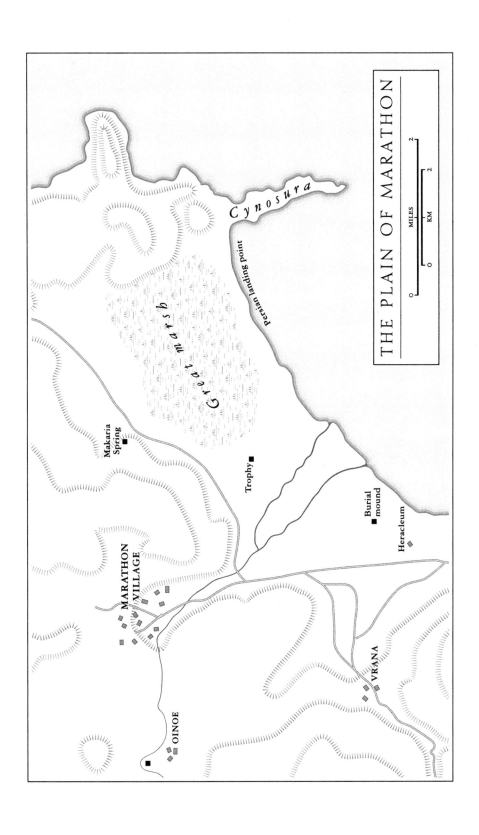

THE PLAIN OF MARATHON

Cynosura

Persian landing point

Great marsh

Makaria
Spring

Trophy

Burial
mound

Heracleum

MARATHON
VILLAGE

VRANA

OINOE

and final goal was Athens, which was only twenty-six miles or a day's march away. They would flick aside any armed opposition that might present itself en route, as with a fly whisk. They would then sack the city and burn to the ground its temples on the Acropolis.

As twilight came on, from high on the mountainside overlooking the plain of Marathon, someone lit a beacon. It gave watchers in Athens the alarming news that the Persians had landed.

How was the city to react? It was clearly the underdog and needed to think of some way of turning the tables. It could only muster a total of nine thousand hoplites, less than half the number of invaders. What is more, Athens had neither cavalry nor archers, whereas the Persians are estimated to have brought with them about one thousand horsemen and a detachment of bowmen. Cavalry was primarily trained to fight other cavalry, but could do a great deal of damage on the flanks of an infantry phalanx. In Greece, only the rich could afford horses and cavalry was identified with the aristocracy; it would be no surprise if the new democracy preferred, even if a little unwisely, to place its trust exclusively in its citizen hoplites.

Military command was in the hands of ten equal generals, as Cleisthenes had ordained, and Callimachus, the polemarch, or "war chief." This offered the unappealing prospect of conducting a war by committee. The most battle-hardened of these commanders was Miltiades, scion of the wealthy and powerful aristocratic clan, the Philaids.

It was his uncle and namesake who had led some Athenian settlers in the days of Pisistratus to the Thracian Chersonese at the invitation of a local tribe and established a tyranny there. Miltiades' father, Cimon, famously won the four-horse chariot race at the Olympic Games three times in a row, a feat achieved only by one other sponsor. He dedicated one of his victories to Pisistratus, who gratefully allowed him back to Athens from exile. But Pisistratus's sons, Hippias and Hipparchus, evidently neither liked nor trusted him and had him murdered; assassins waited for him one night near the Town Hall, the *Bouleterion*, and ambushed him. Cimon was buried outside one of the city gates beside the grave of his victorious mares.

In about 524 Miltiades went out to recover the family domain, which had fallen back into Thracian hands. He became a vassal of the Great King and took part in Darius's Thracian campaign. However, his loyalty was skin-deep, and he apparently joined the Ionian Revolt, during which he won control of the volcanic island of Lemnos (nicknamed the "smithy of Hephaestus," god of fire and crafts). He brought Athenian settlers to live there and, in effect, made the island and its small neighbor Imbros an Athenian possession.

After the suppression of the revolt, Miltiades thought it wise to avoid the ire of Darius and sailed back to Athens. With his military experience and his knowledge of Persian ways, he was an obvious candidate for high military command in the present emergency. But being an aristocrat he had enemies in democratic Athens, who prosecuted him for having run a tyranny over Athenian citizens in the Chersonese. He was acquitted. This was lucky for two reasons. He was in fact guilty as charged and, if convicted, he could never have been elected general.

Callimachus understood that the war would not be won under the command of eleven decision makers, and he had only a modest opinion of his own capabilities. After all, as one of the Archons, he had been appointed by lot. At his suggestion his fellow-commanders agreed to give up their day of command, which they held in rotation one after the other, to Miltiades.

But what strategy should be adopted? In the interval following the terrible news from Eretria, the *ecclesia* debated the question probably more than once. One option was to hunker down behind the city walls and hope to survive a siege. Alternatively, the hoplites could wait for the enemy to approach and fight a battle in front of the walls. These two options smelled of pessimism and defeat. A third, bolder course was to go out and look for the enemy. A central aim should be to contain the beachhead, wherever the Persians were to land. This was the policy of Miltiades and he persuaded the *demos* that he was right. At a crucial meeting of the assembly he proposed that the city's hoplites "provide themselves with rations, set out," and "meet the enemy at once." It was also agreed that a number of slaves should be given their freedom so that they could fight the Persians.

When the message of the beacon was received on that August evening, the generals at once sent Pheidippides on his fruitless trip to Sparta, and a message for help was also dispatched to the tiny Boeotian city-state of Plataea, an unwilling member of the Boeotian confederation north of Attica and very friendly to Athens. The hoplites got ready to march up the coast road to meet their fate, and either left the city under cover of darkness or awaited the early summer dawn. Each man had a donkey and slave to carry his armor, weapons, and equipment for making camp.

The hoplite army entered the plain of Marathon and encamped beside a precinct or shrine to Heracles. It was a strong position with easy access to water at a spring in the hills and at Marathon village. Trees were felled and piled up on either flank as a protective barrier against the Persian horse. The first phase of a successful campaign had already been achieved, for the coast road to Athens was now guarded and the Persians were held to their beachhead. There was nowhere they could go but away, unless they were to beat the Athenians in battle.

A force of between six hundred and one thousand Plataeans arrived in the Athenian camp, a timely response to the previous day's appeal. But there was bad news as well. Pheidippides had returned to Athens and it was now certain that the Spartans could not be expected for another six days or so.

At this point both sides had good reasons for holding off from a full, set-piece battle. The Athenians were waiting for the Spartans to finish their festivities and join them. Also, the generals were nervous of taking the field when the Persian cavalry and archers would be free to attack their infantry from the flanks and the rear.

As for Datis and Artaphernes, they were uneasy at the prospect of pitting their probably inferior infantry against the heavily armed hoplites with their reputation for invulnerability—the "bronze men" as they were nicknamed. Also, promisingly, they were in touch with Athenians who supported a return of the tyranny and were willing to betray the city and open the gates to them when the circumstances were right.

It has never been established who these potential traitors were. Many at the time believed they were the Alcmaeonids, but this seems unlikely. As Herodotus points out, the clan had been consistently hostile to the tyrants over the years. Its head, Cleisthenes, had been responsible for the introduction of democracy and in that way had ensured a continuing place for the Alcmaeonids in the public life of Athens. It is true that some members of the family were to be victims of ostracism in the coming years, but turning coat at this stage would have been extraordinarily shortsighted.

So for several days nothing happened. The armies faced one another two or three miles apart and waited. There was no word of the Spartans, but we may assume that Datis and Artaphernes were aware of their probably imminent arrival, an event that would tip the balance of advantage away from the Persians. But there was also no word from the pro-Persian conspirators in Athens.

The Persian high command decided to make a move. To all intents and purposes Athens was undefended; it was obvious that every spare soldier was at Marathon. On the night of August 11/12 Datis embarked a task force with some infantry and the bulk of the cavalry and set sail for the Athenian harbor at Phaleron. He intended to take the city by surprise. Luckily Ionian scouts on the Persian side slipped away from their posts before dawn and delivered an urgent message to the Athenian camp: "The cavalry has gone."

Suddenly Callimachus and Miltiades were short of time. In the absence of the Persian cavalry the prospects for a hoplite victory were much improved. It would probably take Datis and his fleet up to twelve hours of daylight sailing to reach Phaleron and a further hour or so to disembark. Would it be possible for the Athenians to fight and win a quick battle in the morning and then rush back and defend their city in the evening? Miltiades had no doubt that the answer to the question was a loud yes, but the ten generals were evenly divided. Callimachus as polemarch bravely cast his deciding vote for attack.

By about half past five in the morning the Greek army was drawn up across the plain and faced the Persians, who had left their camp and the great marsh behind them. If Miltiades' plan was to work, the battle would need to be done and won by about nine o'clock. He guessed that, following the Persian habit, Artaphernes would place the best troops of his polyglot army in the center of the line with weaker formations on the wings. And so it happened.

Hoplites were usually massed eight deep, but the numerically superior Persians had a much longer front than that of the Athenians. So, to avoid being outflanked, Miltiades as operational commander thinned his center to three or four ranks at most while strengthening his wings.

He decided to make a virtue of necessity and laid a trap for the enemy. The Persian center would be allowed to press forward and the hoplites would gradually retreat. Meanwhile the Greek wings, one of which included the plucky Plataeans, would defeat the enemy forces in front of them and then wheel about to attack the Persian center from its sides and rear.

At the sounding of a trumpet, the Greeks set off in a brisk march. They broke into a run when they came within range of the archers. The battle proceeded exactly as Miltiades had designed it to do. His center fell back under pressure from the Persians. His wings routed the Persians. The Athenians and Plataeans, writes Herodotus,

> having got the upper hand, left the beaten barbarians to make their escape and then, drawing the two wings together into a single unit, they turned their attention to the enemy troops who had broken through the center.

The last stage of the battle was butchery. The Greeks pursued the enemy to their camp and their ships, already launched and ready for departure. Callimachus was killed and the brother of the tragic poet

Aeschylus, who was also present, had his hand cut off as he was catching hold of a ship's stern. Many Persians were struck down and the sea went red with blood. We are told that 6,400 of them lost their lives, but only 192 Greeks.

The defeated general picked up his wounded and sailed away. He had long been waiting for a sign from the Athenian traitors and at last a bronze shield flashed from a mountaintop. Presumably this was a prearranged message, announcing that antidemocrats at Athens were now in a position to hand over their city to the aged Hippias. In response, Artaphernes was seen to turn his bruised armada southwards. A strong wind and a following sea blew them down to Cape Sunium. All might yet be well, he hoped.

It was not much after nine in the morning. A runner was sent to give the good news to Athens (perhaps the services of Pheidippides were used again) and the exhausted victors followed after him as fast as their legs would carry them.

When his ships hove to off Phaleron later that day, Datis spied to his dismay the hoplite army, travel- and battle-stained. It stood outside the city at the Cynosarges, an open-air gymnasium and shrine to Heracles, and looked southwards to the sea and the enemy. The Median commander saw he had lost the race, and also, he now knew, the campaign. There was nothing more to be done than for him and Artaphernes, who arrived with the main fleet, to set a course for home. With them went Hippias, whose expectation of a return to power was over for good. The traitors, whoever they were, kept their thoughts to themselves. For many years there were to be no more tyrants in Athens.

After their festival and the arrival of the full moon, the Spartans sent a force of two thousand men to help the Athenians, but they arrived too late. They offered their congratulations and gloomily toured the battlefield. It was a humbling experience.

Marathon was a famous victory. More than that, it was an inspiration, for it proved that the new Athens could infuse its citizens with energy and that democracy was not the incompetent shambles its critics had predicted. The *demos* could make and stick to decisions, and win a war. What was more, the Great King's fearsome army had feet of clay. It could be beaten. Free men had overcome the hordes of an oriental despot.

For Darius, by contrast, the defeat was of little or no strategic consequence. It was a pinprick to his prestige, his pride, and his empire, not a wound. However, the setback annoyed him, and he vowed that he would get his own back when occasion allowed.

The Greeks made the most of things. Statues and odes were commissioned. A column was erected to the fallen Callimachus. The few Hellenic dead were cremated and buried under a large, man-made mound, which can still be seen today. Every year a ceremony was held there to honor "those who died in the cause of liberty." The thousands of dead Persians were treated with less respect. The Athenians claimed they had given them a proper burial, but there was no collective tomb. They were thrown hastily into a trench at the northern end of the plain of Marathon (where a German visitor in the nineteenth century reported finding a loose scatter of human bones on the ground).

Just as the Olympian gods joined in the battles between Greeks and Trojans up and down the windy plain of Troy, so various immortals were credited with combating the barbarians on the glorious field of Marathon. These included Athena, the demigod Heracles, and the city's artful founder Theseus. They and other divinities who had given assistance were honored in various ways: Athena was given a bronze statue on the Acropolis and a treasury was built at Delphi with the inscription: "To Apollo first fruits from the Medes from Marathon."

A quarter of a century or so later, a fresco of the battle was painted in the Painted Stoa, a colonnade in the *agora*. It depicted a composite narrative, showing in a single image the different phases of the battle. Miltiades is given pride of place among the ten generals. The guidebook author Pausanias called by in the second century A.D. and has left a record of what he saw. The Plataeans and Athenians are coming to grips with the barbarians: things are about equal. But in the thick of the battle the Persians are fleeing. They are pushing each other into the marsh. The painting concludes with the Phoenician ships, and with Greeks butchering barbarians as they leap into them. The [eponymous] hero Marathon ... is standing there, with Theseus rising out of the earth, and Athena and Heracles.

In the aftermath of victory the Athenians did not forget the epiphany of Pheidippides, for it was reported that the great god Pan had also been seen battling against the invaders. It was essential that he be rewarded and welcomed for the first time into Attica.

A cave near Marathon village was dedicated to his worship and that of the Nymphs, female spirits of the countryside and his amorous companions. The untiring Pausanias said that the place was worth visiting.

The entrance to this cave is narrow and, as you come in, you find "chambers" and "baths" and the so-called Pan's "herd of goats"—rocks mostly resembling goats.

The cave has been rediscovered in modern times, with cavities holding water and stalactites that, with a touch of imagination, can be seen to resemble goats. Finds in the sanctuary include figurines of Pan and female forms, Attic red-figure pottery, and gold jewelry, which date from the fifth century and onwards into Roman times.

Pan was also given a home in a shallow cave on the northwest slope of the Acropolis where every year he was propitiated with sacrifices and a torch race. Other caves sacred to him have been found on various mountains in Attica, the most ornate being on Mount Hymettus. A certain Archedemos described himself as a nympholept, one seized by the nymphs in an ecstatic and erotic frenzy, and covered the walls of the cave with reliefs and dedicatory inscriptions.

Miltiades dedicated a statue of Pan on the battlefield for which Simonides wrote a brief verse.

> *I am goat-footed Pan from Arcadia. I was against the Persians*
> *And for the Athenians. Miltiades erected me.*

One can almost hear the god bleating with delight in the hills.

9

Fox as Hedgehog

The father took his teenaged son for a walk along the beach at Phaleron, the uncomfortably exposed harbor of Athens. He pointed to the rotten carcasses of decommissioned state triremes, pulled up on the sand and abandoned. He knew the boy was thinking of going into politics and wanted to warn him off. He said: "This is how the *demos,* the people, treat their leaders when they have no further use for them."

The youth did not listen to this good advice. His name was Themistocles. Born in about 524, he was ambitious, but suffered from two serious disadvantages. He was half a foreigner, for his mother came from Thrace. Also his father, Neocles, although connected to a good family, was a "man of no particular mark." The democracy was still new and the best jobs still often went to aristocrats and to men of authentic Athenian stock.

What Themistocles lacked in the way of birth, he more than made up in energy and intelligence. Plutarch, his biographer, reports that he was "impetuous, naturally quick-witted and drawn to a life of action and public affairs."

He suffered from discrimination, for boys of mixed descent with a foreign mother were looked down on as illegitimate, or *nothoi*, although they were allowed Athenian citizenship. For their physical training, they were encouraged to enroll at the Cynosarges gymnasium outside the city walls. Heracles, to whom this down-market sanctuary was dedicated, was himself of mixed parentage, being the son of Zeus and a mortal mother. Refusing to accept social disadvantage, Themistocles persuaded some upper-class friends to join him in physical exercise there.

As a schoolboy what he really enjoyed was making mock speeches and learning the arts of the orator, essential for anyone who wished to make his way in the fresh, new, noisy democracy. He showed little or no interest in any subjects intended to be character-forming or where "pleasing accomplishments fit for a free man" were taught (tuning the lyre or playing the harp, singing, dancing, and the like). As a result, he failed to shine at fashionable dinner parties where guests were expected to be competent amateur musicians and play or sing after the meal. Men who thought they were better educated than he was sneered at Themistocles for his boorishness.

His early years in politics were not altogether successful, for he was somewhat too impulsive. In later life he justified himself by saying: "The wildest colts make the best horses, provided that they are properly broken in."

If Themistocles wanted an example of his father's warning of the fate in store for Athenian politicians, one soon came to hand. This was the rise and almost immediate fall of the victor of Marathon, the great Miltiades.

As a grown man in his early thirties Themistocles fought at Marathon in 490. He was philoprogenitive, twice married and with ten children. He seems to have been a happy family man, for otherwise we can depend on his enemies having briefed the ancient sources.

Themistocles never missed an opportunity to make money. He lived in considerable style, entertaining lavishly and showering his friends with gifts. At Olympia he tried to outdo a young playboy, Cimon, son of the hero of the hour, Miltiades, in the extravagance of the dinners he gave, and in the magnificence of his tents and furnishings. This left a bad impression. It was all very well for a rich young man to behave in this way, but not a statesman.

We have a portrait of the man in stone. He is thick-necked and, although we see only his bust, he gives the impression of a stocky build. He has short, curly hair and a short curly beard, proudly surmounted by a heavy, drooping mustache. He eyes are wide open and he has a broad, sensuous mouth, which carries the hint of a smile. Intelligent, ready to learn, and amused, this is exactly how one might have imagined an experienced political operator who had seen everything and knew everyone.

He became a prominent personality in the *ecclesia* and was popular with the masses. The first radical democrat in Athenian history, he served as Eponymous Archon in 493. It was during his term of office, or around that time, that the trial of Miltiades took place under anti-tyrant legislation (see page 121 for more on this). It may very well be that Themistocles had a hand in engineering the acquittal, although he and the old-fashioned aristocrat had almost nothing in common. But Miltiades was the best general around and it was essential that he was available for the approaching Persian invasion. Whoever opposed the enemy was his friend.

But once the battle of Marathon had been fought and won, Themistocles found himself prey to very mixed emotions. When the genius of Miltiades was on everybody's lips, Plutarch writes, for the most part he

was wrapped up in his own thoughts. He became insomniac and refused invitations to the drinking-parties he usually went to. When people asked him in amazement what the matter was, he replied that the trophy set up on the battlefield in Miltiades's honor stopped him from getting any sleep.

It was not just envy that motivated Themistocles. He feared that the rise of a forceful nobleman like Miltiades would threaten the democracy. Fortunately, the victorious general was his own worst enemy.

Such was his popularity that the *demos* happily voted him seventy ships so that he could "make war on the islands that had assisted the barbarians" and, more to the point perhaps, "make them all rich." Miltiades had his eye on the Cycladic island of Paros, famous for its white marble, which had incautiously contributed one trireme to the Persian fleet.

However, he disciplined some other islands first and so forewarned the Parians of what lay in store for them. They had time to strengthen their defenses and when Miltiades gave them an ultimatum to hand over the large sum of 100 talents or face destruction, they gave him a firm refusal. The Athenians laid siege to the port.

The Parians held out. A month passed and they began to waver. Miltiades opened secret discussions with a local priestess on how the island might be taken. He arranged to meet her at a shrine of Demeter, goddess of agriculture, on a hill outside the town. He went there one night, but badly hurt his knee (or, others said, his thigh) when jumping over the sanctuary wall.

Meanwhile the Parians received a boost to their morale, when they misinterpreted an accidental forest fire on a neighboring island as a beacon signal that help from the Persian fleet was at hand and refused to surrender.

The injured Miltiades had no choice but to return to Athens empty-handed. His enemies—and he had plenty, among both other aristocratic clans and democratic leaders—closed in for the kill. For the second time, he was brought to trial. The Alcmaeonid by marriage, Xanthippus, charged Miltiades with defrauding the state.

The knee had not healed and was turning gangrenous. The general was now so ill that he had to be brought into court on a stretcher. It may be that many of his soldiers and sailors had not been paid. If so this must have contributed to a transformation of the public mood. From hero to antihero can be a short ride.

Superfluously as it turned out, the prosecution called for the death penalty, but instead a massive fine of fifty talents was imposed. Miltiades died before he could pay it. His twenty-year-old son, Cimon, settled the account, nearly bankrupting his clan, the Philaids, in the process.

The general suffered an ungrateful end. But at the museum at Olympia there is a helmet on which is inscribed MILTIADES DEDICATED and is probably the one he wore at Marathon. It is a suitable memorial.

Hardly one year had passed since the victory over the Great King.

Many Athenians supposed, self-comfortingly, that the defeat of the Persians was the end of the affair. The barbarians had been given a bloody nose and would not be coming back. Themistocles fiercely disagreed and believed that the recent invasion had been merely a prelude. Like an athlete, wrote Plutarch, he should oil his body and enter the race to be champion of all Hellas. He should put the *polis* into training for greater games. There was not much time to get ready and Athens could not count on more than a few years' grace.

Themistocles was right. Darius had been furious with Athens for its intervention in the Ionian Revolt. He had been looking forward to his revenge, instead of which his armada had been easily repulsed. He was now even angrier.

Soon stories filtered out from the east that another expedition against Greece was in preparation, this time much larger than the first. The Great King sent messengers to the main cities throughout his empire with instructions to provide horses, food, warships, and troop transport boats. Men were enlisted into the army. Taxation was raised to cover costs. Herodotus writes: "The announcement of these orders threw Asia into commotion for three years."

Then fate dealt two disobliging cards. First, in 486 a major revolt, caused by increased taxes, broke out in Egypt, then a Persian province. The Great King was the pharaoh, but a satrap was appointed to run the country. Egyptians were left in no doubt about their subjection. The copy of a statue of Darius in full native regalia has been found in Susa with inscriptions both in cuneiform and hieroglyphs; the original probably stood in Heliopolis. The Persian text reads, in the tones of Ozymandias: "This is the stone statue which Darius the king ordered to be completed in Egypt, so that whoever beholds it in future times will know that the man of Persia has gained possession of Egypt."

Oh no, you have not, replied the Egyptians and prepared to resist the inevitable punitive invasion. But before the insurrection could be quashed, in November of the same year the Great King died at the age of sixty-four after ruling as Great King for thirty-six years. He was buried with all due ceremony in a tomb carved into a rock face high up a mountainside. In an inscription he presented himself in the most favorable possible light:

> What is right, that is my desire. I am not a friend to the man who is a Lie-follower. I am not hot-tempered. What things develop in my anger I hold firmly under control by my thinking power. I am firmly ruling over my own [impulses].

This is not a characterization of the vengeful monarch that the battered Greeks would recognize, but it is a reminder that, provided their subjects were obedient, the Persian kings did offer orderly, predictable, and benevolent government.

Darius's chosen heir was his son, the thirty-two-year-old Xerxes, who was the grandson of Cyrus on his mother's side. His first task was to reconquer Egypt, and this with some trouble he did. He imposed a more oppressive regime than his father had done and, insultingly, declined to assume the title of pharaoh.

In 484, the new Great King turned his attention to Hellas.

The small boy crawled along the claustrophobic tunnels underground, some of them only two or three feet in diameter and too narrow for most fully grown men. He was one of hundreds, perhaps thousands, of slave-miners, who extracted silver-bearing ore from rich seams at Laurium in southeastern Attica.

There were three strata of ore, separated by limestone. Mining had been going on for centuries (Xenophon said, "since time immemorial"), probably open-cast to begin with. During the tyranny of Pisistratus systematic exploitation of the mineral resources of Athens began. Shafts were driven down into the ground and galleries opened where slaves, chained, naked, and branded, worked the seams illuminated only by guttering oil lamps. An unrecorded number were children. It was a miserable, dangerous, and brief life.

The mines were state-owned and leased to wealthy speculators. We know of one leading Athenian statesman in the fifth century who rented out a thousand slaves, for one obol per head per day, to a Thracian mine manager, whom he had probably bought and then freed. (An obol could buy a jug containing about six pints of wine; three obols would purchase time with a prostitute.)

The mines brought the state welcome income. Then in 484/3 a shaft was dug through the second limestone crust to reveal the bottom stratum, an apparently inexhaustible new source of silver. Untold riches were to cascade onto Athens and its citizens, like the beautiful Danae whom Zeus visited in a shower of gold. After only one year's exploitation, the additional annual revenue from Laurium may have been as much as 100 talents or some two and a half tons of pure silver.

It was a miracle and Themistocles had every intention of making the most of it. He knew exactly how the windfall ought to be spent.

Archilochus, a seventh-century poet from the island of Paros, whom some compared favorably to Homer, once wrote: "The fox knows many things, but the hedgehog knows one big thing." Themistocles certainly had the fox's cleverness and cunning, but in truth he was also a hedgehog. Throughout the length of his political career he promoted a single overriding idea.

Athens had a navy of sorts, but was more proud of her land army, her hoplites. After all, not so long ago, they had won what many came to regard as the greatest land battle in Hellenic history. But Themistocles believed he had good grounds for arguing that the future of Athens lay elsewhere—at sea.

His thinking was both strategic and tactical. The population of Athens was still growing and, as we have seen, Attica's bony, largely mountainous landscape was not producing enough food for it. The *polis* depended increasingly on imports of grain; these were most readily available from the fertile arable lands along the northern littoral of the Black Sea. There was no way that hoplites could guard a long maritime supply line. It would have to be protected by a much stronger fleet.

In addition, more had to be done to encourage trade. Solon had taken action, but it had not been enough. If Athenian warships policed the Aegean Sea they would make sailing safe and so create a favorable climate in which Athens's merchant navy could carry on its business.

And then, of course, there were the Persians. If and when the Great King came back, the city's hoplites would be massively outnumbered and would probably be unable to prevent him from invading Attica and even capturing Athens itself. To judge from Marathon, one could not depend on military powers like Sparta. Should the worst come to the worst, a large Athenian fleet could evacuate the population to a neighboring island, such as Salamis, or even sail to Italy and found a New Athens. If it was joined by the navies of other maritime city-states in the Aegean Sea, the Greeks would be able to muster enough triremes to hold off the fleet of Xerxes.

As Chief Archon in 493 Themistocles was in a position to promote his big idea. The first step was to build a new, defensible harbor to replace Phaleron, whose only advantage as a port was that it was visible from Athens. The fleet had to be pulled up the beach, placing it at the mercy either of high seas or hostile ships. It was not fifteen years since the ferocious islanders of Aegina had set fire to the fleet there.

Not far along the coast at Piraeus and five miles from the city there were three closely grouped natural rock harbors. Hippias had already seen the advantages of the site, for this was where he had built his emergency getaway castle. Themistocles persuaded the *ecclesia* to finance the fortification of Piraeus and the development of the triple harbor. It was a tremendous enterprise, which took sixteen years to complete. Solid walls with finely dressed masonry rose from the ground, which were wide enough to allow two wagons to pass each other abreast.

However, his proposal that, if the *polis* was threatened by land, the seat of government should be moved from Athens to the new port met with less favor and was shelved. To abandon the Acropolis and the shrines of the gods would almost be sacrilege.

The Archon also laid out a plan to maintain a larger fleet. This was not only expensive but politically sensitive, and failed to win support. If cavalry was the costly prerogative of the aristocrat and the heavily armed hoplite was a member of the affluent middle class, warships were reserved for the poor, the *thetes*. They were the rabble that had the unenviable task of rowing them. Plato, writing a century later, expressed his disapproval in the offended tones of the respectable rich. Themistocles, he wrote, "deprived the Athenians of the spear and the shield and degraded them to the rowing bench and the oar." The *demos* was ready neither to finance more of the greedy poor nor to entrust its own future to the inconstant waves.

However, the new seam of silver at Laurium, when it was discovered nearly ten years later, and continuing fighting with its nearby trade rival, Aegina, changed its mind. The island had not been forgiven for medizing during the Marathon campaign.

A popular suggestion for spending the income from Laurium was to distribute it equally among all the citizens of Athens. It would be the dividend from a highly successful commercial enterprise. Themistocles insisted at the *ecclesia* that this would be an unpardonable waste. He told the assembly why this "fountain of silver," as the tragedian Aeschylus called it, would be better spent on the navy. But Aegina, although a genuine nuisance, was only his cover story; his real concern was with Persia. He did not broadcast this partly because he had to purchase wood for his triremes from Macedonia, then a Persian protectorate, and partly because his fellow-citizens refused to take the threat from Xerxes seriously.

Despite strong opposition, approval was finally given in 483/2 to the construction of two hundred triremes. Athenians took the view that if they could not beat the Aeginetans at sea, they could at least outbuild them in the number of warships and in that way overawe them.

It has been estimated that at top speed the shipwrights of Athens could build between six and eight triremes per month. Aegina did not have the resources to compete and watched with dismay the mass production of a navy that would treble the size of their own and the creation of a great port where it could safely shelter. As for Xerxes, he was probably not informed of these events, but if he was he will have dismissed them. His fleet far outnumbered the best that Athens could provide and it was manned by the most respected and feared sailors in the Mediterranean, the Phoenicians.

The trireme ("triple-rower") was a three-banked warship and although it had two square-set sails it was primarily a galley powered by oars. It has been well described as a glorified racing eight. Highly specialist, it was lightweight, rapid, and agile.

A development from the penteconter, an old-fashioned vessel with a single row of twenty-five oars on each side, it appeared around the year 600 and may have been invented by the Egyptians. It was exclusively designed to fight other triremes either by ramming them or boarding them. Its main weapon was a heavy bronze beak fastened to the bow at the waterline and designed to pierce an enemy's hull.

A trireme was about 120 feet long and 15 wide. Any longer and it would be too heavy and less maneuverable; any shorter and it would have fewer oarsmen and so would have been slower. Its crew typically numbered 170 rowers, usually drawn from the lower classes but also from foreign recruits, some officers, and ten marine hoplites.

The oarsmen sat one above the other in three rows, the two lowest inside the hull and the top row on an outrigger. The men on the outriggers were the only ones able to see the oars strike the water and they supervised and managed the two oarsmen below. The word "trireme" refers to these groups of three.

A trireme could reach eight miles an hour, but cruise more comfortably at about six—or four if rest breaks were rotated for the crew. Everything depended on the weather, but should they row for eight hours, they might travel between eighty and a hundred kilometers in a day. In an emergency and with an experienced crew and a new ship, this distance could be doubled.

The trireme had some near-fatal shortcomings. First of all, it was labor-intensive and extremely expensive to run. A crewman might earn a daily rate of one drachma, and so it could cost a talent to fund merely one trireme for a month. It follows that a flotilla of ten galleys would cost thirty talents for a three-month campaign. A fleet of two hundred ships employed up to forty thousand men and would quickly bankrupt the treasury of most Greek city-states as well as using up more or less all their manpower. A serious defeat or the destruction caused by a storm could produce eye-watering casualties.

Technical deficiencies weakened the potential of the trireme. It required costly and time-consuming upkeep. Sails, rudders, ropes, oars, and masts sometimes had to be replaced in mid-campaign. Hulls would become waterlogged if they stayed in the sea for too long. In order to prevent this from happening, ships had to be pulled from the water every night to dry out. The use of light woods meant that this could be done without too much difficulty, but it left them vulnerable to surprise attacks.

Also the space on board was so cramped that the oarsmen had to be allowed to disembark for various necessary purposes. There was only sufficient storage space for water (two gallons a head per diem) and crews ate and slept ashore. A modern replica of a trireme has been taken out to sea. Volunteer rowers found the stench and heat in their close quarters almost unbearable (of course, we may have higher expectations of tolerable conditions than people did two thousand years ago).

Designed for speed rather than durability, triremes were more likely to be damaged and sunk by storms than by the enemy. Katabatic, or "fall" winds, which rush down vertically at hurricane speeds out of a blue sky, were as lethal then as they are to today's holiday yachts. No Greek fleet would venture out of harbor during the winter months.

In effect, the trireme was a day boat suitable only for summer sailing.

The personality of Aristides could not have been more different from that of his political rival, the wily and imaginative Themistocles. He was a conservative and incorruptible—so much so that he was nicknamed the Just. He was a close friend and follower of Cleisthenes, but if he applauded his democratic reforms at the time he later changed his mind. The man he most admired was the (probably) mythical author of the Spartan constitution, Lycurgus, and he had little sympathy with popular rule.

He made a point of refusing to give or receive favors. Once he was prosecuting a personal enemy in the courts. The jury refused to listen to the defense and insisted on delivering a verdict immediately. Aristides jumped up and supported the defendant's right to a hearing. On another occasion, when he was acting as arbitrator between two parties, one of them observed that his opponent had done Aristides considerable harm.

"Don't bother me with that," he replied. "Tell me what harm he has done you. I'm here to judge your case, not mine."

Relations between Aristides and Themistocles were cool. Apparently in their youth they fell in love with the same teenager, one Stesilaus of the island of Ceos, and their rivalry continued long after the boy had lost his looks.

The fact that they could not get on with one another is not enough to account for their disagreements. They quarreled on policy too, although the ancient sources do not spell this out. There was a distinction of class, with Aristides defending the aristocracy and Themistocles the lower orders. It is likely that Aristides spoke for the affluent hoplite and attacked the expensive new maritime policy that Themistocles was promoting.

He was not its only opponent. Domestic politics in the ten years following Marathon were poisonous and at last someone seized the weapon of ostracism that Cleisthenes had invented at the time of his reforms, but had lain unused for nearly twenty years (see page 104). In vote after vote, there was a ruthless clear-out of aristocratic political leaders, usually on the grounds that they were "friends of the tyrants." This is odd because some of those ostracized were Alcmaeonids either by blood or by marriage. How can this be, one wonders, when the clan had consistently opposed Pisistratus and his sons for many years past and had suffered exile and persecution as a result?

The answer can only be guessed, but it is a plausible guess. Thanks to the fact that old Hippias, well past his use-by date, had settled at the Persian court and had hoped to be restored to power by Datis and Artaphernes during the Marathon campaign, to be a "friend of the tyrants" meant having pro-Persian sympathies rather than actually wanting to bring back the superannuated system of tyranny. This was why some said it was an Alcmaeonid who flashed a bronze shield from the hills above the battlefield at Marathon. However, it is perfectly conceivable that the Alcmaeonids profoundly disagreed with Themistocles' confrontational attitude towards the Great King. It was no treason to judge that Athens would not be able to repel a new invasion on a larger scale than the first time around and to argue that it was foolish to provoke Xerxes. In fact, it could be seen as common sense.

It is likely that Themistocles was behind the ostracisms, but he surely knew he was taking a terrible risk. He was deploying a weapon that could easily rebound on the one who wielded it. But he must have felt he had no choice: he knew that his policy to create a large fleet was right and he would do anything to ensure that it was implemented.

. . .

Modern archaeologists have unearthed a treasure trove of more than eleven thousand *ostraca,* or potsherds, among the city's ruins, on which are scratched the names of those proposed for exile. Some fragments fit together; curiously the names of political enemies appear on adjoining pieces. At first sight this is mystifying; but evidently commercially minded Athenians manufactured *ostraca* for general sale to citizens during ostracism campaigns.

Some potsherds have gossipy comments scratched on them as well as names. So the young Alcmaeonid Megacles, nephew of Cleisthenes, is accused of adultery, greed for money, and an offensively lavish lifestyle. He was stigmatized as being "accursed" (the long-ago crime of murdering the followers of Cylon in sanctuary still stirred high emotions). He was even criticized for rearing horses. This seems unfair, for in 486, not long after his ostracism, he won the chariot race at the Pythian Games in Delphi, which not only conferred great prestige on the victor, but also on his *polis.*

Pindar, poet laureate of athletes, celebrated the event in language of which the fiercest Athenian patriot would approve. He opened:

> *"Athens, the mighty city!"*
> *For the strong house of the Alcmaeonids*
> *This is the finest prelude*
> *To lay as foundation stone*
> *Of my chariot song.*

Pindar went on to hint at his subject's troubles, writing of "envy requiting your fine deeds," but the ode implies that Megacles felt neither shame for his exile nor resentment against his city.

In 482 the last and greatest of the enemies of Themistocles fell victim to an ostracism. On this occasion, in the run-up to the vote, an illiterate farm worker from the countryside went up to Aristides. He handed over his potsherd and asked him to write the name of Aristides on it.

Aristides was taken aback and inquired of the man what harm Aristides had ever done him. "None at all," he replied. "I don't even know him. I am just sick and tired of hearing everyone call him the Just." Aristides scratched his name on the *ostrakon* and handed it back without a word.

By far the largest number of unearthed potsherds (more than 4,500) for these years name Themistocles. Citizens must have voted against him at every opportunity, although never a majority of them. He will have guessed that his immunity would not last forever, and that one day he would share the fate of the rotting triremes on the beach at Phaleron.

But for now he had work to do if he was to transform Athens into the greatest naval power among the Hellenes, for from 484 onwards news trickled in from the east: the Great King was indeed preparing a vast military expedition.

In all the shipyards of his domains, in Cyprus, Egypt, and the great ports of Phoenicia, along the coastline of Asia Minor, and on the southern littoral of the Black Sea, keels were being laid down and triremes and military transports launched in their hundreds. An advance force of engineers and workmen was busy digging a canal about one mile and a half long through the peninsula of Athos. When finished it was wide enough to allow two triremes to pass one another. Ten years previously Darius's navy had come to grief trying to round Athos; this time history would not be allowed to repeat itself. Also from the Hellespont to Greece roads were constructed or improved and rivers bridged or furnished with ferries.

Nobody needed to ask what destination Xerxes had in mind. There was little time for Themistocles to deliver *his* ships.

10

Invasion

Xerxes, the Great King, was something of an aesthete and, when he first considered the matter, not in the least interested in leading a fresh invasion of Greece.

Like all upper-class Persians he preferred to cultivate his gardens.

In October 481, en route to Sardis where his army was mustering for the campaign, he passed Callatebus, a town famous for a sweet confection made from wheat and syrup of the tamarisk. Along the road he happened upon a magnificent plane tree. He was so impressed by it that he decorated it with gold ornaments, necklaces and bracelets, and (it is reported) even one of his royal robes. He detailed a member of his army's elite corps, the Immortals, to stay there and guard it.

To treat a tree as if it were a beautiful woman who needed protection seems like odd behavior, but Persians loved to manage nature and were enthusiastic gardeners. A Persian prince later in the century boasted that, whenever he was not on military service, he regularly did some gardening before dinner. Every imperial palace came with a walled park. Irrigated by water flowing along narrow channels, this was an oasis of green, shady cool in dry landscapes. A combination of a garden and open land well stocked with animals, it was a pleasant place for taking exercise; for hunting with spears and arrows from specially constructed towers; or just going for a ride.

Mardonius, who had lost his fleet in a storm on the way to invade Greece and been discharged from military office, returned to favor under Xerxes and often put the case for a new, more ambitious expedition against the Greeks. To the usual argument for revenge against the Athenians, he added:

> Europe is a very beautiful place. It produces every kind of garden tree. The land there is everything that land should be. In short, it is too good for any human being except the Great King.

In other words, Mardonius, going somewhat beyond the evidence so far as rocky Hellas is concerned, was tempting Xerxes with the prospect of acquiring a vast new *paradeisor,* or paradise.

These exchanges between monarch and commander are retailed by Herodotus and may be no more than a happy *trouvaille*. But they give a picture of a ruler who regarded his empire as recreation ground on the largest possible scale, who decided everything, but did not take the trouble to do anything himself. That task was left to the servants.

On this occasion, though, after the embarrassing failure at Marathon, the Great King took the highly unusual decision to lead the expedition against the Greeks in person.

Xerxes committed himself to the invasion of Greece no later than 484 after rebellious Egypt had been reclaimed. The work of preparation that then began was interrupted by an insurrection in Babylon. But at last, towards the end of March 480 the Great King and his expeditionary force started out from Sardis on the long march up to the Hellespont, through Thrace, and down into Thessaly and Hellas.

It made a splendid and overpowering spectacle. Almost all the adult male members of the royal family were present in one position of command or other. For anyone to apply for exemption from service was to risk terminal disapproval. A multimillionaire, who was a generous donor to the Achaemenid cause and high in favor, told the Great King that all his five sons had joined up.

"I am an old man, Majesty," he said, "and beg you to release my eldest son to look after me and my property."

Xerxes lost his temper over what he saw as rank disloyalty. He ordered that executioners should seek out the son, cut him in half, and place the two halves on each side of the road and have the army march off between them.

The procession of men in column of route must have taken hours to pass through this grisly display. First came the baggage and technical units, followed by a mixed body of soldiers from every nationality. It was a colorful, multilingual throng. They accounted for more than half the army. A gap ensued to separate them from the Great King and his entourage.

Two crack brigades of cavalry and spear-bearers, with golden pomegranates on their spear butts, led the way. Ten sacred horses from Media followed, and eight grays drew a sacred chariot for Ahura Mazda, lord of the universe. No human being was allowed to ride on it, so the charioteer walked behind on the ground holding the reins. Then came the Great King himself in his chariot accompanied by a charioteer. When he felt like a rest and some privacy he got down and took his seat in a covered carriage.

After him marched another thousand spear-bearers, with either gold or silver pomegranates on their spear butts, and then another thousand cavalry. The royal escort was completed by the Immortals, ten thousand heavily armed foot soldiers. They were so-called because their number was never allowed to slip; if anyone dropped out as a result of death or illness they were immediately replaced.

The Immortals were well looked after. They were magnificently dressed with lavish gold adornments. Their high status entitled them to bring covered wagons on campaign for their mistresses and to employ well-dressed servants. Camels and other beasts of burden carried the Immortals' special rations.

An interval of two furlongs preceded the rest of the army, which brought up the rear—another large body of horse and a column of infantry divisions.

A question arises. How numerous was this vast mass of humanity? It is a hard one to answer, for government records have not survived and classical historians gave absurdly inflated numbers. Herodotus reports that Xerxes assembled 1,700,000 infantry and 80,000 cavalry. To this he added 20,000 for camels and chariots and 300,000 for Thracians and Greeks recruited en route. As for the fleet, 1,207 triremes at 200 oarsmen per ship add up to an estimated 241,400 men and 36,210 marines at 30 per ship. Additional warships required crews totaling 284,000. Herodotus then doubles the total to allow for camp followers and their animals and hangers-on (among them, we are told, eunuchs, female cooks, concubines, and Indian dogs). This produces a grand total of 5,283,220 souls.

Herodotus must have guessed there was something wrong with his calculations. He wonders: "What body of water did the forces of Xerxes not drink dry except for the greatest rivers?" The logic of logistics, especially regarding the supply of water, argues powerfully against such a multitude. Eating was less of a problem than drinking, for, during the long preparation, large food dumps were placed at suitable intervals along the route from Asia Minor to Greece.

One theory is that Herodotus confused the Persian terms for *chiliarch,* commander of one thousand, and *myriarch,* commander of ten thousand men. Remove a zero from the totals given above and the numbers become much more reasonable.

170,000 infantrymen
8,000 cavalry

2,000 camels and chariots
30,000 Thracians and Greeks
_____
210,000

For different reasons modern scholars have come up with similar esti-mates. If these are more or less correct, Herodotus's claim would be justified that the army suffered seriously from thirst only three times during the long march to Greece.

So far as the fleet was concerned, Herodotus provides figures that, on the one hand, look as if they are authentic and, on the other, are far too high for the warships that reached the narrow waters of Hellas. As noted, he reports a grand total (excluding commissariat boats and transports) of 1,207 warships plus an additional 120 contributed by collaborationist Hellenes from colonies in Thrace and the islands lying off its coast. But we are told that only 600 or so triremes made it to their destination.

The discrepancy is easily explained. About half the fleet was com-mitted to a truly astonishing feat of engineering, which removed them definitively from the battle line. Somehow the Great King and his army had to cross the Hellespont, a stretch of water that separates Asia from Europe. Two pontoon bridges were installed, one some 4,200 yards in length and the other measuring 3,500 yards. Two lines of 360 and 314 triremes and fifty-oared galleys, respectively, were anchored from shore to shore and lashed together.

Gaps allowed merchant ships to sail to and from the Black Sea. Tough but flexible suspension cables, six for each bridge, made from papyrus and esparto grass, were laid on each row of boats and tight-ened by capstans. Wooden planking, brushwood, and earth with wooden side screens were placed on the cables to create roadways. The cables were pressed down onto the boats, but took some of the weight as well as sharing the strain on the anchors.

The first attempt at a bridge ended badly. It blew away in a storm, provoking Xerxes into an unhinged rage. If we are to believe Herodotus, he had the clerks of the works beheaded. He also ordered that the Hellespont itself should be punished with three hundred lashes and that a pair of shackles be dropped into the sea. The engineers tried again, hoping to keep their heads on their shoulders, and this time they succeeded. It was an absurd case of paranoid majesty.

By June 480 the Great King and his army had arrived at Abydus, a town on the Hellespont near the two bridges. It was from here that legendary young Leander, who had no need for military engineers, used to swim nightly across the channel to spend time with his girlfriend, Hero, until one time he lost his way and drowned.

The Great King held a review of his land and sea forces—or at least a representative fraction, if we bear in mind that fresh water was limited. He had the people of Abydus make him a throne of white marble and place it on a rise of land. As he looked down, the sea was almost invisible for ships. A race was organized, which Phoenicians from the powerful city-state of Sidon won. The coastline and plain were packed with men.

Xerxes congratulated himself for being such a lucky man. But he was under severe strain and a moment later burst into tears.

The Great King's uncle, Artabanus, asked him what the matter was. Xerxes replied: "I was thinking, and it struck me how pitifully short human life is. Not one of all these people here will be alive in one hundred years from now."

The king changed the subject and asked his uncle, who had advised against the war, what his opinion was today. His reply was well reasoned, even if the conversation is an invention of Herodotus. Artabanus said: "I am frightened of two enemies."

"Who do you mean? Is there something wrong with my army? Isn't it big enough?"

Artabanus explained that the enemies he was thinking of were the land and the sea. Where they were going there were no harbors with the capacity to receive the fleet, and the land would become more and more hostile the further the Persians advanced. If the Greeks failed to give battle, after a short time rocky Hellas would not be able to feed the army, which would starve.

The Great King was much put out and sent his uncle back to the imperial capital, Susa, in disgrace. The order was given to march into Europe. The first to test the bridges were the Immortals, wearing garlands. It took seven days and seven nights for everyone to pass over to the other side.

The army, always shadowed by the fleet, set off on its long westward trek.

The Greeks were well aware of black clouds gathering in the east, but (like free states throughout history) dillied and dallied. There was a single exception; thanks to the foresighted Themistocles, by 481 Athens had completed its planned shipbuilding program, intended in the first instance for the war against Aegina, and continued to lay down new triremes.

In August of the same year the *polis* consulted the oracle at Delphi about the impending crisis. After its delegates had entered the inner shrine and taken their seats, the Pythia, a woman called Aristonice, delivered a terrifying message from the god, according to Herodotus:

> *You are doomed. Why sit around? Escape to the ends of creation.*
> *Leave your homes and the citadel your city circles like a wheel.*

The oracle was on good terms with Persia and it seems that it took the view that resistance to a major invasion by the Great King was futile. It was not alone. The god took care to be well informed and many Greeks were of the same opinion.

The Athenians were devastated by what they had been told, but kept their presence of mind. They took olive branches and went back for a second consultation. "Lord, give us a better oracle," they asked.

The Pythia tried again. This time, she said, her words would be serious ("adamantine"). She offered a ray of hope, although it was hard to interpret what she meant.

> *Zeus the all-seeing grants to Athena a wall of wood.*
> *It alone will not fall, but help you and your children.*

She added a parting shot.

> *O divine Salamis, you will destroy women's sons*
> *When Demeter's grain is sown or gathered in at harvest.*

Although less negative than the first oracular statement, it was also less comprehensible. What was the wooden wall and whose women's sons were to die at Salamis? When the envoys returned to Athens and reported to the *ecclesia,* those were the questions that had to be answered.

The strategic position facing the Greeks was challenging. There were three places where they might be able to hold up the invader as he marched down from Thrace.

First, there were numerous entrances into northern Hellas and the broad plain of horse-rearing Thessaly. The most important of these was the Vale of Tempe, a five-mile-long defile, but it would be hard to halt the Persian advance there because it was easy to turn this defensive position by passing through another access point not far away. Unsurprisingly, most of the states in the area did not look forward to armies fighting on their own land. They were minded to capitulate to the Great King and medize.

Then, leading out of Thessaly and into central Greece was a narrow pass between the sea and mountains at Thermopylae ("hot gateways," so-called because of hot springs). The waters were narrow too at Artemisium, northern cape of the island of Euboea. The two places had the signal advantage of being close enough to one another for reasonably speedy intercommunication (a distance of about forty miles by water).

And, third, a last-ditch defense could be mounted at the Isthmus of Corinth between mainland Greece and the Peloponnese peninsula. It was four miles wide and could be fortified.

Any commander planning how to beat the Persians needed to bear some factors, both positive and negative, in mind. The Great King's men needed food and drink and, of course, had not been able to establish food dumps on enemy territory. However, so long as he maintained command of the seas, transport ships could bring in regular supplies. If anything were to happen to the fleet, the army would find itself in serious difficulties. Xerxes would want to complete a conquest as quickly as possible. If the Greeks could hold up the invaders for long enough they might be able to force a Persian withdrawal.

The Persian fleet was keeping pace with its ground forces. Unless it could be stopped from doing so, it could sail ahead and land troops in the rear of the Greek military positions. Defending successfully the Isthmus of Corinth would do no good if the Persians could simply sail past it and open a bridgehead on the Peloponnese, perhaps from a base on the island of Cythera off its southern coast. On the other hand, there were few large harbors on the peninsula and the Persians were unfamiliar with the lie of the land. We must never forget that people knew little of geography in those days of slow, uncomfortable, and sometimes dangerous travel.

One final consideration: a brand-new Athenian fleet alongside those of other Greek *poleis* could now put up a good show against the Persians. About forty thousand men were needed to man the city's two hundred triremes. The number of adult male Athenians at this time has been estimated at between forty and sixty thousand (probably at this period nearer the former). Most oarsmen were *thetes,* members of the lowest socioeconomic class. There were also about 25,000 *metics,* or long-term foreign residents, who could be conscripted. Both citizens and *metics* underwent intensive training. Manning all the boats at once was feasible, but placed a serious strain on Athenian manpower.

However, the Greeks were still outnumbered and their warships were heavier and less maneuverable than their Phoenician counter-parts. These were good reasons for avoiding battle in open waters. There were only two stretches of sea where it would be safe to fight—Artemisium, as already mentioned, and in the cramped waters between the coast of Attica and the island of Salamis.

It was all too easy to scare oneself into a defensive frame of mind. If the Persian threat was to be eliminated, the question was rather how to win the war than how to avoid losing it. It was to this that the most imaginative political and military mind of the day was looking for an answer. It was the mind of Themistocles.

Sparta, by common consent the leading *polis* of the Hellenes and un-matched on the battlefield, and Athens, the victor of Marathon, con-vened what they called a Congress of Representatives at Corinth. It met in the autumn of 481 while Xerxes was still training his forces at Sardis. Sparta was in the chair and thirty-one states attended. The Con-gress's task was to decide what measures to adopt for a common resis-tance to the invader. It was an exceptional occasion, for it was almost unheard of for Greek city-states to try to agree on something, or in-deed on anything, but without at least a semblance of unity they had no hope of success.

The allies announced an end to their endemic mutual feuds, and in November Athens and Aegina abandoned their on-off, low-level hos-tilities. Themistocles had a main hand in this general accord, for which Plutarch rightly gives him generous credit:

> The greatest of all his achievements was his putting a stop to the wars among Greeks and reconciling Greek city-states with one another. He persuaded them to postpone their differences be-cause of the war with Persia.

We will not go far wrong in also attributing to Themistocles a deci-sion of the Athenian *ecclesia* to recall all the ostracism exiles: Aristides and Xanthippus were patriots and were to play leading parts in the approaching struggle. Reconciliation abroad was to be matched by harmony at home.

The Congress sent spies to investigate the Great King's preparations in Asia Minor. They were caught, but, instead of executing them, Xerxes astutely had them shown around his camp so that they could report back the huge scale of the expeditionary force (apparently they did not see the fleet, which meant that the Greeks were much less well informed about Xerxes' naval strength).

Persian ambassadors were doing their best to persuade Greek city-states to submit in advance to the Great King. In response, the allies voted to confiscate the territories of all that did not join the struggle for survival. They sent their own envoys to bring around those that were reluctant to join an anti-Persian coalition, among them the Thessalians, Argos, Sparta's longtime bête noire in the Peloponnese, and Thebes together with the other cities in Boeotia.

Appeals for assistance were sent to Crete, Corcyra, and the rich and powerful city-state of Syracuse, which dominated eastern Sicily. Nothing came of these initiatives, and it may well be that Xerxes entered into a pact with Syracuse's archenemy, Carthage, which was planning an invasion of Sicily. The idea was that Syracuse would come under attack at the same time as the Great King invaded mainland Greece, so preventing it from sending help.

The Congress met again in the spring of the following year. It was time to decide the structure of command in the coalition forces. Everybody accepted that Sparta should have supreme command of the army, but Athens, now the largest Greek naval power, had hoped to be given command of the navy. However, other delegates threatened to leave the coalition if they had to serve under an Athenian. Themistocles, whom the Athenian *ecclesia* had elected as general (typically, he bribed another likely candidate to stand down at the elections in February), waived his city's claim in the larger Hellenic interest. He accepted a Spartan, Eurybiades, as overall commander of the allied fleet.

Herodotus wrote that the Athenians gave way from the best of motives:

> They considered the survival of Hellas to be of supreme importance and, if they quarrelled over the leadership, Greece would face destruction. They were absolutely right. Just as war is worse than peace, so civil strife is much worse than a united war effort.

Spartans saw themselves as a land power and knew next to nothing about naval matters. However, as the historian Diodorus Siculus put it, Eurybiades was in charge, but Themistocles gave the orders.

The northern states made it clear that they would be forced to medize unless Sparta sent some troops to defend the Vale of Tempe. Before the Great King had crossed from Asia to Europe, a force of ten thousand was duly dispatched, but it stayed only a few days. Locals were unhelpful.

Also the troops soon realized that there were other passes from Macedonia into Thessaly that the Persians were more likely to use than Tempe. The last thing they were willing to risk was to have their position turned and to find the enemy in their rear. So they withdrew south to the Isthmus of Corinth and all the northern Greeks and the Boeotians immediately submitted to Xerxes, still some hundreds of miles away.

The sacred snake was missing. It inhabited an enclosure at the temple of Athena on the Acropolis. Every day it was given a share of the first fruits of sacrifices to the goddess, usually a honey-cake. Then the priests noticed that the food was being left untouched. They looked around, but could not find the snake anywhere. Was this a bleak portent for the city? Was the goddess abandoning Athens in the face of the Persian invasion?

More likely it was a trick of Themistocles. One would not be surprised to learn that the snake was locked up in a box in his house. He was certain of his war strategy; his problem was to persuade the *demos* he was right. He believed that the war could only be won at sea and there was a good chance that Xerxes could not be stopped from invading Attica. The departure of the snake was a forewarning that the Athenian population would have to be evacuated for the duration of hostilities, most probably to the island of Salamis and the small state of Troezen across the Saronic Bay from Attica. This was a traumatic prospect that his fellow-citizens found hard to accept.

Themistocles was perfectly willing to manipulate the supernatural to back his rational arguments. So when the delegates to the oracle at Delphi returned home with their mysterious advice, he tried to turn the Pythia's hexameters to his advantage. It was obvious, he told the *ecclesia,* probably in the summer of 481, that the wooden walls did not refer, as some thought, to the fence on the edges of the Acropolis. It was a metaphor for the fleet. In the sea lay safety.

And as for the sinister allusion that Salamis would destroy many mothers' sons, Themistocles disagreed with the idea that the god was predicting a Greek defeat in the island's waters. If that had been the meaning of the oracle, the verse would have read "O cruel Salamis . . ." or something of the kind. The phrase "divine Salamis" clearly pointed to a Greek victory and heavy Persian casualties.

The assembly preferred Themistocles' analysis to that of the oracular experts. At last, he had won the day, for if he was right about the oracle he was also right about his policy of victory at sea and civilian evacuation.

Although there is no evidence, the suspicious mind may detect his secret hand at Delphi. The oracle was on good terms with the Persians. In an edict Darius had written: "The god [Apollo] had spoken complete truth to the Persians." Themistocles will surely have taken steps to present the Greek point of view, arguing that Greek prospects were greatly improved following the formation of the anti-Persian alliance. Palms may well have been greased to override Apollo's first disastrous response to Athenian inquiry.

The debate that took place in Athens in 480 was one of the most important in the history of the democracy. Herodotus summarized what the citizens agreed by a substantial majority.

> After their deliberations about the oracle, they decided to confront the barbarian's invasion of Hellas with all their people and their ships in obedience to the god, together with those of the Hellenes who were willing to join them.

"Obedience to the god" was formal wording for fighting at sea and abandoning their beloved city. Detailed arrangements were agreed, and publicized; old men and movable property were to be sent to Salamis and women and children to Troezen. Adult citizens and resident foreigners (*metics*) were to join their ships, "starting tomorrow." It must have been at this agonizing juncture that the temple serpent slithered its way down from the Acropolis (or was smuggled out in a box). A dramatic intervention, whether divine or human, had a good chance of stiffening the common will.

A general evacuation probably began in June with Athenian warships acting as ferries. It was a complicated and lengthy operation. The well-to-do who could afford the disruption must have gone first. Farmers will have waited until the harvest was in before leaving. Former Archons on the Areopagus council raised a subscription for those who ran out of money.

Dogs howled at being left behind. Xanthippus, back from exile, sailed off in his trireme and his hound plunged into the water, swam alongside the boat, and staggered out of the waves at Salamis, only to collapse and die.

Political opponents rallied to the common cause. Cimon, the handsome young son of Miltiades with a head of thick and curly hair, and a group of his noble friends who were all riders in the cavalry staged a demonstration to assert the loyalty of the aristocracy and its backing for Themistocles. They dedicated their bridles at the temple of Athena on the Acropolis and then walked down to the coast—to symbolize the fact that "what the city now needed was not brave horsemen but men to fight at sea."

While most of the population readied itself for departure, a few obstinate old men, who thought they knew more about oracles than Themistocles, joined the officials on the Acropolis and barricaded themselves in.

There was another group whom Themistocles had to win over to his point of view—his allies in the Peloponnese. Many of them believed that it would be best to fortify the Isthmus of Corinth and defend the peninsula. This would mean leaving mainland Greece, including Attica, to its fate. Themistocles made it clear that this was completely unacceptable. The Athenian fleet of two hundred triremes would leave the alliance and probably sail to Sicily where the city would be refounded. This was a serious threat, for the rump of the Greek fleet would be no match for the Persians, who had unchallengeable mastery of the seas.

It was eventually agreed that a stand would be made at the pass at Thermopylae and the waters around Artemisium, exactly what the Athenians wanted. Time was running out and a small army, under the command of the Spartan king Leonidas, marched off north at once. It was now August 480 and the Carneia festival was on again, and this year the Olympic Games, in theory a time of truce. But on this occasion at least some troops were allowed to leave Sparta. Meanwhile the Greek fleet of about 270 frontline warships also set sail (a reserve was left behind to guard Attica, Aegina, and Salamis).

The Great King was pleased with himself. With impressive planning and logistical support, a huge army and fleet had been assembled. He did not believe they would face much resistance. Traveling with him was Demaratus, the Spartan king who had been unjustly deposed through the machinations of his fellow-monarch, the late Cleomenes. In 491 he had escaped to Persia where Xerxes' father, Darius, had given him a warm welcome. For the Persian court Demaratus was a mine of information on all things Hellenic.

"So tell me," Xerxes asked him, "will the Hellenes stand their ground and use force to resist me?"

"Majesty, shall I tell you the truth or what will please you?"

"Tell me the truth."

"While I commend all Greeks, what I will say now applies only to the Spartans. There is no way they will accept your stated intention of enslaving all Hellas. Even if the other city-states come to see things your way, the Spartans will certainly oppose you in battle. Even if they can field only one thousand hoplites they will fight you."

"Demaratus, how can you say such a thing? One thousand men fight *my* army!"

The Spartan replied that his fellow-countrymen were governed by law, by the rules of their community, and that prohibited them from fleeing in battle. He concluded:

"I am quite willing to shut up, but you did ask me to speak my mind."

Xerxes made a joke of the conversation and sent Demaratus away gently. But, he told himself, the man was talking rubbish.

11

"The Acts of Idiots"

There was a strange smell in the air at Thermopylae—a mixture of copper and bad eggs, the heavy perfume of broom growing everywhere and a salty undertone of sea. At the foot of a steep cliff hot, sulfurous springs gushed out and ran along gullies cut into the ground. These were called locally The Pots and an altar above them was dedicated to Heracles. A tourist visiting the site in the second century A.D. recalled: "The bluest water I have ever seen was at Thermopylae."

This was where the Spartans and allies decided was the best place to prevent the Persians from entering central Greece. It was an astute assessment. Thermopylae was a coastal passage; on one side mountains ran down to a narrow strip of land and on the other was the tideless sea, full of marshy banks and shoals.

At the western end of the pass, which Xerxes was approaching, the entrance was only two and a half yards wide. For about a mile the land then opened out to about sixteen yards in width and culminated in an ancient, dilapidated, drystone crosswall with a gateway (the wooden gate itself was long gone). The wall ran along a low spur to the sea.

Beyond it stood a mound some 150 feet high. Another stretch of beach and scrub followed, leading to a final eastern passage only wide enough for a cart to drive through.

King Leonidas was a younger son and so had not been brought up as a future king. He underwent the fearsome *agoge* like any other Spartan male child, and only inherited the throne after the death of his half brother, the able but mentally fragile Cleomenes. A "man much concerned with his courage," as Diodorus Siculus puts it drily, he arrived at Thermopylae at the head of a force of four thousand men. These included a royal bodyguard of three hundred Spartiates. They were probably supported by nine hundred *helots*. Because of the Carneia no larger number was allowed (and even that was stretching a point), but after the full moon on September 18, 480, and the end of the festival major reinforcements were promised.

The Spartans were accompanied by more than two thousand hoplites contributed by other Peloponnesian states and on the way they also picked up two Boeotian contingents, including four hundred soldiers from Thebes. Leonidas was especially insistent on the conscription of Thebans, for their city was strongly suspected of siding with the enemy and his call for fighting men would smoke out their true allegiance. In fact, the authorities at Thebes simply sent the king all their malcontents and political opponents.

On arrival at Thermopylae, Leonidas decided to make his stand at the wall, which he had his men repair and strengthen. This was a wise choice, for while the western and eastern passes were narrower, the land alongside them sloped upwards only relatively gently. For all that, Thermopylae was a wonderful defensive position. To his dismay, though, the king learned that the pass could be turned. There was a pathway through the hills that the Persians, if they discovered it, could use to take the Greeks in the rear. To avert that danger some local allies, Phocians, were ordered to occupy a strongpoint on the pathway and repel any outflanking force the Great King might send.

Leonidas was ready.

...

Across the water from the Hot Gates on the northern tip of the island of Euboea stretched a long shelving beach, ideal for drawing triremes out of the water to dry out. Behind lay shallow hills. On a headland a small temple faced the dawn. It was dedicated to Artemis, goddess of wilderness, huntress, a virgin who watched over women in childbirth. The weather could certainly be wild there, as an ancient sunken ship, discovered in 1926, bears witness; it carried one of the masterpieces of Greek art, the famous just over life-size bronze statue of Zeus (or possibly Poseidon) fashioned only twenty years after the Persian invasion. Northwards across the water lay the island of Sciathos and the peninsula of Magnesia, which curled up on itself around the gulf of Pagasae.

It was here at Artemisium that the Greek fleet gathered, apart from the flotilla left behind to guard home waters. After all the Great King might not fall in with the wishes of the Greeks, but, bypassing them, sail out into the Aegean and island-hop towards Attica and ultimately the Peloponnese.

Behind Eurybiades and Themistocles and their ships lay friendly Euboea and an easy escape route south between the island and the mainland. The main disadvantage was that the waters at Artemisium were a little too open fully to counteract Persia's maritime superiority.

Three Hellenic triremes were stationed at the harbor of Sciathos, a small island north of Artemisium, as lookouts. As Xerxes' fleet proceeded down the exposed littoral of northeastern Greece, ten of his fastest warships were sent on ahead to locate, if possible, the Greek fleet. When the captains of the triremes saw them approaching they fled. But it was evidence of the great speed of Persian (or perhaps more accurately Phoenician) ships that they had little trouble in catching the three enemy boats.

The Persians picked out the best-looking sailor on the first boat they seized, took him forward, and slit his throat as a human sacrifice. The second crew had rather more luck; one of its marines resisted until he was nearly cut to pieces. When at last he was overcome, his admiring captors coated his wounds in myrrh and bound them up in linen bandages (their other prisoners they treated simply as slaves). The third ship ran aground, but its crew got away and returned by land to Athens via Thessaly.

This success was more than countered by a natural disaster. Reassured by reports from its ten advance warships, the Persian fleet sailed down towards Sciathos and Artemisium. Early one morning, probably on September 11, a northeasterly gale blew up out of a clear sky. An unaccommodating coastline meant that although some ships were out of the water on narrow beaches many were at anchor eight lines deep. The storm was fierce and lasted for four days. There was no chance of riding it out. Those captains who had sensed what was about to happen drove their ships onto the shore; but a large number were driven off their moorings by a rising swell and smashed against rocks. Herodotus claims that four hundred triremes and penteconters were lost "at the lowest estimate." He exaggerates, but there is no doubt that Xerxes had been dealt a blow.

It was rumored that the Greeks had appealed for assistance to Boreas, god of the north wind. If so, he had listened.

At Thermopylae a Persian rider approached the repaired wall behind which Leonidas had made his camp. Some Spartiates happened to be on duty at the time and the scout counted them. He noticed to his surprise that some were stripped naked for exercise and others were combing their hair (which they wore long). How frivolous, he thought. Once he had finished his survey he trotted off and reported back to the Great King, whose army was waiting in Thessaly.

Apparently Xerxes was bewildered by the briefing:

The truth, namely that the Spartans were getting ready to die and to hand out death themselves with all their strength, was beyond his comprehension, and what they were doing seemed to him the height of folly, the acts of idiots.

Xerxes sent a letter to the Spartan king, calling on him to surrender. He wrote: "Hand over your weapons!" "Come and get them," came the laconic response. On September 17, after four days of fruitless waiting either for the Spartans to withdraw or for all his army to arrive, Xerxes launched a full-scale attack on Leonidas and his tiny force.

Wave after wave broke on the Greek defense, to no effect. Even the famous Immortals were unable to make an impression. The Greeks had longer spears than the Persians and more impenetrable armor. Above all, the Spartans were good at drill. They would turn their backs on their opponents and pretend to be retreating in confusion. The Persians would fall for the trick and rush forward with a great clatter and roar. Then, just at the last minute, the Spartans would about-turn, catch the pursuers off-balance, and inflict heavy casualties.

Xerxes, seated at a vantage point, watched the course of the fighting with growing dismay. After a stormy night, the Persians resumed the onslaught, but with no better luck. The Great King faced an unbreakable stalemate and he had no idea what to do next. Autumn was approaching and the fighting season would be over. And it would not be possible to provision his huge army and navy indefinitely. Unless his luck changed, he would be obliged to make a humiliating withdrawal. Then, unexpectedly, it did change.

A local man called Ephialtes came forward, doubtless as a result of Persian appeals, and volunteered, for a handsome consideration, to show the Persians a track that ran through the hills to just beyond the eastern end of the pass. That very night, with Ephialtes as guide, a detachment of Immortals was dispatched along the route. The Phocian guard heard them rustle dead oak leaves in the dark as they walked along, but Persian archers showered the irresolute defenders with arrows and they immediately fled up the mountainside.

At dawn lookout men came running down from the hills and informed Leonidas of the defeat of the Phocians. He realized that it would not be long before he and his troops were encircled and convened a council. The end was near.

Different opinions were expressed at the meeting, but the king took the view that it would be "unbecoming" for him, his Spartans, and their *helots* to desert their post. End of discussion. He sent away most of the other contingents, but kept the doubtful Thebans and another group from a Boeotian city hostile to Thebes. Perhaps this was to show that Greek unity could survive the certainty of annihilation. Leonidas told the men who were staying, with dour Spartan wit: "Have a quick breakfast, for you will be eating dinner in the underworld, in Hades."

To give the Immortals time to come down from the mountain and seal off the back of the pass, the Great King did not resume the onslaught until an hour or so before noon. When his troops reentered Thermopylae they found that the Greeks had advanced in front of their defensive wall. Herodotus tells the stirring tale.

> Many of the barbarians fell; behind them the company commanders flogged them indiscriminately with their whips, driving the men forward. Many fell into the sea and were drowned, and still more were trampled alive by one another. No one could count the number of the dead. The Greeks, who knew that the enemy were on their way round by the mountain track and that death was inevitable, put forth all their strength and fought with fury and desperation. By this time most of their spears were broken, and they were killing Persians with their swords.

Leonidas fell fighting bravely and a Homeric struggle ensued to rescue his body, echoing the fight over the corpse of Patroclus in the *Iliad*. It was recovered just before the approach of Immortals in their rear. Soon completely surrounded, the surviving Greeks withdrew to the mound behind the wall, where they fought tooth and nail to the last man. That is to say, all except for the Thebans, who after fighting bravely (it has to be admitted) stood aside and surrendered.

Anecdotes throw light on opposing attitudes to soldierly honor. Once the last Greek was safely dead, Xerxes toured the battlefield and made his way among the corpses, among them that of Leonidas. Resentful at all the trouble the Spartan king had caused him, he had his head cut off and impaled on a stake. He worried that visitors would see the high price he had paid for his victory and ordered that most of the Persian dead should be buried in shallow trenches or covered with earth and leaves, leaving only one thousand visible.

Two of the three hundred Spartans were suffering from acute inflammation of the eyes (a common ailment in classical times) and, before the fighting started, had been sent back to a village in the rear to recuperate. One of them, when he heard that the Persians had turned the pass, ordered his batman, a *helot,* to lead him to the battlefield. He plunged into the fray and was killed. The other, a certain Aristodemus, lost his nerve and stayed where he was. When he returned to Sparta he found himself in disgrace. No citizen would offer him a light to kindle his fire or speak to him. He was nicknamed the Trembler.

The allies at Artemisium watched the huge Persian fleet sail into Aphetae, a bay on the northern coast of the strait, and saw the land swarming with enemy infantry. By a lucky chance thirteen Persian ships mistook their opponents' fleet for their own and sailed into captivity, but that was only a minor boost for morale. It did not stop the Greeks from panicking. Perhaps the expedition north had been foolhardy, they thought. Surely they should make their excuses now and leave? But even critics of the forward strategy could recognize the danger in such a move. If the fleet abandoned Artemisium, Leonidas would be left isolated to fend for himself.

However, if Herodotus is to be believed, Eurybiades lost his nerve and decided on flight. The terrified Euboeans petitioned him to wait a little while before leaving so that they could evacuate their women and children to places of safety. When he refused, they had a word with Themistocles and offered him a bribe of thirty talents if he could persuade the high command to stand and fight. He pocketed the money and went to see Eurybiades. He stiffened the Spartan's resolve with a backhander of five talents, which he pretended to have found from his own pocket (throughout this history we shall find Spartans who were brought up in austerity at home and fell for gold when abroad). The fleet would stay. Themistocles never saw any harm in making a profit from doing the right thing.

On September 17, the same day as that on which the Great King launched his first assault on Leonidas at Thermopylae, the Persian fleet did not come out to fight. This was despite the fact that it had made good, so far as possible, the damage caused by the great storm. Also its commanders now knew that for all their losses they still massively out-numbered the Greeks.

But there was a good reason for inactivity. That afternoon two hundred Persian warships set sail northwards from Sciathos. Once the Greeks lost sight of them, they turned east out to sea and then sailed down the hundred-mile length of Euboea. The plan was to round the island's southern tips and proceed up the channel between Euboea and the mainland. Their destination was Euripus, a strait only wide enough to allow a single ship to pass through at a time. Here they would wait.

Once the flotilla was in position on the following day, the Great King's main fleet was to attack and rout the Greeks at Artemisium, whose only escape route was down the channel towards the Euripus narrows. They would be caught in the jaws of a lethal trap.

That was the idea, but secrecy was essential. Luckily, a dissident Greek diver in the Great King's service swam or rowed unnoticed across the few miles of water from Aphetae to Artemisium and re-vealed the stratagem. After they had briefly considered a plan to lay an ambush themselves at the Euripus narrows, Eurybiades and Themis-tocles made the intelligent and brave decision to offer battle at once. It was essential to discover the enemy's battle tactics and to test the effi-cacy of their own.

The Persians made no move, so the Greeks challenged them. They rowed into open water from their beach in a line more than two miles long. The Persians responded by coming out themselves and forming an even longer line. They began to outflank and envelop the Greeks, who on a signal backed water and formed themselves into a circle, with all the ships' bows pointing outwards. This made things difficult for the Persians, who liked to come alongside enemy triremes and board them. By contrast the Greeks preferred to row forward and disable their opponents by ramming them in the side or stern, and for this their hedgehog layout was ideal.

It was a short engagement, which came to an end at dusk. The Greeks captured thirty enemy warships, a minor but significant victory and a boost for morale.

That night Boreas made his second intervention. A tempest raged, torrential and continuous rain poured down, and thunder pealed around the mountain peaks. The main Persian fleet at the open anchorage of Aphetae was badly hit. Apparently corpses and wreckage got entangled with ships' prows and oars, panicking crews and marines.

The detachment of triremes that was sailing around Euboea was caught in open seas opposite the island's dangerous southwestern coast. The wind blew them along in the sodden darkness. They had no idea where they were heading and most of them crashed against the barren lee shore. It seems that not one ship survived. If there had been any still afloat, they would have been mopped up by the Athenian reserve of fifty-three warships. Its job had been to guard home waters, but, now that it was obvious that the Great King was not intending a sudden southern push by sea against Attica, it was en route to join the fleet at Artemisium.

The Persians gave themselves twenty-four hours to recover from their latest battering, but, fearful of the Great King's wrath, they came out from Aphetae again at noon on the following day. Still numerous, they formed up into a crescent and as before tried to outflank the enemy. The Greeks engaged them and fierce fighting ensued. The two sides were just about an even match and both sustained serious losses, but the allied fleet under Eurybiades and Themistocles seems to have had the better of it, for after the fighting was over it controlled the site of the encounter with its corpses and wreckage.

Sore and exhausted, they had reason to congratulate themselves on their performance. But then, as the sun sank, a thirty-oared cutter turned up at Artemisium. It had been stationed off Thermopylae and its job was to report to the fleet any important developments on land. It brought news of Leonidas's last stand the day before, when, ironically, everything had been quiet at sea.

There was no longer any reason to stay. Themistocles ordered the men to leave their campfires burning so as to deceive the enemy of their intentions. Then the allied warships slipped away as quietly as possible under cover of dark and made their way down the Euripus channel.

With a squadron of the best Athenian triremes Themistocles brought up the rear. He could not stop thinking of cunning plans. The Ionian Greeks had been compelled to contribute triremes to the Great King's fleet, and the Athenian admiral told his fellow-commanders that he had thought of a way of dislodging their loyalty. At every coastal site where there was drinking water, he had his men carve a message into the rocks. It asked the Ionians to change sides and join their fellow-Hellenes. If they could not do that, they should at least adopt a posture of neutrality. "Fight on purpose like cowards."

Even if this propaganda had no direct effect, it might at least plant seeds of suspicion in the mind of the Persian high command.

The sea fighting at Artemisium was not decisive, but it had the great advantage of substantially reducing the Persians' numerical superiority. Even more important, it gave the Greeks in general and the Athenians in particular some valuable experience of the realities of warfare at sea. Despite the odds, they saw that they could, just possibly, win. Plutarch wrote:

They learned from their own achievements in the face of danger that men who know how to come to close quarters and have the will to fight have nothing to fear from numbers of ships, brightly painted figureheads, boastful shouts or barbaric war-chants. . . . Pindar understood this when he wrote that Artemisium was

Where the brave sons of Athens erected
The radiant cornerstone of liberty.

12

"O Divine Salamis"

The war was as good as over.

The Great King swept through central Greece in the autumn of 480, meeting no resistance. Despite the fact that the oracle at Delphi was on excellent terms with Persia, most of the local population felt that discretion was the better half of valor and left town. The priests themselves consulted the Pythia as to what to do, and were tersely informed that the god knew how to protect his own property.

And so he did. Although Xerxes probably did not intend to sack Delphi, he sent some troops to secure it. When the soldiers approached, a violent rainstorm broke out that set off an avalanche of rocks; they hastily retreated.

Other places were not so fortunate. Not only did the army help itself to provisions wherever it found them, it also burned and pillaged as it went along. Those who had not yet quit Athens for Salamis or Troezen did so now.

When the Persians entered Attica, they ravaged the countryside, burning temples and villages. Athens was a ghost town. Only the few people on the Acropolis remained. Members of the family of Pisistratus, the long-dead tyrant, were still hoping against hope for a restoration to power. They proposed an honorable surrender, but to no avail. Persian archers occupied the hill of the Areopagus, which faced the entry to the citadel; they shot flaming arrows at the defensive wooden stockade and set it alight. But the Acropolis was almost impregnable and the invaders were unable to storm it until some Persians noticed a path up a steep cliff where the defenders had not bothered to post guards.

When the Athenians saw that enemy soldiers had climbed up onto the Acropolis, they gave up hope. Some threw themselves off the cliffs and died, while others escaped into the inner sanctuary of Athena, where they were found and massacred. Then all the buildings on the citadel were set alight.

Xerxes had accomplished his mission. He had destroyed the holy places of Athens in revenge for the firing of the temples at Sardis all those years ago. It was the most prominent objective of the campaign and he had met it. He sent a jubilant message to the court at Susa and, especially, to Artabanus, whom he had sent home earlier in the year as punishment for his pessimism. The news was received with public rejoicing. People strewed the roads with myrtle boughs, burned incense, and gave themselves over to sacrifices and pleasure. Xerxes was victorious and everyone was going to know about it.

But if he was victorious, the Great King had yet to win. That is to say, he had managed to sack Athens and lay waste to much of Hellas, but had not defeated his opponents in a decisive engagement either in the field or on the waves. Would they see sense and surrender, he wondered, or would he have to do some serious fighting?

As for the Greeks, they had not yet lost the war, but they could very well do so in an afternoon. They were unsure what was their best course of action. After sailing down from Artemisium, they put in at the Salamis narrows on the express request of Themistocles. This gave his triremes time to evacuate any remaining fellow-citizens across the water from Attica, after which he joined the others.

A little later, the Persian fleet arrived at Phaleron bay where, according to Herodotus, Xerxes paid it a personal visit. He wanted to meet his commanding officers and seek their guidance for his next step. He asked his commander-in-chief, the great survivor, Mardonius, to chair the discussion. Most of those in attendance, guessing what the Great King really wanted to hear, advised an early engagement with the Hellenes. A dissenting voice was raised. This came from Artemisia, fiery queen of the Greek city-state of Halicarnassus in southwest Caria. She had taken power after her husband's death and shown herself to be a capable ruler.

In her opinion, Xerxes should not offer battle at sea. "The Greeks will not be able to hold out against you for very long," she said. "I hear they are running short of food on the island." The main army was marching threateningly towards the Isthmus and she predicted that the Peloponnesians would think better than to hang around at Salamis just to please the Athenians.

If her intervention is historical, she was making good points. The Greeks were indeed quarrelsome and were finding it hard to maintain their unity. Feeding all the refugees on Salamis island, the entire Athenian *polis,* was a very difficult task.

But Xerxes had his own problems. With September drawing to a close, the campaigning season would soon be over. In the ancient world, when the weather at sea during the autumn and winter months deteriorated, warships knew better than to venture out of harbor. To be marooned on the cold and windy beaches of Phaleron until the following spring was an unappealing prospect. Not only would the Persian fleet be in danger of further demolition at the hands of Boreas, but merchant vessels would no longer be able to guarantee a reliable supply of imported food. Local provisions would soon run out, if they had not already done so. The Great King's hordes might face starvation.

Opposition at the Isthmus, now fully fortified with a rampart along its width of four and a half miles, would be fierce. Thermopylae had taught Xerxes a lesson about the enemy's defensive capability. In theory the fleet could turn the position by landing on the Peloponnese south of Corinth, but this would be difficult for so long as the Greek navy remained intact. The coasts were inhospitable and uncharted. The island of Cythera to the south of the peninsula was well known to Phoenician traders and had plenty of beaches; in theory, it could make a Persian base for operations against Sparta, but both weather and waters were treacherous.

In sum, Xerxes felt he could not afford to wait. A quick victory over the Greek fleet, holed up in Salamis and still heavily outnumbered, was more likely than one against the hoplites behind their wall on the Isthmus. It would, in fact, make a land battle unnecessary. Assuming a Greek defeat, he began work on a mole designed to stretch from the shore of Attica to the island; this would enable his foot soldiers to cross over quickly to Salamis and slaughter the thousands of Athenian refugees there.

A very similar debate, in reverse, was being held among the allies. A general war council, attended by commanders of all the allied contingents, sat in almost permanent session. News of the invasion of Attica and the sack of Athens was announced at the meeting and set off a panic. All who contributed an opinion advised retreat to the Isthmus. Eurybiades so decided and the meeting broke up.

Themistocles hurried to the admiral's ship and argued that the order for withdrawal would break Hellenic unity and if dismissed, the various flotillas would simply scatter to their individual homelands. He persuaded Eurybiades to recall the council. A heated discussion ensued during which Themistocles put the case for fighting the Persian fleet in the narrow waters at Salamis where Greek triremes would have the best chance of victory. He told his colleagues: "If you do not remain here, you will be the ruin of Hellas, for the whole outcome of the war depends on the ships."

When he saw he was making little headway, he issued an ultimatum. If the decision to leave Salamis was not canceled, the Athenians would renounce the alliance and leave with their families for Italy. There they would found a new *polis*. This was not a new idea, but had already been in his mind when arguing the case that Athens should invest in a fleet.

The allies had to take the threat seriously, although we do not know how seriously Themistocles meant it. The Greek fleet with approximately 380 warships would be impotent without the two-hundred-and-more Athenian contingent. It would be unable to stop the Persians from sailing wherever they wanted. Wall or no wall at the Isthmus, the Peloponnese would lie open and defenseless to the enemy. Eurybiades rescinded his decision.

A day passed and opinion slid again. The Great King moved his fleet from Phaleron to take up position just outside the Salamis narrows where the Hellenes lay. This was alarming and late in the afternoon another council was called. Once again voices spoke up for reconsideration and retreat. Themistocles feared that Eurybiades might once more feel compelled to alter his ruling.

So he took matters into his own hands. He sent a household slave of his, who was a *paedogogus* and looked after his children, one Sicinnus, on a special mission. Either a Persian or a Persian speaker, he rowed a boat under cover of darkness to the enemy fleet and delivered a message for Xerxes. He probably gave it to the nearest officers he could find and made a quick exit, but he may have been escorted into the presence of the Great King. Either way, the carefully crafted words of Themistocles reached their intended recipient. In the version of Herodotus they read:

> I have been sent here by the Athenian commander without the knowledge of the other Greeks. He is a well-wisher of your king and hopes for a Persian victory. He has told me to report to you that the Greeks are terrified and are planning to escape. All you have to do is prevent them from slipping through your fingers, and you now have an opportunity of unparalleled success. They

are at daggers drawn with each other, and will not stand up to you.

As every spy knows, the best cover story is the one nearest to the truth. Themistocles' account was embarrassingly accurate, but nevertheless it was a trap. The Great King stepped onto the snare and the noose tightened. He ordered his fleet to stay at sea all night outside the narrows to prevent the Greeks from sailing off and sent a detachment to guard the western end of the Salamis bay. Picked Persian infantry was placed on an island called Psyttaleia, which partly blocked the opening of the Salamis channel. Escape was no longer an option for Eurybiades.

Themistocles' political adversary, Aristides, back from exile like Xanthippus and serving in the armed forces, had just sailed in from Aegina and had noticed Persian triremes gathering off the western coast of Salamis. He called the Athenian admiral out of the council and told him what he had seen. Themistocles asked him to go into the meeting and report that the Greeks were surrounded—they were much more likely to believe Aristides than himself. This he did, but the commanders were unconvinced. Only when an enemy warship defected and gave a full account of Persian movements did they accept the fait accompli. The atmosphere at the council lightened and became constructive.

Attention began to be paid to tomorrow's battle. Now the allied commanders listened to Themistocles, for whom years of planning were at last coming to fruition. His chief anxiety was to find a way of enticing the Great King's armada into the narrows. It had to appear that the allies had suffered a catastrophic blow to their morale and were ready simply to be mopped up.

Once Xerxes had accepted the bait, the actual battle should be fairly straightforward. It would be fought in constricted waters, in this way preventing encirclement and lessening the inequality of numbers. A crescent formation would give the Hellenes room for maneuver and opportunities for ramming. The Athenian crews had trained for speed off the mark and for quick turning. Their triremes were lower in the water than those of the Persians and more stable in choppy seas.

The narrows of Salamis describe a semicircle leading from the Aegean Sea to the bay of Eleusis. Their opening, past Psyttaleia, is about two thousand yards wide between the coast of Attica and a long thin headland on the left (from an entrant's point of view), Cape Cynosura (another dog's tail). The channel narrows somewhat because of a second headland farther back on the left, on which stood Salamis town. Although the water then apparently widens again, the presence of a small island named today after Saint George, once again on the left, effectively reduces the channel to a little over one thousand yards. The water then opens up once more and leads on into the bay of Eleusis. The general effect is of a funnel.

Well known to a local like Themistocles but not to the Persians, a southerly wind, the sirocco, tended to blow in the morning and a swell would push up the channel from the open sea. This was usually followed in the afternoon by a brisk westerly.

With dawn on September 29 the Greek commanders gave pep talks to their marines. The oarsmen pulled the hulls down into the water from beaches on the Salamis coastline. Meanwhile Xerxes seated himself on a gilded stool that had been placed on a spur at the foot of Attica's Mount Corydallus; a golden parasol warded off the sun. From here he had a splendid and uninterrupted view of events. He was escorted by guards and a bevy of secretaries who noted down instances of heroic or cowardly behavior.

He could see everything the Greeks were doing despite the fact that they were out of sight of the Persian fleet, which had not yet entered the funnel. And what the Great King saw confirmed everything he had heard about disunity and fear among the Greeks. He watched them launch their boats and confusedly make their way northwards towards Eleusis, as if they had no stomach for the fight. A faint-hearted flotilla broke off at top speed and sailed into the distance.

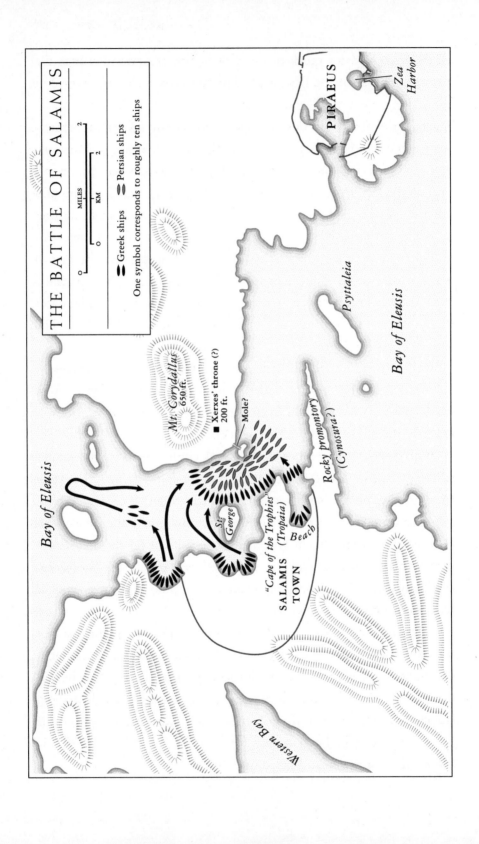

THE BATTLE OF SALAMIS

MILES
0   2
0   2
KM

⚔ Greek ships
⚔ Persian ships
One symbol corresponds to roughly ten ships

Bay of Eleusis

Bay of Eleusis

Mt *Corydallus*
650 ft.

■ Xerxes' throne (?)
200 ft.

Mole?

St.
George

Psyttaleia

Rocky promontory
(*Cynosura?*)

"Cape of the Trophies"
(*Tropaia*)

Beach

SALAMIS
TOWN

Western Bay

PIRAEUS

Zea Harbor

The Persians were certain they would have little trouble disposing of a disorganized and frightened enemy and their vast fleet formed up in close order and tried to squeeze into the funnel. It did so by moving sideways. The highly skilled mariners from Phoenicia held the right wing and advanced obliquely along the coast of Attica up to the point where Xerxes was sitting; they happened to pass an islet that partly isolated them from the body of the fleet. Ionian Greeks were on the Persian left wing; as they maneuvered past Cape Cynosura, they got caught in a traffic jam.

Meanwhile, the Greeks altered their dispositions. They were out of sight of the enemy, but in full view of the Great King, although it was too late for him now to issue new orders. The flotilla that had appeared to be fleeing was in fact holding itself ready in the bay of Eleusis to protect the main fleet from a possible assault by the Persian squadron that was blocking the western end of the channel that separated Salamis island from Megara and the mainland.

The remaining three hundred or so warships changed course and rowed southwards, probably in ten columns. They redeployed into line abreast and, as planned, adopted a crescent-shaped configuration, masking Saint George island. The Athenians on the left wing faced the Phoenicians next to the mainland coast, and triremes from Aegina were on the right across the mouth of a small bay just north of the Cynosura headland.

Then something extraordinary happened. A deafening war chant among the Greek ships warned Xerxes and his sailors that they had badly misjudged the mood of their opponents. Eight years later, the tragic poet Aeschylus wrote a play, *The Persians,* in which he has a messenger arrive at the Great King's court at Susa and describe the course of the fighting. It is an eyewitness account, for like practically every other male Athenian citizen the author was there and pulling an oar.

> *Then from the Hellene ships*
> *Rose like a song of joy the piercing battle-cry,*

And from the island crags echoed an answering shout.
The Persians knew their error; fear gripped every man.
They were no fugitives who sang that terrifying
Paean, but Hellenes charging with courageous hearts
To battle. The loud trumpet flamed along their ranks,
At once their frothy oars moved with a single pulse,
Beating the salt waves to the bosun's chant; and soon
Their whole fleet hove into view.

Before rowing into battle, the Greeks waited for the expected morning breeze. This created a choppy swell and blew the Persian vessels, which were higher and more top-heavy than their Hellenic counterparts, off their bearings and broadside on to their eager opponents. The allies fought in an orderly fashion, ramming enemy warships with their bronze beaks and slicing through banks of oars. The crack Phoenician squadron was pushed towards the Attica shore, broke and fled; Athenian triremes pushed through the resulting gap. Ships in the Persian front line turned back to run before the wind as it veered into a westerly. But there was no space for them and they crashed into those behind them which were pushing forward to join in the action under the Great King's gaze. On the right the Aeginetans began to curl round into the long Persian flank, so that the Hellenic crescent became a closing circle.

The Persians, who had been at their oars on guard duty through the night (while their opponents had slept by their boats on the beaches of Salamis), were beginning to tire. The wind gradually pushed wreckage out to sea. The Great King's admiral and half brother, Ariamenes, was downed by a spear and thrown into the water. His body was picked up by plucky Artemisia, who was having an exciting if not altogether constructive time. Her ship was on the point of capture, so she took down her colors and rammed and sank a friendly trireme. Her Athenian attacker turned away, assuming that she was either Greek or had defected. The Great King watched this feat and praised Artemisia's courage, assuming that she had destroyed an enemy ship. He could see that the tide of battle was turning against the Persians and Herodotus tells us that he remarked of her: "My men have become women and my women, men!"

This was unfair, for the Persians fought bravely, but gradually a confused melee mutated into a confused rout. The funnel emptied. The sea was carpeted with wrecks and drowned men (few Persians could swim). Aeschylus's Persian bearer of news again:

The Hellenes seized fragments of wrecks and broken oars
And hacked and stabbed at our men struggling in the sea
As fishermen kill tuna or some netted haul.

Aristides landed a detachment of hoplites on Psyttaleia where the Great King's picked troops were waiting, marooned and helpless. They were all put to death. The rout became general and a ragged pursuit continued till twilight. The battle was over.

It was a famous victory—so famous that we easily forget that Xerxes still possessed a formidable navy. He had lost two hundred ships with an unspecified number captured and the Hellenes only forty, but he still had plenty left. The significance of what had happened was unclear to people at the time and the allied high command feared that the Persians were perfectly capable of refitting, regrouping, and fighting again. And this is what they did. The army marched on towards the Isthmus and work continued on building a mole and boat-bridge to the island of Salamis where the evacuated population of Attica were nervously awaiting their fate. It looked as if Xerxes was continuing his campaign.

But the spirit had been knocked out of the armada. The best of it, the Phoenician contingent, had been more or less wiped out, and a headstrong decision of the Great King to blame their surviving commanders for the whole debacle and behead them provoked understandable resentment. Some ships may even have deserted. On October 2 there was a partial solar eclipse, which added to the atmosphere of unease and gloom.

The logistical problems had not gone away and the campaigning season, at least at sea, would soon be over. The reasons that, not many days previously, had impelled Xerxes to attack now persuaded him to leave. On top of that, he was not altogether sure that he still commanded the seas, for he could not count on winning a renewed engagement. The Greeks might well take it into their heads to sail to the Hellespont and destroy the boat-bridges, in which case he and his army would be cut off from home. They would be stuck in hostile territory at the mercy of vengeful Hellenes and insurgent Thracians.

The most sensible course was to declare victory and return speedily to Susa. And who could gainsay him? The Great King did indeed control mainland Greece bar the Peloponnese; he had killed a king of Sparta and had fired Athens. He had substantially extended the empire's bounds.

If there had been collusion between Persia and Carthage to vanquish the western Greeks of Sicily as well as those in Hellas (see page 154), as there may well have been, it did neither of them any good. News arrived during these days that Gelon, the tyrant of Syracuse, and his friend Theron of Acragas, had repelled a major Carthaginian invasion. A decisive battle had been fought at Himera, a Greek city of the island's northern coast (not far from today's Palermo). It probably coincided with the Thermopylae campaign. An instinct both for public relations and for neatness fostered an inaccurate belief that it took place on the very day of Salamis.

The Great King set off for home. He returned the way he came and was accompanied by a substantial escort of perhaps as many as forty thousand men. To his dismay, the boat-bridges had been swept away by a storm soon after Salamis, but the returning fleet ferried the Persians from Europe to Asia. Brazenly, Xerxes held splendid victory celebrations when he arrived in Susa. He left Mardonius in Thessaly with an army (it is estimated) of about sixty thousand horse and foot. His task would be to maintain the occupation and, in the following year's campaigning season, to bring a Hellenic army to battle and destroy it. Much of the Persian horde was demobilized and Mardonius kept only the Iranian troops and some other handpicked detachments. In due course the escort returned to his command after delivering its master to the safety of Asia.

Meanwhile Xerxes dispatched his disheartened fleet to Cyme, a port on the coast of Asia Minor, and the island of Samos where it was to await further orders.

It was sign of his loss of authority that the sacred chariot of the god Ahura Mazda and its eight grays disappeared. Xerxes had left them not far from Macedonia on his way to Greece, but when he returned to pick them up they had gone. The chariot had been given to Thracian inlanders and the horses had been rustled. There was nothing he could do about it.

When the Greeks woke up one morning some days after the battle in the narrows, they sent out scouts to locate the enemy navy. The roadstead at Phaleron was deserted. The Great King's ships had vanished. Eurybiades and Themistocles, who was the hero of the hour, led their fleet in pursuit, although they did not hurry and they did not go far. They laid siege to the medizing island of Andros that lies south of Euboea, but with no success.

Themistocles argued that they should sail to the Hellespont and cut off Xerxes before he could leave Europe. Eurybiades wisely disagreed: it was too late in the sailing season, and despite Salamis the allies were still heavily outnumbered and almost all the islands in the Aegean were on the Persian side. Themistocles gave way. Shameless, and ignorant of the fate of the bridges, he sent a message to Xerxes claiming to have prevented their destruction.

The allies decided to call it a day and returned to Salamis, where they wintered. With the arrival of spring 479, Hellenic unity came under renewed strain. The fleet, still commanded by a Spartan but with an Athenian admiral, the former exile Xanthippus, sailed east to Delos. Oddly, they numbered only 110 ships. Perhaps the allies wanted to save money, for navies were labor-intensive and painfully expensive to maintain. Alternatively and much more probably, Athens temporarily held back its own contingent for political reasons.

It would be no wonder if they did. Paradoxically, Salamis had secured Sparta, a land power, and her allies on the Peloponnese, but it had done nothing for Athens, a sea power, which needed a victory on land before it would be safe for its evacuees to return to Attica. It looked very much as if Sparta was disinclined to risk its hoplites on a military campaign to expel Mardonius from central and northern Greece. The Isthmus was now well fortified and this defensive position could no longer be turned now that the Persian fleet had departed.

The only card in the Athenians' hand was their triremes. Mardonius tried to persuade them with generous terms to switch sides; he would rebuild the city and the burned temples, give them additional territory, and allow them to govern themselves. They answered with a firm negative and a man who had the temerity to suggest that the *ecclesia* should at least consider the proposals was stoned to death, along with his wife and children. They pointed out to the Spartans that they could not resist Persia forever, exiled as they still were from their own native land. If the rest of Hellas sat on its hands, they might be obliged to accept Mardonius's terms. It was hardly necessary to add that 110 ships were far too few to resist Xerxes should he ever send his fleet back to Greece. There would be no second Salamis.

Sparta was delayed from taking military action by yet another religious festival, but eventually and with apparent reluctance it conceded. A substantial army, consisting of 10,000 hoplites, of whom 5,000 were elite Equals (perhaps two thirds of all full adult citizens), plus 35,000 light-armed *helots,* was sent north under Pausanias, nephew of Leonidas and regent for the dead king's son, who was still a minor. He picked up contingents from other city-states as he marched along. At Eleusis the united allies swore an oath of fidelity and comradeship: "I shall fight as long as I live, and shall not consider it more important to be alive than to be free."

Mardonius ravaged Athens for a second time in retaliation for his advances having been rebuffed. Modern archaeologists bear witness to the thoroughness of the destruction wreaked by the Persians: in the *agora* seventeen wells have been discovered filled with debris of the private houses they once supplied with water. On the Acropolis dozens of broken and smoke-blackened statues have been unearthed, and the unfinished predecessor of the Parthenon was demolished (its fluted column drums can still be seen).

The Persian general was delighted that Sparta and its friends had been tempted to come out from behind the wall at the Isthmus, now more or less impregnable. He immediately pulled his forces back from Attica and chose a battle venue in Boeotia where the land was fairly flat and suitable for cavalry maneuvers. He placed his troops in a five-mile line along the northern bank of the river Asopus and built a large square camp in the rear protected by a wooden stockade. He waited expectantly for the enemy to arrive. This would be the decisive contest of the war.

On the southern side of the river a ridge bordered a gently undulating plain that stretched to the foot of a mountain range dominated by Mount Cithaeron. Passes led down into the plain from the Isthmus and Attica. Mardonius had his men clear the area of trees and shrubs that would get in the way of his horsemen. To the southeast stood the small, vehemently anti-Persian and pro-Athenian town of Plataea.

Pausanias commanded a force of an estimated 38,700 heavy-armed infantry and 70,000 light-armed skirmishers with contingents arriving daily from various patriotic *poleis*. He encamped in order of battle on the lower slopes of Mount Cithaeron. Sparta held the place of honor on the right and Athens with plucky Plataea on the left. Here the allies hoped they would be safe from the attentions of the Persian cavalry.

Some hope. After a few days of inactivity, Mardonius flung his dangerously efficient cavalry at them. Their commander, Masistius, rode ahead of the line, splendidly attired in a corselet of golden scales and a crimson tunic over it. Unluckily, his horse received an arrow in its flank and reared up in pain, throwing its rider. Athenians swarmed over Masistius, who fought bravely for his life. He was protected by his armor, but someone spiked a javelin through the eye-hole of his helmet, whereupon he collapsed and died. His body was put in a wagon and paraded up and down the Greek lines. Herodotus comments: "It was worth seeing for its size and its beauty."

Pausanias then moved his army from the foot of Cithaeron to the ridge just across the Asopus from the Persians. This was not an ideal position. Its chief advantage was copious water, especially at the Gargaphia spring a little to the south. But by moving so far forward the Greeks were no longer able to protect the passes through which essential food supplies were transported. Also the Persians could outflank the ridge, enter the plain unopposed, and cut Pausanias's line of communications. In theory, Mardonius could interpose his entire force between the Greeks and the hills.

Neither side made a move for more than a week, and then the worst predictably happened. The Persians destroyed a party of five hundred draft animals carrying provisions as it came down a pass from Megara to Plataea and blocked future convoys. Mardonius launched another great cavalry attack against the ridge and had the spring fouled and choked. Hoplites had no answer to mounted archers and the Greeks did not have any cavalry with which to counter the enemy horse. If they wanted to eat and drink the allied forces would have to quit the ridge.

Mardonius was not without troubles himself. Under cover of darkness Alexander king of Macedon rode from the Persian lines to tell the Greeks that the Persians too were suffering from shortages. He wanted to make sure that, whoever won the imminent battle, he was on the winning side.

Pausanias decided to shift his position for a second time to high ground two miles south in front of Plataea. Surrounded by streams, it was nicknamed the Island and water was plentiful. To avoid the enemy cavalry this complicated maneuver was conducted by night, a difficult feat.

Of course, things went wrong. The center (comprising small contingents from many *poleis*) seems to have lost its way in the dark and eventually found itself standing outside the walls of Plataea. We do not know whether this was where it was meant to be, but it was able to protect the traffic coming down the passes, no bad thing.

For some reason the Spartans and Athenians on the two wings did not move, and by first light they were still on the ridge. Herodotus explains that, for reasons of honor, the commander of a Spartan battalion refused to obey the order to retreat. Pausanias spent the night trying to make him change his mind. More probably, he learned that the center had gone astray and was not sure exactly where it was. Much wiser to await the clarification of dawn. Once he had located the mislaid troops, he gave the belated order for the Athenians and Spartans to march, with the supposedly recalcitrant Spartan battalion acting bravely as a rear guard to ward off any Persian attempt to interfere.

Mardonius was in the best of humors. Like the Great King at Salamis, he misinterpreted what he saw as disunity, low morale, and incompetence, and ordered an immediate general advance across the Asopus. Were the confusions on the Greek side an accident or a trick? We can never be certain, but it is at least possible that Pausanias wanted to give an impression of disarray. This would encourage Mardonius to take a risk and attack an enemy satisfactorily established on high ground.

Pausanias was devout and at every stage of the campaign he sacrificed to the gods and made a move only when the omens allowed it. Now of all moments, as the Persian troops marched up towards his line, the omens stayed resolutely unfavorable. His men were under instructions to sit quietly with their shields in front of them, and await the order to advance. The priest killed victim after victim to no effect and Pausanias turned his face, all tears, to a nearby shrine of Hera, queen of heaven, and begged her intercession. In the nick of time the sacrifices turned propitious and the Spartan general unleashed his men just before they were overrun.

The lines met and clashed, and the Spartans soon found themselves hard-pressed. They sent for help from the Athenians. They would have come, but had just been attacked by Mardonius's Ionian Greek division (which included medizing Thebans, who knew what fate awaited them if the battle was lost). The Spartans with support from the men of Tegea, an aggressive city-state in the Peloponnese, fought dourly on. The Persians discharged innumerable arrows from behind a barricade of wicker shields.

It slowly became clear that lightly armored Persians were no match for bronze-encased hoplites. The terrain sloped downwards to them and (it seems) it was not possible to deploy the cavalry. The wicker shields were overturned and, although they fought bravely, the men were pushed back. Mardonius on a gray was very visibly in the thick of things, but he was struck down by a flung rock. His wing turned around and fled back en masse to the stockade camp. On the left, the Athenians endured a fierce attack from their fellow-Greek opponents, but in the end, after a bitter resistance, these too gave way and ran straight to Thebes. The troops outside Plataea, which had originally been the Greek center, did not enter the battle before its closing stage.

The cautious Artabanus, who had escorted Xerxes to the Hellespont and returned to Mardonius, had held his forty-thousand-strong force in reserve on the Asopus ridge, from where he could watch the entire field of operations. Once he saw that all was lost, he faced about and marched without stopping until he reached Asia. He outstripped the news of his defeat and nobody attacked him on his journey home.

The Greeks captured the camp inside which tens of thousands of men were trapped in a confined space and spent hours methodically killing them all. They took no prisoners and by the end of the day, it was claimed, nine tenths of the enemy lay dead. Hellenic losses amounted to a modest 1,360 together with an unreported number of wounded.

Pausanias ordered his *helots* to collect everything of value they could find inside the stockade and on the field. According to Herodotus, they

> spread out through the whole camp. Treasure was there in profusion—tents adorned with gold and silver; couches gilded with the same precious metals; bowls, goblets, and cups, all of gold; and waggons loaded with sacks full of gold and silver basins. From the bodies of the dead they stripped anklets and chains and golden-hilted daggers, but they took no notice at all of the richly embroidered clothes which, amongst so much of greater value, seemed of no value.

Someone suggested that the body of Mardonius should be given the same treatment that had been meted out to Leonidas—namely, that his head should be cut off and impaled on a pole. Pausanias replied angrily: "That is an act more appropriate to barbarians than to Hellenes. Don't ever make a suggestion like that again and be thankful that you are leaving without being punished."

The Spartan general visited an elaborate, richly furnished tent that Xerxes had left behind for Mardonius, perhaps as a token of his intended return. He ordered the Persian chefs to cook a meal and was astonished by the lavish banquet they produced. He contrasted it with the simple fare his staff prepared for him. "What a fool Mardonius was," he reportedly remarked. "This was his lifestyle and he came to deprive *us* of our poverty-stricken way of life!"

King Leotychidas of Sparta had been sitting tight on the island of Delos with his 110 ships. He was joined at last by the rest of the fleet—namely, the two-hundred-odd Athenian triremes, under the command of the Alcmaeonid Xanthippus. These had been held back until Sparta and her allies had done the decent thing and marched out of the Peloponnese bound for Boeotia and victory at Plataea.

Some envoys from the Greek island of Samos came secretly to see the king and persuade him "to deliver the Ionians from slavery and expel the barbarian." After some thought, he agreed and set sail for Asia Minor.

The Persian fleet was much smaller than at Salamis. Morale among the crews, which included a large number of doubtfully loyal Ionians, was very low. The survivors of the Phoenician contingent were so dispirited that they had been sent home. When the Persian commanders at the island of Samos learned the Hellenes were on the move, they decided they were no match for them and withdrew to the shelter of the nearby Mycale headland. There they joined forces with an infantry division that Xerxes had ordered to watch over Ionia during the army's absence in Greece. They beached their ships and erected around them a stockade of rocks and timber.

The Greeks sailed close inshore to the Persian encampment and had a herald shout to the Ionians to "remember freedom first and foremost" and mutiny. They then disembarked not far off. Marines from Athens and other *poleis* marched along the beach towards the stockade. Meanwhile, out of sight of the enemy, the Spartans led about half their men up a gully into the hills and along a ridge to come down on the Persians from inland. The idea was not simply to stage a surprise attack, but, by giving the impression that the Greeks were fewer than they actually were, to tempt the Persians into taking the offensive.

The Persian commander nervously confiscated the Samians' weapons and sent an equally untrustworthy contingent from Miletus to guard the passes that led from the Persian position out of the mountainous promontory. But he could not dismiss all his Ionians.

Just about now a rumor spread through the Greek fleet that Mardonius had been defeated in a great battle. This may have been a pious fiction invented by Leotychidas or possibly genuine news of the defeat of Masistius some days earlier. But it is equally plausible that the information could have been conveyed by a chain of beacons across the

Aegean, for it appears that the battle of Plataea and this engagement at Mycale took place on the same day.

The Persians ate the bait and came out from their camp to fight, expecting a quick and easy victory. They planted a wicker shield-wall, as at Plataea, and shot arrows at the oncoming attackers. There was hard fighting with heavy casualties, but as the Athenians and others began to gain the upper hand, the unarmed Samians and other Ionians switched sides. By the time the Spartans turned up at the top of the ridge, there was little for them to do but mop up.

The victory was total. The camp was stormed and all the warships burned. For now, the Great King no longer had a fleet; when he heard what had happened he went into a state of shock. Elite Persian troops had more or less been wiped out and the Ionians went back to their cities with no intention of being conscripted again.

Leotychidas sailed north to the Hellespont to destroy Xerxes' bridges, in case they had been rebuilt. Even if they had not, he could usefully confiscate the bridging material and capture the massive papyrus and flax cables.

The defeat of Xerxes was now complete. This was Greece's finest hour. For all their squabbling and moral squalor, the allies had stuck together. Over time an idea grew of a historic fight for liberty, waged by a few, the happy few, against the barbarian many. It became a myth that shone ever more brightly with the passage of time. But it was closer than most myths are to the reality of what actually took place. The Persian Empire *was* an expansionist despotism (if a relatively civilized one) and the Greeks *did* seek to realize a certain idea of freedom. For Athens victory was proof that its democracy worked.

The Greeks had shown that a hoplite army, even one without cavalry, was more than a match for the best that the Achaemenids could throw at them. This was not a lesson quickly forgotten. The brilliant opportunism of Themistocles and his decision to make Athens into a sea power transformed the geopolitics of the region. The Greeks now ruled the waves. While the failure of Darius's raid in 490 could properly be discounted as no more than an offense to the Great King's *bella figura,* Xerxes had lost the Aegean Sea and most of its islands and could anticipate a new and more successful Ionian revolt along the seaboard of Asia Minor.

At last the Athenians could thank their hosts at Troezen and Salamis and, after long months as hard-up refugees, go home. Thucydides wrote:

> The Athenian people, after the departure of the barbarian from their country, at once proceeded to bring over their children and wives, and such possessions as they had saved, from the places where they had deposited them. They prepared to rebuild their city and their walls. Only isolated portions of the circumference had been left standing, and most of the houses were in ruins, though a few remained, in which the Persian grandees had lodged.

In fact, the Spartans feared that Athens would get above itself and they had relished any opportunity to interfere militarily in its domestic affairs. Their own city was famous for being without walls and they asked the Athenian *ecclesia* not to build any themselves, and to join them in knocking down the fortifications of other city-states. Their stated motive was to make sure that if the Persians invaded for a third time there would be no strong places that they could capture and use as bases.

A likely tale, thought Themistocles; they simply wanted to keep the Athenians weak. Before he could be stopped, he put to work the entire male population on urgent wall construction and on improving the defenses of Piraeus. The perimeter of the city was enlarged, to accommodate a growing population. Gravestones, column drums from an unbuilt temple, and other miscellaneous material were cannibalized. Only when the work reached the lowest defensible height, at least so far as Athens itself was concerned, did he inform the Spartans what had been done. Privately, they were annoyed, but said nothing.

Twenty years later, very much in the spirit of Themistocles, who (in Plutarch's metaphor) "attached the city to the Piraeus and made the land dependant on the sea," two massive new walls were constructed to lead from Athens to the new port five miles away, and to the bay at Phaleron and so literally link the city to the sea. Later a third wall, parallel to the first, was added, creating a corridor two hundred yards wide. So long as its mercantile profits and the silver of Laurium allowed it to maintain its fleet, the *polis* would in effect become an unconquerable island. It would no longer have to worry about land powers, such as Sparta or Argos or disgraced Thebes. The Long Walls, as they came to be called, were very probably the wily statesman's original idea—even if a generation had to pass before it was realized.

There was one exception to the general renewal of the sacked city. When the allies swore their oath before the battle of Plataea every Athenian was reported to have vowed: "I will not rebuild a single one of the temples which the barbarians have burned and razed to the ground, but will let them remain for future generations as a memorial of their impiety."

So the Acropolis stayed a charred ruin. "Lest we forget" was the visible message that loomed above the city. There was little chance of that, as the Great King was to find out.

The Athenians had not finished with him yet.

THE EMPIRE
BUILDERS

———

13

League of Nations

Nobody underplayed the resonance of victory. It echoed and re-echoed. Monuments, shrines, odes, and elegies proliferated.

Simonides of Ceos specialized in public poetry and was so much in demand that, despite his murky track record as celebrator of the Pisistratid tyranny at Athens, he became the unofficial poet laureate of the Persian Wars. He (probably) wrote that most celebrated of epitaphs in honor of the Spartan king and the famous Three Hundred. Leonidas and his comrades were buried in 480 where they fell on the mound behind the ancient wall at Thermopylae. A stone lion commemorated the king. The poem's terseness can, paradoxically, move the reader, even today.

> *Go tell the Spartans, passer by,*
> *That here obedient to their laws we lie.*

A Thermopylae memorial was erected in Sparta, which listed the names of all the Spartiate dead (of course, no acknowledgment was made of the bravery of the conscripted *helots,* an unwise decision as would appear later). Statues of Leonidas and Pausanias stood nearby (modern archaeologists have uncovered the head and torso of a Greek warrior, almost certainly the Spartan king).

The twin demigods, Castor and Pollux, were brothers of Helen of Troy, beautiful wife of Sparta's king, Menelaus. Statues of them traditionally accompanied armies on campaign, as the poet implied in an elegy on the battle of Plataea. The men of Sparta, he wrote,

> *Did not forget their courage . . .*
> *And their glory among men will be immortal.*
> *Leaving the river Eurotas and the town of Sparta,*
> *They hastened, accompanied by the horse-taming sons of Zeus,*
> *The heroes Castor and Pollux and mighty Menelaus . . .*
> *Led by the noble son of king Cleombrotus . . .*
> *Pausanias.*

For Salamis, Apollo was given a statue of himself holding in his hand the stern ornament of a trireme. Sanctuaries at Salamis, Sunium on the southernmost tip of Attica, and the Isthmus were each allocated a captured warship. Pausanias donated bronzes of Zeus, king of the gods, and his brother, the sea-god Poseidon.

His most munificent, if boastful, gift was the Serpent Column at Delphi. Three intertwined snakes, worked in bronze, stood about twenty feet high, with a golden tripod on top. The names of thirty-one Greek states that had fought the Persians were inscribed on the coils. Originally, an inscription on the tripod read: "Pausanias, commander-in-chief of the Hellenes, dedicated this monument to Apollo, when he destroyed the army of the Medes." Who did the destroying? The commander or the god? The grammatical ambiguity was intentional. The Spartan authorities had the inscription erased.

Simonides did not leave out the fallen Athenians:

> *If the greatest part of virtue is to die nobly*
> *Then Fortune granted this to us above all others,*

For after striving to crown Greece with liberty
We lie here enjoying praise that will never grow old.

Nobody was surprised that Themistocles blew his own trumpet, but what was odd was the resentment and annoyance it caused. As the man of the hour, who had engineered the defeat of the Persian fleet at Salamis, he was invited by the Spartans to take part in their victory celebrations. While Eurybiades, the local boy, won the prize for valor, they awarded Themistocles one for wisdom; in each case this consisted of nothing more elaborate than a wreath of olive leaves. More substantially, though, he was given the finest chariot in town and, when he left for home, three hundred young men escorted him to the Spartan frontier. These were exceptional honors for a foreigner.

Such accolades irritated the Athenians, who felt that Salamis had benefited people in the Peloponnese far more than it had themselves. Themistocles made matters worse by building a small temple and altar to the west of the Acropolis, not far from his house in a popular residential district. Inside he placed a statue of himself. Unblushingly, he dedicated the shrine to Artemis of the Best Advice. Public opinion took against this swanking.

The popularity of Themistocles among the Spartans soon evaporated too. He opposed their argument that all states which had medized should be excluded from the Greek alliance, for he realized that that would give them and their allies in the Peloponnese an automatic voting majority in their councils. He also appears to have extorted money from a number of islands in the Aegean.

A poet of Rhodes wrote some scathing verses about the Athenian leader's partiality for money. Called Timocreon, he had been banished for medizing. His chances of returning home were scuppered when, he alleged, Themistocles, then sailing with the fleet, took a hefty bribe to veto his return from exile. What made this betrayal particularly scandalous was the fact the two men were guest-friends. He prayed for redress to Leto, mother of the gods Apollo and Artemis and the protectress of oaths. She

> *can't stand Themistocles,*
> *Liar, cheat, and traitor, who, though Timocreon was his host,*
> *With shitty lucre was persuaded not to bring him back*
> *To Ialysus [in Rhodes], his native land,*
> *But grabbed three silver talents and went cruising off.*

Themistocles felt for himself the ingratitude of the *demos,* just as his father had foreseen. He learned what it was like to be a redundant trireme. Except once in 478, he was never again elected *strategos;* his naval policy was still followed, but new politicians were coming forward and Themistocles was yesterday's man.

Eventually he fell victim to the political device he had made good use of himself. In 472 or 471 he was ostracized and exiled from Athens for a period of ten years. Potsherds reveal various scratched opinions of the great man; one citizen condemned him, counterintuitively, "because of his esteem" or high reputation. Another simply added "Asshole" (the Greek word implies a shameful liking for being buggered) after his name, and a third that he was a "pollution to the land."

The other hero of the war, Pausanias, the victor of Plataea, also got into trouble. Like other fellow-countrymen he kicked over the traces when he was abroad and temporarily liberated from the iron constraints of Spartan society.

He was appointed admiral of an allied squadron with Aristides in command of the Athenian contingent. His general brief was to liberate Greek islanders and the Ionians of the Asian coastline from Persian control and, after Mycale, to do everything possible to keep the Great King on the run. He made good progress, expelling a Persian garrison from the city-state of Byzantium, which was strategically placed on the shores of the Bosphorus, the narrow passage of water leading to the Black Sea. Whoever controlled Byzantium, controlled the grain trade. He also campaigned successfully in Cyprus and freed most of this large island from Persian rule, for the time being at least.

Unfortunately, Pausanias, young, energetic, and delighted with himself, started misbehaving. He accidentally killed a Byzantine woman he had taken for sexual purposes. He acted insolently and oppressively. When Aristides questioned his conduct, he scowled, said he was busy, and refused to listen. He took to wearing Persian dress and eating Persian food, sinister signs of ideological unreliability from a Greek point of view. People suspected Pausanias, correctly as it turned out, of making overtures to the enemy. He was alleged to have secretly returned some of Xerxes' friends and relatives, whom he had taken prisoner at Byzantium. He sent the Great King a private letter promising to "make Sparta and the rest of Hellas subject to you," if Persia would help him. The king wrote back enthusiastically, promising unlimited financial support.

A widespread feeling grew among the Ionian Greeks that they would be better off if they were led by Athens rather than Sparta. It was after all the former who had made the all-important commitment to sea power. It was its triremes that were the mainstay of the fleet. As we have seen, the city was widely reported to be the originator of the Ionian "race." The Ionian Greeks looked up to Athens, and Pausanias's poor performance was their cue to seek a transfer of command.

It was also thought that Pausanias was tampering with the *helots,* promising them freedom if they helped him become sole monarch of Sparta. The fact that their contribution to the war effort had not been recognized would have loosened any loyalty they may have felt to their masters. If there was one thing that frightened the authorities, it was the prospect of the enslaved peoples of Messenia rising once more in revolt.

Hearing these reports of their admiral's misconduct the *ephors* recalled him, but they had insufficient proof to charge him with any offense. Pausanias slipped away on a trireme to the Bosphorus and took command at Byzantium, where he still had some support. The Athenians angrily ejected him, and in 470 the *ephors* again summoned home their errant regent. But they still had too little hard evidence to convict him—until one of his former lovers came forward. This man showed them an incriminating letter that he had been instructed to deliver to the Great King. He had noticed that all Pausanias's previous messengers to Xerxes had failed ever to reappear. He undid the latest letter and found the postscript he had expected—an order to put the carrier to death.

Even now the *ephors* hesitated. No contemporary tells us this, but we may surmise that Pausanias was popular either with the *helots* or with the Spartiate hoplites with whom he had fought at Plataea—or with both. The Spartan establishment did not want to risk a popular rising.

So a sting was devised. The messenger went as a suppliant to Taenarum (now Cape Matapan), a promontory on Sparta's southern coast sixty miles or so from the capital. Here a celebrated temple of Poseidon was built inside a cave that was said to lead to the underworld. An oracle enabled petitioners to summon and consult the dead. Taenarum was the chief sacred place for *helots* and *perioeci,* where they could seek sanctuary. It was a well-chosen refuge for someone in trouble with the authorities.

Pausanias's onetime boyfriend took up residence there in a hut. The regent, doubtless a little alarmed when he heard about this, traveled down from Sparta, entered the hut, which had a partition behind which some *ephors* were hiding, and asked the man what he thought he was doing. In the conversation that followed Pausanias admitted his guilt. He guaranteed the messenger his safety and sent him on his way.

Back in Sparta the *ephors* now had all the evidence they could require and moved to arrest Pausanias in the street. But when he saw them approaching he guessed from the expression on an *ephor's* face what his mission was and another gave him a secret warning sign. He ran to a nearby temple of Athena, goddess of the Brazen House, and sought sanctuary there.

The authorities walled him up and starved him to death. Just before he drew his last breath they pulled him out, hoping to avoid polluting a sacred space with mortality. They were disappointed, for Apollo at

Delphi ruled otherwise and laid the Spartans under a curse. Having stolen one body from the goddess's protection they were told to expiate the sin by giving her a couple in return—in the shape of costly bronze statues.

Themistocles became entangled in the downfall of Pausanias. Compromising documents were found among the regent's possessions, which the *ephors* handed over to the Athenians. The *ecclesia* summoned their savior to stand trial for treason and issued a warrant for his arrest. At the time he was based at Argos, where he seems to have been making trouble for the Spartans, traveling around the peninsula and very probably fomenting discontent.

Well-informed as ever, Themistocles learned in advance what was afoot and fled to Corcyra. Still not feeling safe, he traveled north to the backward kingdom of the Molossians, where life had not changed much since the days of Agamemnon and where, as in Homer, guests were sacrosanct. Here he was given asylum, despite the fact that in the past he had angered the ruler, Admetus, by not doing him some favor he had requested. His wife and children joined him from Athens, although the man who arranged their escape was executed for his pains.

Themistocles had to move on, though, for the long arm of Athens would eventually and inevitably reach him wherever he was in the Balkans. The only realistic solution was to head for the Persian Empire, but what kind of reception could the Great King's nemesis expect to receive? He made his way east cross-country to the Macedonian port of Pydna north of Mount Olympus, where he took ship for Asia. Narrowly escaping an Athenian squadron off Naxos, he arrived at Ephesus. He arranged for cash to be sent to him from friends in Athens and from "secret hoards" at Argos. Money stuck to him like glue and he never appears to have been seriously embarrassed for funds.

Themistocles wrote a letter to the Great King at Susa. This was now Artaxerxes I, third son of Xerxes, for in August 465 his father had been assassinated in exotic and obscure circumstances. Apparently, the com-

204 / THE RISE OF ATHENS

mander of the royal bodyguard had hanged the crown prince on Xerxes' orders. Having killed the son, he then feared that he would get the
blame and so killed the father.

According to Thucydides, Themistocles was unabashed. Referring
to the supposedly helpful messages he had sent Xerxes just before and
after Salamis, he claimed: "For the past you owe me a good turn. For
the present, [I am] able to do you great service. It's because of my
friendship for you that I am here, pursued by the Hellenes."

Artaxerxes bit on the bait and welcomed the Athenian statesman to
his court. His defection was a public relations coup and his background
briefings on Greek affairs will have been useful, although he had been
out of government too long to have any "live" secrets to tell. He was
made governor of the wealthy city of Magnesia on the Ionian coast not
far from Ephesus, where he died in 459. A surprising fate. Who could
have predicted that the architect of Salamis would have ended up as a
Persian high official?

Taken at face value, the stories of how the two undoubted heroes of
the Persian Wars, Pausanias and Themistocles, met their ends are bizarre. These perfectly rational politicians appear to have lost their
senses, made grave errors, and followed suicidal or at least eccentric
courses of action. But one grand idea, unspoken admittedly, united
them and could provide a solution of the mystery.

If there was a lesson to be learned from the Persian Wars it was that
Greece had been extremely lucky. The multiplicity of tiny states, prone
to ceaseless wrangling, prevented the Hellenes from pursuing a common goal. It was only at the last minute that a precarious unity had been
achieved at Salamis. It would hardly be surprising if intelligent men
began to wonder how Greece could be integrated into a single powerful
state. This might be most readily achieved by encouraging one or other
of the leading powers, Athens and Sparta, to establish a hegemony.

Pausanias felt that constitutional reform at home was essential if
Sparta was to play an effective international role; and Themistocles

foresaw the creation of an Athenian empire among the islands of the Aegean and on the Asian coastline. They both understood the difficulties that lay ahead and realized that Persian military and financial support could offer them a handy shortcut to attain their ends. But to their cost they underestimated the opposition they would arouse from reactionaries at home. They cast the dice and lost.

The Spartan was by far the lesser figure of the two. His contemporaries recognized that Themistocles was the greatest man of the age. He was no traitor, although he would take money from anyone and do business with anyone. The historian Thucydides was a cool judge of men, but he believed that the Athenian statesman transcended his flaws, large and brightly colored as they were. He was

> a man who showed the most unmistakable signs of genius; indeed, in this respect he was quite exceptional and has an unparalleled claim on our admiration. . . . Whether we consider the extent of his natural powers, or his speed of action, this extraordinary man outdid everyone else in his ability intuitively to meet an emergency.

But to the Athenians he *was* a traitor and as such, according to law, could not be buried in the national territory. In Magnesia, though, he remained popular even after his death and a magnificent memorial was built in his honor in the main square. As late as the first century A.D. his direct descendants were still receiving a pension from public funds. It was reported that his family removed his bones to Athens and buried them secretly.

At some stage a monument to him, known as the Tomb of Themistocles, was erected on a headland near the Grand Harbor at Piraeus. It looked rather like an altar and stood on a stone plinth. With touching aptness for the father of the Athenian navy, sailors would set a course by the tomb when it appeared on the horizon. The comic poet Plato wrote towards the end of the fifth century, addressing him directly:

there you look down
Upon the outward and the inward bound,
And galleys crowding sail as they race for home.

The war with Persia did not end at Plataea and Mycale. Greeks at the time celebrated their victory, but they did not feel safe. The Hellenic heartland had been saved, but for how long? The invasion had cost the Great King a mass of treasure, but his empire was rich and he could well afford to build another fleet and equip another army, if he so chose.

What was more, the whole story had begun fifteen years previously in Darius's day with the revolt of the Ionian cities of Asia Minor—but they were still in chains and still waiting for them to be struck off. Would they ever be free? Finally, the Greeks were *not* rich, and now that they had the upper hand they looked for opportunities to make up the cost of the war by pillaging the Great King's lands.

So the idea of a maritime league dedicated to continuing the fighting at sea and (now that the infuriating Pausanias was safely out of the way) led by the leading Ionian power, Athens, received universal support. States around the Aegean pressed it to accept the challenge, but in truth it needed little persuasion. What other use did it have for its two hundred triremes?

Even Sparta, dislodged from its leadership role, was content to allow matters to take their course. It recognized that Persia needed to be treated firmly and welcomed the emergence of a standing allied fleet, even if it were to play little part in its operations. The Athenians had acted bravely and, for a Greek *polis,* more or less disinterestedly. They might as well take charge, even if some nationalists back in the Peloponnese were anxious about the long-term consequences.

Founded in 478, the league's administrative headquarters and treasury were established on the holy island of Delos in the Cyclades—hence the name by which this association of Greek states is known, the Delian League. It was an appropriate choice for here was the birthplace of Apollo, divine patron of the Ionians, for whom it was a cult center. Delegates met in the god's temple there, and each of them, whatever the size and wealth of the state he represented, had a single vote. Member states were autonomous and Athens guaranteed their independence. We do not know how many joined the league in the first instance, but in its heyday later in the century they may have numbered as many as two hundred.

The league was a full offensive and defensive alliance. Some members provided ships for the fleet, and others—especially those miniature island states that could not afford to fit out even a single trireme—made a financial contribution to Athens. To begin with it was agreed that members who paid in cash rather than kind should in total cover the costs of one hundred triremes, estimated at 460 talents annually. As the years rolled by more and more league members found that their citizens disliked military service and absence abroad. They preferred, writes Plutarch, "to stay at home and become farmers and peace-loving merchants instead of fighters, and all through their short-sighted love of comfort." They switched from providing ships to handing over money. This was greatly in the interest of Athens, for the triremes that membership income financed came under its direct control and were, in effect, an addition to its fleet. In time only three members, the rich and large islands of Lesbos, Chios, and Samos, insisted on contributing their own small but effective navies.

Aristides, the Athenian statesman and old rival of Themistocles, was detailed to determine the assessments member by member. He fixed them according to their assets and their ability to pay. He seems to have done the job fairly as his nickname, "The Just," testifies. He was not a rich man when he went into the process nor, tellingly, when he came out of it. Aristides once told an unregenerate Themistocles that "the quality which makes a real general is the power to keep his hands clean." No doubt irritated that he had not been given the assessment commission himself, he in turn sneered that Aristides' reputation "suited a money-box rather than a human being."

Athens led expeditions and appointed its own treasurers to record and manage the league's income. Probably the council met to agree on a plan of campaign for the year ahead, but after a time these sessions were discontinued and Athens took all the key military decisions itself.

Another method of control, indirect but powerful, lay in the administration of justice. Each *polis,* however tiny, had its own judicial system, with different kinds of court, definitions of offenses, and punishments. What was to be done when citizens of one jurisdiction were sued or tried in another? Normally states entered into bilateral agreements. As leaders of the alliance the Athenians insisted that commercial lawsuits involving their citizens should be tried in their own courts. It seems that juries acted fairly and there were few complaints, but the arrangement only added to a shift of power from the periphery to the center.

A critic of the democracy, fierce but clear-eyed, wrote that "the Athenian people are thought to act ill-advisedly in this matter, namely, in forcing the allies to sail to Athens for litigation." But in fact there were advantages to the arrangement. It kept the law courts busy, filled boardinghouses, increased income from harbor dues, and guaranteed juror fees. He continued: "Sitting at home without sailing out on ships, they control the allied cities."

We have already seen that a remarkable feature of the Athenian democracy was the indestructibility of the upper crust. In other Greek states the arrival of popular rule usually meant the extinction or at least the expulsion of the old families. In Athens the inventor of democracy, Cleisthenes, was an Alcmaeonid and that rich and ambitious clan, nicknamed "accursed" because of its role in the Cylon affair 250 years previously, still flourished. Another clan, the Philaids, were wealthy conservative landowners, and the celebrated Miltiades, victor at Marathon, had been of their number. Now his son Cimon, the new chief of the Philaids, took center stage in the politics of Athens. It was telling that he married an Alcmaeonid, granddaughter of the Megacles who was suspected of Medism after the battle of Marathon and was exiled in 486. The "best people" (literally, "the beautiful and the good") knew that it was in their interest to stick together.

During the 470s the Athenians continued on their upwards imperial path, but the dramatis personae changed. Themistocles was no longer employed and, as we have seen, by the end of the decade he was ostracized. Xanthippus's final command was in 479 and that of Aristides in the following year. It seems they merely grew old. The dates of their deaths are unknown, although Aristides lived to see the expulsion of his great competitor.

New personalities emerged, and Cimon was the dominant figure. Born in 510 to a Thracian mother, he had a miserable inheritance. Being only half a Hellene, he was looked down on as a second-class citizen. His father had been fined by an Athenian court the enormous sum of fifty talents (for the details see pages 132 and 133) and immediately died. His son, then scarcely more than a boy, paid the fine and must have been nearly bankrupted. For a time, he and his sister, Elpinice, lay low. There was not enough money to marry her off with a good dowry, and the siblings lived together in the family home.

The young Cimon sowed wild oats. According to Plutarch,

He earned himself a bad name for delinquency and heavy drinking. He was said to take after his grandfather Cimon, who, they say, was so stupid that he was nicknamed Moron. Stesimbrotus of Thasos, who was a contemporary of Cimon, says that he did not receive an advanced education, and had none of the other liberal and typically Greek accomplishments. He did not show a trace of Athenian cleverness and fluency of speech.

However, he adds that his public manner was dignified and straightforward. In fact, the essence of the man was more Peloponnesian than Athenian. As Euripides wrote of Heracles, he was

Plain and unadorned,
In a great crisis brave and true.

Cimon was highly sexed. He was rumored to have committed incest with Elpinice, but this may mean no more than that they gave the appearance of being a couple because they lived together in the same house. In any event he married his sister off to one of Athens's richest men, Callias, who provided slaves to work the state-owned silver mines at Laurium.

Cimon recouped the family fortune, perhaps from his family's interests in the Chersonese, although it was said that Callias had agreed to restore his wealth in return for Elpinice. Cimon won high praise for bravery at the battle of Salamis. He also spent some of his fortune on public works: he transformed a parched grove of olive trees outside the city walls, called the Academy, into a well-watered gymnasium, equipped with running tracks and shady walks.

On the north side of the *agora* he erected a handsome colonnade as a civic amenity and named it after his brother-in-law. Its long back wall was decorated with paintings by the finest artists of the day. These depicted Athenian military exploits from the days of the Trojan War to the present. The Painted Stoa, as the colonnade came to be known, was rather like a modern war museum and, as well as history paintings, mementos of victories, such as captured bronze shields, were on display. It became a popular rendezvous and we hear of jugglers, sword-swallowers, beggars, and fishmongers gathering there.

Over time Cimon became very popular, perhaps because of the ordinariness of his tastes. His record as a playboy amusingly contradicted his admiration for the austere Spartan way of life. Even a satirist such as Eupolis was affectionately scurrilous:

He was not such a scoundrel as they go,
Only too lazy and fond of drinking,
And often he would spend the night in Sparta
And leave Elpinice to sleep alone.

• • •

As time passed, war-weariness set in. Allied states started to grumble at the high standards of efficiency expected of them and some sought to leave the alliance—or, as the Athenians saw it, revolted. Thucydides reports that the chief reasons for these defections were failures to produce the right amount of tribute or the right number of ships, and sometimes a refusal to produce any ships at all. The Athenians insisted on obligations being exactly met and made themselves detested by bringing the severest pressure to bear on men who were not used to continuous labor, and not disposed to undertake it.

Once the rebels had been brought to heel they realized to their dismay that they had lost all freedom of action and in future had to do as they were told. From these small beginnings an alliance of independent states gradually grew into an empire.

The first ally to announce unilaterally its secession was the powerful island of Naxos. The Athenians made it clear that a *polis* was free to join the league, but not to leave it. They besieged the island and forced it back into allegiance. In effect, Naxos became a subject state. Thucydides noted dourly:

> This was the first time that the League was forced to enslave [i.e., remove the independence of] an allied *polis*. The precedent was followed in later cases as circumstances dictated.

Secession was also a reaction against an Athenian policy of sending out small detachments of settlers (the Greek word was *cleruchy*) to different parts of the Eastern Mediterranean. These were different from ordinary colonies in that the settlers remained Athenian citizens and were not altogether independent of the home country. They acted as military garrisons and often competed economically with local city-states.

(*Cleruchies* did not invariably thrive. A substantial force of Athenian citizens was sent to Amphipolis in Thrace at about this time; on moving inland they were attacked by local people and wiped out.)

Athenian arrogance caused bad blood. In about 465, when the Athenians sought to place a settlement in Thrace, the prosperous island *polis* of Thasos, which had commercial and precious metal mining interests in the region, was furious and revolted. It had a sizable fleet and felt it was well able to defend itself. But after a three-year siege the island surrendered to Athens. Its city walls were demolished, its fleet was confiscated and so were its mines. In place of supplying the ships it now no longer had, the Thasians were compelled to pay the annual league membership fee. Their fate was the most egregious example of Athens acting selfishly under the veil of league policy.

Although they had abdicated the command of the seas, the Spartans were finding the growth of Athenian power hard to take. They tried to conceal their bitterness, but in 464 secretly—and slyly—agreed to help Thasos by staging an invasion of Attica to divert the Athenians' attention. However, earthquakes in the Peloponnese distracted them (for more on this see the following chapter).

Even states that declined to join the league could be dragooned into membership: this was what happened in 472 to Carystus, a small *polis* in southern Euboea. It was only a few miles across the water from the coast of Attica and its refusal was seen as an all-too-visible insult.

The league did not spend all its time pursuing defaulting members; it also did its proper job and harried the Persians until, if we are to believe Plutarch, the Chersonese fell to the allies and there was "not a single Persian soldier along the southern coast of Asia Minor from Ionia to Pamphylia." To enable him to operate amphibiously, Cimon, then in command of the navy, redesigned the traditional Athenian trireme, giving it a broader beam and creating more room to carry armed hoplites. At an unknown date sometime during the first half of the decade, the Persians gathered together a large army and a fleet of 340 warships at the mouth of the Eurymedon River (in today's southern Turkey) and in response Cimon sailed out to meet them.

With only 250 league triremes he routed the Persians, capturing two hundred of their ships and twenty thousand prisoners of war, and destroying others. The remnant fled to Cyprus where they abandoned their vessels and escaped inland. Evening was falling, but Cimon was not finished. He placed some Persian ships in his vanguard, dressed the crew in Persian uniforms, and sailed up the Eurymedon to where the enemy was encamped on the riverbank. The trick worked. The Greeks landed without opposition and their hoplites fell on the unsuspecting Persians. There was no moon and the night was dark. Many did not know who was attacking them and, in fact, were unaware that the league fleet was carrying infantry. The slaughter was immense.

This stunning double victory in or about 466 removed any lingering threat to Hellas and its liberties. As usual, Simonides was invited to praise the fallen with a moving verse:

These men lost the splendour of their youth at the Eurymedon.
Spearmen, they fought the vanguard of Persian archers,
Not only on foot but on their swift ships.
Dying, they left the most beautiful memory of their valour.

Nevertheless, more as symbol than from any real need, the Athenians decided to fortify the Acropolis, and the spoils from the Eurymedon paid for the work. The torched temples, though, were left as they were, still untouched.

During these triumphant postwar decades, Theseus, the national hero of Athens, put in a reappearance. He had long been honored as a demigod and hoplites fighting at Marathon believed that they saw him in full armor, leading the charge against the barbarians.

Then came a new development. In 476, the authorities consulted the oracle at Delphi. The Pythia demanded that the bones of Theseus be found and reinterred in Athens. Their approximate location was known—the island of Scyros off Euboea in the Aegean. In the misty days of myth, the aging Theseus decided to settle there and its ruler, seeing him as a rival, had pushed him off a high cliff to his death. But where precisely the body had been buried was a mystery.

Cimon understood the importance of Theseus to the Athenian brand and, after a successful campaign in Thrace in the same year as the Pythia's ruling, restored his shrine at Athens. At this juncture, the league decided to invade Scyros and expel its inhabitants.

The reason was this. The island was largely barren and its inhabitants were inefficient farmers; so instead they made their living from piracy and disrupted peaceful trade. The high seas were not a safe place and maritime banditry was commonplace and almost respectable. To be a pirate was to be somebody in the world; whenever a ship arrived at port, the first question anyone would ask the captain was: "Are you pirates?" If he was, he would be confidently expected to acknowledge the fact. As Thucydides observed, there was "no sense of shame in the profession, rather a glorying in it."

The last straw came when pirates confiscated the goods of some merchants from Thessaly, who had dropped anchor at the port of Scyros, and threw them into prison. The merchants managed to escape and, furious at their treatment, complained to the Amphictyony of Delphi, an association of states in middle and northern Greece—in effect, a federation of neighbors.

Judgment was given in their favor and the authorities at Scyros, anxious to avoid retaliation, named the actual culprits and instructed them to return their plunder. Panic-stricken, the robbers wrote to Cimon and promised to betray the island and hand it over to him, presumably in return for a pardon.

This was too good an offer to resist. Cimon arrived with the allied fleet, captured Scyros without trouble, and removed the population (exchanging it with Athenians and so, in effect, annexing the place). Now that he was there, and mindful of Apollo's commandment, the admiral set about looking for the lost king. It was hard to know where to start until (or so the story goes) he saw an eagle pecking about on the top of a mound. He immediately dug there and unearthed a coffin containing the bones of an unusually tall warrior, a bronze spear and sword at his side.

Evidently Cimon had found his man and, with his sacred cargo on board his personal trireme, he set sail for Athens. His fellow-citizens were thrilled. There were massive celebrations, splendid processions, and sacrifices as if the once and future king were coming back into his own. A monument was built where his remains received the worship due to a hero or a demigod. Plutarch writes:

> And now he lies buried in the heart of the city . . . and his tomb is a sanctuary and place of refuge for runaway slaves and all poor men who stand in fear of men in power, since Theseus was their champion and helper throughout his life, and listened kindly to the pleas of the needy and downtrodden.

How much of this tale should we take at face value? We may suspect Cimon to have had Theseus in mind when planning his raid on the pirates. No doubt what he found was an ancient barrow of some kind or the fossilized remains of a prehistoric creature, easily interpreted as the outsize skeleton of a hero. He knew the value of public relations.

Theseus was a talisman for the *demos* and the new philosophy of government. His legend showed him to have been indomitable, imaginative, popular, ruthless, and quick-witted. These were the values of the contemporary Athenian. He was a metaphor in human form of the democracy. Through him the glorious and mythic past blessed the imperial present.

14

The Falling-Out

One might think that nothing could be done to unwalled Sparta, that haphazard collection of dusty villages, to make it even more unimpressive to look at than it already was. But then, probably in 465, that all changed.

The place was flattened by a series of tremendous earthquakes. The peaks of neighboring Mount Taygetus broke away. The entire city was demolished, except for five houses. Where there had been little to look at there was now nothing to look at. Some young men and boys were exercising together at the time under the colonnade of a gymnasium; just before the earthquake struck, the boys' attention was distracted by a hare and, still naked and covered in oil, they ran after it into the open. But the men were all killed when the gymnasium collapsed on them.

There was huge loss of life—twenty thousand deaths according to one source and, wrote Plutarch, "all the *ephebes* or military cadets." Full adult male Spartan citizens, the invincible Equals, were in short supply.

For the *helots*—the enslaved population of the southern Peloponnese—the catastrophe was a god-sent opportunity. They immediately rose in revolt. Some in the countryside nearby headed at once for the city, where the survivors were trying to rescue those caught under rubble and masonry or to retrieve their possessions. The twenty-four-year-old king Archidamus astutely anticipated trouble and had the trumpet blown to herald an imminent enemy attack. When the *helots* arrived they faced an armed force and withdrew.

However, rebellion spread and many *perioeci,* free men but without civic rights and under Spartan rule, joined it. The Spartans were unable to put out the flames themselves and asked their allies to assist. The appeal was extended to the Athenians in spite of the fact that it was only a short while since they had themselves been planning an invasion of Attica. It was lucky that the men of Thasos kept their mouths shut.

The comic playwright Aristophanes has one of his characters amusedly recall the day "when Pericleidas the Spartan came here once and sat at the altars petitioning the Athenians, with a white face and a scarlet cloak, begging for an army." There was lively debate in the *ecclesia,* some arguing that it would be good for Sparta to be taken down a peg or two. But Cimon, Plutarch writes, "put Sparta's interests before his own country's aggrandizement" and persuaded the assembly to send out an expeditionary force, under his command.

At this point things went mysteriously and very wrong.

The insurgents were gradually pushed back to their heartland and their final defensive position, Mount Ithome deep inside Messenia, where they built stockades and prepared to make a last stand. The Athenians had the reputation of being good at siege operations and this was the main reason for asking for their help. They arrived in force with four thousand hoplites, but before they could achieve anything the Spartans had a startling change of heart.

They abruptly sent the Athenians home, alone of all the foreign troops that had come to help them. They were perfectly polite and merely said that they no longer needed them. According to Thucydides they "grew afraid of the enterprise and the unorthodoxy of the Athe-

218 / THE RISE OF ATHENS

nians and . . . feared that, if they stayed on in the Peloponnese, they might listen to the people in Ithome and become the sponsors of some revolutionary changes."

There may have been some truth in this. The whole point of Athenian policy, and that of its maritime league, was to free Greeks and not to oppress them. The *helots* of Messenia were Greek. Why were Cimon's hoplites helping Sparta to re-enslave them? It is quite possible that they were in touch with the rebels, if only from shame. It is hard to see what else can explain the apparent stupidity of Sparta's action.

Predictably, the Athenians were deeply offended and, just as predictably, the consequences fell on the head of the statesman most associated with their pro-Spartan policy.

This was Cimon. He believed in the dual leadership of Greece, a partnership between equals, in which the Spartans dominated by land and Athens by sea. As we have seen, he greatly admired the plain Lacedaemonian way of life—and even named one of his sons Lacedaemonius. A natural oligarch (remember his family background), he was uneasy with the extreme democracy of his homeland. He was unpopular among populist politicians. On his victorious return from Thasos in 462, he was vindictively hauled before the law courts for bribery. He defended himself with vigor and candor:

> I am not, like other Athenians, the spokesman of wealthy Ionians or Thessalians, to be courted or paid for my services. Instead, I represent the Spartans, whose simplicity and moderation I love to imitate—and I do so for free.

Cimon was acquitted.

Now he was in more serious trouble. His dismissal at Mount Ithome discredited his Sparta-friendly policy and helped put an end to his political career. "On a slight pretext," according to Plutarch, the *demos* took its public revenge on Cimon. He was ostracized, and so compelled to leave Attica for ten years. An *ostracon* has come to light that raises an old slander: "Let Cimon take his sister Elpinice and get out." It was a typical irony of democratic politics that absence made the heart fonder. In exile, the lost leader was soon forgiven.

As for Sparta, it paid a price for its incivility. Athens abrogated its alliance that had been agreed during the Persian Wars and made pacts with its enemies. Although the Spartan army eventually put down the Messenian revolt, the fortress at Ithome never fell. The defenders marched out proudly under an armistice. The Athenians took them under their wing and mischievously resettled them at Naupactus, their naval base on the northern coast of the Corinthian Gulf; from this point of vantage the former serfs kept the Peloponnese under their watchful gaze.

The swell created by the Persian Wars was still rolling. It pushed the excited democrats at Athens to further logical extremes. A new leader was emerging who was determined that every citizen be enabled to be politically active, that the democracy should be made even more democratic. He was to become the greatest of the city's statesmen.

Typically, he was another aristocrat and, yet again, a member of the accursed clan. He was the son of Xanthippus, the Alcmaeonid by marriage who had been brought back from a period of ostracism to help fight the Persians, had displaced Themistocles as commander of the Athenian contingent of the allied Greek fleet, and fought at the crowning mercy of Mycale. The boy's mother, Agariste, was of equally high birth. She was the niece of Cleisthenes, who had introduced the city's (and the world's) first democratic constitution.

Pericles, for that was his name, was born about 495. He was good-looking, except that his head was rather long and out of proportion. It resembled the bulb of the squill, a perennial herb common in Europe and the Middle East, and satirists nicknamed him Squill-head.

With this malformation, he was lucky to have survived the first few days of life, for Greek parents took disabled (or indeed for any reason unwanted) children outside the city bounds and left them to die in some unfrequented open space. On the fifth day after his birth the newborn Pericles was welcomed to the household and placed under the protection of the household gods. In a special ritual called the *Amphidromia,* or the Running Around, his father had to run around the domestic hearth holding the child in his arms and consecrating him to the goddess of the hearth, Hestia.

Like other little Athenians, Pericles will have been brought to the Anthesteria, a Flower and Wine Festival, in the early spring of the fourth year of his life. There he was presented with a wreath to wear on his head, a small jug from which he drank his first sip of wine, and a toy cart. This ceremony was a rite of passage, leading him from the privacy of the family to the open community of citizens.

For it to operate efficiently, the democracy depended on a population that could read, and for this reason if no other the Athenians paid great attention to the education of children. From about the age of seven Pericles was probably tutored at home, although small schools catered for ten or fifteen pupils. The curriculum concentrated on reading and writing, athletics together with music and the arts. Students used waxed tablets on which they scratched letters and texts with a stylus. Pottery sherds also served the function of scrap paper. Literature was taught by rote and Pericles will have learned substantial chunks from the classics of Greek poetry, drama, and epic verse, especially by Homer. But at least Xanthippus did not force him to memorize the whole of the *Iliad* and the *Odyssey,* some 27,000 lines, as the father of one hapless youth insisted.

From the age of seven Athenian boys went to a sports ground or *palaestra* (literally, "wrestling school") where a professional trainer or *paidotribes* took charge of their physical health and introduced them to competitive athletics. There they ran and threw discuses and javelins, boxed and wrestled. The very best young men would enter for the Olympic Games and the other athletic festivals.

Little Pericles' upbringing was interrupted at the age of ten, when he and his family accompanied his ostracized father. He was soon back home in 481 after Xanthippus's truncated exile. At fourteen he was introduced into a *phratry,* or brotherhood, one of thirty such mutual societies or associations. Members met for religious ceremonies and gave each other assistance when in trouble.

At the age of eighteen Pericles was registered at his *deme,* or local council, which functioned as if it were a miniature *polis,* as a full citizen, son of an Athenian father and an Athenian mother. He entered the adult world with enthusiasm. As a teenager he was much influenced by his music and arts teacher, Damon, who also discreetly introduced him to the world of politics. He remained a close adviser of the adult Pericles and, Plutarch writes, "played the role of masseur and trainer for this political athlete."

Pericles was an intellectual and took a lively interest in philosophical questions. He studied under the Italian thinker Zeno of Elea, a Greek colony on the southern Italian coast. Zeno is credited with having invented the dialectic—that is, a method of inquiry based on question and answer. A cynical commentator remarked:

> *His was a tongue that could argue both sides of a question*
> *With an irresistible fury.*

He also devised a number of subtle and profound "paradoxes," in which logic contradicts the evidence of the senses. The most famous of these tells of Achilles, the great warrior, and a tortoise.

Achilles is racing the tortoise. He gives it a head start of one hundred yards. By the time he has run the one hundred yards, the tortoise has advanced (say) by one yard. It takes Achilles some more time to cover the additional yard, during which the tortoise has advanced a bit further still. So at each point that Achilles reaches, the tortoise has moved forward and, as there is an infinite number of points, he will never overtake the tortoise. (But in real life, of course, he does. The paradox, which has tested the finest philosophical minds for two millennia, reveals a mismatch between the way we think about the world and the way the world actually is.)

With teasers like this Pericles titillated his mind. But although he admired Zeno, he also became a close friend of Anaxagoras, a philosopher from Clazomenae, a *polis* in Asia Minor. He was credited with having introduced philosophy to Athens, where he settled in the mid- to late 460s. He was more interested in scientific inquiry than the pursuit of reason or metaphysical speculation. He believed that everything in nature was infinitely divisible and that mind was a substance that enters into the composition of living things and is the source both of all change and also of motion. He was the first to understand that moonlight is reflected from the sun.

Pericles enjoyed lengthy discussions with another of the age's great thinkers, Protagoras, born in Abdera, an important Greek *polis* on the coast of Thrace. His ideas were controversial and deeply offended right-thinking, right-wing Athenians. He was skeptical about the supernatural and was a moral relativist. "About the gods," he wrote, "I have no way of knowing whether they exist or not, nor what form they may have: the subject is very hard to understand and life is short." He also made the bold claim that "man is the measure of all things: of those which are, that they are, and of those which are not, that they are not." This left little room for the Olympians.

Sitting at the feet of men like Anaxagoras and Protagoras, Pericles learned to abandon magical explanations of natural events for rational ones. Once an eclipse of the sun took place when he was sailing in a ship. The helmsman panicked, as did everyone else on board, and did not know what to do. Once the eclipse had passed, Pericles held his cloak in front of the helmsman's eyes and asked: "Is this a terrible omen?"

"No, it is not," came the reply.

"Well then, what is the difference between this and the eclipse— except that the eclipse was caused by something larger than my cloak?"

HEROES OF HOMER

The *Iliad,* an epic poem composed toward the end of the eighth century B.C., was a bible that set out ideals of courage, honor, loyalty, and the competitive pursuit of excellence that generation after generation of Greeks sought to realize in their lives. The hero of the *Iliad,* Achilles, chose to be a warrior, win glory, and die young rather than lead a long, peaceful but ignoble life. Here he bandages the arm of his friend and lover, Patroclus, who has been wounded by an arrow. *Attic red-figure vase by the Sosias Painter, about 500 B.C., Altes Museum, Berlin.*

ATHENS IN ITS GLORY

A reconstruction of the Acropolis, the citadel of Athens, as it was at the beginning of the fourth century, after the completion of the Parthenon and the other great buildings of the age of Pericles.
A. Parthenon; B. Erechtheum; C. Propylaea or monumental gateway; D. Art Gallery; E. Temple of Athena Nike (Victory); F. Ramp; G. House of the Arrephoroi; H. Clepsydra fountain; I. Eleusinium, a shrine for the Eleusinian Mysteries; J. *Agora,* or marketplace; K. Areopagus, or the "Rock of Ares," a hill where the council of the Areopagus met; L. Theater of Dionysus; M. Unfinished Temple of Olympian Zeus. *Akg-images, Peter Connolly.*

HOUSE OF
THE VIRGIN

Athena was the goddess of
wisdom and war. She was the
patron of the city of Athens,
and the Parthenon temple was
dedicated to her. It is the
masterwork of Athenian
architecture. Battered and
mutilated after many centuries
of neglect and ill-treatment,
it retains its power to awe the
spectator.

Sculpture in ancient Greece was painted in bright colors, as
the Victorian artist, Lawrence Alma-Tadema demonstrates in
his *Pheidias Showing the Frieze of the Parthenon to His Friends.*
The spectators stand on scaffolding to view the reliefs and
include the young Alcibiades and Socrates (*left*) and Pericles
with his mistress Aspasia (*center right*). *Birmingham Museum and
Art Gallery.*

Inside the main hall, or *cella,* of the Parthenon,
stood a colossal gold and ivory statue of
Athena Parthenos (the Maiden) by Pheidias.
It disappeared in the fifth century A.D. and
was presumably destroyed at some point
thereafter. However, a re-creation in 1990 by
Alan LeQuire, inside a full-scale replica of the
Parthenon in Nashville's Centennial Park,
gives a sense of the overwhelming impact of
the original.

GREAT MEN

With its sensuous lips, quizzically intelligent look, and rough-and-ready appearance, this portrait of Themistocles evokes the qualities of the most successful statesman Athens ever produced. Always ready to accept a bribe, but not necessarily to fulfill his side of the bargain, he had the guile, the boldness, and the strategic forethought to win the struggle against Persian invaders in 480 and 479 B.C. *A Roman copy of a fifth-century Greek original, Museo Ostiense, Ostia, Italy.*

Nicknamed the "Olympian" for his mastery as an orator in the citizens' assembly, Pericles ruled Athens during its golden years between the Persian Wars and the Peloponnesian War—despite the fact that, at any moment, the people could dismiss him from office. His defensive military policy toward Sparta and its allies was a failure, and he died in 429 B.C. a disappointed man. *A Roman copy of a Greek original, Museo Pio Clementino, Vatican.*

Demosthenes was the most celebrated public speaker in the Greek world. He saw himself as following in the footsteps of Pericles. But a century had passed since the great days of Athens, and his ambitions exceeded his city's capacity. The rising power of the age was Macedon, but instead of allying Athens with the newcomer he did everything possible to thwart its king, Philip, and his son and successor, Alexander. In 338 B.C. Philip crushed the Greek city-states at the battle of Chaeronea, and Athens lost its independence. Demosthenes deserves a large share of the blame. *A Roman copy in marble of a bronze original, about 200 B.C., by Polyeuctus. Glyptotek, Copenhagen.*

Ostracism was a remarkable political device invented by the Athenian democracy in the sixth century B.C. The people voted on whether or not to banish a leading citizen for ten years. If convicted, he could come home after serving his sentence and resume his career. Ostracism removed unpopular politicians or those believed to threaten the constitution. Votes were cast by scratching a citizen's name on a broken piece of pottery and depositing it in a voting urn. More than 11,000 of these potsherds, or *ostraca,* have been found. Some of them bear the name of Megacles, son of Hippocrates, a controversial aristocrat, as in these examples. In 486 B.C. he was ostracized. However, he was not shaken by this setback, for in the same year he won the prestigious chariot race at the Pythian Games at Delphi. The *ostracon* on the left names Themistocles, son of Neocles. In 472 or 471 B.C. the savior of his country was voted out and ended his days as a pensioner of his old enemy, the Persian Great King. *Stoa of Attalus Museum, Athens.*

ARMS AND THE MAN

Only wealthy aristocrats could afford to run a horse, and it was the heavily armed infantryman, the hoplite, who fought for and represented the people. He was, in fact, the democratic citizen in arms. He bought his own equipment: helmet with a horsehair crest; bronze body armor; a spear and a sword; and a round shield made from bronze, wood, and leather. Here we see a fully equipped warrior pouring a libation to the gods before his departure for the wars (or perhaps commemorating his death). *An Attic red-figure oil jar from between 480 and 460 B.C., Museo Archeologico Regionale, Palermo.*

The Greeks were inordinately proud of their victories over the armies of the Persian Great King and liked to represent their defeated enemy as weak, decadent, and overdressed instead of proudly nude, as in this pottery drinking cup of about 480 B.C. *Triptolemus painter, National Archaeological Museum, Athens.*

Two great battles frame the rise and fall of Athens. After the famous victory at Marathon in 490 B.C. the Athenian dead were buried on the field and covered by a tumulus, which survives to this day. The triumphant Athenian general Miltiades dedicated the helmet, which he (almost certainly) wore on the day, to Zeus at Olympia. It is inscribed with his name. *Olympia Museum, Greece.*

The second battle, this time at Chaeronea in central Greece, brought the fiercely independent city-states of Hellas to a bloody close. In 338 B.C. Philip, king of Macedon, routed an allied Greek army. The statue of a lion was erected on the battlefield in honor of the Sacred Band, a body of male lovers from the Greek city of Thebes, which was almost wiped out during the fighting.

The endless wars between the Greek city-states severely depleted the adult male population. Here a tombstone, erected about 460 B.C. in the heyday of Athenian power, shows the city's tutelary goddess deep in thought in front of a stone slab. She is probably paying her respects at the grave marker of a fallen soldier.

Three ancient Athenians still have a living influence on today's world. Socrates, one of the towering originators of Western thought, said, when on trial for his life: "The unexamined life is not worth living." For him ethics lay at the heart of philosophical inquiry. He wrote nothing down, asking and answering questions of anyone who was willing to talk with him in the city's streets and the *agora*. He was a critic of the democracy. *A Roman copy of a lost Greek original, British Museum.*

Plato was the most famous of Socrates' many disciples. In a series of brilliantly written dialogues, he devoted his life to recording and promoting his master's philosophical method. Over time he developed his own ideas and it can be difficult to decide where the historical Socrates ends and Plato's independent thinking begins. It is hard to exaggerate Plato's influence. A leading twentieth-century thinker remarked: "The safest general characterization of the European philosophical tradition is that it consists of a series of footnotes to Plato." *A Roman copy after a Greek original, Glyptotek, Munich.*

In the fourth century B.C. Athens became a base for various philosophical think tanks. The young Aristotle studied at Plato's Academy before setting up his own school at the Lyceum. He and his team conducted scholarly research of all kinds, including ethics, metaphysics, and the natural sciences. His works on logic remained current and valid until the nineteenth century. Like many philosophers of his day, Aristotle intervened in political affairs and for some years was tutor to the teenaged Alexander the Great. *Roman copy of a lost bronze by Lysippus, Museo Nazionale Romano.*

THE DAILY ROUND

Pottery is our best source of what it was like to be an ordinary ancient Athenian. Skilled craftsmen painted vases, bottles, bowls, and plates with the scenes of everyday life. Thousands have survived and even a random selection gives the flavor of a vanished world.

Every self-respecting youth would spend much of his time at the open-air gymnasium developing his physical skills. In a typical scene, a boy gets ready to throw a discus. Nearby a pick will be used to prepare the landing ground for the long jump. A pair of dumbbells, hanging from a hook, will help the athlete keep his balance during the jump. The legend reads: "Kleomelos is beautiful." *Attic red-figure drinking cup by the Kleomelos Painter, between 510 and 500 B.C., Louvre Museum.*

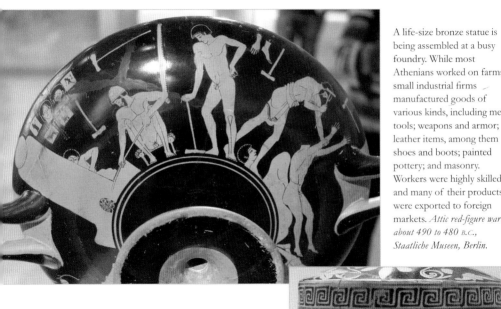

A life-size bronze statue is being assembled at a busy foundry. While most Athenians worked on farms, small industrial firms manufactured goods of various kinds, including metal tools; weapons and armor; leather items, among them shoes and boots; painted pottery; and masonry. Workers were highly skilled, and many of their products were exported to foreign markets. *Attic red-figure ware, about 490 to 480 B.C., Staatliche Museen, Berlin.*

Most women spent their lives at home running their households and looking after the children. They could not vote or play an active part in public life. Here a slave hands a baby over to its mother. *Red-figure olive-oil bottle from Eretria, about 470 to 460 B.C., National Archaeological Museum, Athens.*

There was one class of women that broke the convention of seclusion. The *hetaira* was a high-class courtesan who was expected to offer companionship and intelligent conversation as well as sex. As this depiction of haggling customers shows, the relationships were essentially financial. *Vase by the Kleophrades Painter, about 490 to 480 B.C., Staatliche Antikensammlungen, Munich.*

A priest, wearing a wreath, and a boy prepare to slaughter a young boar at an altar. The Greeks were very religious. Their gods were human in appearance and in behavior. Like forces of nature, they were dangerous. They needed to be placated at every opportunity with offerings and burnt sacrifices. *Drinking cup by the Epidromos Painter, about 510 to 500 B.C., Louvre Museum.*

A guest at a dinner party, or symposium, listens to a musician playing. His bag hangs beside his stick and a cup of wine stands on a table next to his couch. Gatherings of this kind were popular among upper-class Athenian men. Serious conversation and drinking often followed a meal, but if handsome waiters and dancing girls were present, the proceedings could degenerate into something approaching an orgy. *Attic red-figure drinking cup by the Colmar Painter, about 490 B.C., Louvre Museum.*

THE VILLAGE

For many centuries after the classical era, Athens was no more than a dozy village encumbered by ruins. It occupied a neglected corner of the Ottoman Empire, until Greece won its independence in 1832. One year later, the German artist Johann Michael Wittmer painted the Acropolis as seen from the Temple of Olympian Zeus. The dusty backwater he evoked had just started out on its new career as the Hellenic capital. Today, it has grown into a metropolis of more than four million inhabitants. *Benaki Museum, Athens.*

. . .

Pericles was in his early twenties when he first entered the political stage. In the spring of 472 he was chosen to be *choregos,* or theatrical investor and producer, for the tragic playwright Aeschylus. By then his father was dead and he was in charge of the family fortune.

Like other wealthy citizens Pericles was expected to undertake a *liturgy* (the Greek for "work for the people"). This entailed undertaking a costly task for the state at his own expense. There were two kinds of liturgy—responsibility for running a trireme in the navy for one year and funding some aspect or other of a festival (a banquet or an athletic team or, as in this case, a chorus for a musical or dramatic performance). This was a typically ingenious means of encouraging public-spirited expenditure in place of an unpopular tax.

Pericles was *choregos* at the Great Dionysia drama festival and he was the financier and producer of three plays by Aeschylus, one of which survives, *The Persians.* Most Greek dramas were set in the legendary past, but in this case Aeschylus chose as his subject the victory at Salamis, only eight years after the battle had been won and lost. The action takes place at the imperial court in Susa, one of the Persian Empire's capital cities, and its centerpiece is a long description of the battle by an eyewitness (see pages 179–181). It gave plenty of opportunity for splendid and barbaric spectacle. We may imagine that the young Alcmaeonid spared no expense.

It was in this year or thereabouts that Themistocles was ostracized, and it may well be that Pericles used the play to remind the *demos* of the great man's achievement and restore his popularity. If so, it was a bold political move for a newcomer and, as we know, it failed. Themistocles was soon voted out of Athens and obliged to leave his native land.

As a young man Pericles was the coming hope of the nobility, but he took up the people's cause from motives of self-preservation and ambition. He came to act as aide to the leading democratic personality of the day, a man called Ephialtes. Little is known of him, but (unusually) he was probably not of aristocratic stock. Unlike most public figures of the day he was incorruptible. He was the guiding spirit behind the trial of Cimon. Pericles was appointed one of the ten prosecutors, although his heart seems not to have been in the task. Cimon's sister begged Pericles to be gentle with her brother. He replied with a smile: "Elpinice, you are too old, much too old, for this kind of business." In front of the jury he did not press the accusations against Cimon very hard.

For the two democrats there were serious flaws in the way the constitution was working. The first concerned the role of the antique council of the Areopagus. Its members were former Archons, public officials appointed from the two richest social classes in the *polis*. It was not directly elected and the less well-off were excluded from participation. This was against the spirit of the age and action was called for. The council should be either abolished or reformed.

Ephialtes opened the campaign against the Areopagus by bringing individual members to court for corruption and fraud. Having weakened the council's self-confidence, he moved in for the kill. He chose his moment with care. In 462, when his leading opponent, Cimon, was away in Messenia on his unsuccessful mission to help the Spartans, Ephialtes persuaded the *ecclesia* to pass a package of bills that stripped the Areopagus of all its powers that were of political significance. These included its right to punish elected officials if they broke any laws while in office, to supervise the administration of government, and to ensure that the laws were obeyed. Its power to inquire into the private lives of citizens was also abolished.

The functions of the Areopagus were transferred either to the *ecclesia*, the *boulē,* or the jury courts. The council itself was left in being, but its only real, remaining function was to try cases of homicide. To add insult to injury, it was charged with looking after the sacred olive trees of Athena and helping to safeguard the property of the goddesses Demeter and Persephone at Eleusis in western Attica, where annual Mysteries in their honor were held.

Victory was gratifying, but short-lived. In 461, not long after the reform of the Areopagus, Ephialtes was kidnapped one night and murdered. According to Diodorus, it was never clear "just how his death came about"—a mysterious phrase, implying either that his body was not found or that the cause of death was unclear. In any case, his killer or killers were never caught. Plutarch reported that a certain Aristodicus of Tanagra was to blame, but nothing is known about him. It is a fair guess that Ephialtes fell victim to embittered oligarchs who wanted to avenge the emasculation of the Areopagus.

But what if we apply the test *cui bono*? To whose advantage was the murder? The obvious answer was Pericles, who inherited the leadership of the democratic faction. Malicious rumor suggested that he had arranged the assassination. Plutarch dismissed it as a "poisonous accusation" and he was right to do so. Pericles was a law-abiding man, self-righteously so.

At the age of thirty-three Pericles picked up the baton that had been seized from Ephialtes. For year after year during most of the next three decades, he was elected one of the city's ten generals. Although he was by no means a despot, he was by far the most influential political figure in the *ecclesia* as well as being an able and aggressive military commander. In the last analysis, though, he operated in a direct democracy and advised rather than governed.

Pericles immediately proceeded to further reforms. There were three areas where he was sure improvements could be made.

First, he introduced a citizenship law. The franchise was restricted to those both of whose parents were Athenians. Previously a foreign mother had been no bar to civic status; Cleisthenes, Themistocles, and Cimon had all had foreign mothers. The *polis* was home to a large number of resident foreigners and Pericles' aim was to limit access to the benefits of citizenship. Athens was internationally influential and there were practical advantages in turning citizens into a more exclusive closed group. It is also possible that immigration was unpopular (foreigners stealing jobs is a familiar complaint down the ages).

Henceforward, most public officials were appointed annually by lot rather than by election. This had the huge advantage of ensuring equal opportunity for all and of discouraging the creation of political factions or pressure groups. But when Solon introduced sortition for the Archons (see pages 65 and 103), it was only applied to a directly elected long-list. He wanted to ensure the quality of candidates and a willingness to serve, but for Pericles these factors were less important than ensuring that all citizens had the chance of playing a part in public life. Loyalty outdid competence by a long chalk. So preliminary elections were abolished and appointments to the *boulē* and of Archons were made purely by lot.

This new arrangement would only work smoothly if office holders were paid, for otherwise the working poor would be unable to find the time required to fulfill their public duties. So Pericles brought in pay for those serving as Archons and *boulē* members.

Any male citizen above thirty years of age could offer to sit as a juror in the courts. Six thousand of these volunteers were appointed by lot at the beginning of a year (six hundred from each tribe), from which jurors were enrolled for individual cases. Juries were large—1,501 for the most important trials and between 201 and 401 for private suits. Pericles introduced jury pay at the living wage of two obols a day (later in the fifth century this was raised to three obols).

Numerous other officials, who received state salaries or sat on committees, were appointed by lot. These included the Treasurers of Athena, who were responsible for the imperial exchequer with its vast income flows; the Vendors, who farmed out public contracts to work the silver mines at Laurium; the Receivers, who collected public revenues and distributed them to the appropriate officials; the Accountants, who checked all the public accounts; the Examiners, who sat in the *agora* to receive complaints against office holders; and the Commissioners, who maintained the public sanctuaries. The *polis* also employed market inspectors who monitored the quality of goods on sale, commissioners of weights and measures, and grain inspectors.

Only military and some technical financial responsibilities, where competence was absolutely essential, were not subject to appointment by lot.

The Greek alphabet first came into use during the eighth century when reading and writing were relatively novel skills. The Spartans used written records as little as possible to the amused scorn of other Greeks. But without high levels of literacy it would not have been possible for the Athenian democracy to function. A complicated constitution that prioritized openness, participation, accountability, and a busy economy dependent on international trade required reliable systems of reporting and documentation. Citizens had to be able to add and subtract, and understand script. We must assume that even many poor Athenians were, or under force of circumstance became, basically literate.

The democracy was very expensive to run. It has been estimated that by 440 up to twenty thousand citizens, about one third of the total or more, were in receipt of some form or other of state pay. This made a change of constitution unlikely, for there were so many citizens who had a vested interest in the democratic system. The point did not escape a caustic critic of the new order of things. "The poor, the men of the people, and the working class are doing very well and in large numbers, and so will increase support for the democracy."

This was important, for Athenian democrats felt embattled. They went in constant fear that their constitution would be overthrown. The "best people" thought that the democracy was a completely unnecessary innovation; it was unfair, incompetent, and open to the worst kind of demagogue. It was a rogues' charter. The same commentator, attributed (probably wrongly) to Xenophon, puts the argument:

> ... everywhere on earth the best element in society is opposed to democracy. For among the best people there is minimal wantonness and injustice but a maximum of scrupulous attention to what is good. However, among the people there is a maximum of ignorance, disorder, and wickedness. This is because poverty

leads them to disgraceful behavior, and thanks to a lack of money some men are uneducated and ignorant.

The once dominant noble clans would have liked to see a return to oligarchy, to government by a well-bred minority, but they mostly kept their opinions to themselves and, like the lordly Cimon, served the state uncomplainingly.

A broken inscription survives that catalogues the dead from one of the ten Athenian tribes, the Erechtheis, in the year 460 or 459. Usually the fallen of all the ten tribes were recorded onto one stone slab or stele, but the large number of casualties probably explains the use of separate stelae. The inscription opens with a list of the various campaigns, which Athens was fighting simultaneously; the final phrase was in spaced-out capital letters for astonished emphasis.

> Of [the tribe] Erechtheis
> Those died in the war: in Cyprus, in Egy-
> pt, in Phoenicia, at Halieis, on Aegina, at Megara
> I N T H E S A M E Y E A R.

There then followed the names of eight generals and 179 soldiers in three columns. Halieis refers to an unsuccessful foray into the territory of Argos in the Peloponncse. In the mid-fifth century the number of adult male citizens may have totaled as many as sixty thousand, but the *polis* had no hesitation in risking overextension.

Of about the same date is a small, beautifully carved marble relief that shows the goddess Athena, melancholy and in mourning (see the illustration). She may be reading a casualty list on a stele or contemplating a hoplite's gravestone. Either way the image seems to embody the pity of war.

But, for all their grief for the fallen, as the Delian League gradually morphed into an empire, the Athenians became extraordinarily self-confident and aggressive. There was no question of fighting only on a single front, but on as many fronts as cared to present themselves.

An irresistible opportunity for cutting the Persians down to size arose almost by chance. The Egyptians always resented being a colony of the Achaemenids and, when they heard of the assassination of Xerxes in the summer of 465 and the confusion this was likely to cause at Susa, raised the standard of revolt under the leadership of Inaros, a young Libyan prince. The decision to do so was taken in the autumn of 464 and the winter was given over to careful planning and raising a preliminary military force. The Persian administration in Egypt was removed in the summer or autumn of the following year.

A large allied fleet of two hundred triremes happened to be campaigning off Cyprus and, when they learned of the revolt, abandoned what they were doing and sailed to Egypt to support the rebels. This was not altogether an opportunistic decision. To poke a finger in the Great King's eye was always a pleasure. But the growing population of Athens depended on imported grain and Egypt was a breadbasket of the ancient world. If it could be pried from Persia's grasp the land of the pharaohs could become a valuable supplier and supplement the Black Sea trade.

To begin with, fortune favored the Greeks. The fleet sailed up the Nile, gained control of the river and of the onetime capital city of Memphis, just south of the Delta, except for its Persian garrison in a fortification called the White Tower.

The Great King tried to bribe the Peloponnesians to invade Attica, but to their credit they declined, while pocketing an advance payment. The Delian League helped repel a Persian expeditionary force, but Artaxerxes sent another one in due course. The Egyptians and their allies were driven from Memphis and besieged on a river island in the Nile Delta for a year and a half. Eventually the Persians drained the marsh waters and captured the island by infantry assault. Most of the league fleet was lost and after six years the Greek expedition ended in complete failure.

Despite the evidence of Thucydides, it would seem that many Athenians escaped albeit not with their boats, for otherwise fifty thousand lives would have been sacrificed (as we have seen, a trireme needed a two-hundred-strong crew). Although some of the oarsmen must have come from allied states, losses on such a scale would have prevented the *polis* from pursuing the active military policy it actually did in the coming years. But the disaster was indeed a blow to league morale.

Ever resilient, Athens resolved to become a land power in Greece as well as a sea power in the Aegean. The strategic aim was to control the bottleneck of the Isthmus and so prevent invasions of Attica led by Sparta. For a time it based a hoplite force in Megara and built Long Walls to connect it with its port, Nisaea. With harbors on both Megara's northern and southern coasts, Athens now controlled the Corinthian gulf. It defeated its longtime rival, the island of Aegina, confiscated its navy, and compelled it to join the league as a paying member. This was the last chorus of an old song.

Finally, Athens conquered all of Boeotia except for its powerful *polis*, Thebes. Sparta watched these developments with growing fury. Between about 460 and 445 it and its Peloponnesian allies engaged in on-off fighting with the new boastful imperial power (named too generously as the First Peloponnesian War). The Athenians did not hold on to their mainland acquisitions for much longer than a decade. In 447 an important battle was lost at Coronea in Boeotia, with heavy upper-class casualties including Cleinias, an Alcmaeonid. Athenian hegemony in mainland Greece came to an abrupt end. Luckily a revolt in the important and nearby island dependency of Euboea was speedily put down.

With astute anticipation of failure, the Athenians made sure they could protect themselves. The Long Walls connecting Athens to Piraeus and Phaleron were completed in 457. From now onwards, so long as its fleet ruled the waves Athens was invulnerable. Themistocles' vision of his city transformed into a maritime power was at last fully realized. In the 440s the so-called Middle Wall was built, which created a narrow and probably more defensible corridor to the port.

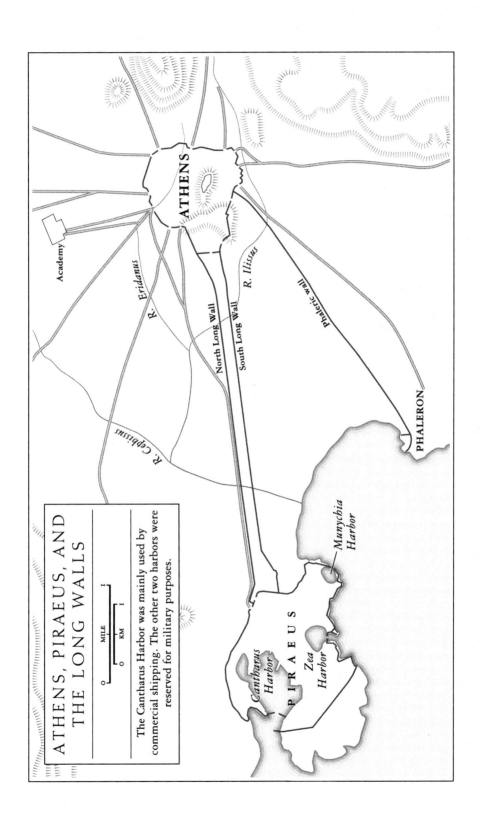

ATHENS, PIRAEUS, AND THE LONG WALLS

The Cantharus Harbor was mainly used by commercial shipping. The other two harbors were reserved for military purposes.

MILE

KM

Academy

R. Eridanus

North Long Wall

South Long Wall

R. Ilissus

Phaleric wall

R. Cephissus

ATHENS

PHALERON

Munychia Harbor

Cantharus Harbor

P I R A E U S

Zea Harbor

Meanwhile on the far side of the Aegean, Cimon, back home after his ten years of ostracism, proved once again that, although never the convinced democrat, he was ever the democracy's proud servant. He was given command of an amphibious expedition against the Persians on Cyprus; but in 450 he fell sick or was wounded and died. At his suggestion on his deathbed, the news was kept secret to give the Greeks time to extricate themselves and abandon the campaign unimpeded.

An epitaph for the fallen, in the manner of the late Simonides, makes much of Cimon's last hurrah.

From the time when the sea divided Europe from Asia
And wild Ares dominated the cities of mortals,
No such act by men of this earth ever took place
On land and sea at one and the same time.

The lines refer to the Cyprus campaign, but they would be a fitting if overstated *envoi* to this whole era of Athenian overreach. For all the gallantry and all the glory in these middle years of the fifth century, how much was really achieved? The answer is mixed.

In fact, Athens had reached the limits of its capacity. At one point the *polis* was so short of manpower that men as young as eighteen and as old as sixty had to be called up as reinforcements. In 456 it contemptuously sent a fleet to sail around the Peloponnese and set fire to Sparta's naval yards at its port of Gytheion. However, in 451 it agreed to a five-year truce with Sparta. A couple of years later an advantageous accord was struck with the Great King, the Peace of Callias (so named after the politician who negotiated it, Cimon's multimillionaire brother-in-law). The Greek cities of Asia Minor were to be free and subject to their own laws, except for Cyprus, permanently lost to Persia—a bitter pill. In effect, Athens had abandoned its ambitions in the Eastern Mediterranean.

On the credit side, Persian military forces were not allowed to come nearer the Mediterranean coast than one day's journey by horse, were not to sail past the Blue Rocks at the entrance to the Black Sea (so protecting the grain trade) nor past the islands that lay between Lycia and Pamphilia (thus excluding the Persian navy from the Aegean). In a word, Artaxerxes agreed to keep out of the Hellenic world.

Neither belligerent could claim a total victory, but fortune overall favored the Greeks. Fifty years had passed since Athenians raided Sardis and aroused the ire of King Darius, but at long last the Persian Wars were over. Joy was not altogether unconfined, though, for peace brought Athens a new threat. In island after island across the Aegean Sea people were asking themselves what was the point of their expensive maritime alliance now that the Great King was no longer a serious threat. Why should they go on paying Athens large sums of money for a fleet that was not needed?

In 446 the truce between Athens and Sparta was converted into a Thirty Years' Peace, based on recognition of the status quo. The two great powers in Greece were following very different paths. Once upon a time partners, even friends, Athens and Sparta had not trusted one another for years. Now they were on tolerable terms again, but it did not take a clairvoyant to see trouble ahead.

Sparta was greatly admired throughout the Hellenic world for its self-discipline and austerity. But it was introverted and obsessively resistant to change. Its system was the expression of barely concealed fear. The subject peoples of the Peloponnese were always seething; at any moment they might boil over and Lacedaemon would be overwhelmed. It was this ever-wakeful nightmare that underwrote its virtues.

The Peloponnesian earthquake exposed the flaws of their system, but the Spartans survived. With a convulsive effort, they vanquished the *helots* and re-enslaved them. But then they found themselves facing another sudden violent shaking, as the revolutionary energy of the Athenian democracy upset the balance of the Hellenic world. It not only controlled the seas, but for a time had established a land empire in central Greece that locked Sparta into its southern peninsula. And the hungry giant of the Persian Empire had been tamed. Athens was well on its way to unifying Greece.

No wonder that at some point during the 440s Pericles proposed a Panhellenic congress. All Greeks, whether from Europe or Asia, were invited. The agenda was to include the future of the Greek sanctuaries burned down by the Persians, the fulfillment of vows made to the gods during the Persian Wars, and, most important of all, the security of the seas. The underlying purpose of the congress was obvious—to win consent to the Athenian hegemony. Unsurprisingly, Sparta sabotaged the plan and the congress never took place.

The constitutions of most states cost time and effort only from a minority of citizens, a political class. The complete democracy that Pericles and his predecessors had installed demanded the full-scale participation of every member of society. Even the meanest and stupidest citizen might find himself, by the haphazard workings of the lot, at the head of government. He had no choice but to pay attention.

The energy that this mass involvement in the public sphere released showed itself not just through an aggressive imperialism, but also in the life of the city. The arts and culture thrived as never before.

15

The Kindly Ones

I t is night, a little before sunrise. A watchman stands on the roof of the palace at Argos in the Peloponnese, bored and tired. He prays: "Gods! Release me from this long and weary guard duty. Gods! do it."

He has spent a year, night after night, scrutinizing the heavens—what he calls (for he has a way with words) the "nocturnal conference of stars." He is waiting for a sign, for something that could be mistaken for a new star, but would in fact be a beacon flaring from a distant hilltop.

The war at Troy is in its tenth year and it has been agreed that if and when the city falls to the Greeks a chain of beacons will be lit. They will island-hop across the Aegean Sea and almost instantly bring the good news to Queen Clytemnestra, wife of the expedition's leader, Agamemnon.

Then, suddenly, he sees a flame shooting up on the horizon. Victory has come. The queen is woken to see the beacon. She rejoices, or does she?

. . .

So opens *The Oresteia,* one of the greatest and earliest dramas in the history of Western civilization. Written by Aeschylus, it was a trilogy that told the bloodstained saga of the ruling family of Argos. Its first performance took place in 458 at the annual festival devoted to the god Dionysus, the Great Dionysia. It is the only complete trilogy to survive.

The origins of the festival are obscure, but the story appears to open at Eleutherae, a small, well-fortified town on the debatable border between Attica and Boeotia. Its people were always being bullied by the Thebans, who throughout their history worked tirelessly to unify Boeotia under their rule.

Eventually in the middle of the sixth century they applied, in the end successfully, to join Attica and become Athenian citizens. Their tutelary deity was Dionysus, the patron of wine and intoxication. As part of the assimilation of Eleutherae into the Athenian state, the god, in the shape of an ancient wooden statue, was transported to Athens. He was carried in procession for the twenty-eight-mile journey and was installed in a tiny, specially built temple on the southern slope of the Acropolis.

In expiation for an initial reluctance to absorb Eleutherae, an annual festival was founded called the Great Dionysia (as already reported, it may have been initiated or enlarged by the tyrant Pisistratus). The original procession was partially restaged every year in March. The statue was escorted from the Academy, the sacred grove of olive trees dedicated to Athena and athletics ground, not far from the city walls. Young men dressed up as satyrs. These were the mythical male followers of Dionysus; partly animal with horse's tails or goat's feet, they were exclusively interested in drinking and having unrestrained sex. Wearing goatskins, they danced alongside the cart carrying the statue. Wooden or metal phalluses were carried on sticks. Sacrificial animals were killed, roasted, and eaten. Wine flowed. The night passed in revelry and dancing to the accompaniment of harps and flutes.

The next day, Dionysus, in his incarnation as a statue, was carried into the theater so that he could watch the proceedings. These included choral performances. The pretend-satyrs danced around the altar singing what was called their "goat song" (from *tragos,* or goat, and *oide,* or song, *tragoidia,* whence in due course tragedy). Over time, the leader of the dancers, who also composed the song, spoke or sang to his choir, which in turn sang back to him. He took on the identity of some personage associated with the events being celebrated and wore an appropriate costume.

As explained earlier, the introduction of dialogue was attributed to Thespis. These proto-dramas were meant to feature Dionysus, but over time the myths of other gods and heroes were performed. On rare occasions contemporary events were chosen as a theme. The general impression in these early years was of a staged oratorio.

This was how tragedy was invented. As the form developed and became more subtle and sophisticated, Greek thinkers tried to define its essence. According to Aristotle,

> tragedy, then, is an imitation of an action of high importance, complete and of some amplitude . . . acted not narrated; by means of pity and fear effecting the purgation of these emotions. [It shows] the kind of man who neither is distinguished for excellence and virtue, come to grief not on account of baseness and vice, but on account of some error; a man of great reputation and prosperity. . . . There must be no change from misfortune to good fortune, but only the opposite.

By about 500 two actors worked together with the chorus, each playing a number of different roles; later in the ensuing century a third actor was added to the company. A chorus of twelve or fifteen men would sing and dance and stayed onstage throughout the action. Three authors each presented three tragedies and a satyr play. The tragedies were usually trilogies connected in subject matter and were performed one after another. They were followed by the satyr play, in which Silenus, chief of satyrs, superintended an uproarious burlesque or farce.

Five comedies were also presented during the festival. These were topical and heavily satirical. Leading politicians and public figures like the philosopher Socrates had to put up with crude but very funny caricatures of themselves and their opinions. In the hands of a literary genius such as Aristophanes comedies were also imaginative, almost surreal fantasies. Dialogue made the most of bodily functions and was unhesitatingly obscene.

Actors lasted most of the day. There were no intermissions and the patience of audiences must have been tested.

Performers and chorus members, who were all male, wore masks, which had slightly opened mouths and suggested the personality of the character in the play. Masks were made from strips of glued linen and molded on the actor's face, and were then painted. Women's masks were usually white. For tragedy, costumes resembled those of everyday life, a tunic and a cloak; but for comedy the tunic covered, or revealed, potbellies, huge buttocks, and enormous phalluses.

The Great Dionysia was a five-day festival and tragedies were presented on three of them. Men and boys also sang choral works. The productions were competitive and ten judges (or *crites,* hence our critics) awarded prizes: to reduce the risk of corruption and to let the god have a say the votes of only five judges, chosen at random, were counted. Performances were enormously popular and tourists flocked into the city (shipping started up again in March after the inactive winter months when sailing was too dangerous).

During the fifth century, the heyday of Athenian power and prestige, plays were performed only once. Every Great Dionysia was a sequence of premieres. If you didn't catch it you missed it, although texts were available for the literary-minded.

A winter festival in honor of Dionysus was staged every January with prizes for comedy and after 432 for tragedy. This was the Lenaea or Country Dionysia; it catered only to the local Athenian public.

Wealthy and public-spirited men, like Pericles with *The Persians,* were appointed as *choregoi* (literally chorus leaders) by the Chief Archon. Each would finance and produce a tragic trilogy and satyr play, or a comedy or a choral concert and dance. They vied with one another for the most lavish productions and some said that Athens spent more on theater than on its fleet (an exaggeration, but an understandable one).

A *choregos* was allocated a playwright and up to three actors. He hired a professional trainer for the chorus, paid for the actors' costumes and those of the chorus, and commissioned the decor and props. The state picked up the bill for the actors' wages. Star performers became increasingly professionalized and acted in arts festivals throughout the Greek world. They commanded high fees and were men of status; being well traveled, they were sometimes employed as state ambassadors. The crafts of theater—writing, production, and acting—often ran in families.

Theater had an important community dimension as well. It has been estimated that as many as 1,500 persons were involved one way or another in the production and presentation of plays in a single year's Great Dionysia.

To be a *choregos* was no passing honor. If he won a prize, he was crowned with a garland and given a bronze tripod. He would set this up on a column or in a miniature circular temple in the long Street of the Tripods, which led from the theater eastwards around the Acropolis. A surviving inscription has recorded the name of one proud prizewinner and those of his creative team.

Lysicrates, son of Lysitheides of the Kikynna deme, was the sponsor. The tribe of Akameantis won the boys' chorus. Theon played the flute. Lysiades the Athenian directed. Euaenetus was Chief Archon.

In this way, the generosity and artistic taste of a *choregos* were placed on permanent display. His memory would live forever.

Large numbers of citizens—perhaps as many as twenty thousand—attended performances at the Great Dionysia. Originally plays were presented in the *agora,* but at some stage during the fifth century they were transferred to a space just north of the temple of Dionysus. Here the slope leading down from the Acropolis formed a natural, semicircular, open-air auditorium (a *theatron,* or seeing space). It was centered on a circular area, called the *orchestra,* which resembled a traditional threshing floor. This was where the chorus chanted and danced.

In the early years there may have been wooden benches at the front for dignitaries, but most spectators sat on the ground. Later, it appears, fixed wooden seating was installed. The first fully stone theater was not built until the fourth century. The entrance fee was good value at two obols, the equivalent of a worker's daily wage. As a rule, audiences were male, although women seem to have been allowed to attend in the fourth century. Wine and confectionery were on sale and audiences ate and drank during performances. They consumed most when bored.

Beyond the orchestra was a raised stage and at its back a *skene* (whence our scene: literally, a booth), a timber framework on which painted scenery could be hung. Usually, a building or buildings were depicted, with two or three doors through which actors could enter or exit. They could also appear on the roof. A crane was installed that brought gods down from on high and carried them off again (we still use the phrase *deus ex machina,* Latin for "the god from the machine," for an abrupt and surprising conclusion to a narrative). This was quite an elaborate piece of equipment: in Euripides' *Medea,* the eponymous heroine brought the play to a spectacular close by flying away in a chariot, probably drawn by winged serpents and accompanied by the corpses of her dead children.

Violent death was never shown onstage. So, for example, Agamemnon and Clytemnestra meet their respective fates inside their palace; then the *skene* was opened wide and a platform, the *eccyclema,* on which their corpses were displayed was wheeled out.

. . .

We are told that Aeschylus called his plays "slices from the great banquet of Homer." His masterpiece, *The Oresteia,* was based on the legendary story of the House of Atreus, but retold in a way to catch the attention of the contemporary theatergoer.

The family lives under a curse and terrible crimes have been committed in each generation. King Agamemnon is the latest to live out a doomed, repetitive pattern of sin and retribution. The Greek fleet gathers under his command at Aulis, a port in Boeotia, but storms prevent it from setting sail to Troy.

> *. . . ships and ropes rotted, cables parted,*
> *Men wandered off.*

The Greek seer Calchas tells the king that he has offended the goddess Artemis and must sacrifice his daughter, Iphigenia, if he wants a favorable wind. Frightened for the fate of the expedition, he puts on the "harness of necessity." At the altar Agamemnon calls for someone to bring a gag to stop his daughter from shouting anything that might cast blame on the House of Atreus. The girl has her throat slit, the goddess forgives, the storm subsides, and the ships sail.

Despite the passage of ten years Clytemnestra has neither forgotten nor forgiven her darling daughter's terrible fate at her father's hands. Several days pass after the news was brought by the beacon and Agamemnon returns to the palace in his pomp. Clytemnestra has made all the necessary arrangements: he that's coming must be provided for, in the words of a later chilling lady.

Her husband takes a bath and his queen volunteers to help him. Like a fisherman with a net, she envelops him in a splendid and voluminous robe and then, having caught him up in it, stabs him again, again, and again. Iphigenia has been avenged.

Clytemnestra has a lover, Aegisthus, a cousin of Agamemnon with a grudge against him. After Agamemnon's murder, the couple live together and reign in Argos. So ends the first part of the trilogy; the second is entitled *The Libation Bearers*.

Seven years have passed. Agamemnon's two children are grown up. Electra, who adored her father, lives on miserably at Argos. Her brother Orestes, the legitimate heir, is a threat to the usurpers but after Agamemnon's death was smuggled out of the country to safety.

He faces the most painful of moral dilemmas. As a son he is obliged to avenge his father by killing his murderer. But that is his mother, Clytemnestra, and matricide breaks the gravest of taboos. Whatever he does, then, he sins. This impossible choice is an example of how fate trips up and entraps human beings, even those who have the best of intentions.

Orestes is ordered by the god Apollo at Delphi to put his mother and her paramour to death in retribution for Agamemnon's assassination. He is horrified by what confronts him, but dutifully returns to Argos accompanied by his friend Pylades. He meets his sister and they plan what is to be done.

The two young men present themselves at the palace, disguised as foreign traders and speaking with a Delphian accent. Obeying the usual etiquette of offering hospitality to strangers, the queen comes out and welcomes them. "As our guest, call this your home," says Clytemnestra, with unknowing irony. Orestes informs her of his own (supposed) death in Phocis. "Oh misery!" keens the queen in conventional mourning, unconsciously prophetic. "Your story spells our total destruction."

Her defenses down, she ushers her guests into the house. Orestes first puts Aegisthus to death. Clytemnestra, hearing noise, comes out of the women's quarters to find out what is happening. She begs her son for her life. Hard-pressed, Orestes asks desperately: "How shall I escape my father's curse, if I relent?" She yields to her fate. "You are right. I waste my breath."

As soon as he has struck her down, Orestes decides to go back to Delphi to beg the god to purify him, for even if innocent he is polluted by what he has done. As the play ends, Orestes runs off, pursued by the ancient, pre-Olympian Furies. These hags, dressed in black and wreathed with serpents, pitilessly avenge wrongs done within the family. Despite their age they seem never to have grown up, for they have no sense of the compromises and uncertainties of adult life. Whatever Apollo may say, they mean to hunt Orestes down and never let him go.

In the last play of the trilogy, the scene shifts to the temple of Apollo at Delphi. For now, Orestes has outrun the exhausted Furies, who lie on the temple steps growling in their sleep like dogs. Apollo arrives and, when they wake up, he argues with them, fruitlessly, about the fugitive's fate. The god claims to have purified him of pollution, but agrees that the court of the Areopagus in Athens shall decide whether to clear Orestes of guilt or to convict him of murder. (The audience will have been aware that one of the reformed Areopagus's few remaining powers was to try cases of homicide.)

We now move to Athens, where a jury of ten Athenian citizens hears the case. Athena presides. A chorus of the Furies prosecutes and Apollo defends. The jurors vote by dropping a white or a black pebble into one of two different urns. The votes are counted and found to be equal. Athena's casting vote goes for acquittal.

The Furies are furious. "The old is trampled by the new!" they wail. "A curse on you younger gods who override the ancient laws."

Athena talks them down from their rage and persuades them to settle as honored guests in Athens. "Share my home with me," she says, and gives them a cave on the Acropolis to live in.

But she warns them solemnly not to

provoke bloodshed in my land. It damages young hearts, maddening them with a rage beyond drunkenness. Do not transplant the hearts of fighting cocks in my people, the spirit of tribal war and boldness against each other. Let them fight foreign enemies instead.

After so much letting of blood we have, finally, a happy ending. The curse of the House of Atreus has run its course thanks to the new democracy of Athens. In a full and confident hope, the Furies are rechristened the Kindly Ones (in Greek, the Eumenides, also the play's title).

During the opening ceremony of the Great Dionysia, the ten generals or *strategoi* poured libations and, according to a fourth-century inscription, offerings were made to such political abstractions as Democracy, Peace, and Good Fortune. Key priorities of the Athenian state were given memorable visual expression. It was on this date that the annual payments for the upkeep of the allied fleet fell due. The money was carried into the theater and shown to the audience. We have seen that it did not take long for the Delian League to transform itself into the Athenian Empire. This display, in front of representatives of league members and other international visitors as well as *metics* and citizens, showed very clearly who was now in charge.

Orphan sons of Athenians who had fallen in battle were brought up at the state's expense and on reaching adulthood were given a set of costly hoplite armor. They were now formally presented to the audience and were a striking reminder of the military power of the *polis*. This was Athens being regenerated.

Before the tragedies began, the names of men who had in some way benefited the Athenian state were read out, and they were awarded crowns or garlands. This public honoring emphasized the value the *polis* placed on loyalty and patriotism.

Taken as a whole, the Great Dionysia was a political event of high importance. Of course, in the first place it was a religious service in honor of the gods. But it is no accident that the invention of drama occurred at about the same time as the invention of democracy. Tragedy and comedy were an additional means by which the *demos* could think about the great social and ethical issues of the day, without having to take political decisions at the same time. In a word, it was the *ecclesia* at leisure.

Aeschylus is a case in point. We should remember that he knew Pericles well. He was a democrat, as he made clear in *The Oresteia*. He diverted the course of the old myth so that it ended up in Athens. What the playwright was doing was to endorse the controversial reform of the council of the Areopagus, pretending that its main role had *always* been to hear murder cases.

He has Athena say:

Since this is how matters have turned out,
I will select sworn judges of homicide, and
I will establish this court for all time.
So summon your witnesses and proofs
Which support your case; I will ... choose the best
Of my citizens, for them to decide this matter truly.

Over and above the particular case of the Areopagus, Aeschylus repeatedly emphasizes the importance of reconciliation. An old order is passing, to be replaced by the new. Violence and despotism have given way to justice delivered by the people. The outmoded principle of vengeance, of an eye for an eye, has been overtaken by the light of reason. The ancient Furies have been persuaded to become good-natured, loyal powers, their night outshone by the brightness of Apollo's sun.

Athens was not the only *polis* where democrats were competing with aristocrats and tyrants. Emotions were running high throughout the Greek world. Revolutions were overturned and reaction set in. The outcome was often civil strife and bloodletting.

In the *Eumenides,* the culmination of his trilogy, Aeschylus has the Furies eat their words and preach peace.

Never let civil war, which eats men,
Rage in Athens; never let its soil
Soak up its people's blood

And murderous passion for revenge
Destroy the state. May its people find joy
In each other, a common will for love.
And when they hate, they must do so with one mind.

The show ends with a procession. Music plays and torches blaze. The Furies don the scarlet ceremonial robes of the *metics,* the city's foreign residents. Everyone sings a final song of welcome as the two divinities, Apollo and Athena, take these "ancient children" into their care and lead them joyfully to their new home.

16

"Crowned with Violets"

Pericles was a contradiction in terms—an aristocrat by temperament but a democrat by conviction or, perhaps it might be better to say, from enlightened self-interest. From the death of Ephialtes in 461 until his own thirty years later he dominated Athenian politics.

How did he accomplish this feat? Part of the answer lies in his personality—or at least how he presented it to his fellow-citizens. After entering politics he adopted a new austere lifestyle, writes his biographer Plutarch.

On one street and on one street only was he to be seen walking, the one that led [from his house] to the *agora* and the Council chamber. He declined invitations to dinner and any other kind of social get-together. During the long period that he was at the head of affairs he never ate a meal at a friend's house—except when his relative Euryptolemus held a wedding banquet. And then he only stayed to the end of the meal and as soon as the serious drinking started he stood up and left.

He cultivated the image of a hardworking public servant. He was known for his politeness, which he maintained even when abused and insulted. Corruption and bribery were rife in the Athenian political system and Pericles made a point of his incorruptibility. He was careful not to make himself too familiar a figure in public life. He did not speak at the assembly on every possible occasion, as some politicians do, but addressed it only at long intervals. This meant that people did not tire of him and, second, he was not held responsible when things went wrong.

Power was in his hands, but there was nothing unconstitutional in the behavior of Pericles. He showed no signs whatever of aspiring to be a new Pisistratus. Every year he had to be reelected as one of the ten generals, or *strategoi*. These were the only major posts to escape the lot and were decided on merit. The senior executive officers of the democracy, they were coequal in their authority and there was no chief *strategos*. The competition for position was fierce. The *ecclesia* was in charge and could dispense with a man's services whenever it wished. Power was on loan.

Pericles was an able orator and, according to Plutarch, he equipped himself with a formal style of speaking that "harmonised with his way of life and the grandeur of his ideals." He made use of the philosophical and scientific ideas that he drew from the thinkers and scientists he knew personally. His addresses to the people were marked by a high seriousness and had something of the quality of lectures delivered by a well-informed expert. He refused to dumb down to his audience. This earned him credit, and even when he had something unpopular or disagreeable to say Athenians listened to him with attention.

He was very careful over his use of words and left none of his speeches or papers behind him in writing. He seldom used memorable phrases, although he once appealed to the *demos* to remove "that eyesore of the Piraeus," the island of Aegina, and on another occasion said that he could already see "war rushing down at us from the Peloponnese."

Pericles did not have a quicksilver temperament like Themistocles, open to human foibles, and the Athenians respected him rather than warmed to him. He was nicknamed the Olympian and, when he spoke at the *ecclesia,* the comic poets of the day made jokes about him thundering and lightning like Zeus, king of the gods.

After the catastrophe in Egypt and the end of their brief domination of central Greece, the Athenians took stock. Casualties had been very high and they did not have the manpower to back overambitious military and naval schemes. Now they explicitly recognized the fact and concentrated on keeping what they still had—namely the Delian League, which had in effect become their empire. The league treasury was removed to Athens from the island of Delos in 454, the same year that Persia had regained its Egyptian province. The pretext was that the Great King had been greatly strengthened and his fleets might well decide to try their luck again in the Aegean. It was only a pretext, for Pericles had his eyes on the money.

In theory, the Peace of Callias meant that there was no longer any need for the league. Inscriptions survive which show the annual financial contributions that members made to the upkeep of the powerful allied fleet; but the quota list for 448 is missing and perhaps there was a temporary remission of fees. It is tempting to see this as a consequence of the end of the war with Persia.

From 447 onwards Athens worked hard to recapture its league income. This it succeeded in doing, but at the cost of causing considerable resentment. In fact, it would have been foolish to wind up the league, for the allied fleet ensured the freedom of the seas, something of value and profit to all trading states. Also in the long run Persia remained a potential threat and it was as well to remain prepared for trouble. Pericles was unrepentant. The answer he gave his critics, Plutarch wrote, was that "the Athenians were under no obligation to account for how the allies' money was spent, provided they carried on the war for them and kept the Persians away. 'They don't give us a single horse, nor a soldier, nor a ship,' he said. 'All they give us is money.'"

A decree was passed in 448 regulating payments to the Athenian treasury. The proposer was Cleinias, a member of the Alcmaeonid clan and so a relative of Pericles. He had fought bravely at Artemisium in 480, captaining a ship he had commissioned and paid for, and was soon to lose his life at the battle of Coronea in 447 (see page 232). Cleinias wanted to tighten up the financial administration of the league. This was not simply a question of making sure the assessed quotas were correct, but also that opportunities for fraud were reduced. Efficient management benefited the debtors as well as the great creditor.

To a certain extent the empire rested on consent, however painfully wrung from the island states of the Aegean. The fact was that the allied, or more accurately, the Athenian fleet, did keep the waterways open for trade and ensured peace and stability in the Aegean and the Black Sea. The city-states of Asia Minor knew well that the Persians, even if inactive now, lay in wait and their liberties depended on the Athenian hegemony. Few seriously doubted that in its absence the Great King would be back.

But in the last resort the empire was held in place by the implicit application of force. This was exerted not simply by the fleet, but also by the establishment of small colonies of Athenian settlers, the *cleruchies*. We have already encountered them in connection with the revolt of Thasos, but Pericles used them extensively as a control mechanism, paying special attention to guarding the grain route. There is evidence for at least twenty-four settlements and perhaps as many as ten thousand citizens emigrated as *cleruchies* (or as colonists of new or existing cities). Plutarch comments:

> In this way he relieved the city of lazy busybodies or agitators, helped alleviate poverty and by imposing garrisons deterred rebellion.

In 436 Pericles staged an ambitious show of force in the Black Sea. He sailed there with a large and splendidly equipped fleet. His object was to display "the size of the Athenian forces, their confidence to go exactly where they pleased and the fact that they ruled the waves." He negotiated useful arrangements with local states and barbarian kingdoms on behalf of the Greek *poleis* along the coastline.

Pericles left a permanent reminder of his visit. A force of infantry and thirteen warships helped a group of democratic exiles to expel a tyrant from the important Black Sea port of Sinope; when that was done, six hundred Athenian volunteers joined the inhabitants and divided among themselves the houses and lands that had belonged to the former regime.

In 440 the threat of imperial violence was renewed. On this occasion the guilty *polis* was the island of Samos one mile off the coast of Anatolia and the rugged ridge of Mount Mycale. It was one of the very few league members that still supplied ships to the allied fleet rather than a cash subscription.

Samos was a rich and powerful Ionian state and was well known for its culture and luxury. Its wine was highly prized as was its red Samian pottery. In the sixth century the island had been governed by an ambitious tyrant, Polycrates, who was responsible for the building of an aqueduct, more than half a mile long and tunneled through a mountain, which supplied the capital city with fresh water. Being underground, it could not be detected by an enemy and the supply cut off. Famous Samians included the philosopher Pythagoras and the teller of fables Aesop.

The island was in hot dispute with the wealthy port of Miletus, which lay not many miles away near where the Maeander River debouched into the sea. The bone of contention was the small *polis* of Priene on the slopes of Mount Mycale.

The Milesians had the worst of the fighting and went to Athens to lay a complaint against the Samians. All the parties were members of the league and, as is usual in family quarrels, feelings ran high. The Milesian cause was supported by some private individuals from Samos who wanted to overthrow the oligarchic form of government. The affair called for a quick response to head off a possible insurrection, which could well spread, if unchecked, throughout the empire: Byzantium, a *polis* on the European side of the Bosphorus, seized the hour and rebelled from the league.

The Athenians immediately dispatched Pericles with forty ships to Samos, threw out the ruling aristocrats, and established a democracy, which they ordered to abandon hostilities with Miletus. To ensure good behavior they took fifty boys and fifty men as hostages and sent them to the island of Lemnos. Before sailing home, Pericles left behind a garrison of Athenians to deter troublemakers.

Some Samians managed to escape to the mainland and made their way to the Persian governor of Sardis, who promised his assistance. Presumably this came in the form of ready money, for they immediately raised a force of seven hundred mercenaries and crossed the narrow strait to Samos under cover of night. They rescued their hostages and handed over the Athenian garrison to the Persians. They then resumed their war with Miletus.

On hearing the news Pericles wearily returned to Samos. He found that the islanders had raised their sights and were now determined to wrest command of the seas from Athens. But they were beaten in a naval engagement and Pericles laid siege to their capital, the port of Samos. The islanders were undaunted. They sallied out and fought under the city walls. But when reinforcements from Athens arrived the city was completely encircled.

The Persians seem to have been still supporting the rebels. Hearing that a Phoenician fleet was on its way to relieve the island, Pericles took sixty ships and sailed away to meet it. This was an incautious move, for the Samians, commanded (in the true Greek manner) by a philosopher, took advantage of his absence and the fewer Athenian ships, and put out to sea in a highly successful surprise attack. They captured the Athenian camp, which was unfortified, and took numerous prisoners, whose foreheads they branded with the symbol of Athena, the owl, and destroyed many enemy ships.

Pericles hurried back to the rescue and once more defeated the Samian fleet. To avoid continuing casualties, he built a wall around the city and settled down with his men to a long siege. Eventually after nine months the Samians surrendered. They were given a heavy fine, their fleet was confiscated, and the city walls were demolished; Byzantium then capitulated too. Plutarch mentions a report, only to dismiss it, that the Athenians acted with great brutality and crucified Samos's captains and marines in the main square of Miletus. But they had been given a bad fright, which tends to make men behave badly.

Thucydides believed that Samos came within an inch of depriving Athens of its command of the sea, but apparently his victory gave Pericles a prodigiously high opinion of himself. It had taken Agamemnon ten years to capture Troy, but (he reflected) he had reduced the greatest city of Ionia in less than one. It is hard to agree with him, for the campaign had been marked by one miscalculation after another.

Back home, Pericles presided over funeral honors for all those who had lost their lives in the war. He won high praise for the speech he delivered. For once he found a memorable phrase, which even today touches the heart. With the deaths of these young men, he said, it was "as if the spring had been taken out of the year."

As he stepped down from the speaker's rostrum, women mobbed him. They clasped his hand and crowned him with garlands and hair ribbons as if he were an athlete and had won a prize at the Games.

A sentry runs to the ruler of Thebes with bad news. Someone unknown has covered the corpse with dry dust where it lies in front of the city walls. It was the duty of a good Greek to bury the dead and a sprinkling of earth was the least he was obliged to do. Without this rite the unhappy spirit would be forever caught between the upper air and the underworld.

But, in the legendary story, King Creon had forbidden any such ceremony, he was so furious with the dead man. This was his nephew Polynices, who had led an invasion against his native city. His brother

Eteocles had patriotically commanded the defense. The invasion was repelled, but the two princes met in single combat and, as luck would have it, killed one another. Eteocles was awarded a full burial, but his sibling was left to the birds and the dogs.

It turned out that the illegal burier was the men's sister Antigone. She was hauled before the king and asked to explain herself. Their exchange sets the theme of a memorable tragedy by Sophocles, successor of Aeschylus and the leading Athenian playwright of the mid-fifth century.

Only seven of his plays have survived and this one, the *Antigone*, first performed about the time of the revolt of Samos, is a masterpiece. Sophocles was a public figure as well as an artist. He served as a national treasurer and fought as a general during the Samian campaign. His work displays an optimism, an intellectual curiosity, and honesty typical of the age of Pericles. It could only have been written under a democracy.

The chorus sings a justly famous hymn to the vitality of humankind.

> *Wonders are many on the earth, and the greatest of these*
> *Is man, who rides the ocean and takes his way*
> *Through the deeps . . .*
> *The use of language, the wind-swift motion of brain*
> *He learned; found out the laws of living together*
> *In cities . . .*
> *There is nothing beyond his power.*

Sophocles makes it clear that humanity is capable of evil as well as good. Overall, the portrait he paints bears a striking resemblance to his fellow-Athenians in their pomp.

The debate between Creon and his niece explores the proper limits of political power and the rights of the individual. It raised imagined issues for the *demos* that it had to answer for real.

The king asks if Antigone knew of his order not to bury Polynices. She replies that she did.

Creon.
> And yet you dared to contravene it?

Antigone.
> Yes.
> That order did not come from God. Justice,
> That dwells with the gods below, knows no such law.
> I did not think your edicts strong enough
> To overrule the unwritten, unalterable laws
> Of god and heaven.

Creon insists that the needs of the state take priority over the laws of conscience and condemns his niece to be buried alive in a cave. Eventually he is persuaded to relent, but too late. Antigone hangs herself. Creon's son, who is her fiancé, and his wife both commit suicide. The broken monarch staggers back into his empty palace.

Creon has been guilty of *hubris,* an offense that was regarded as a serious crime in Athens. It signified gratuitous harm inflicted by someone who is, or thinks he is, superior to and more powerful than his victim.

Sophocles draws no direct comparison with the life around him, but Creon's behavior echoes the pride and violence of some Athenian imperialists. His fate, the playwright means us to understand, was a lesson the victors of Samos would be wise to learn.

One woman in particular was pleased that the Samian crisis was over. This was the beautiful Aspasia. She was, allege the ancient sources, a high-class prostitute or *hetaira* (literally, a "female companion"). *Hetairai* were usually educated women who were expected to offer intellectual and emotional support to their patrons as well as sexual services.

The appellation was unfair or at least overstated, for Aspasia appears to have been born to a "good" family in the powerful *polis* of Miletus on the coast of Asia Minor. However, there is no doubt that she lived with Pericles as his mistress.

Public opinion blamed Aspasia for egging on Pericles to take the Milesian side against the Samians. We have no conclusive evidence, but it would be surprising if Aspasia did not raise the topic with her lover. On the other hand, Pericles was not the kind of man to mix politics with pillow talk. Whether Aspasia used her influence or not, the defeat of Samos meant some release from the imputations of scandal.

Mystery and slander surround Aspasia and the more we look the less we see. Nothing is quite as it appears. She was probably not born before 470, and so was twenty-five or so years the junior of Pericles. She may have moved in with him as early as 452 or 451. This was all highly irregular, and out of character for a well-conducted aristocrat.

To the conventional Greek, the female of the species was lethal to the male. She was sexually rapacious and needed to be kept under strict control. According to the eighth-century poet Hesiod, the first woman was invented by the gods as a living punishment.

> *From her comes all the race of womankind*
> *the deadly female race and tribe of wives*
> *who live with mortal men and bring them harm,*
> *no help to them in dreadful poverty*
> *but ready enough to share with them in wealth.*
> *... Women are bad for men, and they conspire*
> *In wrong.*

It is true that women had authority to manage their own households and that there were happy heterosexual relationships, Aspasia and Pericles being a case in point. For every murderous witch, such as Medea, who killed her children to punish her husband, there was a Penelope, the faithful, brave, and intelligent wife of Odysseus, who waited twenty years for her husband to return from Troy; or an Alcestis, who volunteered to die in place of her spouse. But the misogyny was pervasive. Greek society was indelibly sexist.

Marriages were usually arranged and were designed to advance a family's standing or to acquire property. To preserve an estate an heiress and only child would wed a close relative (she was known as an *epikleros,* or "a woman attached to the *kleros,* or estate"). The bride came with a dowry that was repayable in the event of divorce. Men often waited until they were more than thirty years old before marrying. Their wives could be as young as twelve.

An upper-class woman's chastity was very carefully guarded. She spent most of her time at home, supervising the household. She spun wool and made her husband's and her own clothes. When she went out shopping she would take care to be accompanied by servants and slaves. She attended religious festivals and funerals, which were among the few occasions when she might meet men outside the close family circle (her unavailability may help to explain the prevalence of pederasty among young men).

In his dialogue *The Estate Manager,* Xenophon has a husband give instructions to his new wife:

> ... your duty is to stay indoors. You must send out those servants who have outdoor jobs and supervise those who are working in the house. You must take in the produce that comes in from outside, and distribute or store it as necessary. When wool is delivered make sure that those who need clothes get them and that grain is made into edible provisions.

In spite of the fact that Pericles led an unconventional private life, he summed up the subordinate status of Athenian women in a funeral speech for war dead that he delivered in 431. Advising the men's widows, he said:

Perhaps I should say a few words about the duties of women . . .
the greatest glory of a woman is to be least talked about by men,
whether they are praising you or criticising you.

Men did not insist on sexual satisfaction from their wives. As the
great Athenian orator Demosthenes put it bluntly in the fourth century:

We have *hetairai* or mistresses for pleasure, an ordinary prostitute to service our bodies' daily needs, and wives so that we can
breed legitimate children and have trustworthy guardians of our
domestic possessions.

A marriage was a purely private affair and neither priests nor state
officials played any part in it. Weddings were often solemnized in the
depth of winter during the Greek month of Gamelion (January to
February). The bride dedicated a lock of her hair to the protectors of
marriage, Zeus and Hera, and pledged her childhood toys to the virgin
goddess Artemis (who heartily disapproved of sex and marriage and
needed to be placated).

On her wedding day the bride took a ritual bath in holy water and
then attended a banquet that her father gave for the two families and
their friends. She sat apart from the men alongside a duenna who
guided her through the ceremony. Little cakes covered in sesame seeds,
believed to make women fertile, were handed round. Towards sunset
the groom led his bride to her new home in a wagon drawn by mules
or oxen. They were preceded by a torchlight procession. Noisy wedding hymns were accompanied by flute and lyre. On arrival at the bride-
groom's house the happy couple were showered with nuts and dried
figs. They entered the bridal chamber and only then did the new wife
remove her veil. Outside the door, teenagers of both sexes sang a nup-
tial praise song, or *epithalamium* (literally "at the bedroom") loudly
enough to mask the woman's—or more often girl's—cries as her husband penetrated her.

...

The young Pericles obeyed convention, marrying an Alcmaeonid relative (possibly a woman called Deinomache, who later married the Cleinias who fell at Coronea). However, they were not a loving couple and, although they produced two sons, Xanthippus and Paralus, the marriage came to an end in the second half of the 450s.

The boys do not seem to have turned out well. Plato has Socrates hint that they were simpletons and Xanthippus, the firstborn, was on poor terms with his father. He felt that the allowance he received was insufficient (his wife was high-maintenance). Pericles was uninterested in money and, to avoid having to think about it when busy on public business, had an agent manage his estate. He preferred to watch it tick over rather than strain for large profits.

Xanthippus borrowed a substantial sum from one of Pericles' friends, pretending it was for his father. Pericles knew nothing about the matter until the friend asked for the sum to be repaid. The great man not only refused, but took his son to court. A furious Xanthippus told amusing and discreditable stories about life at home, making his father into a figure of fun.

The real reason for his divorce was that Pericles had fallen in love with Aspasia. This tale of a middle-aged man in his fifties shacking up with an attractive bimbo had satirical potential. The gossips of Athens and the city's comic poets made the most of it.

The allegation they put about was that the general's live-in lover had been a hooker. The well-known comedy writer Cratinus wrote:

To find our Zeus a Hera, the goddess of Vice
Produced that dog-eyed whore Aspasia for wife

"Dog-eyed" was a cruel parody of Hera's usual Homeric epithet, "ox-eyed." Aspasia was reported to be the madam of a brothel on the side, and procured freeborn Athenian women for Pericles (sex outside marriage with a freeborn Athenian woman was illegal and taboo).

However, there is another possibility. We know that Aspasia's father in Miletus was called Axiochus, a rare Greek personal name. There happens to have been another Axiochus in a branch of the Alcmaeonid family. He was the son of a man called Alcibiades. It seems likely that this Alcibiades, who was ostracized in 460, spent some or all of his exile in Miletus where (we may suppose) he married into Aspasia's family. In fact, he must have wed a daughter of Axiochus and a sister of our Aspasia. A son, we can reconstruct, was born of the union, who was named Axiochus in honor of the infant's Milesian grandfather, as was the Greek custom.

Now a gene-proud Alcmaeonid was highly unlikely to wed a prostitute, even a high-class one. So we must assume that Aspasia was a Milesian aristocrat, or at worst belonged to a respectable family. From Pericles' point of view she was a family friend and all the stories about her disreputable sexuality were libels put about by his enemies or were inventions of the Athenian stage.

Whatever her origin, there *was* something bold and out of the ordinary about Aspasia. Being a foreigner, she was free from the social restrictions placed on Athenian women and was able to lead something like a public life. She was intelligent and Plutarch pointed to the "great art and power this woman had, that allowed her to manage as she pleased the foremost statesmen of the age and even gave philosophers a theme for lengthy and high-minded debates."

This is nothing less than the truth. Socrates knew her well and apparently recommended a wealthy friend of his to send his son to study politics under Aspasia's guidance (perhaps here we have the twisted origin of the brothel-keeping libel). Plato has the philosopher credit her with writing Pericles' speeches for him:

Yesterday I heard Aspasia composing a funeral oration for the fallen. For she had been told, as you were saying, that the Athenians were going to choose a speaker, and she repeated to me the sort of speech which he should deliver, partly improvising and partly from previous thought, putting together fragments of the funeral oration which Pericles spoke, but which, as I believe, she composed.

Ancient sources present her as a female Socrates who applied his celebrated technique of conversational cross-examination to her friends.

These stories may well be exaggerations and jokes, we cannot tell. But Aspasia was evidently a remarkable personality. Displays of emotion between the sexes were felt to be embarrassing and unmanly, but we know that Pericles loved her and was willing to show it to the world. It was reported that when he left for work every day in the *agora* and when he returned home he gave her a kiss. To an Athenian, this verged on the improper and the ridiculous. However fine Aspasia's mind, we may guess that their relationship was fundamentally erotic and emotional.

Another unexpected person, a three-year-old baby this time, joined the household of Pericles. This was a grandson of the Alcibiades who had married (I conjecture) into the Milesian family of Aspasia. His elder son, Cleinias, as we have seen, lost his life at Coronea in 447, leaving behind an infant orphan, called Alcibiades after his paternal grandfather. Members of the Alcmaeonid clan looked after one another when trouble struck; Pericles and his brother were appointed the boy's guardians, and Pericles took him in and brought him up.

Little Alcibiades proved to be a handful. He was strikingly good-looking. According to Plutarch,

regarding his beauty, we need only say that it flowered at every season of his bodily growth in turn, and gave him grace and charm, alike as a boy, a youth and a man.

He was badly spoiled and became used to getting his own way. Once as a small boy he was playing knucklebones in the narrow street with some friends. Just when his turn came to make a throw, a loaded wagon approached. Alcibiades ordered the driver to stop as his dice had fallen in its path. The driver took no notice, but urged his team on. The other boys scattered out of the way, but Alcibiades threw himself down on his face in front of the horses, stretched out his body, and told the man to drive over him if he cared to. The driver lost his nerve and pulled up. Shocked bystanders ran across and grabbed the child.

As he entered his teens Alcibiades became a scandalous role model for his contemporaries. Although a reasonably conscientious student he refused point-blank to learn to play the flute. His explanation was that, unlike the lyre, it distorts the face and makes it ugly. "Leave the flute to the Thebans," he said in a reference to a stock *polis* of stupid foreigners. "They don't have the slightest idea of how to hold a conversation."

Alcibiades was athletic, but too competitive not to cheat. When hard-pressed in wrestling he set his teeth into his opponent's arm so hard that he nearly bit through it. The boy let go his hold and complained that he cheated because he was weak: "Alcibiades, you bite like a woman." "No, like a lion," came the reply.

A malicious, but not necessarily untrue, report suggests that the arrival of puberty and numerous male lovers made matters worse. He ran away from home to stay with one of his admirers. It was suggested that the town crier should announce his disappearance. Pericles stayed cool and said no. "If he's dead, we'll merely get the news a day sooner. If he's alive, he'll have lost his reputation for good." The boy was no respecter of persons. Once he came across his guardian looking worried and asked him what the matter was. Pericles said: "I'm trying to work out how to produce a statement of public accounts." Alcibiades replied: "You should not be bothering about how to produce such a statement—but how not to."

Socrates took Alcibiades under his wing and introduced him to philosophy. Plain-living and ugly, he was a merciless friend. He told the young man awkward truths, unlike the flatterers who surrounded him, and constantly pointed out his moral weaknesses. Nobody had treated Alcibiades like that before and he was entranced. Socrates made no concessions and his reproaches often reduced the boy to tears.

Handsome teenagers attracted much attention and a youth such as Alcibiades was expected to play a highly visible role in the city's lavish festivals.

Every fourth December in the depth of winter, the priestesses of Athena and four little girls of high birth set up a loom on which a new tunic, or *peplos*, was to be woven—a gift for Athena, the all-wise protector of the city. They worked on it with help from some women weavers, or *ergastinae*. The material, a simple rectangle six and a half by five feet, was embroidered with the splendid and brave deeds of the goddess and, in particular, featured the great war of the Giants who fought Zeus and the new Olympian deities for control of the universe.

Nine months later in the heat of August the garment was ready for delivery. This was the time of the Great Panathenaea, the quadrennial festival in honor of the goddess. First, there were poetry and music contests, introduced by Pericles. Men and boys sang to the lyre and the flute. Athletic competitions, on the model of the Olympic Games, followed in the *agora*, where Cimon had planted plane trees to give welcome shade for spectators.

The first four days of the festival were open to foreigners, but the fifth was restricted to the ten Athenian tribes. A popular event was a male beauty contest, the *euandria*, in which the tribes competed for a generous prize of 100 drachmas and an ox (most victorious athletes at the games were only awarded an amphora, or large two-handled jar, filled with olive oil). Male beauty was highly prized in ancient Greece and not merely among boys and youths, but also men in the prime of life. Old men too were chosen for their handsome looks and were selected to carry an olive branch, sacred to Athena, in the ceremony that brought the Panathenaea to an end. Another team event was the Pyrrhic Dance, in which youths, naked except for helmets, shields, and unbated swords, mimicked the offensive and defensive moves of battle—and sometimes accidentally cut one another.

Nighttime festivities were held during which choirs of boys and girls sang and teams of runners competed in a torch relay race. On the following and final day, a long procession formed to carry the new tunic up to the Acropolis and clothe an ancient wooden statue of the goddess. Crowds gathered before dawn at the Double-Arched or Dipylon Gate. The *peplos* was conveyed in a life-sized ship, which was wheeled along at the head of the cavalcade. A long train of women carried gifts. Victors at Greece's various games were present, and so were the winners of the male beauty contests. Leading citizens, priests and priestesses, musicians, bearded elders and army commanders holding olive branches, young cavalrymen with their horses, charioteers, *metics* in their scarlet cloaks who carried trays of cakes and honey as offerings, all proceeded singing hymns to Athena along the Panathenaic Way, a broad street leading from one of the city gates via the *agora* to the Acropolis. Ordinary citizens assembled in their *demes* and brought up the rear.

Sacrifices were offered en route. The *peplos* was taken from the ship up the steep slope to the Acropolis. There the little girls handed the tunic to the women weavers, who carried the wooden divinity down to the seashore where they washed both it and the tunic. After further sacrifices, the *ergastinae* dressed the statue in the new *peplos*. The proceedings ended with a feast attended by invitees chosen by lot from each *deme* in Attica. They ate the cooked meat of the sacrificed animals together with bread and cakes.

In each of the three years between festivals a smaller celebration was staged for citizens only, but the Great Panathenaea with its athletic and arts contests open to all spread the name of Athens throughout the Greek world.

. . .

It was a pity that the city looked such a mess. The state buildings in the marketplace were adequate to purpose, but no one would call them grand or well suited to the capital of an empire. The Athenians were as good as their word when they and the other allies had sworn their famous oath before the culminating victory over the Persians at Plataea thirty years previously.

According to one of its clauses, they had vowed not to rebuild any of the burned and demolished temples but to leave them as a memorial. The only new monument to the war was a colossal bronze statue of Athena Promachus ("she who fights in the front line"), which stood on the Acropolis about thirty feet high and could be seen by sailors at sea. It was created by the internationally known sculptor, painter, and architect Pheidias. Otherwise, the Athenian citadel remained a plateau of broken and blackened marble debris.

The peace treaty with the Persians of 449 changed the mood. Pericles moved that the oath of Plataea be rescinded. Once the Delian League members had been bullied and cajoled into obedience again and resumed their annual payments for maritime protection, Athens found that it was becoming richer and richer. The reserve fund had grown from nothing in 478 to 9,700 talents, when it was transferred from the island of Delos to Athens in 454. The end of the war boosted trade, the silver from Laurium continued to flow into the treasury, and in the absence of an enemy it was no longer necessary to dispatch large fleets to sea. In quiet years the Athenians only sent out a flotilla of sixty ships.

The *demos,* guided by the Olympian, decided to go on a spending spree. They would rebuild all the temples, not only those in the city, but across Attica. The end of the war had driven up unemployment and this massive construction program would not only beautify the city, but also create many jobs. However, there was opposition. Thucydides, son of Melesias (not the historian), who was an aristocrat and a relative of Cimon, led the conservative faction in the *ecclesia*. He developed the clever tactic of getting his supporters to sit together at assembly meetings in one bloc and to react and applaud in unison—a first step towards a political party. According to Plutarch, they argued:

> . . . the Greeks must be outraged. They must consider this an act of bare-faced tyranny. They can see that, with their own money, extorted from them for the war against the Persians, we are gilding and adorning our city, as if it were some vain woman doing herself up with precious stones and statues and temples worth millions of money.

Thucydides felt that Pericles shaped his policy to bribe citizens with benefits, constantly giving them pageants, banquets, and processions and "entertaining the people with cultural delights."

Pericles acted decisively. Using his in-built majority in the *ecclesia,* in 443 he arranged for Thucydides to be ostracized. For the time being that put an end to carping about the *grands projets* that were to occupy the Olympian's attention for the next twenty years. History hears no more of Thucydides, who is reported to have settled in a Greek city in southern Italy.

Pheidias was placed in overall charge of the Athenian building program and Pericles seems to have collaborated closely with him. Distinguished architects were hired for specific developments as well as a large team of first-rate sculptors. The work proceeded at great speed and many different kinds of business and craft skills were in high demand, as Plutarch reports:

> The materials to be used were stone, bronze, ivory, gold, ebony and cypress-wood, while the skilled labor needed to work these materials up were those of carpenter, moulder, coppersmith, stone mason, dyer, worker in gold and ivory, painter, embroiderer, and engraver, and in addition the carriers and suppliers of

the materials, such as merchants, sailors, and pilots for maritime traffic, and cartwrights, trainers of draft animals, and drivers of everything that came by land. There were also rope-makers, weavers, leather-workers, road-builders and miners.

In one way or another much of the city's workforce was involved.

An inscription survives that lists sculptors of the Erechtheum and their earnings. Built between 421 and 406, this complicated little structure, also on the Acropolis, replaced a destroyed archaic temple of Athena, with shrines to various divinities and divine heroes, and was the home of the wooden statue of Athena. They include:

> To Praxias, resident at Melite [a city *deme*], for the horse and the man seen behind it who is turning it—120 drachmas.

> To Mynnion, resident of Agryle [a *deme* on Mount Hymettus], for the horse and the man striking it. He afterwards added the pillar (for which he was paid a little more)—127 drachmas.

The Acropolis was transformed. Intended to rival the temples of Artemis of the Ephesians and of Hera on Samos, the Parthenon, a huge brand-new edifice, was one of the first construction projects and was completed in 443/2. It was made entirely from local Pentelic marble, which takes on a golden tint in sunlight, and was in the Doric style. Wide fluted columns stood without a base directly on the flat platform (the *stylobate*) on which the temple was built and were topped by plain stone slabs. The temple was decorated with sculptures painted in bright colors. Their purpose was educational as well as aesthetic, for they celebrated contests of Lapiths and Centaurs, Greeks and Amazons, Gods and Giants, all of them symbols of the triumph of civilization over barbarism. On the triangular pediments at either end of the temple the birth of Athena was displayed and the rivalry between the goddess and her uncle Poseidon for the right to be the patron deity of the city.

Inside the colonnade were two large windowless inner chambers. High up on the outside of their walls a long frieze, depicting the Panathenaeic procession, ran around the temple; sacred shrines were usually reserved for gods and heroes, but here ordinary Athenians were depicted. The larger of the rooms, the *cella,* was the home of a forty-foot-tall statue of Athena Parthenos, the virgin goddess, created by Pheidias. Her flesh was represented by ivory (because of the dry atmosphere this had to be regularly dampened with water) and her full-length tunic by molded gold plates (in total the gold weighed a little more than one ton and belonged to the Athenian treasury; it could be removed for use in a financial crisis). Gleaming in the gloom, Athena was an awe-inspiring sight.

The temple was beautifully constructed, with refinements often invisible to the human eye. Its horizontal lines curve slightly upwards to avoid an optical impression of sagging, the columns bend and tilt inwards, which creates a sense of height and grandeur, the corner columns thicken so that they stand out when seen against the sky. These modifications are barely perceptible, but they give the building greater presence.

It must be remembered that Greek sculpture did not look as it does today, plain unvarnished marble or bronze. It was painted in brilliant colors. Traces of red, blue, and yellow paint have been found on the Parthenon. So, for example, the background of the *metopes* (square spaces let into the marble lintels that lie on top of the temple pillars, on which carved reliefs were displayed) appears to have been blue or red. The skin color of males was usually a ruddy brown and of females, white. The overall effect was bright, if not gaudy.

The Parthenon was not simply a monument to victory, it was also a storehouse for state valuables. In the smaller back chamber the income from the league was stored and all kinds of trophy and valuable oddments were kept in the *cella*. These included a gold crown, five gold libation bowls, two nails of gilded silver, six Persian daggers, a Gorgon mask, twelve stalks of golden wheat, thirty-one bronze shields, seven

Chian couches, ten Milesian couches, miscellaneous swords, breastplates, six thrones, and various musical instruments. The treasurers who provided this inventory in 434/3 also noted without comment "eight and a half boxes of rotten and useless arrows."

The next building to be constructed on the Acropolis was a new monumental entrance, the Propylaea (literally "that which is before the gate" or more generally "the gate building"). The visitor climbed broad steps up to a stone façade that looked like an echo of the Parthenon, with six columns and a pediment. He entered a large covered porch through which he stepped out onto the Acropolis. A little way off to the right the Parthenon towered.

Other new shrines worth noting include the tiny temple of Nike, or Victory, perched on the edge of the Acropolis next to the Propylaea (it was tended by a priestess for an adequate part-time salary of fifty drachmas a year). It is in the Ionic style with elegantly slender fluted pillars surmounted by a carved capital resembling ram's horns. Also built in the fifth century are a very well-preserved temple on the edge of the *agora,* in honor of Hephaestus, the god of blacksmiths, artisans, and sculptors, where he and his half sister Athena were worshipped, and a temple of Poseidon on the headland of Sunium. Like the Parthenon, these were both in the heavier Doric style.

Not all public spending was dedicated to temples and statues of the gods. The *polis* also supported secular and social projects. It had once been natural in the days of Cimon to look to the great aristocratic families for patronage, but the city's democratic rulers believed it was now their role to make life easier for citizens at state expense. New amenities such as gymnasia and baths were opened to all. Perhaps the most striking of these developments was a concert hall for music events. This was the Odeum, next to the theater of Dionysus, and it was designed to accommodate the music competitions during the Panathenaea. A large square building with a pitched roof rising to a single point and supported by ninety columns, it echoed the design of Xerxes' great war tent, which had been brought to Athens after the battle of Plataea.

The exact total expenditure on these public works throughout Attica is unknown, but was very considerable. Most of it was drawn from the league reserve. Some badly fragmented inscriptions of accounts survive, from which we learn that the gold and ivory statue of Athena cost between 700 and 1,000 talents. The Parthenon that housed it may have cost about 500 talents. To offer a military comparison, the war against Samos and Byzantium cost 1,400 talents.

The *demos* was proud of what it had achieved, and so was its leader. By the end of the 430s, Athens enjoyed a visual splendor that set it apart from the rest of mainland Greece, and especially from its great competitor Sparta and the collection of dim little villages that made up its capital. Its impotent "allies" could only look on as their Athenian hegemon spent *their* money on its magnificence.

Pericles well understood the importance of "soft power" and of Athens as a visitor destination. He advocated an open society. Unlike the introverted rigidities of the Spartan system and the impenetrable labyrinth of the Persian court, his city made a point of being readily accessible to all. Secrecy was discouraged so far as possible, even in matters of war and peace where an enemy might be able to gain an advantage by foreknowledge. Spies were welcome.

Thucydides puts into the mouth of Pericles opinions the great man held even if the historian gave him the words. "Mighty indeed are the marks and monuments of our empire which we have left. Future ages will marvel at us, as our present age marvels at us now." A politician's rhetoric usually has a short shelf life, but the judgment of posterity shows that on this occasion the speaker turned out to be telling the plain truth. The city became a masterpiece.

The great fifth-century poet Pindar evoked the glamour of Athens to his fellow-Greeks in less abstract terms. He will have done so with some reluctance, for he was a man of Thebes in Boeotia and so ought to have been an inveterate enemy of the ambitious new imperial power. But he found an unforgettable if mysterious phrase, when he wrote in praise of Pericles' extraordinary *polis:*

Brightly shining and crowned with violets and beloved of poets
The bastion of Greece, famous Athens, god-favoured city.

What did he mean by "crowned with violets"? Pindar died before the city's architectural rebirth and was perhaps inspired by the spectacular dawns and sunsets of Attica's dry and dusty air. The glowing paintwork of the temple sculptures only enhanced the atmospheric glories of the Acropolis. Athens was the *ville lumière* of the ancient world.

THE
GREAT WAR

———

17

———

The Prisoners on the Island

In the 430s, the politics of Athens began to change. For the time being we hear no more of disgruntled noblemen who were always carping at the democracy. A new breed of politician emerged and Pericles found that, to use the jargon of modern politics, he had enemies on the left rather than, as usual, on the right.

These were men of the middling sort, who had made their fortunes as traders or manufacturers. They rose to prominence on merit and by giving well-received speeches in the *ecclesia* or the law courts. They were fully committed to the democracy; they just wanted more of it. They were hawkish in foreign affairs and criticized Pericles for being over-cautious in his policy towards Sparta and the Peloponnesians. One of their number was Cleon, probably the son of a wealthy leather merchant and tanner. He was a pushy, able, and lucky political improviser, whom Thucydides described as being remarkable "for the violence of his character." Respectable opinion at the time disapproved of him and history too has been unkind. Aristotle (or one of his students) commented:

more than anyone else he corrupted the people by his wild impulses. He was the first man who, when on the speaker's platform [at *ecclesia* meetings on the Pnyx], shouted, uttered abuse and made speeches with his clothes hitched up [so that he could move about more easily], while everybody else spoke in an orderly manner.

During this decade, a series of prosecutions against the associates of Pericles was brought. Their purpose was to destabilize his position and we may suppose that they originated in this new opposition. According to Plutarch, one of the sculptors working for Pheidias accused him of embezzlement in regard to the statue of Athena in the Parthenon. Pericles ordered that the gold plates attached to the sculpture be removed and weighed. It was found that the weight was correct and no gold was missing. Pheidias was also accused of having sacrilegiously or at least improperly carved a self-portrait among the figures on the goddess's shield and, half hidden, a likeness of Pericles.

It would appear that Pheidias was acquitted or else fled the country. He is next heard of at Olympia where he created for the temple of Zeus a colossal chryselephantine statue of the god enthroned. It was listed among the Seven Wonders of the World in tourist guidebooks of the second and first centuries B.C. By a remarkable chance the remains of Pheidias's workshop at Olympia have been found. Pieces of ivory, tools, and terra-cotta molds have been recovered, and a mug inscribed "I belong to Pheidias." The floor plan is the same size as that of the temple's *cella* and is where the statue was assembled.

Opponents of Pericles ventured even closer to home. They attacked Aspasia. Although we do not know the details, she faced two charges: impiety and pimping freeborn women for Pericles (unless the latter offense qualified as impiety). Prejudice against her, especially in the light of rumors about her role during the Samian revolt, meant that a fair trial might be difficult. Pericles was so alarmed that he came to court in person and, breaking down in tears, pleaded, successfully, for his lover's acquittal.

As we have seen, the Olympian and his circle had a reputation for advanced thinking, which offended religious conservatives. In 438 a certain Diopeithes, whose head was well stocked with ancient prophecies, introduced a law to the effect that "anyone who did not believe in the gods or taught theories about celestial phenomena" should be prosecuted. He presumably had Pericles in mind.

Probably in 437/6 Pericles' friend the scientist Anaxagoras was charged with impiety by Cleon and it appears that Pericles defended him in person. He narrowly avoided the death penalty, was fined five talents and expelled from Athens. He ended his days teaching at the city of Lampsacus on the Hellespont.

The real target now came under direct fire. The *ecclesia* approved a bill instructing Pericles to make his public financial accounts available to the *boulē* (lucky that he had paid no attention to the advice of young Alcibiades on the subject of accounts) and, under an unusual religious procedure likely to ensure a conviction, to answer a charge of stealing sacred property. However, an amendment was passed to have the case heard before a jury of ordinary citizens, who had long admired and trusted Pericles. An acquittal could now be confidently expected and no more was heard of the accusation.

So the Olympian rode out the attacks on his leadership. Having followed his guidance for more than two decades, the *demos* was not about to abandon him now. But these domestic dissensions coincided with, and may have been caused by, a deteriorating international situation. Sparta and its Peloponnesian allies had been watching with alarm the rising power of Athens. For a long time they were unsure how to counter it, but a drift towards war was increasingly evident—although, as one was a land power and the other a sea power, it was hard to see how it could be waged.

Thucydides had little doubt that a breakdown in relations was inevitable. In the fifty years since the Persian Wars, he writes, the Athenians

succeeded in placing the empire on a firmer footing and greatly added to their own power. The Spartans were fully aware of what was happening, but only opposed it for a little while and remained inactive for most of the period. They were always slow to take up arms and in any case were hampered by wars at home. In the end, the growth of Athenian power could not be ignored when it began to encroach on their allies. At this point they could no longer tolerate the situation.

Pericles did not want war, but he too believed it was coming and had a plan for fighting it. Since the debacle in Egypt and the collapse of the land empire, he had discouraged any further foreign adventures. In the coming conflict with Sparta and her Peloponnesian allies he wanted to avoid needless risks and did his best to delay hostilities. He ran a secret fund of ten talents a year; officially it was "for sundry purposes," but in fact he spent it in Lacedaemon on calming key personalities.

Looking ahead, he developed a strategy that he said would guarantee victory. Sparta could field a large confederate army of thirty thousand first-rate hoplites without counting reserves, to which Athens could only respond with thirteen thousand (an additional sixteen thousand were needed for various garrisons and the defense of the city itself). So there was no point offering battle on land. The Spartans were likely to invade Attica and they should not be resisted. Farmers and their households were to abandon their fields and retire behind the city's defenses, which included the Long Walls to the Piraeus and could easily resist any siege. Command of the seas would ensure food imports. The city would not starve. In a sense, Pericles was offering a rerun of the policy of Themistocles during the Persian Wars—abandon the land and rely on the navy.

Athens's strength did indeed lie in its ships and their well-trained oarsmen. In addition to flotillas contributed by league members Lesbos and Chios, it had three hundred triremes of its own. Most crew members were probably Athenian citizens, but there were not enough of them to man the fleet and many were recruited from the Greek islands. Of the Peloponnesian alliance only Corinth had a fleet, but it was small, inexperienced, and outclassed.

Pericles said of his fellow-citizens: "If they bide their time, look after their navy, refrain from trying to add to the empire during wartime and do nothing to put their city at risk, they will prevail." In 434/3 strict limits were set on public expenditure and the city's finances were placed on a war footing. In the Parthenon treasury there were substantial reserves of coined silver. "If the worst came to the worst," he added, "they will even be able to use the gold on the statue of Athena herself."

According to Pericles, Sparta would give up on any war long before Athens ran out of money. Provided that the *demos* was patient, victory or at least a safe draw with few casualties was more or less guaranteed.

Epidamnus was a place of no importance, but it lit the greatest military conflagration of the age.

Built on the slope of a hill that descends into a picturesque valley, the *polis* enjoyed a superb setting and commanded one of the largest harbors on the eastern coastline of the Ionian Sea (today it is Durres in Albania). High stone walls protected the city. However, it was off the beaten track and on the way to nowhere. Its inhabitants traded with native Illyrian tribes in the hinterland. They bartered Greek goods such as pottery, weapons, fabrics, and furniture in return for foodstuffs, wood, pitch, copper, and slaves. Epidamnus remotely thrived.

Or it would have done so were it not politically unstable. The city lost a war with the Illyrians and entered a time of political and economic decline. Then, shortly before 435 there was a democratic revolution and the aristocratic ruling families were expelled. They made common cause with neighboring tribes and launched a series of piratical attacks on their own homeland. It looked as if civil war would destroy the city.

Epidamnus had been founded, or as the Greeks put it, "colonized" by the island of Corcyra, a maritime *polis* lower down the coast. It boasted a fleet of 120 triremes, which, most unusually, it maintained in peacetime. It was the region's most formidable sea power after Athens. As we have seen, from the eighth century new Hellenic communities had been established around the Mediterranean in large numbers. Unlike modern colonies, they were independent of their mother *polis,* but were expected to be respectful, friendly, and cooperative. They might ask it for help in time of trouble.

This is what the citizens of Epidamnus did. They sent an embassy to Corcyra that begged for support in negotiating a peace with the old regime outside their gates. But the Corcyraeans refused even to listen to the envoys. Not knowing what to do, the Epidamnians asked the oracle at Delphi for advice. The god advised them to apply to the rich mercantile state of Corinth, the founder of Corcyra and so the "grandmother" of Epidamnus.

This guidance was thoroughly irresponsible, for the international experts at Delphi must have known that Corinth and Corcyra were not on speaking terms. The islanders looked down on their founder, claiming that they were much stronger militarily and that their wealth put them on a level with the greatest Hellenic states.

The Corinthians were delighted to disoblige their colony and sent a force of soldiers and volunteer settlers from various different *poleis,* who rescued the democratic regime at Epidamnus from its attackers. They had no strategic interests at stake and their motive was simply to annoy Corcyra. In this they succeeded, only too well.

In a furious reaction the island *polis* sent forty warships to besiege Epidamnus and proposed that the quarrel be put out to arbitration. The Corinthians refused and with help from their allies assembled seventy-five warships and two thousand hoplites. With their remaining eighty triremes the Corcyraeans met the Corinthian fleet and routed it off the headland of Actium. Epidamnus surrendered and the aristocracy was restored.

No mercy was shown the defeated: all the soldiers and settlers sent by Corinth were executed except for Corinthian citizens, who were kept on as prisoners and bargaining counters. Corcyra now commanded the Ionian Sea and sailed around damaging the allies of Corinth.

Feelings ran high in Corinth and the authorities there could not just let matters rest. They spent the next two years building warships and recruiting crews in the Peloponnese. The Corcyraeans heard of this and panicked. They had no allies of their own and unlike Corinth were not members of the formidable Peloponnesian confederation. Where could they find a powerful friend? There was only one feasible answer—Athens.

So in 433 a Corcyraean embassy made its way to Athens to seek support. The Corinthians got wind of this and were alarmed. They instantly sent an embassy of their own. Both of them put their respective cases to the *ecclesia*. A decision would not be easy. According to the terms of the Thirty Years Peace, a signatory was entitled to ally itself with any state that was not already affiliated either to the Spartans or to the Athenians. But common sense argued that it would be against the spirit of the treaty, if not the letter, for one side to ally itself with a state such as Corcyra that was already at war with a member of the other.

At first sight the affair was a local one and should have been of little interest to Athens. The *demos* was not spoiling for a fight and the Corinthians hoped for an abstention. As it turned out, the *ecclesia* voted to help Corcyra. On mature consideration, there was a good reason for this unexpected outcome. If there was one thing Athens could not permit it was a shift in the maritime balance of power, and that was what a large new Corinthian fleet signified.

However, the *ecclesia* did not go the whole way. After two debates it decided on a policy of minimum deterrence and offered no more than a defensive alliance. Athens would fight Corinth only if it attacked Corcyra and ordered a token squadron of ten triremes to sail to the island. To reassure the Peloponnesians, Lacedaemonius, son of the pro-Spartan Cimon, was appointed its commander. This was certainly an attempt to avoid breaching the treaty and we may detect the hand of Pericles behind these dispositions. He would do what he could to avoid war, or at least the blame for war.

Events now followed their course. A large Corinthian fleet of 150 triremes, the result of all that preparation, sailed against 110 Corcyraeans. The Corcyraeans were worsted, so the Athenian flotilla intervened. Mystifyingly the Corinthians then withdrew. An explanation soon presented itself; the *ecclesia* had had second thoughts and twenty additional Athenian triremes had appeared on the horizon as reinforcements. Discretion being the better part of valor, the Corinthians returned home the next day. On their way they captured a Corcyraean colony, Anactorium, a place in the Ambracian Gulf, and installed settlers.

The international crisis deepened. Corinth turned its anger from Corcyra to Athens and Pericles decided he needed to take precautionary measures on the peninsula of Chalcidice in the northwestern Aegean. This was an important staging post on the way to the Black Sea and all its cities were members of the Delian League.

Unfortunately, one of these was a Corinthian colony called Potidaea. Athens ordered it to pull down some of its fortifications and to abolish its practice of appointing Corinthian officials. It refused and revolted. Prompted by the neighboring king of Macedon, all Chalcidice followed suit. Corinth, anxious not to be seen to break the peace, recruited an international "volunteer" corps to help the rebels. Athens sent out an expeditionary force, won a battle against the Potidaeans and the volunteers, and placed the city under siege.

The situation was delicate. Pericles took what he saw as a diplomatic step that, without the threat of violence, would warn off allies of Corinth and Sparta from interfering in Athens's business. The little state of Megara, friendly to Corinth on its western frontier, had been for many years on extremely bad terms with its much bigger eastern neighbor, Athens. The *ecclesia* passed a decree excluding Megarian ships and goods from all ports in the Athenian empire. For an exporter of cheap woolen goods around the Mediterranean the embargo would bring economic collapse.

Pericles probably intended his démarche to calm the situation, but in fact the effect was incendiary. Ten years later the comic writer Aristophanes set out the common opinion of how the war between Athens and Sparta began. In his play *Peace* the god Hermes is asked who caused the war. He replies that Pericles was frightened that he would follow his friends and associates and face prosecution in the courts.

> Before anything could happen to him, he threw a little spark into the City marked "Megarian Decree" and in a moment it was all ablaze, with him fanning the flames, and the smoke drew tears from the eyes of every Greek, at home or abroad . . . nobody could halt the disaster and Peace just vanished.

The notion that Pericles started the war only for personal reasons is highly implausible. However, it is true that politicians have been known to elide personal and public motives for action. The waning of his popularity may have formed the background to a hardening of Pericles' foreign policy. Adventures abroad are often popular with voters.

The cautious Spartans were not bellicose and, for the avoidance of doubt, they sent to Delphi to ask the god whether it would be wise for them to go to war. Apollo replied that if they fought with all their might they would win, and that he would be on their side—a surprisingly firm prediction (did money change hands?). Then in autumn 432 they convened a conference to discuss the deteriorating international situation and to decide if Athens had broken the Thirty Years Peace. Although Corinth and Megara complained bitterly about their treatment, it was not altogether clear that it had done so. If anyone was guilty of a breach it was Corinth, which had meddled more or less openly in Chalcidice.

But the fact was that both sides were insensibly edging towards war, whatever the wishes of the politicians. Some Athenians happened to be in Sparta ostensibly on other business and won leave to speak. They made no concessions to their audience. Thucydides has them say: "We have done nothing extraordinary, nothing against the way of the world, in accepting an empire when it was offered to us—and then in refusing to give it up."

The Spartans asked everyone else to withdraw and considered the matter among themselves. King Archidamus, who was a personal friend of Pericles and a moderate, advised caution, but a hardline *ephor,* Sthenilaidas, disagreed: "Others may have a lot of money and ships and horses, but we have good allies, and we ought not to betray them to the Athenians." As with elections, serious decisions at Sparta were decided in assembly by acclamation. Those who shouted loudest won the decision. In this case the roar was for war.

The Spartans then issued an ultimatum that they knew could not be accepted. Remembering that Pericles was an Alcmaeonid, they told Athens to drive out the "Cylonian pollution." In other words, they were to exile the family of Megacles, who had massacred the supporters of Cylon in the seventh century (see page 55). The Athenians repaid the compliment by calling on the Spartans to expel the "curse of Taenarum"; some suppliant *helots* had been sacrilegiously forced from sanctuary in the temple of Poseidon at Cape Taenarum in the southern Peloponnese and executed.

Neither side budged. The Hellenic world gathered its forces for a letting of blood. Fourteen years had passed since the Thirty Years Peace had been agreed.

Preparations against the invasion of Attica by a Peloponnesian army went ahead. Valuable artifacts from countryside shrines were moved to the Acropolis, and sheep and cattle were transferred to Euboea and other islands off the coast. People brought their movable property into the city. The disruption was unpopular, according to Thucydides:

Most Athenians still lived in the country with their families and households and as a result were not at all inclined to move, especially as they had only just re-established themselves after the Persian invasion. It was anxiously and resentfully that they now abandoned their homes and the time-honoured temples of their historic past, that they prepared to change their whole way of life.

Some of the rural incomers had houses of their own in the city and others were able to stay with friends. But most had to settle down on land that had not been built over or in temples and shrines (although not on the Acropolis, which was out of bounds). There was terrible overcrowding.

The first hostilities—and another glaring violation of the peace—were the siege of the valiant little town of Plataea by Thebes; as we have seen, this longtime ally of Athens distinguished itself in the battle of the same name, which saw off the Persians in 479. The Plataeans resisted the Thebans, but in 427 following an attack by the Peloponnesians they surrendered, not before reminding their conquerors that, in the aftermath of the battle, the Spartan general Pausanias had decreed that Plataea was holy ground and should never be attacked.

"You will get no glory, Spartans, from such behavior—not for breaking the common law of the Hellenes, nor for sinning against your ancestors, nor for killing us, who have done you good service," Thucydides has a Plataean spokesman tell the Spartans. Nevertheless, their commander had all his prisoners put to death. Some two hundred Plataeans had escaped earlier and were given Athenian citizenship in compensation for the loss of their *polis*.

For most Athenians the reality of war only struck home in the last days of May 431 when the corn was ripe. King Archidamus led a huge army of about sixty thousand heavy infantry into Attica, albeit without much enthusiasm. In case Archidamus spared his estate, whether out of genuine friendship or to make mischief, Pericles made it over to the *polis*. Meanwhile, tit for tat, an Athenian fleet sailed round the Peloponnese ravaging coastal settlements. The old rival, Aegina, was ethnically cleansed. The inhabitants were driven out and replaced by Athenian settlers. The island was annexed.

These were minor victories when compared to the psychological impact of the invasion of Attica. This was far greater than the actual damage done. Citizens were outraged at having to watch their farms being torched while being forbidden to offer any resistance (although some Thessalian cavalry were sent out to do what they could to harry the enemy).

Pericles remained certain of the rightness of his war strategy, but could see that the *demos* was furious with him for not leading them out to fight the Peloponnesians. So he took care not to summon the *ecclesia* in case "a general discussion resulted in incorrect decisions being taken."

On a winter's day every year a ceremony was held in honor of the glorious dead. It must have held a special meaning in 431, the first year of the war. The bones of those who had fallen were brought into a tent where relatives could make offerings in their honor. They were then placed in cypress coffins, one for each of the ten tribes. For those whose remains had not been recovered an empty bier was provided.

Two days later a procession of wagons, carrying one coffin apiece, made its way to the Cerameicus suburb that lay just outside the city's Dipylon or Double Gate. Here was the public burial place where all the city's military dead were interred, with the exception of the men killed at Marathon: their achievement was so signal that they were buried with full honors on the battlefield itself.

Once the bones had been laid to rest, a distinguished citizen was invited to deliver an oration in praise of the fallen. This year Pericles was chosen and, at a crisis in the city's affairs, he delivered a ringing encomium of Athens itself and its values. It must have lifted morale and, in the hands of Thucydides, the speech as it has come down to us was a literary masterpiece.

At the heart of the Athenian achievement, Pericles claimed, lay its democratic constitution.

When it is a question of settling private disputes, everyone is equal before the law; as for social standing, what counts is not membership of a particular class but a person's ability. Class is not allowed to interfere with merit, nor is poverty an obstacle. If a man is qualified for public service, his humble origins will not count against him.

Pericles extended the principle of meritocracy to an Athenian's private life. Provided he obeyed the law, he could do as he liked. The city was culturally rich and commercially, too, for it imported the world's produce.

We are lovers of beauty with economy; and of things of the mind without growing soft. . . . For us wealth is for use rather than ostentation and poverty is no disgrace, unless we are not doing anything about it.

His message was that out of democracy grew the vitality that led to empire, to wealth, and to the benefits of civilization.

I declare that our city is a liberal education to Greece and each one of our citizens excels all men in versatility, resourcefulness, brilliance and self-reliance. That this is no hollow boast for the occasion, but the actual truth, our city's power bears witness.

Pericles' rhetoric rose to an extraordinary metaphor of sexual desire; he saw the city as an *eromenos* and the citizens as a collective *erastes*.

Think of the greatness of Athens, as you actually see it day by day, till you fall in love with your *polis*.

The speech glossed over certain unpleasant characteristics and some inconvenient qualities, but its theme, that Athens had been going through a golden age thanks largely to its democratic constitution, seems to have been true enough.

But there was another, much less palatable truth that was about to strike the Athenians. In the summer of 430 during the Peloponnesians' second invasion when farmers crowded the city and lived huddled in shacks and stifling tents, people began to fall ill and die. The symptoms of the epidemic were horrific, as Thucydides, who had been infected himself and survived, described in detail. Perfectly healthy men and women suddenly began to have burning feelings in the head; their eyes became red and inflamed; inside their mouths their throats and tongues bled, and they had unpleasant breath.

Next came sneezing and hoarseness of voice, and before long victims developed a chest pain and a cough, and then a stomachache. They vomited up every kind of bile.

The skin reddened and broke out into pustules. It felt cool to the touch, but inside sufferers felt burning hot. After seven or eight days a severe diarrhea set in and was often fatal. Thucydides writes: "Nothing did the Athenians so much harm as this or so reduced their strength for war."

We are not sure what the infection was. It seems to have originated in Egypt and spread through the Persian Empire. Its symptoms resembled those of pneumonic plague, measles, typhoid, and other diseases, but fit none of them exactly. One thing is sure; the "plague," which is what people called it, was often lethal. The death toll is uncertain. Thucydides gives totals for the cavalry and infantry classes—4,400 infantry out of the 13,000 for the field army. In addition, at Potidaea 1,050 men died in forty days. Three hundred cavalrymen died out of an active total of 1,200. The poor probably suffered most and for them there are no figures. It has been estimated that between one quarter and one third of the population died. It was a terrible blow.

"It was the one thing I didn't predict," remarked a despondent Pericles. The plague raged for two summers, took a break, and then resumed in 427 before finally running its course.

Few doubted that the war and the plague were connected and that the gods were punishing Athens for some offense. Everyone could recall the anger of Apollo in Homer's *Iliad,* and the punitive plague he inflicted with his twanging arrows on the Greek army before Troy.

Sophocles' new tragedy, *Oedipus the King,* was performed at the Great Dionysia of 429 when the plague was at its height. It was no accident that it opens with Apollo at his murderous work again. The play didn't win first prize, but many see it as his masterpiece. Aristotle wrote in his study of the art of fiction, *Poetics,* that it best matched his prescription for how drama should be made.

Its hero, Oedipus, becomes king of Thebes by unknowingly killing his father and marrying his mother. Because of the pollution he brings to his kingdom, a terrible pestilence descends on the city. The audience understood all too well the horrors of which the Chorus sings:

> *Beyond all telling, the city*
> *Reeks with the death in her streets, death-bringing.*
> *None weeps, and her children die,*
> *None by to pity.*
> *Mothers at every altar kneel,*
> *Golden Athena, come near to our crying!*
> *Apollo, hear us and heal!*

It was only when the pollution was traced back to Oedipus and he had blinded himself and been expelled from the city that the infection subsided.

People remembered an old prophecy that said:

War with the Dorians [the Spartans were Dorians] and death will come at the same time.

They also recalled that before deciding on war, Sparta had received a favorable response from the oracle at Delphi. Its words appeared to be coming true and it was noticed that the plague scarcely touched the Peloponnese. In the winter of 426 Athens carried out ceremonies of purification at the island of Delos, birthplace of Apollo. All the tombs of those who had died on Delos were dug up and it was proclaimed that in future no deaths or births, both of which were pollutant events, were to be permitted on the island. A five-yearly festival was revived, the Delian Games, and horse racing was added as a new competition.

It comes as little surprise that at this juncture the will of the *demos* wobbled. Peace feelers were extended to Sparta, although they came to nothing. Probably in September 430, Pericles was suspended from his post as *strategos* to which he had been elected in the spring, and charged with misappropriation of public funds. He was found guilty and fined fifty talents. He became depressed and spent his time lying about at home. Young Alcibiades and others had to persuade him to resume political work. In the spring, he was reelected, "as is the way with crowds," Thucydides observed sourly. Pericles was back in office at the start of the new official year in midsummer 429.

The Olympian was felt to be indispensable and he was against wobbling. As always he spoke truth to power—that is, to the *demos*. "Your empire is, not to mince words, a tyranny," he advised. "It may be that it was wrong to take it, but to let it go now would be unsafe."

Pericles was not only unfairly blamed for the plague, he also caught it. He passed the crisis but the disease lingered, and in the autumn of 429 he died. His two unsatisfactory sons had also been infected and preceded him to the grave a year before. So that his direct line should survive, he persuaded the authorities to make Pericles, his unsuffraged child by Aspasia, an Athenian citizen (the young man had fallen foul of the nationality law his own father had introduced all those years ago, which allowed the franchise only to children both of whose parents were Athenian).

Pericles was a great man. Thucydides, who was hard to please, admired him. He gave him a fine eulogy.

Being powerful because of his rank, ability, and known integrity, he exercised an independent control over the masses, and was not so much led by it as himself led it. As he did not win power by improper methods he did not have to flatter them. . . . In short, what was nominally a democracy became rule by the first citizen. His successors were more on the same level as one another, and each of them strove to become the leader.

However, as Pericles himself must have recognized, his career ended in failure. This had less to do with the plague than with his war strategy. It was defensive and wars are seldom won without attack, without looking for the enemy and fighting him. He underestimated the devastating impact on public morale of the annual invasions of the homeland. When he reassured the *demos* before the war that Athens had huge financial reserves, he was factually correct. But here is a puzzle. The city was indeed much richer than its opponents, but Pericles knew as well as anybody else that maritime warfare was prohibitively expensive. By the time of his death the reserves were already running low, and hostilities had hardly opened.

Pericles was cautious by nature and there is only one plausible explanation for his faulty prognosis. His war strategy was that there would be no war—or, rather, a war with very little fighting and one that was likely to end quickly, as soon as Sparta had realized that there were no practical measures they could take to damage the Athenian Empire. In sum, Pericles had been betting on a draw.

It looked as if he was going to lose his stake.

The seemingly endless and ruinous siege of Potidaea did not end until its capture in 430. Costly naval expeditions were needed to counteract the effect on morale of the annual invasion of Attica. Allowance had to be made for future unknowns both known and unknown—in this case it was the plague, but further surprises could be anticipated. These would almost certainly include more bank-breaking rebellions in the empire. Worst of all, the enemy showed no sign of submission. So how was the war actually to be won?

In foreign policy Pericles was a hawk, but he was a cautious hawk. He liked to avoid risk. He would do nothing unless he was reasonably sure in advance of the outcome. Now that he was dead, a new hawk would fly the skies who had no such inhibitions. This raptor saw that Athens had to show real aggression, even to the point of rashness, if it were to defeat the enemy. And it had to grab chances as they came; rather than eliminate luck, it would provoke it. Its name was Cleon, who succeeded Pericles as the chief man in the state.

So far the war had been small beer, a succession of minor encounters and skirmishes by land and sea. Realizing that a strategy consisting largely of invasions of an already thoroughly ravaged Attica brought fewer returns with each passing year, the Peloponnesians decided to build a navy to win allies in western Greece and to challenge Athens's maritime dominance in the Corinthian Gulf. One of Sparta's chief allies, the mercantile city of Corinth, was suffering badly from what amounted to a blockade.

However, a brilliant Athenian admiral called Phormio outwitted and defeated a much larger fleet (his twenty met forty-seven Peloponnesian warships). Athenian triremes were not simply well built, they also had well-trained and experienced crews and tactically clever officers. Sparta was forced to recognize that to compete at sea required a lot more than investment in timber and canvas.

Both sides needed to recover their finances. Sparta, always short of cash, wondered whether the Great King might fund those who were fighting his bitterest enemy, Athens, and dispatched an embassy to sound him out. The very fact of doing so reveals the lengths to which Sparta was now prepared to go. Only half a century had passed since the invasion of Xerxes, and betrayal of the Greek cause to the Persians had become an acceptable policy.

The huge financial reserves of Athens were dwindling at an alarming rate. In 428 the imperial *polis* seems to have been maintaining at sea at one and the same time the largest number of warships that it had ever done, 250 in total. As we have seen, thousands of crew members, marines, and hoplites had to be paid at a rate of one drachma a day (or two if they had a servant). There was no sign of the war ending soon and with the disappearance of Pericles the opportunity arose for a new, leaner method of carrying on the struggle. This entailed an absolute severity in collecting league dues, additional taxes at home, and more carefully and economically designed military expeditions.

Such measures might stave off bankruptcy, but they would not win the war. So Athenian generals became more aggressive and more opportunistic. Unlike Pericles, they were not aiming for a draw, but for victory. They were nimble and sought to apply minimum (and so affordable) force to achieve a decisive objective. They were on the lookout for tightly defined risks that would bring real gains if successful and cause little real damage or expense if they failed.

"War is a stern master," observed Thucydides. Standards of decency were breaking down throughout the Greek world and men turned increasingly to violence and terror as routine political methods. The Spartan envoys to the Great King fell into Athenian hands and were sent back to Athens. As soon as they arrived they were executed without trial or even an opportunity to defend themselves. Their bodies were not given a proper burial, but thrown into a pit. The official justification for this criminal act was that it was retaliation for the Spartan practice of putting to death crews of Athenian merchant ships captured off the Peloponnesian coast. Indeed, at the beginning of the war the Spartans killed as enemies all whom they captured at sea, whether they were Athenians or neutrals.

The polities of Greek *poleis* were breaking down. The first and best example of this trend was the island of Corcyra. The class struggle there that had inadvertently set off the general war continued with vertiginous and bloodstained reversals of fortune, watched over by Peloponnesian and Athenian fleets whose maneuvers at sea pushed the pendulum on land to and fro. In the end the Corcyran democrats prevailed. Four hundred aristocrats and their supporters sought sanctuary in the temple of Hera in Corcyra town and Thucydides reported that the democrats

> persuaded about fifty of them to submit to a trial. They then condemned every one of them to death. Seeing what was happening, most of the other suppliants, who had refused to be tried, killed each other there in the sanctuary of Hera; some hanged themselves on trees, and others committed suicide as they were severally able.

Some five hundred aristocrats managed to escape the carnage and established a fort in the north of the island, from which they launched raids against the democrats. A couple of years later they were defeated with help from an Athenian force. The survivors surrendered after receiving guarantees of their safety. They were then shut up in a large building, taken out in groups of twenty, and led past two lines of armed soldiers who beat them and stabbed them. Eventually, and understandably, those who were still inside refused to come out. So the democrats climbed up onto the roof, threw down tiles on the prisoners below, and shot them with arrows.

History then repeated itself. Most of the victims began to

> kill themselves by thrusting into their throats the arrows shot by the enemy, and hanging themselves by cords taken from some beds that happened to be there and with strips torn from their clothing. . . . Night fell while these horrors were taking place and most of it had passed before they were brought to a conclusion.

The civil strife in Corcyra ended for the good reason that one side in the conflict had been wiped out.

> In theory the crime was the attempted overthrow of the democracy, but in practice people took the opportunity to settle private

scores or grab other people's estates or property. Death took every shape and form. There were no lengths to which the brutality did not go. Fathers killed their sons, suppliants claiming sanctuary at an altar were dragged away or even butchered on it as if they were sacrificial animals. Some were even walled up in a temple of Dionysus and died there.

What happened in Corcyra was repeated elsewhere. As time passed practically the whole of the Greek world was infected, with rival factions in every *polis*. As a rule, democratic leaders appealed to the Athenians for support and oligarchs or aristocrats to the Spartans. It became a natural thing for those intent on a change of government to seek external alliances. Revolutions broke out in city after city.

Thucydides notes the effect these upheavals had on language and shows how the ordinary meaning of words was transformed and debased.

Reckless aggression was now regarded as the courage of a loyal party supporter; to think of the future and wait and see was merely another way of saying one was a coward; any suggestion of moderation was a disguise for unmanliness; an ability to see all sides of a question meant that one was unfitted for action. Fanatical enthusiasm was the mark of a real man.

The Greeks did not understand the concept of a loyal opposition. Politics was a zero-sum game in which the winner took all. Losers were either butchered or went into exile. Large numbers of banished patriots were scattered throughout the Greek world and plotted vengeance against their political opponents. Hellenic unity, always fragile, became a lost cause.

Athens was by no means immune from this widespread coarsening of moral standards. In 428, the fourth year of the war, the *polis* of Mytilene and most of the rest of Lesbos, the third largest Greek island, revolted from the league. It was not a subject state but a "free ally" that contributed its own ships.

People on Lesbos had long been planning an insurrection and watched the fall of Samos with dismay. The governing aristocracy of Mytilene had no special grievance, but were striking out for the principle of freedom. They were waiting until they had narrowed the mouths of their harbors, completed some fortifications, and built more warships, but were betrayed before they were ready to rebel.

From the Athenian point of view this revolt was a challenge to the whole rationale of the empire. It came at the worst possible moment, when the city had been devastated by the plague and the treasury was beginning to run low. Worse, Lesbos entered into an alliance with Sparta.

Nevertheless, the Athenians made a great effort. An emergency property tax was introduced. A sizable expeditionary force sailed to Lesbos and placed Mytilene under siege. The Spartans (very boldly for them) sent out a fleet to help the Lesbians, but its commander was nervous and dilatory and arrived too late to save the city.

What happened was that the aristocrats armed ordinary citizens to help with the Mytilenes' defense. However, these were mostly democrats and, once they had weapons in their hands, mutinied and insisted on surrender to the Athenians. The terms agreed were tough. Athens was accorded the "right to act as it saw fit with regard to the people of Mytilene," but they in turn were allowed to send representatives to Athens to put their case.

The *demos* at Athens had received a shock and was in a filthy mood. On a motion from Cleon, "the most violent of its citizens," it decided to have the entire male population of Mytilene executed immediately and to make slaves of the women and children. A trireme was immediately dispatched to convey the terrible command to the Athenian general on Lesbos.

Overnight there were second thoughts. People worried that the decision was unprecedented and punished the innocent as well as the guilty. It was particularly unjust to kill the democrats, who had in fact opposed the revolt and whose resistance to the government had caused its collapse. The representatives of Mytilene were still in the city and noticed the change of mood. Together with some friendly Athenians, they approached the authorities and asked if the matter could be debated again. They won their point and an immediate meeting of the *ecclesia* was called.

Cleon spoke again to his original proposal. He was unrepentant. According to Thucydides, he told the *demos:*

> By giving way to your feelings of compassion you are putting yourself in danger and your weakness will not win you any thanks. What you do not realize is that your empire is a tyranny exercised over subjects who do not like it and are always plotting against you.

It is interesting to note that whatever their other quarrels, Cleon and Pericles took the same view about the empire—that it was inherently unjust and that their fellow-citizens should acknowledge the fact and live with it. Might was right. Would Pericles have supported Cleon's official massacre, though?

He would probably have shared the opinion of a certain Diodotus, whose only appearance in history is as a contributor to this debate. He did not appeal to the compassion of his audience, but to its self-interest. This was not a question of justice, he argued, but of policy. Cleon was too hasty and too angry. The death penalty was not a reliable deterrent, for it simply made future rebels desperate and less likely to surrender.

"The right way to deal with free people is this—not to inflict some tremendous punishment on them after they have revolted, but to take tremendous care of them before this point is reached—to prevent them even contemplating the idea of revolt."

By a narrow majority the previous day's decision was reversed. A second warship was sent off with all urgency. The envoys from Lesbos plied the crew with wine and food and promised a large reward if they arrived in time to stop the death sentence being carried out. The men were fed as they rowed with barley mixed with oil and wine, and slept in relays while the remainder rowed on. Luckily there were no contrary winds.

The first trireme dawdled on its disagreeable errand and arrived at Mytilene just a little ahead of the second one. The commander there had only had time to read the original decree and to start making the necessary arrangements for a mass execution before he learned that the order had been countermanded. Thucydides remarked drily: "Mytilene had had a narrow escape."

The same cannot be said of what happened to an ancient Greek *polis* in Chalcidice called Scione. Its citizens used to say that their ancestors settled there after being blown off course by a storm on their way home to Greece from Troy. Six years after the Mytilene affair they revolted from Athens and were eventually starved out.

This time nobody in the *ecclesia* is recorded as having objected when all the adult males of Scione were put to the sword, and the women and children sold into slavery. Perhaps to remind the world that Sparta had been the first to practice this kind of atrocity, the empty city was handed over to the homeless survivors of Plataea.

Values had yet further decayed and we hear no more from Diodotus.

A starving wolf met a guard dog of his acquaintance. "I knew what would happen," said the dog. "Your irregular lifestyle will soon be the death of you. Why don't you get a steady job like me, and have regular meals?"

"I would have no objection," said the wolf, "if only I could find one."

"I'll fix that," said the dog. "Come with me to my master and you shall share my work."

On the way to the dog's home the wolf noticed that the hair on the dog's neck was worn away, so he asked him how that had happened.

"Oh, it's nothing," said the dog. "That is where the collar is put on at night to keep me chained up. It chafes a bit, but one soon gets used to it."

"Oh, really?" replied the wolf. "Then goodbye to you, master dog."

This fable is by Aesop, who flourished in the sixth century (if he is not a figure of legend). He was a slave from Thrace and lived on the island of Samos. His exemplary tales mainly featured speaking animals and were immensely popular. Most Greeks would warmly endorse the moral of the encounter between dog and wolf: to starve and be free was far better than to be fat and enslaved.

They knew what they were talking about, for slavery was widespread throughout the Hellenic world. From Homer onwards it was an accepted part of daily life. Aristotle called a slave "a living piece of property." There was some dispute whether a slave should be treated as a domestic animal or as a child.

An old-fashioned conservative like the anonymous author of *The Athenian Constitution* had decided views on the subject. Owners were far too soft with their slaves. They were "allowed to take the greatest liberties in Athens. You are not allowed to strike any of them there, nor will a slave stand aside for you. . . . We have put slaves on terms of equality with free men."

Few slaves would agree to the accuracy of this observation. The majority, who worked in the fields or (worse) the mines, led hard and bitter lives. Boys and girls with good looks could end up in a brothel or at best be compelled to have sex with their owners.

Even poor citizens could afford a slave. Hesiod in the eighth century advised a peasant farmer to "get a house, a bought woman and an ox for ploughing." The averagely affluent Athenian probably owned two or three slaves and the rich could afford between ten and twenty. By encouraging procreation, owners could add to their stock without making an additional purchase.

A minority, with a good education and good luck, were able to get on in the world. Slave sculptors worked alongside free colleagues on the new temples on the Acropolis. Owners allowed trusted slaves to manage businesses and live in their own houses. Sometimes close ties of affection grew between them (and indeed between slave woman and mistress). Slaves were sometimes set free, but we do not know how often this was done.

The state owned a number of slaves, among whom were the Scythian archers responsible for keeping public order; others were notaries, jury clerks, coin testers, and an executioner. These were the fortunate ones, treated with respect and given a degree of independence.

There are no records, but by the fifth century Athenians collectively owned thousands of slaves (some estimate as many as 150,000, not far off the number of the free population). They came from all around the Eastern Mediterranean; some were unfortunate Greeks who were sold into slavery by their enemies in war (Scione, for example) or kidnapped by pirates. Many were not Hellenes; these were mainly "barbarians" from Thrace and such places as Illyria and even faraway Scythia, and may well have been sold by their parents. Others originated in Caria and Lydia.

An auction sale list from 415 has survived. If its numbers are typical, it suggests that slaves were not cheap. A Syrian male was sold for 301 drachmas and a "little Carian boy" fetched 240 drachmas. A slave's average market value stood at anything between 50 and, exceptionally, 1,000 drachmas, with about 200 drachmas an average price.

Most Greeks believed that slavery was ethically acceptable, but Aristotle reports that some argued that "it is contrary to nature to rule as master over slave, because the distinction between slave and free is one of convention only, and in nature there is no difference. This form of rule is based on force and therefore not just."

Few paid attention to such awkward critics. A Hellene's heart may have lain with the wolf, but his mind told him that dogs were very useful acquisitions.

The island of Sphacteria was a remote and lonely spot on the southwest coast of Messenia in the Peloponnese, the enslaved land of Sparta's *helots*.

One great thin chunk of mountainous rock, it was nearly three miles long and about 150 yards wide. The ruins of an ancient prehistoric fortification could be found on a high hill at the northern end, but, with only one spring, the place was uninhabitable and was the exclusive haunt of birds of prey. The soil was red. The stony terrain was wooded and there were no tracks or paths. On the landward side a wall of cliffs tumbled precipitately into the waters of a magnificent natural harbor, which Sphacteria protected from the open sea.

Two channels led into this harbor. The one to the north of the island was very narrow, no more than 150 yards across, and on the far side loured a tall, more or less impregnable headland called Pylos. In the south the passage was about 1,400 yards wide.

One spring day in 425 an Athenian fleet of forty triremes sailed past on its way north with orders to sail to Corcyra and Sicily (for more about the expedition see page 333). Most unusually, it was carrying a private citizen who had a secret plan in mind.

He was Demosthenes, an associate or protégé of Cleon and one of a new breed of military commander. Like the admiral Phormio, he was a dashing and creative improviser. While campaigning in western Greece in the previous year, he had devised a plan to launch a surprise attack on Boeotia from the north, mainly using locally recruited troops. It was a brilliant idea, but poorly executed. It led to an embarrassing defeat and 120 Athenian hoplites were killed. Demosthenes dared not return to Athens to face the fury of the *demos,* but stayed in the region, where he scored victories against a Peloponnesian force and a colony of Corinth. This retrieved his reputation at home.

He was reelected *strategos,* but his term of office would only begin in the summer and in the meantime he conceived another bright scheme. If only Athens could gain a foothold on the coast of the Peloponnese it would go some way to counterbalance the regular invasions of Attica.

The two fleet commanders were given the mysterious instruction to allow Demosthenes to "make what use he liked of this fleet of theirs on its way around the Peloponnese." As they passed by Pylos he pointed it out to them and recommended that it be fortified; it would be a useful base from which local Messenians and those who had been settled in Naupactus in the Corinthian gulf could harry the Spartans.

The commanders were not impressed, but a fortunate storm forced them to take shelter in the harbor. Pylos was a natural stronghold and to pass the time the crews were authorized to fortify its weak spots. When the weather improved after a week, Demosthenes stayed behind with five triremes.

When the news of Pylos's capture reached Lacedaemon the authorities were seriously alarmed. Ships and troops were sent to eject the Athenians. Attacks were launched on Pylos and 420 Spartan hoplites with *helot* servants landed on Sphacteria to prevent the Athenians taking it as a permanent base. Demosthenes had little trouble repelling the Spartans, but he dispatched two triremes to bring back the fleet. When it arrived, it defeated the Spartan ships in short order.

This meant that, in effect, the Spartans on the island were under siege. They numbered less than one thousand in total, if we assume that each of the hoplites was accompanied by a *helot* servant. Of the hoplites themselves, at least 180 were elite citizens or Equals. Two Athenian warships sailing round Sphacteria in opposite directions stayed on permanent patrol to prevent any rescue attempt from the mainland.

To lose so many Equals was inconceivable and some *ephors* arrived in person to assess the situation. It was embarrassingly clear that the hoplites and *helots* on the island could not be freed. Sparta offered a truce during which it would suspend hostilities and temporarily hand over its fleet to the Athenians. A trireme conveyed a Spartan delegation to Athens where they proposed a permanent peace that would bring the war to an end.

Cleon persuaded the *ecclesia* to insist on impossible terms. These were, in effect, the reinstatement of the "land empire" abandoned under the terms of the Thirty Years Peace. The envoys suggested private talks, but Cleon vetoed the idea. The delegation gave up and left town. The truce was ended, but Demosthenes refused to give back the Spartan fleet as promised, alleging some minor infraction. The blockade of Sphacteria continued.

Grain, wine, and cheese were smuggled across the water to the Spartan soldiers by underwater swimmers and small boats. It began to look as if they could survive the siege indefinitely. By contrast, the supply of food was beginning to be a logistical problem for the Athenians. The arrival of winter might put an end to the blockade.

Then at last there was an important, if accidental, development. There were so many soldiers and so little space on Pylos that marines on the Athenian patrol ships used to disembark on the southern tip of Sphacteria and cook their midday meals there. One day they accidentally set fire to part of the wood. The wind got up and the flames quickly spread. Soon the entire island was ablaze.

In the absence of tree cover it was now possible to see exactly how many Spartans there were and where they were encamped in the center of the island near the only well. Demosthenes had been considering an attack, but now he was in a position to prepare a detailed plan.

Time passed and nothing seemed to be happening. In Athens, the *demos* became impatient. Ordinary citizens wished that they had accepted the peace terms, which they had been persuaded to reject. Cleon felt under pressure and blamed a political rival, a multimillionaire businessman, Nicias, who was one of the year's generals.

Born in about 470, Nicias came from the entrepreneurial middle class. He inherited a large fortune from his father. His property was valued at the huge sum of 100 talents and included a labor force of slaves who worked his substantial concessions at the silver mines of Laurium and provided him with a handsome income. He lacked charm and found it hard to make up his mind. He was deeply religious and avoided decisions until he had taken omens. A poor orator, he was thought of as an earnest bore. However, he was extremely public-spirited and became popular because of his generous support of public causes. He made a point of being a hard worker. His lack of charisma stood him in good stead when compared with the opportunism and unreliability of a demagogue like Cleon.

The comic poets enjoyed making fun of Nicias. In his *The Cavalrymen,* Aristophanes has his "Cleon" say:

I'll shout down every speaker and put the wind up Nicias.

Phrynichus, another well-liked writer of farces, writes of one of his characters:

He's the best of citizens, as well I know.
He doesn't cringe and creep about like Nicias.

Nicias inherited the defensive, cautious policy of Pericles. In the debate Cleon put the blame for inaction on him.

"If only our generals were real men," he shouted, "it would be easy to take out a force and capture the Spartans on the island."

Nicias retorted: "As far as the generals are concerned, Cleon can take whoever he likes and see what he can do himself."

Cleon thought this was merely a ploy and said he was perfectly willing to accept the command. But he soon realized that Nicias was in earnest and did his best to wriggle out of the commitment. But finding that the *ecclesia* was insistent he changed tack and accepted the command. Brazenly doubling the odds, he claimed that he would bring back the prisoners within twenty days or kill them.

Everyone laughed to see Cleon hoist on his own petard; but he took the commission seriously and soon set off for Pylos with a substantial force. His critics were delighted. Either Cleon would fail—which was what they rather expected—and they would be rid of him, or if they were proved wrong, they would have the Spartans in their power. Heads I win, tails you lose.

On his arrival at Pylos, Cleon immediately agreed to the plan of Demosthenes (the two men were close and he may already have been briefed about it before the debate in Athens). They waited for a day and then just before dawn landed eight hundred hoplites on Sphacteria. They quickly overran an outpost. Once a bridgehead had been established the rest of the army arrived—up to thirteen thousand hoplites, lightly armed skirmishers (called *peltasts*), and archers.

The Athenians marched against the Spartans in their camp in the center of the island. The skirmishers and archers wore down the heavily armed and relatively immobile hoplites. Clouds of red earth and black cinders created an artificial fog and blinded the defenders, who eventually withdrew to the ruined hilltop fort.

A small group of Messenian exiles from Naupactus knew the terrain and completely surrounded the Spartans. Their position was hopeless. After consulting the authorities on the mainland they capitulated. Of the original 420 soldiers, 128 were dead. The 292 survivors, of whom 120 were Equals, were shipped to Athens as prisoners.

The Athenians set up a trophy. This was routine for a victorious army left in charge of the battlefield. Trophies were usually a selection of enemy arms—helmets, cuirasses, and the like—fastened to a wooden post, which was fixed in the ground on a hill or a rise. Some captured shields were sent back to Athens for permanent exhibition. To prevent rust, they were coated in pitch. They were still on show in the second century A.D. and one of them has been unearthed in the *agora*. The Messenians of Naupactus commissioned a statue of a winged Victory at Olympia, which can still be seen there today.

Cleon had delivered on his mad promise. The impact of the news was colossal. The whole point about Equals was that they never surrendered. Thucydides commented: "Nothing that had happened in the war surprised the Greeks as much as this event."

There was a widespread desire for peace, but two years passed before a treaty was signed.

An infuriated Aristophanes wrote two fierce satires in 425 and

424, *The Acharnians,* in which the protagonist negotiates a private peace with Sparta and enjoys its fruits, and *The Cavalrymen,* a bitter, no-holds-barred caricature of the Athenian political system. Cleon appears in the latter as a comic monster who can be blamed for all that was wrong with the *polis.* The chorus of cavalrymen sing to the assembled *demos:*

> *For everyone that's here,*
> *One thing they'll all agree on:*
> *They'll greet with cheer on cheer*
> *The overthrow of Cleon!*

In the Peloponnese, Athens improved her position still further, winning control of the substantial island of Cythera, the love goddess Aphrodite's birthplace, or so it was said, and Methone, a port on the coast of Messenia. Sparta was under real threat in its home base and the possibility of another Messenian revolt was edging into probability. It was now that the two thousand able and troublesome *helots* were notoriously tricked with the promise of freedom and liquidated in secret. Cautious, pessimistic, and irritated with its allies, Sparta had lost its zest for the war.

Athens did not have it all its own way. Attacks on Corinth and Megara met with only partial success and a botched attempt to invade Boeotia culminated in a bad defeat at the town of Delium. One thousand Athenians lost their lives. The event was notable for the participation of Socrates, the famous Athenian philosopher, at forty-five years nearly too old to fight, and his pupil, the handsome young aristocrat Alcibiades, now in his mid-twenties. Alcibiades, who had been Socrates' messmate in an earlier campaign, recalled the philosopher's valor under fire. "He quietly observed the movements of friend and foe and made it perfectly plain even at a distance that he was prepared to put up a strong resistance to any attack. That is how both he and his companion got off safe." Alcibiades was on horseback on this occasion and rode alongside Socrates until he was out of danger.

Cleon did not last. He was obliged to capitalize on his newfound military reputation by leading an expeditionary force to a strategically important corner of the Athenian empire, Chalcidice. There he confronted a most un-Spartan Spartan. This was Brasidas, enterprising, imaginative, and charming. The only quality he shared with his compatriots was courage.

With some enfranchised *helots* and Peloponnesian mercenaries, he had marched so quickly up the length of Greece that nobody had had time to stop him. Once in Chalcidice he had raised the standard of revolt and, to great alarm in Athens, won the important city of Amphipolis to his cause.

Cleon was no fool, but he was inexperienced and, after Pylos, overconfident. To reconnoiter the terrain, he went too close to the city walls for safety. He guessed what was going to happen next, for he saw the feet of men and horses under one of the gates, but Brasidas was too quick for him. He sortied out quickly and caught the Athenians before they could get away.

Cleon was killed. There were plenty of other so-called demagogues to take his place during this period—among them Hyperbolus, who apparently had been a lamp maker before entering politics, Androcles, and Cleophon, a lyre maker. They have all received a bad press from ancient historians, who were snobbishly contemptuous of middle-class politicians. However, Cleon was a towering figure. Although he never attained the heights of power that Pericles had scaled, his more forceful and energetic approach to the war was an intelligent response to the Olympian's failed war plan.

The Athenian defeat in front of Amphipolis was a disaster for Athens, but with terrible luck for Sparta Brasidas too fell. The symbolism of the opposing generals' simultaneous deaths was not lost on peacemakers. Now that the two liveliest proponents of war had gone, the trouble of agreeing on an accord was greatly eased.

The setbacks at Delium and Amphipolis disarmed the war party in Athens, and the general mood favored a settlement. As for the Spartans, they were desperate to see an end to the war and would agree to almost anything to get their men back from the island.

Discussions went on during the winter of 422. Nicias, now the chief man in the state following the death of Cleon, headed the negotiations and sought a durable peace. A final agreement valid for five decades was announced after the Great Dionysia the following year.

The basis of the treaty was the status quo ante. Each side was to return its gains made during the war. There were some awkward exceptions to the rule that were quietly glossed over. But Sparta would give back Amphipolis, the biggest prize, and a number of rebellious *poleis* in the north. The Boeotians would hand over a frontier fortress. Megara would have to put up with Athens its old enemy retaining the port of Nisaea. Corinth lost some northwestern possessions, now in the hands of Athens. For its part Nicias agreed to give up Pylos, Sphacteria, and its other footholds along the Peloponnesian coastline. All prisoners of war would be exchanged.

The treaty satisfied Sparta's needs very well, but it enraged its allies. They cried foul and refused to accept it. The Spartans knew better; they trusted Athens not to meddle and were convinced that in time the likes of Corinth and Megara would understand that they had nowhere else to go for support but to Sparta. Sooner or later they would stop complaining and form up behind them.

If Pericles in the Elysian Fields learned of the entente, he will have been justifiably pleased. He would have opposed the aggressive policies of Cleon and his like, but they had produced the result he had wanted. The enemy had lost the will to carry on.

Athens was the winner, on points.

18

The Man Who Knew Nothing

Life and leisure in the city carried on despite the effects of war and the plague. The great annual festivals came and went, affluent citizens entertained one another at home, and shoppers haggled in the *agora*. Peace brought a welcome dividend, trade flourished, and tourists flocked to the city of light from all corners of the Eastern Mediterranean. Time passed agreeably.

One afternoon in January of the year 416, the young Athenian playwright Agathon held a dinner party followed by drinks. He had won the prize at the Lenaea or Country Dionysia drama festival with his first tragedy and wanted to celebrate the achievement. The previous day he had thrown a boozy function for the cast, but now, although he was hungover, he invited a few intimates to join him at his house.

Agathon was sensationally good-looking and "the lovely Agathon" became something of a catchphrase. Always well dressed, he cut a distinctive figure. He lived with his partner, Pausanias, and they seem to have constituted that rare thing in ancient Athens, an adult gay couple (later in life he is said to have been the partner of the aged tragedian Euripides). Nothing of his has survived, except for the stray quotation.

His guests included the comic playwright Aristophanes and one of the butts of the comic stage, Socrates. The events of the evening and the conversation that unfolded were described in a slim volume entitled *The Symposium* (taken from the Greek for "a drinking-together"), by Plato, a disciple of Socrates and an even greater philosopher than he.

Plato was said (perhaps mistakenly, but it is hard to be sure) to have written an erotic epigram about Agathon.

Kissing Agathon, my soul was on my lips.
It tried, stupid thing, to cross over into him.

The *Symposium* was written no earlier than 385 and is a masterpiece of world literature. It is a work of fiction, but Plato tricks out his account with all kinds of plausible detail, and perhaps faction is the better word. The playwright's victory is historical and it is more likely than not that he marked it with a party. The guest list may have been different, but Plato's description of upper-class hospitality in the fifth century is true to life. Those attending were, for the most part, well-known personalities and we may suppose that the opinions their literary avatars express echo those of the real-life personages.

There were no pubs or bars in ancient Athens, so far as we can tell. Apart from at public festivals, alcoholic refreshment was provided in private. In the houses of the well born and well-to-do, there was a men's room (or *andrōn*). Here, at a symposium, writers, politicians, thinkers, and attractive young men could eat, drink wine, and talk; it was an opportunity for the sharing of traditional values and for homosexual bonding.

Those taking part wore garlands and reclined on couches, one or two apiece and leaning on their left elbow. Made of wood or stone, there were at least four couches—or room for the host and seven or more guests (women seldom attended and if they did sat on upright chairs). In front of each of them stood a three-legged table where drinking cups were placed and food served.

Food in ancient Athens was plain and simple. Olives, onions, and garlic were popular. Greeks ate a lot of bread with honey, cheese, and olive oil; it was usually made from barley, which was more plentiful than wheat; white wheat bread was the preserve of the wealthy. Milk was used in cooking, but seldom drunk. Fruits and nuts were readily available.

Produce familiar to us had not yet been discovered and exploited—potatoes, rice, oranges and lemons (although Jews are recorded as pelting a high priest with lemons in the first century B.C.), bananas, and tomatoes.

Plato does not give us Agathon's dinner menu, but it might have included eels from Lake Copais in Boeotia. There were other possibilities. Dried or salted tuna, mackerel, and sturgeon were imported from the Black Sea and baked in olive oil with herbs. Anchovies and sardines were fished close to the Attic shore. Simple casseroles of poultry and game were often served, but for roast meat the Athenian had to await a religious sacrifice and so it was rarely on the menu at home. Everyone who attended a sacrifice received a portion of meat (the less edible parts of an animal were reserved for the gods, who seemed not to mind).

A gastronomic writer from Sicily, Archestratus, in the fourth century, approved of pork and roast birds. He observed:

> As you sip your wine, let these delicacies be brought to you, pig's belly and sow's uterus, spiced with cumin and vinegar and silphium [probably a variety of fennel and used as a contraceptive as well as a seasoning], together with the tender species of roast birds, as each is in season.

Drinking wine was a serious, even a religious, business for the responsible Athenian. It was almost always mixed with water and could be artificially sweetened (sugar being unknown, its place was taken by honey or dried figs). A symposium was not an informal gathering at which everyone set out to get drunk; rather, it was governed by strict ritual.

Each stage of the proceedings was marked by an acknowledgment of the power of the gods. After everyone had eaten and the food had been cleared away, and before the wine was mixed with water, those present drank a few drops in honor of the *agathos daimon,* a kindly supernatural power or Good Spirit. They prayed to the *daimon* that they might do nothing indecent and not drink too much. They then poured three libations of wine—to Zeus of Olympus and the other Olympian gods, to the heroes (exceptional human beings who were regarded as divine), and to *Zeus Soter,* or Savior and Deliverer from Harm. This was followed by a hymn to Hygieia, the goddess or personification of health, cleanliness, and hygiene. "I pray that you be a gracious inmate of my house."

One of those taking part in a symposium could be appointed Master of Drinking, or *symposiarch.* He was chosen by the throw of a die and would usually not be the host. He was a lord of rule, rather than of misrule, for he set the regulations for the evening. He determined the amount of water to be mixed with the wine and the number of cups to be drunk. His decision obviously influenced the tone of the party. It could be a serious discussion group that debated the issues of the day and indeed aristocratic symposia gained a reputation for antidemocratic activism. Alternatively, songs were sung, with well-known poems supplying the lyrics. The occasion could be something of a knees-up; entertainment was often laid on in the shape of a flute girl or two, or there could be dancing. Slaves, sometimes chosen for their good looks, went around serving wine from a large mixing bowl. On racier occasions clothes might be loosened or discarded.

Games could be played. One of these, *kottabos,* called for considerable skill. The rules differed, but in a popular version, a wooden pole was set in place, with a small figurine on its apex. Halfway down was a plate or pan; toasting an attractive young man, a player would flick some wine from his cup and try to knock down the figurine so that it fell on the pan and made a musical sound.

Another game demanded a good knowledge of Greek literature and casts light on the high level of cultural awareness among upper-class Athenians. The first player recited a famous line from a poem, and the second had to cap it by quoting the following line. The third had to quote from a passage on a similar theme by another poet.

Socrates was, unconsciously if we are generous, the most unreliable of guests. On this occasion, he had taken the trouble to have a bath and put on shoes, both quite rare events with him. But then he became lost in his thoughts and asked a friend whom he had met on the way to walk ahead, gate-crash the party, and tell his host that Socrates would be along later.

Agathon took all this in good part and welcomed the unbidden guest. After waiting for a time, he sent out a servant to find Socrates. The philosopher was standing under a neighbor's front porch, but was deaf to the man's entreaties to come in. Eventually everyone lay down to dinner and, about halfway through, Socrates arrived, without a word of apology. Then the usual libations were poured and hymns sung.

There was general agreement that after the previous day's excesses nobody was at all eager for serious drinking, so a *symposiarch* was not appointed. It was agreed that each man should drink as little or as much as he chose. Socrates was excluded from consideration, for he had an iron constitution and was impervious to alcohol.

A specially hired flute girl was sent away. "Let us entertain ourselves today with conversation," a doctor called Eryximachus said. "My proposal is that each of us, going from left to right, should make the best speech he can in praise of love."

Socrates concurred. "Love," he said, "is the only subject I understand."

One by one the guests delivered their opinions. *Eros* was the Greek word for the passionate, primarily sexual, engagement between two human beings. As a god he was the oldest divinity and inspired lovers to great sacrifices. Love at its finest was that between man and boy, semi-educational, semi-erotic. Nobody spoke up for love between a man and a woman. According to the good doctor, love was a spirit or force that permeated and guided everything in the universe.

The contribution of Aristophanes was a tour de force. Plato allowed him to invent a comical myth to explain the power of love. It exactly suited the playful, fantastical mind of the historical playwright.

In the beginning of things, he said, there were three sexes—male, female, and a hermaphroditic combination of the two. Human beings in that early time were shaped like a circle with two backs, four hands and four legs, and two faces on one head looking in different directions. They could walk backwards or forward but when they wanted to run, Aristophanes said that they "used all their eight limbs, and turned rapidly over in a circle like gymnasts performing a cartwheel."

These eccentric hominids attacked the gods and Zeus was at a loss what to do with them. After much thought, he decided neither to exterminate them nor to let them carry on regardless, but to weaken them by slicing them in two. He proclaimed: "They will walk upright on two legs. And if there is any further trouble from them and they don't keep quiet, I will bisect them again and they will have to hop about on one leg."

Men and women yearn for a return to their primal condition when they were complete, for, according to Aristophanes, "love is simply the name for the desire and pursuit of the whole." They fall in love with their other halves when they can find them or their equivalents. Those who are halves of a male whole pursue other men, while women who are halves of a female whole are lesbians and fall in love with other women. Those men who seek women and vice versa come from a hermaphroditic whole.

Beneath the fantasy and the joking Aristophanes was making a serious point. Everybody loves what is akin to them and most nearly restores their original oneness. Love is a need that transcends sexual attraction. It is a longing for fulfillment, for a return to vanished happiness. These are themes that Socrates picks up later in the evening.

Perhaps the most surprising aspect of Aristophanes' speech was that he was given the opportunity to deliver it at all. One would have thought that he and Socrates were on the worst possible terms and unlikely to have attended the same social event. As a writer of satire he had savaged the philosopher in one of his political comedies, *The Clouds*. He not only destroyed his character, but got his character wrong. A saint would have been offended.

Some years previously, in 423, Aristophanes' *The Clouds* received its premiere at the Great Dionysia. It flopped, but the author was proud of the play and revised it. The final version was finished about the time of Agathon's dinner party.

The protagonist is Strepsiades, a fraudulent farmer who is getting on in years. He has been bankrupted by his expensive wife and a wastrel of a son, Pheidippides, who spends all his money on horses. He believes that Socrates, who is well known for "making the worse cause seem the better," would show his son how to bamboozle his creditors.

Socrates runs a school, the *Phrontisterion,* or Thought Shop, and is happy to oblige. But Pheidippides refuses to enroll, so his father takes his place. Strepsiades learns of Socrates' scientific achievements. These include a new unit of measurement for working out how far a flea jumps, the cause of a gnat's whine, and a new use for a large pair of compasses (to remove cloaks from pegs on gymnasium walls).

Strepsiades begs to be introduced to the great man, who appears like a god in a tragedy suspended in a basket from a rope—the better to scrutinize meteorological phenomena. "I am walking on air," he says, "and attacking the mystery of the sun."

The comedy contains some dangerous allegations. Socrates is made to claim that rain clouds are divine. He tells Strepsiades: "The Clouds are the only goddesses, all the others are pure nonsense." The old duffer replies: "But Zeus! Come on now, doesn't the Olympian god exist?"

"Who's Zeus?" asks Socrates. "You're talking rubbish, there is no Zeus."

A joke is a joke, but the Athenians like other Greeks were pious and resented religious innovations. If this was what Socrates really believed, he was a malefactor and breaker of taboos.

After various comings and goings that involve father and son, the play ends with Strepsiades losing faith in Socrates and blaming the Thought Shop for his troubles. He arms his slaves with torches and spades and leads a frenzied attack on the school. Socrates and his students run away.

What was Aristophanes getting at? Scientists and philosophers remained unpopular with ordinary citizens, as men like Anaxagoras had been in Pericles' day.

Throughout the Greek world intellectual life was in a ferment. Itinerant teachers called sophists wandered around the region and tested traditional values. The word *sophistes* in Greek originally meant a master craftsman and therefore someone with a claim to specialist knowledge. The new sophists claimed that they could impart wisdom, in a general sense, to their students. Gorgias, a famous sophist, claimed to know the answer to any question he was asked.

These public intellectuals embodied three different disciplines. First of all, they taught their late-teen pupils the art of oratory. In direct democracies like that of Athens, persuading the *ecclesia* to adopt a particular course of action or not was an essential talent. Also, there were no professional lawyers, no police force, and no professional prosecution service. Individual citizens brought charges or defended themselves in court. It was self-evident self-interest to learn the principles of advocacy. The impression spread that sophists were cynics who trained young men in rhetorical techniques that would win assent to the most disreputable of propositions.

The better class of sophist rejected this criticism, saying that a good speaker was a good man. Most of them offered to teach virtue or *aretē*.

Virtue had been the prerogative of birth, but now it could be inculcated through training. It is true that, in general, sophists equipped young men with the skills needed to climb the greasy pole of power. However, they were interested in morality, if they failed always to promote it.

The traditional view was that the gods were just and that virtue consisted in establishing their will and obeying it. But Greeks were now asking how divine justice could be reconciled with the evil in the world. Also, could the Olympians make a convincing claim to be morally good? Xenophanes, a fifth-century critic of conventional theology, remarked: "Both Homer and Hesiod have attributed to the gods all sorts of thing that are shameful and a reproach among men: theft, adultery and mutual deception." Readers of Homer could hardly resist this claim, for his gods and goddesses behave like spoiled children.

Many Greek thinkers were early scientists in that they wanted to understand natural phenomena. They asked questions about the nature of the universe and looked for governing principles. Thales of Miletus, whom we met when planning resistance to Cyrus the Great (see page 38), was a geometer, astronomer, political adviser, and businessman; he flourished in the first half of the sixth century and was among the first to reject supernatural explanations featuring gods and goddesses. He proposed general principles and developed hypotheses. He used geometry to calculate the height of pyramids and the distance of ships from the shore. He asked what was the substance or substances from which all things were made. According to Aristotle, he guessed that the "permanent entity was water." The fact that he was wrong should not obscure his claim to be the father of the rational sciences.

There were multifarious theories. Other thinkers argued for air, fire, and earth or all four elements. Pythagoras, who also flourished in the sixth century, and his followers "applied themselves to mathematics, and were the first to develop this science; and through studying it they came to believe that its principles are the principles of everything."

Heraclitus, a younger contemporary and a member of the royal family of Ephesus, posited a constantly changing order of things. "You cannot step into the same river twice," he said, gnomically. As a metaphor of the need for change, he added: "The barley drink separates if it is not stirred." His writings were famously obscure; when Euripides was asked his opinion of them, he replied: "The bit I understand is excellent, and so too, I dare say, is the bit I do not understand; but it needs a diver from Delos to get to the bottom of it." (The island seems to have been famous for its expert swimmers in search of fish.)

Heraclitus also appears to have anticipated an up-to-date version of the Big Bang theory. He believed that the universe "is generated from fire and it is consumed in fire again, alternating in fixed periods throughout the whole of eternity."

By contrast, the Eleatic School (so-called after the town of Elea, today's Velia, in southern Italy) was headed by Parmenides in the fifth century and held that change was only an illusion and that a divine and unvarying unity permeates the universe.

On the other hand, the atomists headed by the fifth-century thinker Democritus of Abdera in Thrace offered a hypothesis that also (remarkably) anticipated twentieth-century physics. They argued that the only things that were unchanging were small, indivisible units called atoms. These came together randomly to form the variousness of the world's phenomena.

There was as little agreement among Greek philosophers as among politicians.

The Socrates of *The Clouds* is obviously a parody of the typical all-purpose sophist—an amoral know-all and phony. Socrates, as he really was, was no sophist except in the sense that he taught young men through argument. Aristophanes was being dangerously unfair.

Sophists were restless travelers, but Socrates was a stay-at-home and never went abroad except when on military campaign. He was born in Attica not far from Athens in 469, and so was fifty-three at the putative date of *The Symposium*. His father, Sophroniscus, was a sculptor or stonemason and his mother, Phaenarete, a midwife. He himself seems to have worked at some stage of his life as a stonemason. He married Xanthippe and was reportedly henpecked. The couple had three undistinguished sons.

His economic circumstances are unclear. As we have seen, he served as a hoplite and so must have been a man of means, but he lived very simply and spent his time talking philosophy. Perhaps we should assume that he lived off the family savings from the masonry business.

Socrates was famously ugly. He had a broad, flat, turned-up nose, bulging eyes, thick lips, and a potbelly. He seldom changed his clothes or washed himself and had a habit of walking barefoot.

His lifestyle and ideas were unlike those of sophists. A teacher such as Gorgias charged his students high fees and was treated as a VIP. By contrast, Socrates spent most of his time out of doors talking to whomever he met. He made a point of not charging fees, although his followers, or perhaps more truly his disciples, tended to be wealthy young aristocrats who could easily afford to pay them. He fancied attractive boys (or at least allowed people to believe he did) and in today's terminology may well have been bisexual; however, he appears not to have had sex with them.

Socrates was not much interested in scientific inquiry and restricted himself to the discussion of ethical questions. "The unexamined life is not worth living," Plato has him say. Unlike the Aristophanes version, he was conventionally religious and respected the gods (especially Apollo) without question. However, unusually, he asserted that right and wrong are established independently of the pantheon. Also, he seems to have held the somewhat eccentric belief that the gods could never injure each other or human beings—in a word, they could do no evil. One can imagine the unquenchable laughter when that news reached Olympus.

Socrates was not altogether a rationalist; he spoke of a "divine sign" or spirit, a *daimonion* sent by the gods. This was an inner voice that turned him back from a given course of action, but never gave its approval to one. It was thanks to his *daimonion,* he used to say, that he steered clear of active politics.

Xenophon's first encounter with Socrates illustrates the philosopher's pickup technique. Born about 430, he was a well born youth, modest and (this always helped with Socrates) extremely good-looking. One day Socrates came across him in a narrow passage walking in the opposite direction. He stretched out his stick to block his path and asked Xenophon where every kind of food was sold. On receiving a reply, he put another question: "And where do men become good and honourable?"

Xenophon was stumped. He admitted he had no idea. "Then follow me," said Socrates, "and learn."

The boy was smitten. From that moment he became a pupil of Socrates and remained so for the rest of his life. In later years Xenophon wrote a memoir of his mentor, in which he drew a sketch of him at work:

> Socrates was always in the public eye. Early in the morning he used to make his way to the covered walkways and open-air gymnasia, and when the marketplace became busy he was there in full view; and he always spent the rest of the day where he expected to find the most company. He talked most of the time and anyone who liked was able to listen.

A familiar figure walking among the plane trees in the *agora,* the philosopher used to visit a shoemaker called Simon who had a shop just beyond its edge or boundary. Boys were not allowed into the square, so they often met in shops of this kind. Simon wrote down Socrates' sayings and was one of the first to publish them as dialogues (sadly, they are lost).

The remains of a building have been found near the Tholos, the circular building where the Prytaneum, the executive committee of the *boulē,* conducted its business; its floor was covered with hobnails and a cup base was found with the word "Simon's" scratched on it. Pericles heard of his writings and offered to pay for Simon's upkeep if he would come and live in his house. Simon refused, on the grounds that he was unwilling to sell his freedom of speech.

Socrates' method of philosophical inquiry was highly original. Unlike Gorgias, who claimed to know everything, he insisted that he knew nothing. He wrote nothing down although many of his followers did, but proceeded by spoken question and answer, the so-called dialectic. Where the sophist would study virtue by means of the art of oratory, Socrates insisted on justifying propositions through reason. He seldom offered an opinion himself, but concentrated on pursuing definitions and demonstrating the wrongness of his interlocutor's views. "What is courage?" he would inquire. "What is justice?" He drew a sharp distinction between opinion (bad) and knowledge (good, but hard to attain).

He seems to have believed that virtue, or *aretē*, was necessary for the fulfilled and happy life. But he always denied that he knew what it was, simply what it wasn't. Understanding the nature of *aretē* was a function of the divine, he sometimes said, and the most that humans can attain is to acknowledge their own ignorance.

Socrates equated virtue with knowledge. The good leads to happiness, or is itself a part of happiness. More than anything else we all want to be happy, so it follows that anyone who has an inkling of what the good is will inevitably choose to embrace it. It is impossible to know the better and follow the worst.

Socrates had little difficulty dismissing the other speakers at Agathon's celebration dinner, but when his turn came to discourse on love he modestly avoided offering his own opinion. Instead, he reported a conversation on the same topic he had once had with a mysterious personage called Diotima.

She was a woman from Mantinea, a town in the Peloponnese. It is not at all certain whether she was fact or figment. All other speakers in Plato's many philosophical dialogues existed in real life, so maybe Diotima did too. Some modern scholars used to speculate that she was a pseudonym for Aspasia, Pericles' companion. Not a very plausible thought, for Diotima appears to have been something of a seer, whose intercession succeeded in postponing the Athenian plague by ten years.

As recalled by Socrates, she claimed that love "is the perpetual possession of the good." It is a ladder between the sensible world and the eternal world. Through procreation a man can have children and win a kind of immortality. But if he can rise above sex, the next rung is to reckon beauty of soul more valuable than beauty of body. He will procreate with his lover (a male *eromenos,* of course) in a spiritual sense by "bringing forth such notions as may serve to make young people better."

In a continuing progression, he will recognize that passion for one human being is beneath him and fall in love with all beauty. He will discern it in activities and institutions and realize that love of a beautiful person is an overrated pastime.

> By gazing upon the vast ocean of beauty to which his attention is now turned, [he] may bring forth, or procreate, in the abundance of his love of wisdom many beautiful sentiments and ideas.

Finally, the seeker after wisdom encounters

> a beauty whose nature is marvelous, indeed the final goal, Socrates, of all his previous efforts. This beauty is first of all eternal; it neither comes into being nor passes away, neither waxes nor wanes; next, it is not beautiful in part and ugly in part, nor beautiful at one time and ugly at another, nor beautiful in this relation and ugly in that, nor beautiful here and ugly there, as varying according to its beholders; nor again will this beauty appear to him like the beauty of a face or hands or anything corpo-

real, or like the beauty of a thought or a science, or like beauty which has its seat in something other than itself, be it a living thing or the earth or the sky or anything else whatever; he will see it as absolute, existing alone with itself, unique, eternal and all other things partaking of it, yet in such a manner that, while they come into being and pass away, it neither undergoes any increase or diminution nor suffers any change.

How much of all this is Socrates and how much the thinking of his great disciple? We will not go far wrong if we agree that Plato offered a speaking likeness, copied accurately his question-and-answer method, and echoed his interest in the correct definition of ethical terms. The historical Socrates probably also advocated the sublimation of sexual desire into some kind of spiritual or (as we respectfully name it) "platonic" love.

But the notion, adumbrated in *The Symposium,* that the everyday world, which seems so real to us, consists only of shadows, is merely appearance, can almost certainly be attributed to Plato. In his *On the State* he makes his thinking clear with a celebrated allegory. Men have been kept as captives in a cave since childhood. Their heads are fixed so that they can only look at the cave wall. Some way behind them a fire is burning and between the fire and the prisoners an array of objects of all kinds casts shadows on the wall. For the prisoners these shadows are reality, but if one of them is released and he turns around, he will be blinded by the fire and the sunlight outside the cave mouth. He will seek to return to the world of shadows. But in fact the objects, what Plato calls "forms," are the real reality and the sun represents perfect knowledge. The flickering shadows are only inadequate copies. We human beings are the prisoners and our task is at least to glimpse the truth that lies behind our backs.

A clatter was heard at the front door and loud knocking. A moment later Agathon and his guests heard the voice of Alcibiades, the onetime ward of Pericles, shouting tipsily from the courtyard. At thirty-four years of age or thereabouts he was now one of the city's foremost politicians. But he was still a spoiled boy and insisted on seeing Agathon.

He was helped into the dining room by a flute girl and some companions. He stood in the doorway with a thick wreath of ivy and violets on his head, from which some ribbons were hanging. He usually wore his hair long and, like most adult males, will have been bearded—a curious combination of masculine and feminine.

"Good evening gentlemen," he said. "Will you welcome into your company a man who is already drunk, completely plastered, or shall we just give Agathon a garland, which is why we came, and go away?"

Everyone shouted for him to stay. He lay down next to Agathon, whom he kissed and crowned with his wreath. Only then did he notice that Socrates was also sharing the couch. Pretending that the philosopher was stalking him, he said: "Good god, what have we here? Socrates? Ambushing me again?"

Alcibiades was asked to improvise a speech in praise of love, but excused himself because he was drunk. Instead, if allowed, he wanted to deliver a eulogy of Socrates, his mentor and *erastes*. "If I compliment anyone but him, he won't be able to keep his hands off me!" "Be quiet," said Socrates.

Having obtained permission to proceed, Alcibiades claimed that Socrates was a more moving orator than Pericles and compelled him to realize that he himself was still a "mass of imperfections." He told a long anecdote about an attempt he made on Socrates' virtue. He gave him dinner and persuaded him to stay the night. When the lights were out and they were alone, Alcibiades threw his arms around Socrates, but failed to get any response. In other words, the philosopher lived up to the fine aspirations in his speech about rising above sexual desire.

Alcibiades went on to speak of Socrates' bravery in battle, not only at the battle of Delium, but at another engagement when he was wounded and Socrates rescued both him and his weapons.

When Alcibiades finished, everyone laughed. The joke was that he had turned upside down the usual order of things in single-sex love affairs. He was the youthful *eromenos,* but instead of being demure and desire-free, as was proper, he had been forward and randy. On the other hand, Socrates was a most passive and unaroused *erastes.*

A crowd of revelers found the front door of Agathon's house open and joined the party in the dining room. All order broke down and the rest of the evening was given over to heavy drinking. By dawn everyone had dozed off except for the host, Aristophanes, and, of course, Socrates, who was still holding forth. Agathon and Aristophanes gave way to his arguments and then fell asleep themselves.

Dawn broke and the philosopher got up and left. He walked to a gymnasium called the Lyceum where he had a wash, spent the day as normal, and towards evening went home to bed.

19

Downfall

A t dawn on a fine June day in 415 almost the entire population of Athens poured out of the city and walked down between the Long Walls to the great port of Piraeus and the sea. They came to see the fleet before it set sail. One hundred warships were anchored in the harbor, a splendid sight. Although the state had paid for their construction, ship captains had spent their own money on carved and painted figureheads and on general fittings. If they were rich enough they may have paid for the making of the ship itself, as a gift to their city. They topped up the sailors' state salary of one drachma a day in order to recruit the finest crews. Each was anxious that his own vessel stand out from the rest for smartness and speed. Everywhere polished armor gleamed and glinted in the morning light.

Sixty triremes were manned for fighting at sea and forty transports for carrying at least five thousand hoplites or heavy infantry, of whom about one third were Athenians and the rest allies, as well as archers and slingers. Up to 17,000 men pulled the oars. There was also a large number of vessels to convey wheat and barley and other items. Surprisingly only one ship was reserved for cavalry and carried a mere thirty mounts; the lack of cavalry was to be made good by allies in Sicily. (Other smaller craft and allied warships had previously been instructed to rendezvous at the island of Corcyra.)

Thucydides observed: "This expedition . . . was by far and away the costliest and most splendid force of Hellenic troops that up to that time had ever been sent out by a single city." It was a hugely expensive military venture, but a few years of relative peace had replenished the city's exchequer. The human capital lost from the plague more than ten years in the past had been restocked, at least in part, with a new generation of young men.

Once the crews and men had gone aboard, a trumpet called for silence. Everyone recited the customary prayers for those in peril on the sea, following the words of a crier, and hymns were sung. Then wine was poured into bowls and officers and men offered libations from gold or silver cups.

Once all this had been done, the fleet set sail in column and triremes raced each other as far as the island of Aegina. The expedition sailed around the Peloponnese en route to its destination—Sicily.

What can Athens have been thinking of, to abandon the main theater of war, the isles of Greece and the Aegean Sea, in favor of an adventure in the faraway west?

Before that question is answered another, more pressing one presents itself. What had happened to the general peace that Athens and Sparta had negotiated with so much trouble in 421?

Aristophanes' exuberant comedy *Peace* captured a mood of enthusiasm that citizens could now safely return to the countryside and tend their farms again and that profiteering city tradesmen were going bankrupt. He makes his hero, a farmer, say:

Now we can wank and sing altogether at high noon, as the old Persian general did, when he crooned "What joy! What bliss! What delight!"

But, as reported, a problem had arisen from the outset. Sparta had promised more than it could deliver. Its allies—Corinth, Megara, and Boeotia—refused to cooperate and hand back to Athens places presently under their control, as stipulated.

In particular, the city of Amphipolis, where Brasidas and Cleon had died, refused to be transferred and the Spartan army there was disinclined to force it to do so and left for home. So, not unreasonably, the *ecclesia* declined to return the prisoners of war captured on Sphacteria.

To the stone inscription of the treaty this sentence was added: "The Spartans have not kept their oaths." They were also becoming desperate. This was not just because they wanted their men back, but because a thirty-year treaty with their old enemy in the Peloponnese, the powerful *polis* of Argos just south of Corinth in the northeastern corner of the peninsula, was about to expire. There was an alarming risk that Argos, freed at last from its entente, might combine with Athens against Sparta. To avert this prospect a Lacedaemonian proposal emerged of going beyond an accord between two belligerents and entering into a full-on fifty-year defensive alliance between Sparta and Athens. Nicias, who headed the peace faction and wanted an enduring friendship with the old enemy, readily agreed. At last the prisoners were sent back, but Pylos and Cythera were retained against the handover of Amphipolis.

This was an unsatisfactory state of affairs and the various parties schemed against one another unrelentingly. For a time a plan was put forward for Sparta's onetime Peloponnesian allies to create a new league headed by Argos and including anyone who wanted to be included (provided, of course, that they were neither Sparta nor Athens). Then Argos, whose record of treacherous neutrality during the Persian Wars had never been forgotten, lost its nerve and sent an embassy to Lacedaemon to negotiate a new long-term treaty.

Meanwhile Athens was furious with Sparta for making up to the Boeotians despite the fact that not only had they not handed back the frontier fort they were meant to do, but had demolished it.

At this awkward juncture a familiar personality intervened, who was determined to make as much trouble as he could—Alcibiades. In 420 he was elected *strategos* for the first time when he was thirty (the earliest legal age) or a little older and, after Cleon's death in 422, became a leading man in the state.

He was prominent among radical politicians who were opposed to the peace with Sparta, and he worked hard to discredit it. Having spent his childhood in a political household, he was well connected and familiar with all the issues. He was also charming, highly intelligent, and a brilliant public speaker; he even turned a lisp to pleasing effect.

Alcibiades put forward to the people of Argos (or Argives) the idea of an alliance with Athens. They promptly jilted the Spartans and chose the better offer. A plenipotentiary deputation from Sparta hurried to Athens to try to ward off this new combination of foes. Alcibiades laid a trap; he told the envoys in private that if they made no mention of their full powers he would arrange for Pylos to be handed back to them. They were taken in and at a meeting of the *ecclesia* said in reply to a question they had come without full powers. The *demos* lost patience and was on the point of choosing the alliance with Argos when the session was interrupted by an earthquake. When it resumed the following day, wiser counsels prevailed. Nicias won the debate and was instructed to negotiate an agreement with Sparta.

Unluckily the discussions failed and, after all, Athens agreed to a pact with Argos and a number of smaller Peloponnesian states. It was not long before Sparta, feeling itself threatened on its home ground, marched with a strong force under its King Agis and met an allied army outside Mantinea, a *polis* in Arcadia. In 418, they won a great battle. The Athenian contingent extricated itself relatively unscathed, but its two generals were killed.

The encounter had two consequences. Argos's uncertain bid to become the leading power in the Peloponnese was over and it had no option but to submit to the Spartans. It was a welcome victory, for it restored some of their battered prestige after the Pylos debacle.

As for Athens little harm had come of its Argive adventure, but little good either. Alcibiades had shown himself to be an opportunist rather than a statesman.

The amusing and affable drunk at Agathon's dinner party may have become a senior politician, but he was no more respectable than he ever had been. He spent the family fortune with abandon. He dressed extravagantly, scandalously trailing long purple robes in the dust of the marketplace. He was well known for financing theatrical productions. In 416, the same year that Plato had him gate-crash Agathon's dinner party, he entered a record-breaking seven teams of horses in the Olympic Games, which took first, second, and fourth places in the chariot race. This extraordinary—and ridiculously expensive—achievement became a talking point throughout the Greek world. "Victory is a beautiful thing," wrote Euripides obligingly in a celebratory ode and the winner thoroughly agreed.

Alcibiades claimed that he was more than a playboy with a talent to amuse, and that promoting his image was good for Athens as well as for him. According to Thucydides, he told the *ecclesia:*

> The Hellenes expected to see our city ruined by the war, but they concluded that it is greater than it really is because of the splendid show I made as its representative at the Games.... It is a very useful type of folly when a man spends his money not just for himself but for his city too.

Alcibiades was reported to act greedily and arrogantly, and to get his way by threats. He was popular, but also feared as a bully. He married well—that is, wealthily. His wife, Hipparete, was the sister of Callias, one of the city's richest men, and she brought with her a handsome dowry of ten talents.

Alcibiades treated her badly and apparently brought his pickups back to the house—whether free women or slaves. This was indeed unacceptable behavior, for a wife's home was her protected domain.

Alcibiades seems to have been addicted to sex. A third-century poet wittily remarked that as a boy he drew husbands away from their wives, and as a young man wives from their husbands.

Hipparete lost patience and left home to lodge with a relative. Almost certainly accompanied by a supportive male relative, she went in person to see the Chief Archon at his workplace, the City Hall or Prytaneum in the *agora,* and asked him for a divorce. Divorce seems to have been uncommon in ancient Athens, although little information has come down to us; when initiated by a woman, it was a public procedure presumably designed to safeguard her reputation.

Alcibiades was having none of this; the last thing he wanted to do was to repay the dowry, as a divorce would have required. Calling on some friends to help him, he carried off his wife from the *agora* by force and brought her back home. It was evidence of the fear he aroused that nobody in the square tried to stop him. We do not know whether he was acting within his rights or not, but his behavior was at the very least high-handed and brutal. Apparently Hipparete died soon afterwards. Relations with Hipparete's brother went into a deep freeze and Callias accused Alcibiades of plotting his death.

From time to time public affairs and his private life overlapped. Melos is a small volcanic island among the Cyclades, famous for the mining of obsidian (and some centuries later for the statue of the goddess of love, Aphrodite, whom we know as the Venus de Milo). The inhabitants claimed to be descended from Spartans, but remained carefully neutral in the war.

The Athenians had tried, without success, to force the island to join their maritime league. Now, also in the same year as Agathon's symposium, they invaded Melos and laid siege to its main town. They promised a general pardon if Melos agreed to join the Athenian Empire. Once again, the islanders declined. Thucydides wrote (perhaps invented) a debate between spokesmen of the two sides. An Athenian justified imperialism with cold candor.

"It is a necessary law of nature to rule where one can," he said. "We did not make this law, nor were we the first to act on it. . . . All we do is make use of it."

When winter came, the Melians surrendered. There was no forgiveness for the trouble they had caused. All adult males were put to death and the women and children sold into slavery. It was an atrocity that shocked the Greek world.

Alcibiades not only actively approved of the expedition and its cruel conclusion, he personally profited from it. He bought an attractive Melian woman as a slave and had a son by her.

A few months later at the Great Dionysia in the spring of 415 the playwright Euripides staged his tragedy *The Trojan Women*. He was a disenchanted rationalist and was noted for his strong women's parts. Like Aeschylus and Sophocles he addressed the issues of the day, usually in mythical disguise. The play hardly has any plot, but it is a masterpiece of grief. Troy has just fallen and Euripides directs his attention to the sufferings of a group of women among the ruins of the plundered city. Headed by King Priam's wife, Hecabe, they are waiting to be distributed among the victors and can look forward only to a life of slavery. One of the queen's daughters is sacrificed on the tomb of Achilles and her darling little grandson, Astyanax, is also slaughtered by the Greeks. Hecabe wails over his dead body:

> Dear, lifeless lips, do you remember your promises? You leant
> over my bed and vowed, When you die, Grandmother, I will cut
> a long curl of my hair for you, and I will bring all my friends to
> honor your grave with gifts and holy words. But you have bro-
> ken your promise, young man.

Euripides was inflaming a sore spot. It is perhaps because his audience recognized echoes of Melos, but refused to admit its guilt for what had been done in its name, that that year the first prize for tragedy went to an execrable poet (in the opinion of Aristophanes, a good judge) called Xenocles.

Payment for the crime would wait.

. . .

The politics of Sicily were complicated. The Carthaginians, an aggressive mercantile city-state based in North Africa, were well established in the west of the island, Greek settlements populated the eastern end (as well as the Italian boot), and indigenous peoples, the Sicels, occupied the interior. The Athenians had long had an on-off interest in Sicily and agreed on bilateral treaties with individual city-states from time to time. Between 427 and 424 in the early stages of the Peloponnesian War they had sent out expeditions to Sicily with a view to gaining allies; they were a little afraid that pro-Spartan *poleis,* such as the great city of Syracuse, founded by Corinth, might aid and abet their enemies in mainland Greece.

But these interventions led nowhere and the fears of Athens were allayed. More pressing matters called for their attention in mainland Greece. Then in 416 the *polis* of Segesta in western Sicily asked the Athenians, with whom it had agreed to an alliance not long before, for assistance in a war they were losing against their neighbor Selinus, which was supported by Syracuse. The *ecclesia* was not especially interested in the details, but was minded to respond favorably to the appeal. According to Thucydides, their unstated idea was "to conquer the whole of the island while at the same time making it look as if their purpose was simply to help . . . their newly acquired allies there."

Pericles' advice not to expand the empire while fighting a war was forgotten. However, there was peace (of a sort) and no immediate threats faced the Athenians from Sparta or its allies. The situation at home was more complicated, but eventually a political consensus was reached.

A war faction led by Alcibiades wanted to continue meddling in the Peloponnese despite the setback at Mantinea; and the less aggressive Nicias made his priority the recapture of Amphipolis. The *ecclesia* could not agree on a consistent policy.

About 416, a radical fixer called Hyperbolus (so like an exaggerated version of Cleon that someone nicknamed him "Cleon in hyperbole") thought he saw a way forward. He would resolve the standoff by proposing an ostracism, which (he calculated) would remove either the chief advocate of the peace faction, Nicias, or (preferably) Alcibiades. Although sworn opponents, the two candidates for ostracism joined forces to ward off the threat. Their combined supporters scratched the name of Hyperbolus on their potsherds and much to his dismay the author of the ostracism found himself in exile. (In retrospect, although this was an amusing outcome, everyone thought he had been the victim of a dirty trick and it seems that the constitutional mechanism of ostracism was never used again.)

So the problem of two opposing policies—one for peace and the other for war—that were more or less equally supported remained unresolved. However, the plan to invade Sicily was so glamorously ambitious that unity was achieved. The *demos* had no hesitation in voting for it and ordering a fleet of sixty triremes. Nicias did his best to dissuade them. He tried to frighten people by exaggerating the expense and said that sixty ships would be too few. Pressed to name his own figure, he hazarded at least one hundred triremes. The *ecclesia* immediately agreed to the increase and voted full powers to the three generals whom it chose to lead the expedition.

In an obvious attempt to encompass the complete range of opinion, it appointed Alcibiades, Nicias, and Lamachus. The first two were brave on the battlefield and had extensive military experience, but they were first and foremost leaders of political factions that disagreed with one another; the third was a nonpolitical "career" commander. In principle this was a good team, although running a military campaign by committee would risk delay and compromise when immediate decisions were needed. Still, the auguries for a successful campaign were good.

One man stood out in opposition, Socrates, who said he had "no great expectation that any good would come to the city from the expedition."

Scattered throughout Athens stood Herms. These curious sculptures offered protection from harm (see page 87). They were venerated and at festival times were rubbed down with olive oil and garlanded. Every neighborhood of the city had them; they stood at boundaries and street corners, in front of temples, gymnasia, porticoes, and in the porches of private houses. There was a row of them beside the Royal Stoa (or Colonnade) in the *agora*.

One May morning not long before the planned departure of the fleet for Sicily, Athenians woke up to news of sacrilege. The faces of many of these statues had been disfigured and knocked about during the night. The identity of the vandals was unknown.

There was worse to come. An instant investigation drew out testimony from personal servants and *metics* of even worse offenses. Although they had nothing to say specifically about the Herms, they reported that young men worse for wear from drink had defaced statues and had conducted a mock celebration of the Mysteries at Eleusis; these were highly secret initiation ceremonies that involved "visions" and the promise of an afterlife. Witnesses claimed that the blasphemous parody had been staged in the house of Alcibiades.

According to Thucydides, those who disliked Alcibiades "exaggerated the whole thing and made as much noise as they could about it. They claimed that the business with the Mysteries and the profanation of the Herms were all part and parcel of a plot to overthrow the democracy and that Alcibiades was behind it all."

As a disciple of the supposedly irreligious Socrates, Alcibiades was convicted in the court of public opinion, despite his furious denials. So far as the Herms were concerned his involvement is, in truth, most unlikely. To commit such a public outrage on the eve of his departure for Sicily would have been the height of stupidity—and whatever else he was, Alcibiades was not stupid. The timing strongly suggests that the perpetrators' aim was to hold up or disrupt the Sicilian Expedition. The vandals could have been paid agents of Syracuse or possibly some of the wilder activists in Nicias's peace camp.

It is not clear when the mock-Mysteries were supposed to have taken place, but if they occurred a good while in the past, one could imagine the teenaged Alcibiades happily joining in a bit of blasphemous fun. In the case of an adult seriously building a political reputation the verdict must be at worst not proven.

Alcibiades protested his innocence and demanded an immediate trial to establish the truth. His enemies declined to take the bait. They wanted to pursue their investigations in the absence of the army, which thought highly of its young general. He was ordered to sail out with the fleet alongside his two colleagues, Nicias and Lamachus. He had no choice but to obey.

Even if we clear Alcibiades of involvement, what the scandal did do was raise fundamental questions about his political beliefs. Was he a true democrat? Was he aiming at establishing a tyranny, as some feared? A contemporary who later admitted to having played a part in the mutilation of the Herms said of Alcibiades that he talked "as though he were a friend of the people" and "a guardian of the constitution," while really favoring an oligarchy. Socrates was no friend of the Athenian democracy, so Alcibiades' association with him did neither of them any good in the popular mind.

Perhaps Alcibiades was happy to play the political game according to the rules laid down by Cleisthenes, but privately reserved judgment and waited on events. Suspicions about his real motives may have been well founded. But for the time being he was a man of the people. It is highly unlikely that he had any active plans for fomenting revolution.

The grand armada sailed via Corcyra to Sicily. The generals were not entirely sure what to do when they arrived. Nicias, whose heart was not in the campaign, wanted merely to press the two opposing *poleis* to come to an agreement, sail about for a while in a show of strength, and then go home. Alcibiades argued that the expedition should first of all recruit allies among the city-states of Sicily. Lamachus, an elderly man but a soldier's soldier and willing to take risks, was all for marching on Syracuse at once, their real object, while they were not yet ready to defend themselves. Even if they could not storm the city they would be able to cut it off by land and sea, and so compel a capitulation. He reluctantly agreed to back Alcibiades' plan in order to outvote Nicias, whose opinion he liked least. But, as it turned out, the recruitment drive failed, for it transpired that the Sicilians were cautious and preferred neutrality. A wasted summer passed with nothing achieved.

Back in Athens the atmosphere was becoming toxic. False evidence inflamed a witch hunt. Young aristocrats were mainly blamed for the sacrilegious scandals. Feeling against Alcibiades grew. It was alleged that he played the part of the high priest of Eleusis during tipsy revels. The *ecclesia* recalled him to face his accusers. This turned out to be a mistake.

The impeachment against the general was still on record in Plutarch's day. It read in part:

> Thessalus, the son of Cimon, of the deme of Laciadae lays information against Alcibiades, son of Cleinias, of the deme of the Scambonidae, that he committed sacrilege against the goddesses of Eleusis, Demeter and Kore [another name for Persephone]. He made a mockery of the Mysteries and put them on show in his own house.

It is noteworthy that the accuser's father was the great Cimon, who lost power for being too pro-Spartan. If he kept up the family tradition, the son will have wanted permanent peace with Sparta as fervently as Nicias. Getting rid of Pericles' ward would go a long way to achieving that.

The state galley, the *Salaminia,* was dispatched to bring home Alcibiades and other co-accused. However, he was not placed under arrest, for he was well liked and it was felt the men might mutiny. At Thurii, on the Italian coast, he disembarked, gave his guards the slip, and went into hiding. When the *Salaminia* returned to Athens without its prize, the *demos* was enraged. Alcibiades was condemned to death in absentia and his estate was confiscated. The sale list of his bedroom furniture has survived; twelve Milesian (that is, high-quality) couches were auctioned along with coverlets, bedclothes, and "six perfume bottles."

It was further decreed that his name should be cursed by all the city's priests and priestesses. When he learned of the death sentence, Alcibiades remarked: "I'll show them that I am still alive."

He was as good as his word. After extricating himself from Thurii he made his way across the Ionian Sea to mainland Greece and settled in Argos where he had friends. Then, fearing for his safety, he decided to renounce his country altogether. He wrote to Sparta asking for asylum. He promised: "I will render you services greater than all the harm I have done you when I was your enemy."

His request was granted, although, not trusting turncoats, the Lacedaemonian establishment was cautious. Alcibiades made his way there and, like a chameleon, quickly turned himself into a proper Spartan. The locals were captivated: according to Plutarch,

> When they saw him with his hair untrimmed, taking cold baths, enjoying their coarse bread, and dining on black broth, they could hardly believe their eyes, and doubted the man they now saw had ever had a cook in his own house, or so much as looked at a perfumier, or endured the touch of Milesian wool.

The treachery of Alcibiades gave his hosts a gift beyond price, as the half peace tipped slowly over into war. As a leading politician, he knew all the secrets of Athens, the unstated policies, the future covert ambitions. He appears to have told the Spartans everything. He showed them all the cards in the other player's hand.

In particular, he gave them two invaluable pieces of advice. First, he persuaded them to send out a competent Spartan general to lead the defense of Syracuse. No time was lost in commissioning a certain Gylippus; his mother may have been a *helot* and so he was probably not an Equal. However, in his childhood he had been trained in the traditional Spartan fashion. When he grew up, he was allowed to join a military mess and, as he did not have the money, a wealthy patron covered his fees.

Second, Alcibiades proposed that the Spartans resume their invasions of Attica and, above all, build a permanent fort at Decelea, a strongpoint near the northern border with Boeotia. Not wanting to be the first to break the peace, they waited for a year before doing as he said, but the effect when it came was dramatic. From now on, instead of making brief annual visits, a Spartan force was always present on Athenian soil. The economic consequences were severe. Food imports from Euboea were interrupted. Farming had to be abandoned altogether and for food supplies the population now relied exclusively on grain from the Black Sea. The production of silver from Laurium was halted. Over the coming years more than twenty thousand slaves, mainly skilled workers, ran away to Decelea (it did them little good: they hoped for liberty, but, cruelly, were resold into servitude at rock-bottom prices).

Thucydides summed up the situation:

> Every single thing the city needed had to be imported, that instead of a city it became a fortress. Summer and winter the Athenians were worn out by having to keep guard on the fortifications. . . . But what oppressed them most was that they now had two wars at once.

Alcibiades had shown his true colors and those who suspected him of being unstable and immature had had their fears confirmed. It was an expensive lesson, for he was doing everything he could to make Athens lose the war. Like an angry child, he was imagining the worst possible revenge for his treatment—saying to himself: "Then they'll be sorry." He did not yet understand that he might also be spiting himself.

. . .

In Sicily the Athenians were doing as well as could be expected when doing very little. Victory in a land battle was not followed up, perhaps for want of cavalry. Winter passed uneventfully. Nicias "kept on sitting around, sailing about, and thinking things over" and so the advantage of surprise was lost.

At last, with the arrival of spring 414, Nicias bestirred himself. His plan was to blockade the city and to achieve this it would be necessary to take control of Epipolae, rising ground that sloped up northwest from the city to a commanding plateau. The Syracusans intended to station six hundred picked troops on these heights, but the Athenians pipped them to the post by landing their entire force north of Syracuse and storming Epipolae. They then began building a wall northwards at speed.

At this rate the Syracusans would soon be sealed off by land as well as by sea. So they constructed a counterwall designed to cut across the Athenian circumvallation. However, the Athenians attacked and destroyed it, and then built fortifications southwards towards the Great Harbor. Once again a counterwall was constructed and once again, in a fierce battle, it was destroyed. The victory came at a high price, for the general Lamachus was killed in the fighting. Now Nicias, the reluctant warrior, was commander-in-chief and alone.

However, victory was in sight. All that remained to be done was to extend the north wall until it met the sea. Thucydides writes: "The Syracusans no longer thought they could win the war, no kind of help having arrived from the Peloponnese, and were beginning to discuss terms of surrender among themselves."

Once again Nicias dithered. He fortified Plemmyrion, a promontory on the southern end of the Great Harbor of Syracuse, a convenient base for the fleet. Unaccountably he did not trouble to complete the wall on Epipolae. This was another grave error, for it allowed the Spartan general Gylippus to slip into the city and take command. He energized the Syracusans and restored their morale.

He realized that his first priority was to regain control of Epipolae and started work on a new counterwall. After a couple of sharp engagements, the Syracusans succeeded in cutting across the Athenian rampart with one of their own. At last, even if the Athenians won battles, the city was safe from complete encirclement. Meanwhile reinforcements arrived to strengthen the defenders. The Athenians found that they were outnumbered and the prospect of victory suddenly receded.

Nicias saw that every day which passed brought new strength to the enemy and increased his own difficulties. He was especially worried about the state of the fleet; the ships were waterlogged and the rowers were no longer in peak condition. He himself had contracted a kidney disease and was in poor physical shape. The strain of sole command after the death of Lamachus was telling on him. He wrote a letter to the *ecclesia* in which he explained the situation. "We thought we were the besiegers, but in fact have become the besieged."

He reported that the time had come either to recall the expedition or to send out another fleet and army as big as the first. Also because of his illness he asked to be allowed to resign his command and for a replacement commander to be appointed. Nicias hoped that his dispatch would persuade the *ecclesia* to recall the entire expedition, but, once again, he was to be disappointed by its bellicosity.

The failure in Sicily was a shock to the democracy, but when offered double or quits it instinctively doubled. Another vast expeditionary force was assembled and Nicias was not relieved of his command. He had always been known for being lucky, and sooner or later, it was felt, fate would relent and turn in his direction. His incompetence and lack of enthusiasm were overlooked. However, two new generals, Eurymedon and the hero of Pylos, Demosthenes, were appointed to join him.

The balance of power was changing. In the summer of 414 Athens brought the peace to a clear and explicit end by raiding Laconia, Sparta's homeland, but surprisingly lost a sea battle in the Corinthian Gulf. The Spartans at last felt free to resume hostilities and it was in the following spring that, as we have seen, they fortified Decelea.

. . .

Meanwhile in the Great Harbor, Nicias's fleet lost a sea fight with the inexperienced Syracusans, whose army captured the fort and supply depot at Plemmyrion.

No longer was the Athenian trireme invulnerable. The situation was becoming decidedly uncomfortable, for Nicias and his men were in some danger of being trapped.

In July 413 there was a massive case of déjà vu. A second superbly equipped fleet, almost as large as the first one, set sail from Piraeus, bound for Sicily. Under the command of Demosthenes, seventy-three warships carried five thousand hoplites as well as three thousand javelin throwers, archers, and slingers. On this occasion the historians did not record crowds of enthusiastic onlookers, and those who were present must have had mixed feelings about the future.

However, the impression the armada made on the Syracusans when it was sighted off the Great Harbor was one of unmixed horror. Plutarch describes the scene.

> The flash of armor, the vivid colors of the ships' ensigns and the cacophony of boatswains and flute-players marking time for the rowers made for a spectacular display, which dismayed the enemy. As was only to be expected, the Syracusans were plunged into despair. They saw ahead of them no end to their troubles except futile suffering and a purposeless loss of life.

Demosthenes knew that in fact the visual glamour of the new fleet was misleading. It was a good example of psyops, a mind game designed to influence the enemy by the use of selective information. It did not reveal the grim reality. Demosthenes studied the Athenian campaign so far and concluded that, unless the Athenians regained control of Epipolae and fully invested the city, Syracuse would never be defeated.

This was more easily said than done. Gylippus had ensured strong defenses on the heights and Demosthenes' first attempt to capture the counterwall came to nothing. Seeing that any assault by daylight was bound to fail, he planned a daring night raid.

One midnight in early August Demosthenes led about ten thousand hoplites and the same number of light-armed skirmishers up the steep ascent to Epipolae. The moon had not yet risen and the Athenians surprised the Syracusan garrison and captured their fort. Some of the garrison were killed, but the rest escaped and spread word of the Athenian attack. The elite Epipolae guard rushed out to meet the enemy, but they too were quickly routed.

The Athenians pressed on, eager not to lose momentum before they reached their objectives. Some began immediately to tear down the counterwall. Gylippus, taken entirely by surprise, arrived with his troops from outworks, but the Athenians pushed them back.

Then something went wrong. The Athenians assumed that victory was theirs and began to lose cohesion. They encountered a band of tough Boeotians, who had crossed seas to come to Syracuse's aid, and for the first time that night the Athenians were thrown back.

There was now a bright moon, but while figures could be discerned in outline they were not recognizable. Also, the defeated hoplites had no clear idea where they were. Large numbers of soldiers of both sides were crowded together on the plateau and it was hard to tell who was friend and who was foe. Soldiers still climbing up onto Epipolae received no orders when they arrived and collided with their retreating compatriots. The noise was confusing, with different groups singing their paeans, or hymns of thanksgiving, at the tops of their voices and shouting out their watchwords.

Thucydides writes:

> After once being thrown into confusion, the Athenians ended by colliding with each other in many parts of the field, friend against friend and citizen against citizen. They not only created panic among themselves, but actually came to blows and could only be parted with difficulty.

Many men lost their lives trying to escape from Epipolae; the descent was narrow and a good number threw themselves down from the cliffs. By the time day dawned, some two and a half thousand Athenian infantry were dead.

Night fighting was always a dangerous tactic in ancient warfare. Even in daylight a battlefield was a mystifying place and most soldiers knew only what was going on in their immediate vicinity. Preliminary surprise could often be achieved, but if a nocturnal engagement lasted for any length of time soldiers could easily lose their bearings. Communication between the high command and the rank and file was usually out of the question.

Demosthenes was a talented general, but as we saw earlier in his career over-optimism could make him careless. He was unfamiliar with the terrain (although Nicias could have explained it to him in detail) and failed to make his orders absolutely clear. He ought to have established way stations to manage the flow of traffic or some other reliable system of information exchange.

There was no point deploring the past. A council of war was held the following day to discuss what to do now—not only in the light of the defeat, but also the army's catastrophically low morale. The camp was situated in marshy ground and many men were ill.

Demosthenes saw, correctly, that the campaign was lost and advised an immediate withdrawal while Athens still had mastery of the seas. He told the meeting: "It is better for Athens for us to fight against those who are building fortifications at Decelea in Attica than against the Syracusans, who can no longer be conquered easily."

Nicias disagreed. He accepted that the expedition was in grave danger, but he had private sources of information in Syracuse which suggested that the enemy was in an even worse way. He was sure that the *ecclesia* in Athens would disapprove of a withdrawal and refused to lead the army away from Sicily. Privately, he was in two minds, but he feared an angry *demos* and knew that it would punish failure. He said he would prefer death at the hands of an enemy to an unjust condemnation by his fellow-citizens. Demosthenes and Eurymedon could have outvoted Nicias, but they let their senior colleague have his way.

Indecision meant delay. Sickness in the camp worsened. Meanwhile Gylippus recruited a large army of native Sicels, and hoplite reinforcements arrived from the Peloponnese. Nicias's resolution to stay put weakened. He now endorsed Demosthenes' proposal that the expedition should sail away from Syracuse to open country where the army would be free to maneuver and attract supplies, which were running dangerously short. Orders to leave were to be given as secretly as possible.

On the night of August 27 between 9:41 and 10:30 the moon was totally eclipsed. As early as the seventh century Greek thinkers and scientists had put aside myths and looked for rational explanations of natural phenomena: Herodotus reports that Thales of Miletus predicted a solar eclipse on May 28, 585. However, many Athenians were superstitious and had laughed at the pretensions of science in *The Clouds* of Aristophanes. Panic-stricken, they saw the eclipse as a warning from the gods against their plan to withdraw from Syracuse rather than as an astronomical event.

According to Thucydides, Nicias was "rather over-addicted to divination and such things." He consulted a soothsayer who recommended that the Athenians should wait "three times nine days" before departing. Not only was this a catastrophic piece of advice militarily, but it was unnecessary. A third-century seer called Philochorus judged that an eclipse "was not unfavourable to men who were fleeing but, on the contrary, very favourable; for concealment is just what acts of fear need, whereas light is their enemy."

If Nicias had been mentally more nimble he would have promoted an interpretation à la Philochorus that would allow the army to leave. But the fact is that in his heart of hearts the commander-in-chief preferred inactivity and feared responsibility, as he had done ever since the invasion of Sicily was first mooted.

The Syracusans soon learned from deserters that Nicias intended to sail away, but was delayed by the eclipse. Sensing a collapse of enemy morale, they decided to force a sea fight in the Great Harbor. After some days training their crews, they sent out seventy-six triremes and at the same time launched a land attack on the camp walls. The Athenians fielded a fleet of eighty-six warships. The gamble paid off handsomely. Although the enemy hoplites were repelled, the Athenians lacked space for maneuver in the Great Harbor and were defeated. Some of their triremes were driven back onto the marshy northwestern shore of the harbor and the Syracusans dragged away eighteen of them. Eurymedon, who was in charge, fell.

The eclipse was forgotten and everyone now wanted to get away as soon as possible. If the Athenians did not make their escape immediately they would be cornered.

But the jubilant Syracusans were not ready simply to let the invaders go. They were determined to capture and destroy the entire expeditionary force. "To conquer the Athenians by land and by sea," they felt, "would win us great glory in Hellas."

They started to block the harbor entrance with a line of triremes broadside on as well as other craft and boats at anchor. They chained them together and laid boards over them. As soon as the Athenians realized what was happening, they decided to leave a garrison onshore defending the smallest space possible and manned their entire fleet of 110 ships with every fit oarsman they had and a large number of archers and javelin throwers.

This was Nicias's finest hour. Although half distraught by the crisis in Athenian fortunes, he behaved as a leader should. He took a boat through the fleet and spoke to each trireme captain individually, doing his best to cheer everyone up. He also arranged for the infantry to line the shore and give whatever vocal support they could to the fleet. Meanwhile elsewhere on the harbor's edge Syracusan soldiers also gathered to watch the oncoming battle. Women and old men looked on from the city walls. Both sides shouted and cheered as if they were spectators at some great sporting occasion at the Olympic Games.

The paean sounded and the Athenians rowed across the bay to attack the barrier. Through sheer force of numbers their ships crowded around and began to cut the chains and break through. The Syracusans came out against them and pushed them off into the center of the harbor and the battle became a series of one-to-one duels. There was little room for ramming or the tactics of movement that had won Athens the mastery of the seas. Fighting was hand-to-hand as marines tried to grapple with and board enemy triremes.

Thucydides has left a famous description of the struggle, so vivid that it must have been based on the evidence of an eyewitness:

> The two armies on the shore, while victory hung in the balance, were a prey to the most agonizing and conflicting emotions. The Syracusans thirsted for more glory than they had already won, while the invaders feared to find themselves worse off than they already were. . . . While the result of the battle was in doubt all kinds of sound could be heard coming simultaneously from this one Athenian army, shrieks, cheers, "We're winning," "We're losing" and all the other different cries one would expect to hear from a great army in great danger.

Eventually the Syracusan fleet had the better of it and chased the enemy across the harbor and back to land, to great shouts and cheers. It was a decisive setback. The panic-stricken Athenians ran as fast as they could from their beached ships. They could see that they had no hope of escaping by land, unless some miracle happened, but they refused point-blank to board the sixty viable triremes that remained and resume the struggle. Such a move would have taken the Syracusans by surprise and might well have succeeded.

Escaping by land was now, in fact, their only if forlorn hope. The Athenians were still dangerous and the Syracusans feared, correctly, that the enemy might leave by night and steal a march on them. So they sent some horsemen who pretended to be renegades; they shouted into the enemy camp a warning not to march that night because the roads were already guarded. Believing the information to be genuine the generals put off their departure for a couple of days.

This was yet another blunder, which they compounded by lingering for a third day to allow time for the men to pack their most essential luggage. They burned some of their ships but left the rest for the enemy to drag away at will. Meanwhile the Syracusans had used the interval to build roadblocks on the likely escape routes. At last on September 11 the bedraggled expeditionary force set off inland on the third day after the sea fight. In all, they amounted to no fewer than forty thousand souls, allies as well as Athenians and oarsmen as well as hoplites.

The generals intended to march inland into native Sicel country before turning northwards for the port of Catana where they could expect a friendly welcome and supplies.

Nicias, ill and in pain, did his best to raise the men's spirits. But they were so fearful and depressed that they left their dead unburied, a grave sin of omission, and abandoned seriously wounded comrades, despite their pleas to be taken with them. The two generals each commanded a hollow rectangle of troops surrounding civilians, camp followers, and the like.

The army fought its way successfully through enemy opposition, but was constantly harried by cavalry and javelin throwers. Food and water were in short supply. Eight miles northwest of Syracuse an obstacle stood in the way—the Acraean cliff, a large plateau accessible through a ravine. The enemy had already built a wall across the ravine, and it was impervious to attack. A torrential downpour soaked the Athenians. The Syracusans began building another wall behind them, threatening to trap them, so the Athenians turned around, prevented its completion, and pushed past to level ground where they encamped.

They gave up their original plan to make for Catana and decided to march south. They lit many fires and crept away under cover of darkness. Unfortunately, during the night Demosthenes' contingent became confused and fell behind. The Syracusans caught up with it by midday and encircled it, as it stood huddled in an olive grove surrounded by a wall. They rained missiles on the Athenians from every direction. There was nothing they could do in response and on September 16 Demosthenes capitulated on condition that none of his men was to be put to death. Once the detailed arrangements for surrender had been agreed, he tried to take his life, but only wounded himself with his sword before it was removed from him. Of the twenty thousand men who had set out from Syracuse under his command only six thousand were left.

Meanwhile Nicias, six or eight miles ahead, was plowing on. A Syracusan herald broke the news to him about the fate of Demosthenes, which at first he refused to believe. He proposed terms of surrender, but they were not accepted. On the following day, the eighth of their march, the Athenians pressed forward under constant Syracusan attacks until they arrived at the river Asinarus (today's Falconara). The men were exhausted and were longing for water.

Many of them broke ranks and ran to the river to slake their thirst. They crowded in so closely that some men were trampled underfoot or killed with their own spears. The water became muddy and full of blood, but they went on gulping it. Syracusan and allied troops were stationed on the far bank and rained missiles onto the confused mass of Athenians and their allies. Some then came down and slaughtered anyone they could find.

Nicias saw that this was the end. He surrendered personally to Gylippus, whom he trusted more than the Syracusans. Of his troops only one thousand survived the Asinarus. Athenian citizens were imprisoned throughout the winter in the city's stone quarries. In this early concentration camp, they were "forced to do everything in the same place." Most of them perished from sickness and a wretched diet (half a slave's rations of meal and water). Some were sold and branded with the sign of a horse on their foreheads.

Against the wishes of Gylippus, who wanted to show them off in

Lacedaemon, the ailing Nicias and the half-dead Demosthenes were put out of their misery and executed. Their bodies were thrown beyond the city gates and lay there in plain sight for all to see.

The Sicilians were great poetry lovers. They were especially fond of Euripides and used to treasure any scraps of verse visitors from mainland Greece could repeat to them from memory. Apparently some of the very few Athenians who returned home safely made a point of calling on the author of *The Trojan Women* to thank him. They told him that they had received their freedom after teaching their masters whatever they could recall of his poetry. Others, after the final battle, had been given food and drink in return for reciting some of his lyrics.

One day in mid- to late September 413, a stranger landed at Piraeus and took a seat in a barber's shop. He began to talk about the defeat in Sicily as if it were common knowledge. In fact, not a word had reached Attica and the shocked barber ran at top speed to the city. He rushed up to the Archons and blurted out the news in the *agora*. Uproar followed and an emergency meeting of the *ecclesia* was called.

The barber was cross-examined, but he could not explain clearly who his informant had been (no doubt the stranger had very sensibly made himself scarce). He was condemned as an agitator and tortured on the wheel until messengers arrived and gave chapter and verse of the disaster. Even then for some time people did not believe what they were told. It had to be an exaggeration. It could not be true.

It is tempting to regard the Sicilian Expedition as an example of pride before a fall, of overreaching ambition justly punished. But terrible as the narrative is even for the casual reader, there was nothing inevitable or even likely about the catastrophe. In fact, it was a catalogue of if-onlys. If only Alcibiades had been allowed to retain his command; if only Nicias had put his shoulder to the wheel, had not sought to shuffle off responsibility, had not delayed, had not been foolishly superstitious; above all, if only old Lamachus had been allowed to launch an attack on Syracuse immediately on arrival, as he wished—with a reasonable degree of diligence all would have been well.

That said, there *was* something deeply irresponsible about the project. It diverted energy and treasure to a policy that was, strictly speaking, unnecessary. The defeat of Syracuse would not help Athens, one way or another, to resolve its broken relationship with Sparta and its allies. What is more, even if the *demos* could reasonably assume victory, how did it propose to govern Sicily once it had conquered it? It is unlikely that it would be able to keep a humbled Syracuse permanently down. Athens would almost certainly collide with the fabulously rich maritime power Carthage, which had a foothold in the west of the island and would certainly have given it a run for its money.

Underlying the Sicilian Expedition lurked an ambition to unite all Hellas under an Athenian banner. The fact was that Athens did not have a large enough population, nor dispose of sufficient and sustainable wealth, to capture and control the Greek world, the lands that stretched from Segesta in the west to Miletus in the east, from Cyrene in northern Africa to Thrace or the frontiers of Macedon. The failure of the Egyptian campaign in the long-ago days of Pericles had convincingly demonstrated that the reach of Athens exceeded its grasp. His successors in power had forgotten the lesson. They learned it again in Sicily.

Counterfactuals are risky, but, if it had vanquished Syracuse, Athens might well have achieved overall dominion of the Greek world, but surely not for long. There would have been endemic instability and revolts. So maybe the incapacity of Nicias saved everyone a deal of trouble in the longer run.

As it was, Athens now had its back to the wall. Thucydides had no doubt of the importance of the disaster. He wrote:

This was the greatest achievement during this war, or in my opinion the greatest we know of in Greek history. For the vic-

tors it was the most brilliant of successes. It was the most ruinous debacle for the losers, for they were defeated comprehensively
and in every way. Their sufferings were on a vast scale. Their
destruction was, as they say, total. Their fleet, their army, everything was destroyed, and few out of many returned home.

20

The End of Democracy?

After so many false starts, the Athenians at last had victory in their sights.

In March or April 410 news arrived at Athens of a glorious engagement at sea off Cyzicus, a *polis* on the southern coast of the Sea of Marmara. A complete Spartan fleet had been eliminated. The Athenian admirals had captured all the enemy's warships, and taken many prisoners (shades of Sphacteria) and a vast quantity of booty.

Although the Spartan commander, Mindarus, was brave and experienced, this had been his third major maritime defeat in a row and he himself had been killed. Within the space of a few months the Peloponnesians had lost between 135 and 155 triremes. Athens had complete control of the seas and had secured the sea routes for food imports from the Ukraine and the Crimea, the wheat that, post-Decelea, was vital for the city's survival.

The Spartan vice admiral had written with laconic brevity to Lacedaemon, pleading for help, for orders, for anything: "Ships gone, Mindarus dead, men starving, don't know what to do." As a final stroke of bad luck, the letter was captured by the Athenians and greatly entertained the *demos*.

Sacrifices were made to the gods in celebration and various festivities were held. Then a high-level delegation arrived in the city from Lacedaemon. It was headed by a former *ephor*, Endius, who addressed the *ecclesia* in direct and simple terms. He wanted the long war, which had lasted on and off for more than two decades, to come to an end. He argued that both sides were suffering, Athens even more than Sparta, and that it was time to halt the mutually self-destructive struggle. He proposed a treaty with Athens.

> Men of Athens, we want to make peace with you, on these terms; that each of us keep what cities we now possess; that the strongholds we maintain in one another's territories [Pylos, for example, and Decelea] be abandoned, and that our prisoners of war be ransomed by exchange, one Laconian for one Athenian.

How could all this be, only two years after the Sicilian Expedition? So huge and so complete had been the destruction of manpower in 413 that most people expected Athens to concede defeat.

In fact, this huge historical calamity did not end the war, but it did transform it. Once the news from Sicily had settled in, the first reaction of the Athenians was to give up hope. The thousands of hoplites, cavalry, and men of military age who had lost their lives could not be replaced until a new generation had grown up. The best and most experienced generals were gone. There were hardly any ships in the Piraeus dockyards and most of the crews were dead. The treasury was nearly empty. There was a widespread fear that a vengeful Sicilian fleet was already at sea and heading for Piraeus. The allies would all surely revolt and the Athenian Empire would collapse.

After thoroughly frightening itself, the *demos* regained its nerve with a titanic effort of will. Despite its limited resources, it decided not to give up the struggle. Somehow or another it scraped together the funds and the timber to put together a new fleet. It raised money and did its best to keep its "allies" loyal.

The old system of an annual subscription fee for members of the Delian League was replaced by a 5 percent tax on imports and exports to or from all harbors in the empire; it was believed that this would raise more money and would be a more equitable system of payment. It underlined the fact that the Athenian "peace" throughout the Mediterranean encouraged trade and economic growth even in time of war. In the city itself the people took measures of economy and reform, appointing a committee of "wise men" to advise the *ecclesia* on the situation. Thucydides summed up the mood drily: "As is the way with democracies, now that they were panic-stricken, they were ready to put everything in order."

And here was the surprising thing. Although there were major revolts, much of the empire stood firm alongside its master. There was good reason for this. Persia had by no means gone away. The Athenians may have been high-handed and arrogant, but they *did* provide protection from the eastern threat. Also they now took more care to treat their subjects well; when they expelled a Spartan garrison from the rebel *polis* of Byzantium, they did not replace it with one of their own—an example of what a contemporary historian called a "new policy of justness and conciliation adopted as a means of recovering the empire."

That said, Chios off the Anatolian coast revolted and other league members on the Asiatic seaboard followed suit. The Athenian fleet laid waste the fertile countryside on the island and besieged the main town. By the spring of 411 the situation was that in the northern Aegean and the Hellespont the empire was intact, but a good number of the Ionian *poleis* had seceded.

The Spartans reacted to the misfortunes of Athens by coming back to life. They had always had a bad conscience about the outbreak of war in 431 because they had not accepted an Athenian offer of arbitration beforehand; but with the renewal of hostilities after the Peace of Nicias they felt it was Athens that had broken the peace treaty.

They had always claimed that their original strategic aim was to free the Greeks, but now an easy victory seemed to await them after which, in the words of Thucydides, "the overthrow of the Athenians would leave them in quiet enjoyment of the supremacy over all Hellas."

This was not just a matter of high politics. Individual Spartans foresaw a chance to make their fortunes. According to tradition, nine thousand Equals or full male citizens received country estates, the income from which paid for training and education and for maintaining their communal messes. Only about five thousand Equals fought at the battle of Plataea against the Persian invader in 479, and no more than 3,500 had fought at Mantinea in 418 against the Argive coalition.

The reasons for this decline are both obscure and various, but it is clear that fewer and fewer Spartans were able to afford the high costs of citizenship and that poverty excluded many males who were otherwise eligible to join the Equals.

Spartans came to hope, writes Diodorus Siculus, that if they won the war they would "enjoy great wealth, Sparta as a whole would be made greater and more powerful, and the estates of private citizens would enjoy a great rise in prosperity."

Poverty was not only an issue for individuals; the Spartan state had insufficient resources to carry on the war, however eager they now were to do so. They could not afford to mount a serious challenge to the Athenians at sea. However, there existed an almost boundless treasure-house of money—the Persian Empire. But if Sparta were to accept the Great King's shilling, how could it maintain its proud role as liberator of the Greeks?

As in all such pacts with the devil they could only access these riches if they were willing to sell their souls.

Until the Sicilian disaster, Athens had ruled the Aegean Sea unchallenged and for many years the Great Kings saw little point in contesting its supremacy. But they had not forgotten the humiliations of Salamis and Plataea that their predecessor Xerxes had suffered, and they still had their eyes on the now independent cities of the Ionian seaboard.

The monarch at this time was Darius II, who had ascended the throne over the dead bodies of various other contenders of the blood royal, one of whom was drenched in alcohol and thrown into a pit filled with glowing embers. He wanted Ionia to return to his rule and Athenian weakness after Sicily offered him the opportunity.

Although a Great King was an absolute ruler, his dominions were too extensive for him to rule personally, and we have seen that, at the center of a feudal web of mutual allegiances, he devolved executive authority to the governors of provinces, or satraps. At this time, the two governors in charge of the western end of the Persian Empire were Pharnabazus and Tissaphernes. The province of Hellespontine Phrygia was to all intents a family possession; Pharnabazus had inherited the satrapy from his father and would pass it on to his son. He may have been descended from one of the co-conspirators of Darius the Great. He was an energetic and honorable ruler.

He was on poor terms with the slippery Tissaphernes, who was the grandson of a general in command of the elite Immortals during the invasion of Greece by Xerxes. Tissaphernes was the satrap of Lydia and Caria. He was loyal to his master, but was an inscrutable and unscrupulous political operator.

Darius II made it known to his satraps that he wished them to collect tribute and arrears from the coastal *poleis* of Asia Minor that Persia had lost after 479. This would mean bringing them back under his rule. The simplest and most cost-effective way of achieving this would be to back Sparta in its war with a seriously weakened Athens.

Rival delegations both from Pharnabazus and Tissaphernes arrived in Sparta at about the same time. They said that the Great King was ready to join the war against the Athenians. Each satrap wanted Spartan support for a rebellion of members of the Delian League in their region.

Throughout the Peloponnesian War, as we have seen, Sparta had always been short of money; it had no silver mines, did not engage in trade, and had nothing useful to export except soldiers. The *ephors* had long believed that they would never defeat Athens unless they built a powerful fleet and destroyed it as a sea power. But they had found out to their cost that warships were expensive and ruinous to maintain as a fighting force. However, if Persia were now to foot the bill, Sparta would renew the war on the waves.

The Spartans decided to do business with Tissaphernes. In 412 careful negotiations were opened. An early draft has survived that showed only too clearly the Great King's intentions. It read:

> All the territories and cities now in the King's possession or formerly in the possession of his ancestors shall belong to the King. . . . The war shall be carried on jointly by the King and the Spartans and their allies. . . . Any people who revolt from the King shall be treated as enemies by the Spartans and their allies.

The final text was more discreet, but the message was clear. Sparta, the liberator of Greece against the invading barbarians, had signed up to help those very barbarians regain the lands they had lost. In return Darius would subsidize a Spartan fleet. Everyone could see that once the protection of Athens was withdrawn the Ionian *poleis* would fall back into his hands like low-hanging fruit. The treaty was evidence of the bitterness and the corruption of values that the long war had engendered.

The Spartans agreed to help the men of Chios, which was in the satrap's theater of operations, with their insurrection. They sent their new fleet to this southern theater of war, and with them sailed Alcibiades, still making trouble for Athens.

His astonishing career now lurched in a new direction. While in Sparta he had apparently had an affair with Timaea, the wife of King Agis,

while he was away on campaign at Decelea. This was discovered probably in February 412, much to her husband's annoyance. It is alleged
they had a son, Leotychidas, whom Agis disavowed, although years
later on his deathbed he changed his mind and acknowledged him as
his. According to Plutarch, Alcibiades

> said, in his mocking way, that he had not done this merely as an
> insult, nor simply to satisfy his lust, but to ensure that his de-
> scendants would one day rule over the Spartans.

His hopes were in vain, for the boy never acceded to the throne. In
any event, Agis was seriously displeased and took against the Athenian
renegade. As a matter of fact, the Spartans had never entirely trusted
him and were now tiring of him. The term of office as *ephor* of Endius,
a family friend, came to an end in the following autumn and removed a
key supporter. Alcibiades had pressed for Sparta's new maritime policy,
financed by the Persians, and had engineered or assisted revolts against
Athenian rule. This was beginning to look like bad advice, for Athens
was taking energetic and largely successful measures to protect its foreign possessions. Chios was not the center of a general uprising as had
been expected, but was under siege and consuming Peloponnesian resources. Athenian sailors were tactically more experienced and imaginative; Spartans were in awe of them and tended to avoid battle when
they could. The notion that the empire was ready to fall over at one
push was proving to be wishful thinking.

A letter was sent to the Spartan admiral ordering him to put the
unruly Athenian to death. Alcibiades got wind of this and without
making any fuss removed himself to the court of Tissaphernes. Ostensibly he continued to work for Sparta, but in fact became the satrap's
confidential adviser.

Typically, he immediately fit into his new environment. He turned
his irresistible charm onto Tissaphernes, who despite his long-standing
hatred of the Greeks was bowled over. Plutarch writes that he

surrendered so completely to Alcibiades's blandishments as to surpass him in reciprocal flatteries. He decreed that the most beautiful park [or *paradeisos*] he owned, which was famous for its refreshing streams and lawns and contained pavilions and retreats decorated in a regal and extravagant style, should be renamed after Alcibiades. Everyone always called it by that name.

In fact, Alcibiades was in a very tricky position. He was running out of options. He could follow the example of Themistocles, who had ended his career as a Persian official, but what if he fell out of the satrap's favor? Moreover, he was homesick. Now that he was no longer *persona grata* in Lacedaemon, it was not in his interest to support a Spartan victory. He began to consider how he might negotiate his recall, despite the terrible damage he had done to his homeland's interests.

Some Athenians were thinking the same thing.

The women of Athens are tired of the long war and thirst for peace. The inspirational and strong-minded Lysistrata persuades them to take over the government of the city. This they do by refusing sexual favors to their husbands and by taking over the treasury on the Acropolis. We learn that they will forswear a popular erotic position called The Lioness on a Cheese-Grater. The men are soon desperate for sex and sport enormous erections. A Spartan herald appears, similarly incommoded, proposing peace talks. An accord is soon agreed. Husbands receive back their wives. Spartans and Athenians join in a celebratory dance and banquet.

None of this happened, of course, for this was the plot of Aristophanes' latest farce, *Lysistrata* (her name means "army disbander"), which premiered in 411. But many Athenians in the audience will have wished that it *had*.

In fact, there was sharp dissension in the city, but not between the sexes. The quarrel was between the classes. The city's aristocrats had endured, but not enjoyed, the democracy, this despite the fact that many of them got themselves elected as generals and government officials. They still believed in their hereditary primacy—what Pindar called "the splendour running in the blood." Now their opportunity had come to abolish the democracy and return to the old order. The *demos* deserved to take the blame for Sicily and respectable people of moderate views felt that popular rule should be reined back. They were willing to support the establishment of some kind of oligarchy.

In Athens the atmosphere was gloomy. A posse of blue-blooded young thugs assassinated leading democratic politicians and terrorized the population. In May, one century after its creation, the *ecclesia* let itself be bullied into abrogating the constitution. It dissolved itself and was replaced by a council of four hundred oligarchs, which took office in June 411. Its leaders promised in due course to establish an assembly of five thousand voting citizens. In the meantime executive authority lay in its hands. Payment for service in almost all public offices was abolished.

The new regime was more unstable than it looked at first glance. Many suspected that it intended to concede an ignominious peace treaty with Sparta. In spite of their exhaustion, most Athenians would see this as treachery, for they had not lost hope in victory or at least a draw. Above all, the ringleaders of the revolution were few and depended on the support of moderates.

One of these was Theramenes, an able and agile politician and the son of a Periclean general. One of nature's compromisers, he was nicknamed Cothurnus, a boot worn by actors that fit either foot. He quickly grew disenchanted with his more radical and unyielding colleagues. He noticed that they were putting off publishing a list of the Five Thousand, as they had promised, and suspected they were dragging their feet, because they knew their power would fade once the new assembly began to meet. The Four Hundred split into two groups, extremists and moderates like Theramenes, who favored a qualified, not an out-and-out, democracy.

The main reason that the oligarchs were able to effect a change of constitution in Athens was that so many citizens were with the fleet in Samos. Trireme captains may have preferred an oligarchy, but rank-and-file oarsmen, when citizens, were drawn mostly from the poorest social class, the *thetes,* and remained staunch democrats. An alternative *ecclesia* was established on the island.

The oligarchs in Athens put out peace feelers to Sparta, which rejected them. When they started work on building a fortress at the entrance to Piraeus's main harbor, people immediately feared that they were planning to let in a Peloponnesian fleet to end the war. Opposition grew and a leading oligarch was struck down by foreign assassins in the *agora.* Crowds demolished the fort and an ad hoc assembly was held on a steep hill at Piraeus. Ironically, a commander named Aristocrates was the first to arrest a senior oligarch.

In the outside world, matters went from bad to worse. An enemy fleet was sighted off Salamis, the important island of Euboea on Athens's doorstep rebelled, and a small home squadron of thirty-six triremes was trounced by the Spartans, a rare victory for landlubbers. Most of the Four Hundred lost sympathy with their radical leaders and hated the situation in which they found themselves. The fleet at Samos insisted that they be abolished.

In September a general assembly met on the Pnyx and dissolved the Four Hundred only four months after they took power. Just as Theramenes wished, they were replaced by a sovereign body, not of every citizen, but of all adult males who could afford to buy their own armor. In effect, this new governing *ecclesia* was equivalent to the phantom assembly of Five Thousand, which was now at last brought into being.

The new system was a great success, enabling Athens to restore not only effective government but also her fortunes in the war. A year later and without one drop of blood being shed, the full democracy was reinstated and its first known document begins with the customary formula—"enacted by the *boulē* and the *demos.*" Everything returned to the status quo ante (including the reinstatement of payment for public service). Thucydides wrote that

> during the first period of this new dispensation, the Athenians appear to have enjoyed the best government that they ever did, at least in my time. There was a reasonable and moderate blending of the few and the many, and this was what enabled the city to recover from her manifold disasters.

The traitor was back. One of the most controversial decisions that the alternative *ecclesia* on Samos took was to depose all the generals elected in Athens and replace them with their own choices.

These included Alcibiades, who they believed would help Athens win the war. The new assembly of the Five Thousand confirmed the vote. This was not to say that all was forgotten and forgiven. Alcibiades had many enemies who feared he aimed at installing a tyranny, but for the time being they had no choice but to keep quiet.

Age and the vicissitudes of his career had improved Alcibiades, who was now in his late thirties. He had grown into a tougher and more mature leader and had put behind him his weakness for easy triumphs and clever tricks. He knew too that this was his last throw of the dice; if it failed, his political career and probably his life would be over.

As adviser to Tissaphernes he had recommended an evenhanded approach to the two belligerents. This had the advantage from the Persian point of view of wearing them both down. While not altogether trusting Alcibiades (who would?), the satrap agreed. He reduced the subsidy on which the Peloponnesian fleet depended and made sure that a promised reinforcement, the Phoenician fleet, never arrived. But he did not agree to a rapprochement with Athens.

Meanwhile Alcibiades had opened negotiations with the fleet at Samos, promising to bring Tissaphernes over to their side. He had first been in touch with the oligarchs, but soon switched his attention to the democrats. An influential, intelligent, and independent-minded sailors' leader, Thrasybulus, argued for his recall.

The satrap learned of this confidential initiative and began to distance himself from his adviser. It was about this time that a revised entente between Sparta and Persia was agreed.

Thrasybulus persuaded the assembled troops and crews on Samos to recall Alcibiades and grant him immunity from prosecution. He collected the former renegade from the mainland and brought him to Samos. It soon became clear that Alcibiades had lost his credit with Tissaphernes, but his energetic leadership and skill at raising funds to pay the men canceled that disappointment.

The Athenians now hit a winning streak.

Tired of Tissaphernes and his half-fulfilled promises, the Peloponnesians sailed northwards to the Hellespont and opened a new theater of war. Here lay the satrapy of the more straightforward Pharnabazus, with whom they were soon on good terms and who took over as Sparta's Persian best friend. Fearful for their grain supply, the Athenians had no choice but to follow suit, led by Thrasybulus and another admiral.

The tumultuous year of 411 concluded in the autumn with two striking Athenian victories in the Hellespont. Then, as we have seen, came the crowning mercy of Cyzicus in the following spring. The three Athenian commanders were Thrasybulus, Theramenes, and Alcibiades, the last of whom deserved much of the credit for the victory. The only disappointments were the loss of Nisaea, the port of Megara, and Sparta's capture that winter of Pylos, the rock fortress on the Messenian coast that Athens had taken as long ago as the year 425.

To everyone's surprise the Athenians now found themselves in a very strong position.

They saw to their relief that they were still a great power and a new self-belief spread through the fleet. They exaggerated. The recovery was hugely to their credit, but Athens was no longer the city of Pericles. Its reserves both of precious metals and of human capital were nearly exhausted, and so was its resilience. It could not go on indefinitely producing new fleet after new fleet. It would have been wise to accept offers of peace from a disheartened Sparta and taken a few years to recuperate. But the old Attic arrogance was as fierce as it had ever been. The *demos* wanted total victory, and it wanted it now.

When the distinguished Spartan Endius headed his delegation to Athens and offered peace to the *ecclesia*, he must have anticipated a warmer welcome from a war-weary people than he received in the event. The restored democracy had lost little of its traditional aggression. The most prominent popular leader of his day, Cleophon, stressed the magnitude of the city's recent successes. "I will use a dagger to cut the throat of anyone who proposes making peace," he is reported to have threatened.

His critics lampooned him as a depraved drunk of low birth, but his father had been an elected *strategos,* so he must surely have come from an affluent and respectable family. The *demos* agreed with Cleophon, and Endius was sent on his way. With Alcibiades at the helm all would yet be well.

It is evidence of Cleophon's confidence in the future that he resumed construction of the Erechtheum, the elaborate little temple complex with female caryatids on the Acropolis, which had been abandoned during the Sicilian Expedition in order to save money. Although this was a comparatively small project he was following in the footsteps of the great Pericles. A new temple on the sacred hill was bound to boost public morale. Also, in honor of Cyzicus, a parapet was built for the tiny temple of Athena Nike.

And for a time all did go well. The Athenians never retrieved Chios and Euboea, but the island of Thasos off the Thracian coast was lost and regained. Variably neutral during the war although a league member, Rhodes finally went its own independent way. With these exceptions, the empire held together, more or less.

In 407 after four years in the field Alcibiades at last decided it was safe to go home. He had proved himself, and his friends in the city guaranteed him a warm and, more important, a safe welcome. When he sailed into Piraeus, a great crowd of well-wishers was waiting—just as they had been the last time they had seen him, leading the fleet as it set off to Sicily on that day of splendor in 415.

He anchored offshore but, fearing an ambush by his enemies, did not immediately disembark. Instead he stood on the deck and kept looking to see if his relatives were there. Only when he recognized a cousin did he go ashore and walk up to the city, surrounded by an informal bodyguard.

With tears in his eyes, Alcibiades said what he could at the *boulē* and the *ecclesia* to explain his actions, but most people were more interested in a glittering future than in the past. A crown of gold was placed on his head and he was appointed commander-in-chief, as Xenophon put it, "on the grounds that he was the man to restore the former power of Athens." The records of his trial and sentence were sunk in the sea, his property was returned, and the priests were ordered to recant their curse.

Since the Spartan occupation of Decelea, the annual procession from Athens to Eleusis to celebrate the Mysteries had had to travel by sea. This year Alcibiades led it along its traditional land route, escorted by troops. The Spartans did not react. It was a doubly symbolic gesture; it showed contempt for King Agis and his men and it gave Alcibiades an opportunity to show his reverence for the Mysteries, which he had been accused (falsely, he still claimed) of mocking. If ever there was a moment when he could establish himself as tyrant it was now, but perhaps he told himself that he would do better to win the war first.

Two developments cast a shadow over Athenian prospects. An intelligent and energetic new Spartan admiral was appointed to the Peloponnesian fleet. This was Lysander. His family was poor and he was a *mothax* (literally Doric Greek for "stepbrother"), a term used for a

Spartan who was too poor to pay for membership of a *syssitia,* or soldier's mess, and was obliged to find a wealthy sponsor. Although not one of the Equals, a *mothax* was allowed to fight alongside them.

Lysander was an imperialist and wanted Sparta to replace Athens as leader of the Greek world. He made the acquaintance of Cyrus, brother of the Persian king Artaxerxes. He complained to the young prince that Tissaphernes was only halfhearted in his support for the Peloponnesian fleet and persuaded him to raise the subsidy for sailor's pay from three obols a head to four. Artaxerxes appointed Cyrus to take over command of the war from Tissaphernes. He was in his late teens, hyperactive and resolutely pro-Spartan. Lysander could be arrogant and overbearing, but on this occasion he obeyed the rules of flattery and deference at court. The Spartan and the Persian became good friends.

At this inauspicious moment Alcibiades lost concentration. His enemies at home, who had been patiently waiting for an error they could exploit, pounced.

An Athenian fleet was standing off Ephesus near the port of Notium. Alcibiades wanted to bring Lysander and his fleet to battle as soon as possible, but they stayed where they were inside the harbor of Ephesus. The Spartan admiral, handsomely financed by Cyrus and able to afford higher wages than the Athenians, had time on his side and saw no reason to risk a fight. By contrast, Alcibiades was the victim of great expectations, for the Athenian public imagined he could achieve whatever he wanted. Also, tempted by Persian gold, his oarsmen were deserting to the enemy in some numbers.

Alcibiades sailed away in his troopships on a brief expedition to look for money and rations, leaving his triremes on guard against any move by Lysander. He placed his helmsman in charge of the fleet, a man called Antiochus, a good pilot but (according to Plutarch) an unthinking lowlife. He was well qualified as a drinking companion, but not as an admiral.

Alcibiades gave him strict instructions to avoid battle at all costs, but Antiochus ignored what he had been told. He sailed across Ephesus's harbor mouth with a couple of triremes, shouting abuse and making obscene gestures. Lysander sent a few boats to chase him away, and gradually both fleets came out to fight. Antiochus was killed and the Athenians lost twenty-two ships. It was a minor but completely pointless setback. Alcibiades rushed back as soon as he heard the news and offered battle to Lysander, but the Spartan declined. He had done well enough as it was, and saw no need to take any more risks.

The skirmish at Notium was the first real reverse since Cyzicus, and the *ecclesia* was dismayed. A speaker blamed Alcibiades for appointing men "who had won his confidence simply through their capacity for drinking and telling sailors' yarns." He was treating the war at sea as if it were a luxury cruise. All his old misdeeds were rehearsed, the assistance he gave Sparta and his collusion with the Persians. He was dismissed from office.

It seems a foolish decision, the *demos* at its flightiest, but the debacle at Notium did no more than throw a harsh light onto a preexisting state of affairs—the divisiveness of Alcibiades. Feelings against him were too strong not to keep reemerging and he could not assemble a broad enough consensus of support in the long run. He knew that his return to Athens had been a huge and dangerous gamble. He saw at once that he had made his last throw of the dice and lost. He was no longer safe. He left the fleet for a castle in the Thracian Chersonese, a bolt-hole that he had prepared in advance exactly against this eventuality.

Irrepressible as ever, Alcibiades paid for some mercenaries and led a raiding party into Thrace, ransoming his captives for large sums of money. But this was child's play to what he had lost.

Two years after the disgrace of Alcibiades, Aristophanes wrote in *The Frogs* of his fellow-citizens' mixed feelings about their lost leader. Athens "longs for him, but hates him, and yet she wants to have him back." But it was too late for that now.

The *demos* continued on its angry, cruel, and unpredictable way.

Lysander's commission expired after its statutory year in 406 and he was obliged to hand over to a new young commander, Callicratidas, who was that rare thing—a traditional Spartan with charm, who had something of the much-missed Brasidas about him. His predecessor was so annoyed at being superseded that he blackened Callicratidas's reputation with Cyrus and gave back to the prince the unspent remainder of the subsidies he had provided.

The admiral disagreed with the expansionist policy of Lysander. He regarded the Persian alliance as a disgrace and was furious when Cyrus refused to meet him. On a visit to Miletus, an anti-Persian *polis* that he made the headquarters of his campaign, he told its general assembly: "It is a sad day for the Greeks when they have to flatter foreigners for cash. If I get home safely I will, to the best of my ability, make peace between Athens and Sparta."

He raised the money he needed to pay for his huge fleet of 140 vessels from Ionian cities, who appreciated his distaste for the Persians. He hunted down the Athenian fleet, now led by an admiral called Conon, and caught it at the harbor mouth of Mytilene, the capital of the island of Lesbos. He captured thirty Athenian triremes, leaving Conon with not more than forty blockaded inside the port. If he had destroyed the entire fleet the war would have been over. Cyrus did not want to see Sparta victorious without Persian help and immediately sent Callicratidas money to pay the crews.

Conon managed to sneak one ship out to report to Athens and ask for more ships. A tremendous effort was made to respond to the crisis. Slaves were freed to row in the fleet and even the aristocrats in the cavalry knuckled down as oarsmen. One hundred and ten warships were built and manned. The allies contributed forty more, including ten from still loyal Samos. As a token of gratitude a marble relief was commissioned of Hera, the tutelary goddess of Samos, shaking hands with an armed Athena.

The relief force arrived off Lesbos and Callicratidas lost his numerical superiority. An engagement took place near the Arginusae Islands in front of Mytilene. It was a blustery day. The Athenians, who formed up in two rows against the enemy, began to outflank the Spartans on the left. In response, Callicratidas divided his fleet into two separate squadrons. This opened a gap in his center into which the Athenians rowed. Callicratidas fell overboard while his trireme was ramming an enemy ship, disappeared, and was never seen again, and the Athenian right drove the Peloponnesians back. Some triremes got away but the Spartans and their allies lost seventy-seven warships, or well over half their fleet. The Athenians lost only twenty-five. It was an extraordinary result, and Diodorus writes that Arginusae was "the greatest naval engagement in history of Greeks against Greeks."

As the long battle ended a storm blew up. It was the explicit duty of victorious admirals to pick up surviving crew members, as they clung to their wrecked vessels or swam around, as well as corpses lying in the water. At Arginusae this amounted to five thousand men.

The eight admirals (to avoid battle by committee, a different one was in overall charge every day) decided that up to fifty triremes, to be commanded by Theramenes and Thrasybulus, both of whom were ship's captains on this occasion, should pick up survivors. But the weather was very bad and the two men decided it would not be possible to obey these orders. Meanwhile the rest of the fleet went off to deal with the Spartan flotilla that was still blockading Mytilene harbor. So the five thousand were lost.

This was a large number and although the *ecclesia* was thrilled by the victory it was furious about the casualties. Theramenes and Thrasybulus swiftly laid the blame on the admirals, who were deposed and put on trial. Their cases were heard together and they were all sentenced to death on a single vote.

To prosecute accused men en bloc violated a decree guaranteeing separate trials. By a remarkable chance, Socrates happened to be sitting on the *boulē* for this year (the only time he ever held a public office). For this month he was also on the subcommittee, or *prytany*, which prepared business for the *boulē* to lay before the *ecclesia*. Even more coincidentally, he was chairman of the *ecclesia* for the very day in question. He refused to put the motion to the assembly on the grounds that it was illegal.

His authority lasted only twenty-four hours, the hearing went ahead, and the admirals were executed. They included Pericles, son of Pericles and Aspasia. One of the condemned men paused before he was led away. With cutting sarcasm, he asked the assembly to remember to discharge the vows to the gods that he and his colleagues had made before their victory, for they themselves no longer had the time to do so.

Only the unpopular philosopher comes out well in this unconstitutional episode.

The loss of life at Arginusae had certainly been substantial, but did Athens have enough talent at its disposal that it could afford to eliminate so many commanders in one fit of rage? As it recognized later but too late, the *ecclesia* had acted cruelly and foolishly. Its conduct makes one miss the rational governance of the Five Thousand. Would *they* have lost their self-control as completely as did the recently reempowered *demos*?

The Spartans once more sued for peace, with each side keeping what they held. They even offered to give up Decelea. Apparently Cleophon intervened again, disastrously. According to the fourth-century author of a study of the *Athenian Constitution,* he prevented "the masses . . . from making peace by going into the assembly drunk and wearing his breast-plate, and saying that he would not allow it unless the Spartans surrendered all the cities they had taken."

The Athenian refusal was yet another unwise decision. The ships that won Arginusae were the last that the Athenians would be able, almost miraculously, to create out of nothing. They had scraped the bottom of the barrel for personnel, matériel, and money. If anything were to happen to the present fleet, that would be the end. No more prodigies would be possible.

How was it that the *demos* did not see this? Perhaps the only answer is exhaustion. Like a punch-drunk boxer, it did not have the energy needed to call a halt.

· · ·

A horseman trotted along the shore to where the Athenian ships lay beached and asked to see the six admirals in command. We may guess that he was not kept waiting for long, for the visitor was none other than Alcibiades and he had come specially to give them some advice.

The place was called Aegospotami (or Goat Streams), a small river debouching into the Hellespont from its northern coast. The castle to which Alcibiades had withdrawn was not far away on what is today's Gallipoli peninsula and he had been able to watch the developing situation.

On the face of it Aegospotami had little to recommend it. There was no harbor and the nearest substantial town where provisions could be found, Sestos, was more than ten miles away. Its only advantage was that it lay opposite the port of Lampsacus, where Lysander, back in command again, and a fleet of two hundred warships were installed.

The Athenians with 180 triremes wanted to fight a battle as soon as possible while they still had money to pay their crews, about 35,000 men in all. If they were to do so, they had to be in a position to challenge the Spartans. For four days they rowed the two miles across the channel from Aegospotami and offered battle. On each occasion Lysander kept his fleet under oar inside the harbor, but did not sally out. It was far too dangerous to attack him there and in the afternoon the Athenians returned to their beach and foraged onshore for an evening meal.

Alcibiades' visit fell on the fourth day. He urged the admirals to move their fleet south to Sestos where there was a harbor and a city. He added that if they gave him a share of the command he would produce an army of Thracians to attack the Spartans by land. Alcibiades was right to warn the admirals that their present position was risky, and a force of Thracians, if one was really available, would have indeed been useful.

However, they could not conceivably have shared any part of their command with a man twice condemned by the *ecclesia*. Moreover, as Diodorus points out, they figured that "they would incur the blame for any defeat, whereas everyone would give the credit for any success to Alcibiades." They told him to make himself scarce. "We are the admirals now," they reminded him.

On the following morning thirty Athenian triremes set out ahead of the main fleet. The admiral in charge was Philocles. His aim was probably to tempt Lysander out to destroy a temptingly easy target and then to be overwhelmed by the main fleet when it came up later. The plan failed for two reasons: deserters betrayed it and discipline among the Athenians had grown lax.

Forewarned, Lysander put out immediately with his full fleet, scattered the Athenian advance guard, and swooped onto the beached triremes before the crews had had a chance to launch them. He also landed some infantry to attack the enemy camp while the Athenians were fully occupied trying to rescue their ships. Most ran off in all directions and made for Sestos.

Of the Athenian navy only ten boats had not been sunk or taken. Between three and four thousand prisoners were captured. It was decided to put to death all who were Athenian citizens. Those previously responsible for atrocities received special attention, among whom was Philocles: he had had a motion passed by the *ecclesia* that after a victory all captives should either have their right thumbs or hands cut off. Also on one occasion he had ordered the crews of two captured triremes to be thrown overboard to drown. Xenophon writes: "Lysander first asked him what he thought he deserved for having begun such uncustomary and criminal actions against the Greeks. He then had his throat cut."

One of the state triremes, the *Paralos*, arrived at Athens during the night and brought news of the catastrophe at Aegospotami. Xenophon memorably describes the scene.

A sound of wailing came from Piraeus and ran up through the Long Walls and into the city itself as one man passed the news to another. As a result, no one slept that night as they wept not only for the dead, but for themselves, thinking that they would suffer the same treatment they had inflicted on others—the people of Melos . . . and many other Greeks.

The great war between Athens and Sparta was nearly but not quite over.

Athens prepared for a siege. The city was impregnable, so it would have to be starved into submission. Lysander threatened death to any Athenian citizen caught outside the city and a stream of refugees multiplied the number of mouths that had to be fed. A blockade of Piraeus halted food imports. Lysander waited. A winter passed and by the spring people were dying in the streets.

What terms would Sparta impose? The fate of Melos had not been forgotten nor other war atrocities. What the Athenians had meted to others should now be meted to them. The Corinthians and Boeotians wanted to see Athens destroyed, "root and branch," the city razed to the ground and the people sold into slavery. The proposition was supported by King Agis and Lysander. But a moment's thought showed this to be against Sparta's interests. If Athens vanished from the map a power vacuum would be created that either the Corinthians or the Boeotians, both of whom had been troublesome during the war, would be the first to fill. There was little advantage in losing one rival superpower only to create another.

What would be best for the Spartans was a tamed Athens. And this was what was ultimately agreed. Athens remained an independent state, but stripped of its Long Walls and the fortifications of Piraeus and of its empire. It was locked into a treaty of friendship with its former enemy that prevented it from having a foreign policy. All exiles (these were mostly oligarchs) were to be recalled.

Athens's chief negotiator was the moderate Theramenes. Radical democrat Cleophon, irrepressible as ever, tried to resist the settlement, but cruel necessity was against him. He was arraigned on a charge of evading military service, found guilty, and executed. Lysander sailed in triumph into Piraeus, and both Athenians and their conquerors worked alongside one another to tear down the Long Walls. Daunted by the Spartan commander's presence in the city, the *ecclesia* did as it was told. It voted out the democracy and appointed a commission of Thirty, headed by a returning exile, an author and oligarch called Critias, to prepare a new constitution. These reactionaries became the de facto government.

And what of the man who had done most to destroy, and then most to try to save, his native land—the man whose volatile and charismatic personality incarnated the spirit of Athenian imperialism?

After Aegospotami Alcibiades knew that he was without a future. The authorities in Sparta wanted to see an end of him. As the fourth-century orator and commentator Isocrates said: "They could not be sure of the loyalty of Athens if they demolished her walls, unless they should also destroy the man who could rebuild them." In other words, he was too dangerous to live.

Alcibiades lay low in his castle in the Hellespont, but, when Thracian raiders mounted an attack and robbed him of his money, he escaped across the water into Phrygia. Here the ever-decent Pharnabazus let him use a house in a village in the countryside. As a last throw of the dice Alcibiades persuaded the satrap to arrange a meeting with the Great King Artaxerxes in Susa. He would try to persuade him to act against Sparta and help Athens to recover from its defeat: his argument would be that as ever it was in the Persian interest to maintain a balance of power in Hellas. In any case he would offer Artaxerxes his services, to whom he could be as useful as Themistocles had been in his day.

Critias had once boasted in a poem that he had put the motion to the *ecclesia* for the recall of Alcibiades, but, as the new ruler of Athens, he changed his tune. He sent a message to Lysander in Asia: "Unless you cut off Alcibiades, none of the arrangements you have made at Athens will stand. So if you want your decisions to remain unaltered, you must have him put to death." In their teens, Critias and Alcibiades had studied under Socrates, and it must have occurred to their teacher that neither of them was a fine example of the study and practice of virtue.

At first Lysander refused to act, but, under pressure from the authorities at home, he told the satrap that relations with Sparta would be broken unless he produced Alcibiades dead or alive. Pharnabazus complied, reluctantly, and asked two relatives of his to deal with the matter.

Plutarch reports that a *hetaira,* or courtesan, called Timandra was living with Alcibiades at the time. One night he dreamed that he was wearing her dress. She had his head in her arms and was making up his face with cosmetics as if he were a woman.

Not long afterwards the men who had been sent to kill Alcibiades came to his home during the night. Not daring to enter, they laid wood against the walls of the building and set it alight. Woken up by the crackling of the flames, Alcibiades tried to smother the fire with clothes and bedding. Then he wrapped a cloak around his left arm and with a sword in his right ran through the blaze without being burned. His attackers backed away out of his reach and shot at him from a distance with javelins and arrows, until he fell and died.

Later when the assassins had left, Timandra took up the body and wrapped it in her own clothes. Then she cremated it in the fire that had been laid to consume Alcibiades when he had been alive.

And so one of the last Alcmaeonids left the stage. The clan fades from the record and whether it died out or survived in comfortable anonymity we may hope that with this blood-stained climax the Cylonian curse was expiated.

A LONG
FAREWELL

———

21

Sparta's Turn

A n Athenian who came back to his home city in 403 after a long absence must have noticed how quiet and empty the streets were. Where were all the people?

The short answer is that they were dead. There were fewer than half as many Athenian men at the end of the war than there had been when it started, even allowing for the arrival over the years, courtesy of the birthrate, of new cohorts of male citizens and the enforced return of citizen settlers, or *cleruchs* (in all probability, there were no more than ten thousand of these). The causes were not only battle casualties, notably during the Sicilian Expedition, but also the mass mortality of the plague in the 420s. Hoplite numbers are estimated to have declined from 22,000 in 431 to about 9,250 in 394. The sea battles in the last years of the war brought even greater losses among the *thetes,* or the lowest economic class. There were about 15,000 of them in 415, but only between 5,000 and 7,000 in 394. Because of the large numbers of oarsmen needed to power a trireme, casualties could far exceed those of a battle on land.

In sum, the number of adult male citizens of Athens after the Peloponnesian War is estimated as being between 14,000 and 16,250. It had been over 40,000 in 434. Its citizen population had fallen by some 60 percent.

After so complete a defeat, could Athens ever recover her position as a great power in the Greek world? It hardly seemed likely.

The city's economy had collapsed. In its heyday, agriculture lay at its heart, and some two thirds of the adult male population owned some land, although not necessarily enough to provide a living. In many cases, smallholders could supplement their earnings by serving as a juror or receiving state payments for holding public offices. They might row in the fleet or work in the shipyards of Piraeus. Alternatively, they could emigrate and join a *cleruchy*, here and there across the empire. The landless poor were even more reliant on income deriving from the war and from opportunities for paid public service at home. Public policy overlapped with welfare funding.

But now the empire was gone and so was the fleet. The gap between haves and have-nots on the land widened. Accustomed inflows of money abruptly dried up. As we have seen, more than twenty thousand slaves had run away. Many of these came from the mines at Laurium, and it was not until the middle of the next century that the extraction of silver came anywhere near the old levels. Also many slaves were given their freedom in return for fighting at Arginusae. When money was short, they could not be easily or quickly replaced. So long as there was the slightest risk of fresh military invasions, large-scale investors may have found loans to merchants and sea traders a safer bet than mining or agricultural renewal.

The league membership payments (or, more honestly, imperial tribute) ended. The subscription charge and other monies collected from the allies had provided the Athenian state with 600 talents in 431; 1,300 talents, after revised assessments upwards, in 425; about 900 talents in 413—and in 403 nothing at all. On the credit side, now that the empire had gone, as it undoubtedly had, Athens was no longer obliged to keep the seaways safe for merchants (one unpredicted consequence of which was a rise in piracy). Income fell, but so to some extent did expenditure.

Athens had never been primarily a manufacturing center and most of its light industry served the domestic market. During the war many firms in such fields as metalwork, carpentry, tanneries, and dockyards, which produced weapons, ships and ship's gear, armor, and the like, had done well and the arrival of peace will have brought with it unemployment and a period of painful readjustment. There was no longer a fleet to build or an army to equip.

There were some slivers of a silver lining. Athenians were able to resume living safely in the countryside and full-time farming started up again. The Spartan army had left the fortress at Decelea and three decades of enemy invasions were at last over. The fields of Attica had been burned and dug up; farm buildings had been dismantled and wood and tiles, tools and furniture removed. Land fell in value, and in 389 or 388 the speechwriter Lysias refers to a landowner, the value of whose estate had fallen from seventy to twenty talents.

The destruction was not quite as bad as it looked. Grain is replanted annually, vines cannot be easily destroyed, and olive trees resist the ax and the flame (although new ones take years to grow). The renewal of agriculture reduced costly dependence on imported foodstuffs from the Black Sea. The wealthier landowners recovered more quickly than the rest, and we hear of several affluent farmers who did well in the postwar era, including somewhat surprisingly Plato, the philosopher and student of Socrates.

Once things had settled down, Athens, or rather Piraeus, reasserted its position as an entrepôt for traders in the Eastern Mediterranean, where goods were imported and reexported. Ports from Carthage to the Crimea sent ships to Athens to buy as well as to sell. However, there was no denying a sharp decline in business. The total annual value of seaborne imperial trade had probably been more than 18,000 talents, of which Piraeus's share was at least 25 percent, or 4,500 talents. In 402/1, though, the port's earnings may have fallen to 1,800 talents, although this was still a substantial sum.

Commerce was supported by bankers and tax farmers, who were often resident aliens, or *metics,* and well-trained slaves (the state did not have an exchequer or a revenue service). Foreigners also came to Athens for cultural reasons, in particular to attend the Great Dionysia. With the end of hostilities, tourists returned. In the long run the provision of services to foreigners was to become the city's most lucrative industry.

A young man from the Bosphorus visited Athens in the mid-390s. His evidence was not untypical.

> When I heard reports about Athens and of the other parts of the Greek world, I wanted to travel abroad. And so my father loaded two ships with grain [to sell here in the city], gave me money, and sent me off on a trading expedition and at the same time to see the world.

So daily life in Athens returned to something resembling normality. Small shoots of economic growth could be detected. But recovery was inevitably constrained by the population collapse and a gloom fell across the future. Partly the disasters of the war knocked back self-confidence, partly there were simply too few people and too little money left to afford a war, an economic revival, an empire, or a cultural renaissance.

One afternoon in 404 Lysias, a wealthy *metic* or resident alien, was holding a dinner party at his home in Piraeus, when the authorities called.

Two members of the Thirty, the oligarchic regime established by Lysander, walked in. They were accompanied by a body of armed men. They turned out the guests and then went off to the arms factory next door, which Lysias and his elder sibling Polemarchus owned. They made an inventory of the 120 slaves who were manufacturing shields. Meanwhile one of the oligarchs, Peison, stayed with Lysias in the house.

The Thirty were short of funds and suspected treachery among the community of resident aliens. They decided to solve both problems with a single blow. Ten prosperous *metics* were identified whose property would be confiscated and whose lives forfeited on spurious criminal charges (for appearances' sake two of them would be poor). Lysias and Polemarchus were among those selected. They came from a rich, respectable, and carefully nonpolitical family of immigrants, whose Syracusan father had been invited by Pericles to settle in Athens. Polemarchus was interested in philosophy and Plato set the scene for his great philosophical dialogue *On the State* at his house.

Lysias asked Peison to let him go free in return for a talent of silver, and Peison agreed. He went into his bedroom and opened a strongbox that contained three talents and other gold coins. Unfortunately, Peison followed him, saw the box, and had his men take it away. So Lysias lost everything. He was handed over to the second oligarch and taken to a neighbor's house. His prospects looked poor; so while his unwelcome visitors were in conversation, Lysias took his chance and slipped off unnoticed to freedom through three doors, which all happened, unusually, to be unlocked. He made his way to the house of a sea captain he knew, who went up to Athens to find out what had happened to Polemarchus. He brought back the news that he had been arrested and taken to prison. So Lysias boarded a boat the following night and crossed over to Megara.

Recalling these events a year later, he spoke bitterly of his brother's fate. "To Polemarchus, the Thirty gave their familiar order, to drink hemlock [a poison used in capital punishment], without so much as telling him the reason for his execution. Still less was he allowed a trial at which he could defend himself." Polemarchus's property was looted (even his wife's earrings) and his relatives had to beg and borrow the necessaries for his funeral.

Critias, the leader of the Thirty, was no ordinary reactionary. This onetime student of Socrates wrote poems and tragedies. In exile from Athens towards the end of the war, he helped establish a democracy, of all things, in Thessaly. Suspected of involvement in the mutilation of the Herms, he was an advanced thinker: a fragment of one of his tragedies survives in which a speaker explains that the gods were a necessary invention to control human beings.

> *Some shrewd man first, a man wise in judgment,*
> *invented for mortals the fear of gods,*
> *in that way, frightening the wicked should they*
> *even act or speak or scheme in secret.*

He believed that virtue should be imposed by force, and that was indeed his policy when he took power. However, force soon came to be applied without the slightest attempt at virtue, as Lysias's story shows.

Once firmly in the saddle the Thirty abandoned any idea of preparing a new constitution, as they had been instructed to do. They confiscated all weapons and armor in the city and instituted a reign of terror. They began by executing known informers, but went on to arrange the deaths of 1,500 men simply for their money or their reputation as law-abiding and politically moderate citizens.

An attempt was made to implicate ordinary Athenians in these judicial murders. Socrates was ordered, along with four fellow-citizens, to arrest a respectable former military officer, Leon of Salamis. At great personal risk, he refused and simply went home. According to Plato, he admitted later that he might have been put to death for this, but, he added: "If it's not crude of me to say so, death is something I couldn't care less about, but my whole concern is not to do anything unjust or impious." The others were not so brave; they brought Leon in and he was put to death. The Thirty were sensible enough to leave Socrates unpunished.

Theramenes had hoped that the Thirty would implement his idea for a limited oligarchy, as in the days of the Five Thousand. He joined them, but soon had a change of heart. To broaden the base of his government, Critias issued a register of Three Thousand supporters, and announced that all other citizens were liable to capital punishment without trial and to have their property confiscated. Theramenes criticized the regime for its cruelty and a split threatened. It was wrong, he said, to kill people simply because they had been popular under the democracy. At last this man for all seasons, the so-called Cothurnus, had made his choice.

Critias acted. He summoned the *boulē* and arrived at the meeting with an escort of young supporters, equipped with daggers concealed in their armpits. After an angry debate, he struck the name of Theramenes off the list of the Three Thousand, for his membership guaranteed him a trial, and ordered his instant arrest and execution. Theramenes ran to an altar and claimed sanctuary. However, he was dragged from it and, protesting loudly and clearly, was dragged through the *agora*.

In the little prison on the edge of the *agora,* he was given a lethal cup of hemlock to drink. As if he were an *erastes* playing a game of *kottabos* (see page 312) at a drinking party, he threw out the dregs as a toast to his murderous *eromenos:* "Here's to the lovely Critias!"

Removing a senior politician in such an arbitrary and violent way was a sign of weakness rather than of strength and the government faltered. Two leading democrats in exile in Thebes decided to intervene. One of them was Thrasybulus, the capable admiral based at Samos in the last phase of the war, and the other Anytus, an influential politician and owner of a successful tanning business. He had had a checkered career: many years previously he had fallen head over heels in love with the teenaged Alcibiades. He was a moderate democrat and in 409 he was elected as one of the year's ten generals. He had the misfortune to be in command when Pylos was lost to the Spartans. He was put on trial for this failure, but apparently paid the jury for an acquittal.

In December 404 the two men crossed over from Thebes into Attica with seventy followers and occupied a hill called Phyle ten miles from Athens. The Thirty sent a force to mount a blockade, but a snowstorm broke it up. Men left the city and joined Thrasybulus and soon he had seven hundred followers. Just before dawn one morning they attacked and scattered some cavalry and members of a Spartan garrison stationed on the Acropolis that had been dispatched to watch Phyle.

Morale among the Thirty fell sharply and they left the city. They took over the border town of Eleusis as an emergency retreat if that became necessary, and massacred the local population. Thrasybulus then marched by night to Piraeus, and Critias followed him to the port with his troops and men from the Spartan garrison. The fighters from Phyle retired in good order to high ground and, although outnumbered, drove off an enemy attack. Critias and seventy others lost their lives.

A confused pause ensued. The Thirty were abolished, but the oligarchs clung to power. Would the Spartans step in and save their cause? Lysander wanted to, but his high-handed behavior after Aegospotami had dismayed his own government. He had allowed Greek cities to offer sacrifices in his honor as if he were a god. He had had a statue of himself erected at Delphi; on its base a boastful inscription read that "he had destroyed the power of the sons of Cecrops [a legendary king of Athens], Lysander who crowned never-sacked Sparta." Perhaps, his enemies whispered, he was meditating a revolution and wanted to set himself up as king or tyrant.

This was un-Spartan behavior and the Agiad monarch, Pausanias, who was in the field with an army, was suspicious. He wanted to do nothing that might enhance Lysander's status. Supported by the *ephors,* he negotiated a peace between the warring parties at Athens. An amnesty was agreed for all past acts, excepting only those of the Thirty themselves and their officials. A constitutional commission restored the democracy. The foreign garrison withdrew. Men of all political persuasions did their best to make reconciliation work.

Only two years had passed since the catastrophe of Aegospotami and Athens was no longer a creature of the Spartans and had taken a long step towards retrieving its old liberties. But could it ever retrieve its old power? Even to fantasize such a dizzying hope, more time was required.

Signs of a changing political climate are illustrated by the careers of two distinguished but disillusioned Athenians—Conon and Xenophon. With the end of the war, many men who had flourished as soldiers or sailors found themselves out of work. For them, going home to a defeated and desolate city was an unappealing prospect, even if their fellow-citizens were to allow them back. They looked for work as mercenaries.

Mercenary troops had been used in the past (for instance, as trireme crews), but they were increasingly employed as hoplites in the fourth century. This was not just that the arrival of peace left large numbers of fit young men at loose ends. Athens was not the only *polis* that had registered heavy casualties and in the coming years states in need of an army had to look for supplementary fighters from abroad.

Also, the misery of the Peloponnesian War seems to have had a moral impact. The deployment of native force to drive foreign policy, an untroubled patriotism, and a willingness to sacrifice citizens' lives freely were no longer part of the Athenian mentality. The fierce, self-sacrificial energy that the invention of democracy seems to have released had run its course. The *demos* would no longer obey a new Cimon or a new Pericles if he wanted to scatter thousands of citizen hoplites around the Eastern Mediterranean. People still loved their country, but they lacked the old passion. Loyalty to the state gave way to a new individualism.

Both Conon and Xenophon, in their different ways, turned their gaze to Persia, which was eager to make use of Greek military skills and men. The former had been an admiral at Aegospotami, and was the only man to have kept his nerve on that dark day. His trireme, seven others, and the state warship, the *Paralus,* quickly boarded all their row-ers and sailed across the narrow sea to Lampsacus, the Spartan base. Here, with great presence of mind, they captured the main sails of Lysander's fleet (sails were usually left in camp before a battle to save space). This meant that his flotilla could not be pursued.

Fearing the rage of the *demos,* not without cause, Conon fled to Cyprus where he placed himself under the protection of King Evago-ras of Salamis, a city-state on the island. Evagoras, who belonged to a long-ruling dynasty, was a competent leader. He took over all of Cy-prus and broke away from Persian rule. The local Greek culture flour-ished. There Conon, who was in his forties, lived quietly, letting time pass, but awaiting opportunity.

Power fills a vacuum. Sparta inherited the hegemony of Athens in the Aegean. It cynically presented itself as the liberator of Greece, but quickly became even more repressive than its predecessor. Lysander threw out democracies and appointed military governors, called *har-mosts,* wherever he went. Like most Spartans when they were let off the leash and allowed to travel abroad, he behaved with a nauseous mixture of self-righteousness, corruption, and high-handedness.

Worse, in order to defeat Athens, Sparta had felt compelled to seek Persian assistance, and above all Persian money. The unprincipled price for that was the sacrifice of Hellenic independence on the Ionian coastline. Both powers recognized the presentational difficulty this cre-ated for the "liberator" and the Great King was content to allow the Ionians a show of autonomy in return for paying tribute to the Great King. But the fact remains that Marathon, Salamis, and Plataea had been for nothing.

However, relations with Sparta were soon to be transformed. In 405 the Great King Darius II died and the Persian court plunged into one of its regular phases of murderous palace intrigue. He had had four sons by his half sister, Parysatis. One of them succeeded to the throne as Artaxerxes II, but the queen mother had other ideas. Her favorite child was Lysander's friend and ally Cyrus the Younger. It was through her influence that in 408 he had been appointed commander of Persian forces in the west although he was only in his late teens. She tried and failed to persuade her ailing husband to make Cyrus his heir.

Tissaphernes detected the prince in a plot to murder the new Great King. Artaxerxes, who was as emollient as his brother was headstrong, forgave him on his mother's plea. This clemency was unwise.

The unrepentant Cyrus began to raise an army secretly, or at least discreetly, which he intended to lead against Artaxerxes and replace him on the throne. He called in his debts with the Spartans and demanded their support. His message to them was simple—I helped you win your war; now you help me win mine. They agreed, placed their fleet at his disposal, and appointed a Spartan general to lead a regiment of more than ten thousand Greek mercenaries, whom Cyrus had recruited to his army.

Xenophon, in his late twenties, had been a cavalryman for the Thirty, but was disgusted by their cruelty and especially by the bloodbath at Eleusis, which he had witnessed. However, he was a natural pro-Spartan oligarch and, to escape the restored democracy at Athens, joined up under Cyrus, of whom he became a great admirer.

He has left a vivid eyewitness account of his great adventure. One spring morning in 401 the armies of Cyrus and the Great King met near a village on the Euphrates called Cunaxa.

> And now it was midday, and the enemy were not yet in sight; but when afternoon was coming on, there was seen a rising dust, which appeared at first like a white cloud, but sometime later like a kind of blackness in the plain, extending over a great distance. As the enemy came nearer and nearer, there were presently flashes of bronze here and there, and spears and the hostile ranks began to come into sight. There were horsemen in white cuirasses on the left wing of the enemy, under the command, it was reported, of Tissaphernes; next to them were troops with

wicker shields and, farther on, hoplites with wooden shields which reached to their feet, these latter being Egyptians, people said; and then more horsemen and more bowmen.

The exact number of participants in the battle eludes us, but Artaxerxes' host was so large that the center of his battle line, where the Great King was placed by tradition, extended beyond the edge of Cyrus's left wing. The Greek mercenaries were on the pretender's right wing and their flank abutted against a river. They were by far the best troops in the field and Artaxerxes' left wing knew the treatment they could expect. They turned and fled before the Greeks even came within arrowshot. Encouraged by this rout and shouting again and again "Get out of the way," Cyrus charged obliquely from the central position in his army at the Great King. In the melee Artaxerxes was wounded and unhorsed. He withdrew on foot to a nearby hill, but Cyrus was killed, and with him gone there was no point in anyone fighting on. The battle ended.

The Greeks had done well and were still a coherent fighting force. Their commanders unwisely accepted an invitation to dinner with the wily Tissaphernes. They were promptly arrested and executed. The mercenaries elected new generals, one of whom was Xenophon, and made their escape as best they could. They marched hundreds of miles through deserts and snow-filled mountain passes and came under frequent attack from Persian troops and angry locals. Finally, they reached the Black Sea, where they took ship to the Aegean and safety.

Sparta's support for Cyrus brought unpleasant consequences. Artaxerxes pulled back from the autonomy-for-tribute understanding and Tissaphernes began to act aggressively towards the Ionian cities. The Spartans had a new, ambitious king, Agesilaus, lame from birth, who as a boy had been Lysander's *eromenos*. He had a typically laconic wit. He was once invited to listen to a man who could imitate the nightingale's song. "No thank you," he replied. "I have heard the bird itself."

Now about forty years old, the king decided to recover Sparta's good name and from 399 to 395 led a successful campaign against the

Persians in Asia Minor. Bearing Xenophon's experience in mind, he aimed at winning

> the person of the Great King and the wealth of Ecbatana and Susa, and above all things to rob the king of the power to sit at leisure on his throne, playing umpire for the Greeks in their wars, and corrupting their popular leaders.

Agesilaus was so successful that his opponent Tissaphernes lost favor in Susa. The queen mother, who seems to have led a charmed life, had not forgiven him for his hostility to her favorite son and persuaded Artaxerxes to have him beheaded for his failure to repel the invader. His fate was a reminder that it is possible to be too clever.

Back in mainland Greece Sparta's allies were losing patience. They had received none of the spoils of war after the fall of Athens and were irritated by Spartan meddling in the north of Greece. Pharnabazus stirred the pot by laying out fifty talents in bribes. In 395 Argos, Thebes, Corinth, and a rather nervous Athens launched a war against Sparta (the so-called Corinthian War). Their fortunes ebbed and flowed. The two most important outcomes were, first, the death of Lysander in battle in Boeotia and, second, the recall of Agesilaus, much to his fury and just as the Great King had calculated.

Meanwhile the Persians had spent some years building a large fleet in the Aegean. Conon was appointed as its commander and, with the Great King's gold, he contributed a squadron of his own crewed by Hellenic émigrés and mercenaries. In August 394 Conon destroyed the Spartan fleet off the island of Cnidus.

It was a triumphant moment for the Athenians, and one to be savored. Conon toured the islands of the Aegean expelling the Spartan *harmosts* and garrisons. He then sailed back to Piraeus where he received a hero's welcome. At great expense (Pharnabazus picked up the bill), he employed the crew of his eighty triremes, about sixteen thousand men, to refortify the port and rebuild the Long Walls.

A little more than one decade had passed since Aegospotami and the loss of empire, and the violet-crowned city was once again a great power. It began to invest in warships. As the patriotic Isocrates remarked: "The Spartans . . . lost their supremacy, Greeks were liberated and our city recovered part of its old glory."

The careers of Conon and Xenophon allowed thinking men to draw two momentous conclusions. First, the pretensions of Sparta, perilously short of citizens as it was, were shown to be hollow. The battle of Cnidus broke once for all its ambition to replace Athens as the ruler of a great maritime empire. Second, the experience of Xenophon and his mercenary comrades exploded another reputation—that of the Great King. Persian soldiery could not rival the professional competence of the Hellenic hoplite (although Persian cavalry had to be reckoned with).

A talented general with enough trained hoplites and a deep pocket would have a good chance of overthrowing the vast and ostensibly invulnerable realm that had once had the Greek world at its feet. Agesilaus might have been that man, had the gods not decided otherwise.

During the years following the fall of Athens, the restored *demos* had recovered much of its self-confidence and bellicosity. Critias and his oligarchs had come and gone, but it had not forgiven, even if it had officially forgotten, the crimes of its domestic enemies. Abroad it tried to exploit Sparta's misfortunes and at home, despite the amnesty after the deposition of the Thirty, it looked about for vengeance. In 399 it found a high-profile target in Socrates, who was taken to court on capital charges.

"I don't know what effect my accusers have had on you, men of Athens," he told the five hundred and one jurors at his trial. "But so far as I was concerned I almost forgot who I was, their arguments were so convincing. On the other hand, there is hardly a word of truth in what they have said."

Socrates might have been forgiven for his puzzlement. The accusations against him were serious enough to warrant the death penalty, but at first reading they seem to contradict everything we know about him. What was going on?

A politician called Meletus, supported by two others, Anytus and Lycon, brought the charges against the philosopher. They read:

> This indictment and affidavit is sworn by Meletus, the son of Meletus of Pitthos, against Socrates, the son of Sophroniscus of Alopece: Socrates is guilty of refusing to recognize the gods recognized by the state, and of introducing other new divinities [in Greek, *daimonia*]. He is also guilty of corrupting the youth. The penalty demanded is death.

Little is known about Meletus. He was young and, according to Plato, had "a hooked nose, and long straight hair, and a poorly growing beard." He was a tragic poet whom Aristophanes attacked, or perhaps the son of one.

We have met Anytus before, hero of the democratic restoration. He was acquainted with Socrates and appears as a character in one of Plato's dialogues, *Meno,* in which he is presented as being hostile to sophists. Lycon was a democrat and an orator. Socrates was friendly with Anytus's and (perhaps) Lycon's sons, and the two fathers may have resented his influence over them.

What is curious about the charges is that Socrates was a religious man and noted for his piety. He was punctilious in observing all the relevant rituals; he took part in the many city festivals and followed the common forms of private and public worship. Although he criticized some sacred legends, he did not reject the existence of the Olympians as some scientific rationalists did, such as Anaxagoras, the friend of Pericles.

It would seem that Meletus and his friends were attacking the "Socrates" of *The Clouds,* whom Aristophanes tars with the same brush as those nomadic intellectuals, the sophists. In fact, the real Socrates was known to be as critical of them as was the average Athenian. It is hard to see how this accusation could have been made to stick.

Did he then introduce new gods, as alleged? Questions of precise belief did not much interest the Greeks and many new cults were imported to Athens without raised eyebrows or cries of heresy. However, Socrates did frequently refer to his *daimonion,* his own supernatural spirit, which gave him personal access to the will of the gods. Once again there was nothing so very unusual for a Greek to consult oracles or other signs.

On the other hand, Greek religion was essentially about the community not the individual. Indeed, it was a means by which the individual signaled his membership of the community. But Socrates' *daimonion* spoke to no one else and was, in effect, his private property. This must have been the offense; no right-thinking citizen should boast a hotline to the supernatural, for it lent too much weight to the individual conscience.

The third and last charge was the easiest to understand. Everyone was aware that, although uninterested in money himself, Socrates was an intellectual honeypot for wealthy young aristocrats. They numbered among them men such as Xenophon and his exact contemporary Plato, who spent his long lifetime preserving, glorifying, and developing his memory and his ideas. But, much worse than that, they included Critias, leader of the Thirty, and his nephew and ward Charmides, an active supporter of the oligarchy who fell with him during the fighting at Piraeus in 403. They both appear in Socratic dialogues by Plato.

Socrates was believed to be *misodemos,* a hater of the democracy, and a good case could be made that his circle was a breeding ground of political reaction. This was unfair, as the philosopher's brave stand against the tyrannical behavior of the Thirty showed, at risk to his own life; and, once second thoughts had set in, even democrats respected his refusal to put the motion to the enraged *ecclesia* to try the Arginusae generals together. Nevertheless, many people blamed him, indirectly at least, for the overthrow of the established constitution. This was the heart of the matter.

There being no public prosecutor nor a police force to detect crime, any citizen was allowed to bring criminal charges against any other (the Scythian archers were only tasked with keeping public order). He would make an arrest (if incapable, a magistrate or Archon would step in). The process was not free of risk, for in the case of wrongful arrest a fine of 1,000 drachmas was levied. The accuser led the prosecution and he could pay for the services of professional speechwriters.

At a preliminary hearing, the plaintiff swore that the charge was genuine and the defendant that he was innocent (he was entitled to enter a counterplea if he so wished). All trials took place in the open air and at different locations in the city (for example, at the Painted Stoa in the *agora* or the Odeum), dependent on the category of alleged crime. They lasted for one day only. The presiding Archon had no powers to give legal directions and simply oversaw due process. Juries, as already noted, were very large in order to discourage bribery. Once each side had delivered its speeches, they cast their ballots in secret and without discussion. The prosecution required 50 percent plus one of the votes to secure a conviction.

We do not have a copy of Socrates' defense, and apparently he spoke off-the-cuff and in a rather offhand manner. He was unyielding and seems almost to have dared the jury to convict him. Both Plato and Xenophon wrote versions of his speech and, although these overlap here and there, they differ markedly from one another. Neither man was present and must have relied on a combination of eyewitness reports and imagination. Whatever his actual words Plato surely captured his spirit when he has him say:

> Men of Athens, I respect you and love you, but I shall obey god rather than you. As long as I live and am able to carry on, I shall never give up philosophy nor stop trying to win you over and pointing out the truth to any one of you I may meet.

Socrates was found guilty by a majority of sixty votes. For some crimes there were fixed punishments, but when, as in this case, there was no penalty fixed by law, the prosecutor recommended one and the defense another. The jury was asked to choose between them. Meletus sought death, as in the indictment. Socrates teased his audience by saying that he had wanted to propose maintenance for life at the state's expense as a public benefactor; but in deference to his friends, including Plato, whom he had consulted, he suggested a fine of 3,000 drachmas. The jury, irritated by his attitude, voted for death by a larger majority than they had for his guilt.

The accusers of Socrates had not in fact wanted his execution. Banishment would have been sufficient. But the philosopher refused to escape abroad, as had been expected. He had always obeyed the law and refused to evade its sanctions now. And in any case he had lived long enough. When his wife complained that he was condemned unjustly, he replied: "Well, would you prefer me to have been condemned justly?"

Socrates spent a delay of some weeks in Athens's small twelve-cell prison (archaeologists have found it) so that a religious festival would not be polluted by his death. He was then told to drink a concoction of poison hemlock. He drained the cup calmly and with no sign of distaste and the small company of close friends in the room broke down in tears.

Plato was absent ill, but his account of Socrates' final minutes as narrated to a friend by an eyewitness, a disciple called Phaedo, is justly famous. Socrates complained:

> "Really, my friends, what kind of behavior is this? Why, that was my main reason for sending away the women, to prevent this sort of commotion; because I am told that one should make one's end in a peaceful frame of mind. Calm down and try to be brave."

This made us feel ashamed, and we controlled our tears. Socrates walked about, and soon, saying that his legs were heavy, lay down on his back—that was what the prison warden recommended. The man (he was the same one who had administered the poison) kept his hand on Socrates, and after a little while inspected his feet and legs; then pinched his foot hard and asked if he felt it. Socrates said no. Then he did the same to his legs; and moving gradually upwards in this way let us see that he was becoming inert and numb. Presently he touched him again and said that when it reached the heart, Socrates would be gone.

The numbness was spreading about as far as his groin when Socrates uncovered his face—for he had covered it up—and said (these were his last words): "Crito, we ought to sacrifice a cock to Asclepius. Make sure it's done. Don't forget."

"No, it shall be done," said Crito. "Are you sure that there is nothing else?"

Socrates made no reply to this question, but after a little while he stirred; and when the man uncovered him, his eyes were fixed. When Crito saw this, he closed the mouth and eyes.

Such, Echecrates, was the end of our comrade, who was, we may fairly say, of all those whom we knew in our time, the bravest and also the wisest and most upright man.

Asclepius was the god of healing and Socrates presumably meant by his last words that he was thankful for being cured of the disease of life.

Some years later, a repentant *demos* executed the leading prosecutor, Meletus, and exiled Anytus and the other accusers for their part in the hounding of Socrates. We are told that Anytus was stoned to death when he visited the Black Sea *polis* of Heraclea and travelers could still visit his grave in Roman times. In Athens later in the fourth century a statue of the philosopher was commissioned from the great sculptor Lysippus. In effect, Socrates had been canonized.

The Corinthian War, which had started in 395, continued to go badly for the Spartans. They had some successes, but in 390 the Athenians annihilated a Spartan regiment. The engagement had no strategic consequences, but 250 hoplites lay dead on the field. Sparta could not stand losses on that scale.

All the international powers were coming under strain. Persia was absorbed by revolts in Egypt and Cyprus, the Spartans had acquired a new fleet that Athens feared would interrupt food imports from the Black Sea. Argos and Corinth were also in difficulties.

Prompted by Sparta, the Great King proposed a general peace. Its theme was independence for city-states, but important concessions were made to special interests. According to the treaty, which was agreed in 386, "King Artaxerxes believes it to be just that cities in Asia should be his, as also . . . Cyprus." All the other cities in the Aegean and mainland Greece were to be independent—except for the islands of Lemnos, Imbros, and Skyros: this reservation ensured the compliance of Athens, which was reluctant to lose these new island acquisitions.

Here we witness Sparta (and Artaxerxes) gaining an interval for drawing breath; Athens was obliged to discontinue its hopes of imperial expansion and a reluctant Thebes had to allow the autonomy of the cities of Boeotia. All Sparta had to do for these gains was to stop fighting the Persians and once more to abandon its Ionian cousins, as Plutarch put it, "in the most shameful and lawless way."

Sparta now had the upper hand to settle various outstanding issues in the Peloponnese, and also in 382 sent a major expedition by land to northern Greece against Olynthus, which headed a growing league of more than thirty *poleis* in Chalcidice. The city was beginning to threaten Spartan supremacy in that part of the Aegean and needed to be cut down to size. After three years of indecisive fighting, Olynthus, hard-pressed by famine, conceded defeat.

On that journey north the Spartans sought permission to pass through Theban territory, which was willingly granted. However, a regimental commander called Phoebidas, who, writes Xenophon, "was not considered to be a man who thought things through or was very bright," was let into the city of Thebes by a dissident oligarch. He and his men occupied the citadel, called the Cadmea, and the democratic government was thrown out.

The coup was a blatant breach of the peace treaty and across Hellas there was a hugely negative reaction. Agesilaus gave it his support while at the same time trickily distancing himself from it. Phoebidas was heavily fined, but Sparta kept the Cadmea.

Athens and Thebes were bitterly hostile neighbors, but both were angry with Sparta. They quickly entered into an alliance and went to war with their common enemy.

Isocrates was the most celebrated intellectual and educationist of the fourth century. When he spoke, many felt he spoke for Greece. And that was how he liked it.

Born in Athens in 436, a few years before the start of the Peloponnesian War, he became one of its victims. His family was rich and his father, Theodorus, gave him a first-class education. He studied under some of the best-known sophists, among them Gorgias, a one-man traveling university whom Plato ridiculed in one of his dialogues for arguing that it was unnecessary to know the truth of things if one had learned the art of persuasion.

Isocrates also fell under the influence of Socrates and in the *Phaedrus,* Plato has Socrates foretell, with a typical touch of Socratic sarcasm, the young man's future fame as an orator or a philosopher.

In the later stages of the Peloponnesian War the family lost its fortune and Isocrates had to cast about for a way of earning a living. He began his career by writing courtroom speeches. He left Athens during the time of the Thirty and taught rhetoric on the island of Chios. He returned to Athens after the restoration of the democracy and shortly before 390 opened a school of rhetoric. The curriculum was unusually wide and he placed a greater emphasis on the importance of morality than most of the teachers with whom he competed.

The school became famous throughout the Hellenic world, where able young men could be "finished." His fees were high and he only accepted a maximum of nine students at a time. Isocrates was a good businessman and made a great deal of money. His only weakness was a poor voice and he lacked confidence as a public speaker. So he tended to write essays in the form of speeches that he published rather than delivered in person.

Isocrates became an influential opinion former. It was his firm belief that Hellas would be weakened, even destroyed, by the inability of its constituent *poleis* to agree on anything among their own citizens or with each other. In 380 he published a celebrated pamphlet, *The Panegyric* or Festival Speech, in which he drew a bleak picture of a broken Hellenic community.

> Who would desire a state of affairs where pirates command the seas and mercenaries occupy our cities? Fellow-citizens, instead of waging war in defense of their territories against foreigners, are fighting each other inside their own city walls? . . . And so far are *poleis* from "freedom" and "autonomy" that some of them are under tyrants, some are controlled by Spartan governors, some have been sacked and razed to the ground and some are under barbarian masters—the same barbarians whom we once punished for their audacity in crossing over into Greece.

Isocrates was an admirer of the Athenian Empire in its most unblushing form and even defended its brutality at Melos. He agreed with Pericles that his city was an education to Greece. He claimed:

> And so far has our city distanced the rest of mankind in thought and in speech that her pupils have become the teachers of the rest of the world. She has brought it about that the name Hellene suggests no longer a race but an intelligence, a way of thinking, and that the word is applied to those who share our culture rather than to those who share a common blood.

The clash of civilizations between Europe and Asia had been a Greek fixation ever since the war at Troy. Isocrates proposed a unification of Greece under two great powers—Athens by sea and Sparta on land—which together would lead a war of liberation against the Persian barbarians.

There was much in this proposition to please the Athenians. For some time they had been wondering if they could reconstitute their maritime league and found that across the Aegean many small states would welcome its return. The seas had become unruly, piracy was widespread, and a return to order was much to be desired. However, Isocrates' fellow-citizens made one reservation. Although in the long run a crusade against the Great King had great appeal, a more immediate enemy had to be tackled first—Sparta, whose behavior as the dominant Greek state was oppressive.

In 378–77 the *ecclesia* passed a decree establishing the principle of a new league. The original stone inscription has survived (in many pieces), which states the aim as being to "compel the Spartans to allow the Greeks to enjoy peace in freedom and independence, with their lands unviolated." The league's sphere of operations was to be mainland Greece and the islands, and the Persians were discreetly left out of account, although they remained at the back of everyone's mind. Troops were levied, and ships commissioned and manned.

The Athenians understood that they had to show contrition for the old empire they had deservedly lost. The allies were to have their own assembly, parallel to, but separate from, the Athenian *ecclesia*. It met in Athens, but Athens was to play no part in its deliberations. A measure passed by one body would only be valid if approved by the other. This double lock meant that, unlike under the first empire, the allies could veto Athenian decisions.

Obviously there had to be a common fund to pay for the fleet, of which Athens would be the treasurer, but payments into it were politely called "contributions" in place of the odious word *phoros,* or tribute. *Cleruchies,* or Athenian settlements on league members' land, were not permitted and no Athenian was allowed to buy or mortgage any real estate there.

The new league was very popular. The first members were already allies and included Chios, Byzantium, Mytilene, Methymna, and the powerful island of Rhodes. Most of the *poleis* on Euboea joined, as did (extraordinarily) Thebes. Among other members were Corcyra off western Greece, and Jason, the energetic tyrant of Pherae in Thessaly. The total membership rose to about seventy.

The league was crucial for Athens. In part this was a question of pride, for it gave the impression that the empire was back. To some extent, though, this was an illusion, for the days of Pericles had passed. Where Athens used to command it now had to consult. However, it *was* able to afford a large fleet that could protect the trade route from the Black Sea, its most important strategic priority.

No doubt Isocrates was pleased by the rise of Athens and the unification of the seagoing city-states, but this meant little to him if Sparta was still the enemy, however badly it had behaved, and so long as the Ionian cities remained under the Great King's thumb.

It was the winter of 379 and the weather was cold and windy, presaging snow. Seven exiles including a certain Pelopidas planned to overthrow a pro-Spartan oligarchy in Thebes and to remove the Spartan garrison in its citadel, the Cadmea. Dressed as peasants, they crossed into Theban territory by night and spent the next day quietly in some unpopulated spot. Then, pretending to be coming in from the fields, they joined other farm laborers who were passing through the city gate at the end of the working day.

With their faces muffled ostensibly against the bad weather, the group made its way to a "safe house" where other local conspirators were already gathered. Their plan was to enter the homes of two leading generals or *polemarchs,* Archias and Philippos, that evening, and assassinate them. That would be enough, they calculated, to overthrow the regime and replace it with a democracy.

A banquet was being held in honor of the *polemarchs,* who were leaving office that day. The celebration was organized by their administrative secretary, Phyllidas, who happened to be among the plotters. At the *polemarchs'* request, he promised to lay on some attractive women (as Xenophon noted sourly, "they were that sort of men"). They feasted and soon, with a little help from their secretary, became very drunk.

A letter came in for Archias, revealing details of the plot. He put it on one side, saying he would look at it the next day. The party shouted for the women and Phyllidas went out for them. He returned with three of the more attractive conspirators in drag and wearing veils and wreaths. They were accompanied by some equally transvestite maids. They insisted demurely that the servants left before they joined the party. Once that had been done the conspirators entered the dining room and lay down next to the *polemarchs,* threw off their disguises, drew their daggers, and slaughtered them. The victims were too befuddled to defend themselves.

Afterwards another guilty man, the Theban oligarch who had let Phoebidas into the city three years previously, was attacked and killed in his house nearby. It was now full night and the townspeople were asleep. The triumphant conspirators tried to rouse them, shouting that the tyrants were dead. As long as it was dark nobody dared to come out, but with daybreak everyone poured into the streets and cheered the revolution.

In the Cadmea the nervous Spartan garrison did not know what to do, but were eventually persuaded to leave town quietly. So ended a scandal that seriously damaged the reputation of Sparta.

When they learned what had happened, the Spartans collectively lost their temper, the classic sign of a guilty conscience. They executed two of their three garrison commanders and banished the third, for capitulating without a fight. They complained to Athens about volunteers that had gone to Thebes to help.

And then, as if to compound the offense of Phoebidas, a Spartan called Sphodrias thought he would compensate for the loss of Thebes by acquiring Piraeus. He decided to march overnight deep into Attica and capture the port of Athens by attacking it from its landward side (despite its rebuilt walls Piraeus still had no town gates). He seems to have been no brighter than Phoebidas; by sunrise he had only reached Eleusis and still had miles to go. He was forced into a humiliating retreat, but not before showing the world what he had intended.

While the star of Athens was in the ascendant, that of Sparta was overclouded. A storm was on its way.

During the 370s, Thebes resisted the might of the Spartan army and grew stronger as a result. It deepened its control over the *poleis* of Boeotia, whatever the Athenians and their new league said about liberty. At sea the Athenian navy scored major successes against the Spartans and their allies, whose prestige slowly declined.

King Agesilaus seems to have harbored an obsessive hatred for the Thebans and a Spartan army invaded Thebes a number of times during this decade, although it was careful to avoid risking too many casualties and undertook no sieges. Meanwhile the Thebans built a defensive rampart around part of their Boeotian territory.

In response to continual Spartan bullying, a Theban general called Epaminondas with his great friend (and possibly lover) Pelopidas developed innovative tactics for hoplite battles. Three hundred male couples, each an *erastes* with his (grown-up) *eromenos,* were brought together in a new elite regiment, the Sacred Band. The theory was that they would not want to act disgracefully in each other's presence. It seems to have worked, for they soon won a fearsome reputation for courage under fire.

In 375 a small but fierce encounter took place during which the Sacred Band and a few cavalry routed a Spartan force of more than one thousand hoplites and killed two of its commanders. This was the first time in history that a Spartan army had been defeated by an enemy of equal or lesser size. The wind was shifting.

The regular formation for hoplites was the phalanx in which men were deployed eight or more ranks deep in a long line (see page 99). Epaminondas tailored his own version, which he marshaled up to fifty ranks deep and placed on one of his wings. The rest of his army was thinned out and stepped back in an oblique formation. The phalanx bristling with long spears drove into its opponents with irresistible force.

In 371 a peace congress was held in Sparta and a general settlement was agreed on the familiar principle of autonomy for individual city-states. The question of the Boeotian League arose. Should Thebes be excluded from the treaty on the grounds that it dominated the other *poleis* in Boeotia? Epaminondas the Theban took the oath endorsing the peace on behalf of all Boeotians. His view was that because Boeotia was a geographical unity it was also and rightly a political unity—just like Laconia, which was governed by the Spartan *polis*.

Agesilaus, who was recovering from a long illness, lost his temper. He asked Epaminondas whether, in the light of the principle of autonomy, he thought it just and equitable for the cities of Boeotia to be independent. The Theban replied with another question. "Does Agesilaus think it just and equitable for the cities of Laconia to be independent?" The king furiously erased the name of Thebes from the treaty text and issued a declaration of war.

According to the terms of the accord, all parties were to withdraw or disband their forces, but Sparta thought otherwise and an allied army of ten thousand hoplites and one thousand horse under King Cleombrotus, Agesilaus's co-monarch, was ordered to march against the Thebans and liberate the Boeotian cities. They encountered Epaminondas and an opposing force of about six thousand men at a village called Leuctra seven miles southwest of Thebes.

Seven Boeotarchs or generals of the Boeotian League were in charge of the Theban campaign (it was typical for Greek armies and navies to have multiple commanders). Epaminondas and two other generals argued for an immediate battle, but three others were in favor of pulling back and looking for a more advantageous position. The seventh Boeotarch was absent guarding a mountain pass. When he returned to the camp he backed Epaminondas, who now had a majority for battle. He prepared a highly original plan that was designed more than to make up for his inferior numbers.

Cleombrotus held a council of war after breakfast on July 6, 371, at which it was decided to accept battle (there was a rumor that wine was drunk). He received a surprise when the armies began to take their positions. As was traditional, the Spartan hoplites, including seven hundred Equals, formed up on the right wing under the king's command. They stood in a phalanx twelve ranks deep. In front of them was a weak squadron of Spartan cavalry.

Astonishingly, though, the Spartan right was confronted by a massed Theban phalanx fifty ranks deep, also covered by cavalry. The rest of the Theban army was echeloned back from this formidable mass of men and was evidently not expected to play a major part in the forthcoming battle.

The Boeotian horse were well trained and in the opening phase of the battle soon cleared the Spartan cavalry from the field. Cleombrotus extended his phalanx farther to the right to outflank the Boeotians. But while he was undertaking this maneuver, the oversized Theban phalanx, headed by Pelopidas and the Sacred Band, ran at the double towards the Spartan king and his staff.

The impact when it bulldozed into the Spartan hoplites was terrible. Almost immediately Cleombrotus fell mortally wounded and his hoplites were overwhelmed. When half the Spartans, including four hundred of the Equals, had been felled, the remainder broke and fled to their camp. The Equals who were still alive wanted to resume the fight, but the allies had had enough.

In a single day, Spartan power had been destroyed. The slaughter of the Equals reduced their number to a point where Sparta could no longer field a proper army. A rout on this scale amazed the Greek world. As the news spread, remaining *harmosts* were expelled and democracies reinstalled throughout the mainland and the Aegean, and even in Sparta's backyard, the Peloponnese.

. . .

Immediately after the battle, a garlanded Theban herald was sent to Athens to bring the good news to the Athenian *boulē,* which happened to be in session at the time on the Acropolis. He asked for their support and said: "It is now possible to take vengeance on the Spartans for all the things they have done to us." But this was the last thing on the councilors' minds. They were dismayed by the fact that Thebes was now the dominant force in mainland Greece and had upset the centuries-old balance of power. They made no reply to the herald and did not even give him a customary meal of hospitality. He returned home, unthanked.

In Sparta they were celebrating the Festival of the Naked Youths (*Gymnopaedia*). Unclothed teenagers and men took part in competitive sports, choral events, and displayed their military skill by performing mock-combat dances. A messenger arrived to announce the disaster during a performance in the theater by the men's chorus. The *ephors* were greatly distressed when they heard the news, but allowed the concert to run its course before revealing the names of the dead to their families. The Spartans reacted with characteristic serenity. Xenophon writes:

> . . . they ordered the women not to cry out, but to bear the calamity in silence. On the following day one could see those whose relatives had died going about in public with bright and cheerful faces. You would have seen few whose relatives had been reported as still alive, and these few walking about with gloomy and downcast faces.

Agesilaus held his nerve. Knowing that every soldier was needed, he suspended the law that removed citizenship from those who fled in the face of the enemy. In 370 he launched an incursion into Arcadia, for the sake of morale, but took care not to lose any men.

Epaminondas and Pelopidas were determined that Sparta should fall never to rise again. The simplest means of achieving this was to prize the Peloponnese from its grasp. This would mean freeing the *helots* and establishing Messenia as an independent state, and doing the same for the Arcadians in the north. In the winter of 370, Epaminondas led a large army into the Peloponnese. It was the first of four invasions in the coming years.

The Thebans and their allies set out for Sparta itself, sacking and burning the countryside as they went. For half a millennium no foreign enemy had ever penetrated the Peloponnese and the shock to Lacedaemonian pride was tremendous. Women who had never cast eyes on a foreigner before could not bear to see the smoke rising from fires in the suburbs. *Perioeci* broke free from their masters. A mere eight hundred or so Equals guarded the unwalled city. As a risky last resort, the aged Agesilaus recruited six thousand *helots* to join the defense. Some long-standing allies, such as Corinth, sent help. As they watched their countryside being laid waste, the Spartans, like the Athenians in 431, wanted to go on the attack, but the king refused to let them. A Theban crowed: "Where are the Spartans now?"

A fierce defense made the Thebans pull back. They bypassed Sparta and marched south to its port, Gythium, destroying everything they came across. Then they went west and liberated Messenia. At long last the *helots* were free. To secure their future Epaminondas decided to build them a well-fortified capital city, Messene, and for its location selected the slopes of Mount Ithome, focus of ancient revolts and symbol of resistance. The omens were auspicious, stone was ordered, and town planners and developers skilled in building houses, temples, and fortifications were hired. In solemn ceremonies, the ancient heroes, or demigods, of Messenia were begged to return to their native land. The loudest summons was for a historical personality, Aristomenes, rebel leader and elected king during the Second Messenian War in the seventh century. Exiles, who had retained their customs and still spoke a pure Doric dialect, were recalled after centuries of absence.

In eighty-five days the Thebans and their allies, guided by the experts, constructed a massive stone perimeter wall; five and a half miles long, with guard towers and two main gates, its remains can still be seen. They also built houses and temples. The men worked to the music of flutes. The bones of Aristomenes were retrieved from their resting place abroad and reburied; it was said that his ghost had been present at the battle of Leuctra and guided the Thebans to victory.

In 368 a fortified city, Megalopolis, was also founded to guard a newly independent confederation of Arcadia. So both to the north and in the west Sparta's onetime subject peoples and compulsory allies were given their freedom as well as the means with which to defend themselves.

The Greeks were used to city-states temporarily losing their authority and influence, but after a while recovering them. But this time it was clear that Sparta could not recover from the decision of Leuctra. It dwindled into a local power in the Peloponnese and would never again bestride the Hellenic stage.

Eventually after three months, the Peloponnesian allies of Thebes began to leave, taking with them as much booty as they could carry. The Theban hoplites, too, began to think of home. Having altered the course of history, Epaminondas called it a day.

22

Chaeronea — "Fatal to Liberty"

Isocrates was a disappointed man.

He had argued for Greek unification and invasion of the Persian Empire. He had proposed in his *Panegyric* that Athens, his own city, and Sparta should join forces, as they had done during the long-ago invasion by Xerxes, and give the Great King his just deserts.

But the years had passed without anything being done. At last, writing in 346, he conceded that Athens had proved to be a disappointment.

> I turned to Athens first of all and tried to win her over to this cause with all the earnestness of which my nature is capable, but when I realized that she cared less for what I said than for the ravings of speakers in the *ecclesia,* I gave her up, although I did not abandon my efforts.

At different points in his long career he identified other candidates for the leadership of Greece. They included the Spartan king,

Agesilaus, who campaigned against the Persians in Asia Minor with some success. Then there was Jason, tyrant of Pherae, a town in Thessaly, in the 370s. He commanded an efficient and well-trained mercenary army with which he dominated Thessaly and even planned a war against the Persians. Xenophon has a fellow-Thessalian say that Jason

> is so intelligent a general that whatever he sets out to achieve— whether by stealth, anticipation or brute force, he does not fail to get. . . . Of all the men I know, he is the one most able to control the desires of the body, so that he is not hindered by such things from achieving what needs to be done.

However, any hopes for Jason were dashed when he was assassinated in 370.

The gaze of the eighty-year-old sage turned to Dionysius I, tyrant of Syracuse, whom he petitioned as the "foremost of our race and possessor of the greatest power," but he too disappointingly died; and then to Archidamus, son and successor of Agesilaus. He sounded him out in an open letter:

> Men of good counsel should not wage war against the king of Persia until someone shall have first reconciled the Greeks with each other and have made us cease from our madness and contentiousness.

But it was obvious that Sparta was a broken reed and was obliged to spend most of its energies trying, and failing, to recover its position in the Peloponnese.

At last, Isocrates found a leader who might indeed call a halt to Greece's quarrels and attack the evil empire. He was Philip, ruler of Macedon in the north, to whom he wrote yet another of his open letters:

I have chosen to challenge you to the task of leading the expedition against the barbarians and of taking Hellas under your care, while I have passed over my own city.

This time Isocrates hit the mark, for Philip did indeed dream of dominating Greece and was seriously tempted by the Great King's fabulous wealth.

So who was Philip? Was he truly Greek? And would he last? In 359 at the age of twenty-two he was acclaimed king of Macedon by his army, the traditional method of confirming the succession. His inheritance was, to put it mildly, insecure.

The kingdom lay northeast of the Greek mainland above the three-pronged peninsula of Chalcidice. Populated by hardy peasants and horsey squires, it was divided into two distinct parts—lowlands and highlands. Lower Macedonia consisted of a flat, fertile plain through which two rivers flowed into the Thermaic Gulf. The land was predominantly pastoral. The climate was warm, timber and minerals were plentiful, and Herodotus praises the "gardens of Midas [named after the mythical king of Phrygia whose touch turned everything to gold] where roses grow wild, each with sixty blossoms and more fragrant than any others in the world."

This was the heartland of the kingdom and was ringed with hills. Beyond them lay the plateaus of Upper Macedonia to the west, which are themselves ringed by mountains. Feudal barons dominated these remote fastnesses. Unlike the lowlanders, they preferred Thracian deities to the Olympian gods and indulged in orgiastic cult practices, not at all dissimilar to those in Euripides' late masterpiece, *The Bacchae,* written in Macedon and premiered in Athens in 405.

To the west and north lived the tribes of Epirus, Illyria, and Paeonia and, farther along on the eastern shore, the coastline of Thrace. These unmanageable peoples were constantly on the attack and placed Macedon under severe pressure. From about 700 the Argead dynasty had provided rulers for the region, but they exercised only a loose control outside the lowlands.

Greeks from their city-states regarded themselves as civilized and looked down on the Macedonians as barbarous and uncouth. They spoke a dialect of what they claimed to be Greek, but nobody else understood it. In fact, although they had no indigenous literature, they enjoyed a sophisticated visual culture. Their craftsmen created very fine gold, silver, and bronze artworks. They also painted murals in their tombs and commissioned superb mosaics depicting stories from Greek mythology or everyday scenes, such as deer hunting. Their feudal warriors had something of Homer about them; they thirsted to excel and placed a high value on military glory for its own sake. They lived the life of an Achilles or a Hector.

The Macedonians insisted that they were members of the Hellenic community, competed in the various international games, and did their best to adopt the best of Greek culture. Both Agathon and the octogenarian Euripides emigrated from Athens to the court of King Archelaus. The king had the reputation of a dissipated homosexual, but he was a busy administrator and a committed Hellenizer; he founded the Olympian Festival, which was dedicated to the Nine Muses and included athletic and musical contests. He invited Socrates to Macedon, but the philosopher was too much attached to his home city and politely declined the offer. He would rather not accept favors, he explained, that he could never repay.

Archelaus did his best to unify Upper and Lower Macedonia. He undertook major military reforms, improving the supply of weapons, horses, and other military resources and building a network of roads. He relocated the capital to the strategic port of Pella.

If other things had been equal, Macedon should have been a great power. But its monarchs were always having to resist the enemies that crowded around the country's borders, and when they were not doing so they faced treacherous pretenders at home. It is something of a mystery that anyone should compete for such a contested and blood-drenched throne. So far as the Hellenic powers were concerned Macedon was a fringe player in the great game of international politics.

After the assassination of Archelaus in 399 a period of anarchy ensued. Five monarchs followed one another on the throne in the space of six years. All the good work of Archelaus had seemingly gone for nothing. Calm was restored under Philip's father, Amyntas III, but upheavals and lawlessness resumed on his death in 369. The kingdom entered another period of dynastic chaos.

For ten years after Leuctra, Thebes was the leading power in Greece, but its predominance was only temporary.

Soon after the battle, Pelopidas was invited to arbitrate between two contenders for the Macedonian throne. The one he chose was swiftly murdered by his rival, who decided that a treaty with Thebes would be advisable.

To demonstrate his sincerity, the usurper sent some distinguished hostages to Thebes. These included Philip, then only fifteen years old and a younger son of the dead monarch. He was a bright and attractive teenager, who appears to have caught the roving eye of Pelopidas. He learned from him the art of polite behavior. His Theban hosts were also intellectuals and it was probably from them that, a little surprisingly in the light of his later violent career, he also developed an interest in the philosophy of the mathematician and mystic Pythagoras.

To more practical effect, Philip watched Epaminondas at work on army affairs and listened carefully to his conversation. He received military advice from another general, Pammenes, in whose house he lodged and with whom he was also rumored to have shared his charms. He was a popular boy. Pammenes admired the Sacred Band, whose self-discipline he compared favorably with the unruly peoples and tribes in Homer. Philip stored in his mind everything he heard at Thebes before returning home in 364.

During the ten years after Leuctra, we have seen that Epaminondas invaded the Peloponnese a number of times. He was determined to prevent a Spartan resurgence. Thebes also turned its attention to central and northern Greece. It built a fleet to rival that of the Athenians and fostered discontent among their allies, Rhodes, Chios, and Byzantium. Pelopidas intervened in Thessaly, where Jason of Pherae's son and successor was behaving aggressively towards his neighbors, but, although the campaign was ultimately successful, the Theban commander lost his life.

People began to tire of Thebes—so much so that there was talk in the Peloponnese of that most implausible event, an anti-Theban alliance between Lacedaemon and its long-standing enemy, the Arcadians. In 362, fearful of losing influence, Epaminondas found himself having to launch his fourth expedition to southern Greece. Once again he threatened Sparta itself. Xenophon compared the city to helpless chicks in a nest without their parents, but luckily Agesilaus was warned in time and came to the rescue.

At Mantinea, Epaminondas faced the army of a grand alliance, led by Athens and Sparta. In terms of numbers, this was to be the largest battle yet fought between Hellenes: the Thebans and their allies came with thirty thousand infantry and three thousand cavalry and ranged against them were twenty thousand infantry and two thousand cavalry. It was a long day, but the Theban cavalry and then the deep phalanx eventually put the Spartans to flight.

The enemy targeted Epaminondas, who was pushing a little ahead of his line and a Spartan wounded him with a spear. He was taken to his tent. Victory in the battle was his, but he knew that he had been fatally hurt. He asked for one of his best generals to assume command, and was told he had been killed; then for another, but he too was dead. "In that case," said Epaminondas before expiring, "make peace."

The loss of Epaminondas and Pelopidas was a heavy blow to Thebes. Its influence ebbed. In the long run, though, this had less to do with victories or defeats in the field than with the fact that it had never managed to unite Boeotia fully into an integrated and loyal whole. One medium-sized *polis* on its own did not have the resources to play a leading role on the international stage for any length of time.

The waning of Thebes left Athens as the strongest Hellenic power. But the old energy was missing. Somehow lifeblood was seeping from the *polis,* the city-state that, in the fifth century, had claimed to be an education to Greece and had not only demanded but received its citizens' active loyalty on the battlefield. The orator Aeschines made a telling point when he said

> the people, discouraged by their experiences, as though they were suffering from dementia or been declared of unsound mind, lay claim only to the name of democracy, and have given away the substance of it to others. And so you go home from the meetings of your *ecclesia,* not from a serious debate, but after dividing the profits like shareholders.

The city was becoming an open-air museum. Visitors came to tour the monuments of the Periclean age. Apart from restoring their fortifications, the Athenians only started major new building works and refurbishments again in the third quarter of the century; these included ship sheds, the arsenal, the great stone theater of Dionysus, and a Panathenaic stadium in a valley southeast of the city—important projects, but not quite on the old grand scale. Wonderful sculpture continued to be carved or cast, but with a difference. Where Pheidias conveyed the majesty of anthropomorphic gods, Praxiteles, the leading Athenian sculptor of his age, portrayed in marble beings that were nominally supernatural but in fact looked like individual men and women, if very beautiful ones. His celebrated Aphrodite at Cnidus was sexy and erotic: so much so that it is said that a young admirer had himself locked up overnight in the temple where she stood and left semen stains on the marble.

Tragedies were still composed, although inspiration was failing and none of them has survived. So far as we can tell, they gradually withered into unactable literary exercises. A tradition grew of reviving the masterpieces of the past, especially the plays of Euripides. The concept of the classic was born.

The scabrous political farces of Aristophanes, which oxygenated the democracy of the fifth century (called by scholars Old Comedy), modulated into something softer, comedies in which innuendo supplanted obscenity (Middle Comedy). These in turn were replaced by a brand-new style of humor—gentle, optimistic, and focused on individuals rather than on politics (New Comedy). A leading practitioner was Menander, who flourished in the second half of the fourth century.

His plays are usually set in Athens or the countryside of Attica and concerned the private lives of affluent middle-class families. The plots are artificial and depend on implausible coincidences. They describe obstacles to true love and center on the young man of the house. Children are abandoned or kidnapped and are finally recognized many years later thanks to some curio or trinket. The characters are stereotypes—the boastful soldier, the irate father, the garrulous chef, the clever but cowardly slave, the good-time girl with a heart of gold. Story lines that could never have happened in real life were made convincing by colloquial and witty verse dialogue. In ancient times, Menander was seen as a realist.

His work has only survived in papyrus fragments that archaeologists have found in the rubbish tips of ancient Egypt—convincing evidence that his work was not only acted in theaters, but also read throughout the Greek world.

By a similar process, the subject matter of red-figure pottery paid less attention to the male body, sex scenes and drinking parties, military images, and mythological stories and more to domestic incidents and the private lives of women. The last figurative pottery was produced in the city no later than about 320.

. . .

A modest prosperity returned to Athens, although there was never quite enough money to pay for its ambitions.

The state's income was sufficient to pay for the administration of the democracy and the law courts. The new league meant that its subscriptions allowed the city to run a peacetime fleet. However, for all the ingenuity of its politicians, Athens was unable to build sufficient reserves to cover the prohibitive costs of a major military campaign or lengthy hostilities. These pressures had the beneficial effect of making the city improve its financial systems (especially under its leading statesmen, Callicrates and Eubulus, during the middle years of the century), and imaginative means were found of bleeding the rich.

Eubulus also devised a cleverly cheap way of helping the poor. He created (or perhaps reinstated) a Festival Fund. Athens had more festivals than any other Greek *polis*. Attendance used to be free, but now charges were levied; the new fund paid for the admittance of poorer citizens. This popular measure has been estimated to have cost no more than thirty talents a year. However, the fund's budget soon rose sharply. As well as its regular income, it received all annual exchequer surpluses and became a powerful agency that eclipsed the official financial institutions, including the *boulē,* and gave grants for all kinds of public purpose.

In a pamphlet on the Athenian economy, Xenophon acknowledged the state's financial weakness and very sensibly recommended measures to increase trade and, above all, "a complete end to war, on land and sea." On the face of it, Athens looked as if it had recovered its fifth-century status, but in fact its supremacy was fragile.

Nevertheless, the shortage of money by no means prevented the city from being busy militarily everywhere, albeit as cheaply as possible and without much effect. During the decade after Leuctra its land forces fought in the Peloponnese most years with varying allies, the general aim being to undermine the dominance of Thebes. It also tried to halt Theban activity in Thessaly and intervened in Macedonia. Athenian generals won campaigns in Samos in 365, the Chersonese from

365 onwards, much of Chalcidice in 364, and Euboea in 357. Among them stood the towering figure of Timotheus, son of the great Athenian admiral Conon. A capable commander and politician during the era of the new Athenian maritime league, he worked hard to revive his city's imperial power.

The city's main defense priority remained to keep clear the sea-lane from the Black Sea to Piraeus. There were two dangerous obstacles along the way: the city-states of the peninsula of Chalcidice needed to be under Athenian control or at least friendly; and the narrow waters of the Hellespont, the Propontis, and the Bosphorus had to be open to Athenian shipping.

In 364 a storm blew up out of an apparently clear sky. The Athenians seem not to have noticed that their heavy-handed behavior was seriously annoying their Aegean allies; although they had promised not to create *cleruchies,* they in fact had done so and the undisciplined activities of mercenaries in their employ whom they failed to pay regularly produced many complaints. Discontent was fomented by the energetic ruler of Caria, Mausolus. The successor of Tissaphernes, he was nominally a Persian satrap, but to all intents an independent power. On his encouragement, some allies of Athens broke away from the league. These were the great islands of Rhodes, Cos, and Chios, which Mausolus wanted to bring into his sphere of influence, together with Byzantium on the Bosphorus.

Athens opened a vigorous campaign against the insurgents in what is called the War of the Allies, but lost decisively two major naval engagements. One of its best admirals was killed and two others, who had avoided battle because of stormy weather, were unjustly brought to trial on a charge of treachery (one was Timotheus, who went into exile to avoid a colossal fine of 200 talents and died shortly thereafter). To raise money to pay his troops, an Athenian general went to the aid of a rebellious satrap, to the fury of the Great King, who threatened war. But the treasury was empty (the city had spent 1,000 talents on mercenaries alone) and in 355 Athens was obliged to agree to a peace.

The three island rebels were allowed to leave the league and the independence of Byzantium was recognized. The dismembered confederation struggled on, but the renewed dream of empire was over.

The lame old man still labored unstintingly as the servant of his country. In 361 Agesilaus, now eighty years old (a very great age by the standards of the day), agreed to lead a Spartan force to Egypt. It had won its independence from Persia some forty years previously and its pharaoh was now going on the offensive against the Great King. He needed some Greek mercenaries to help him.

An unconvincing justification for Agesilaus's accepting the commission was that it would advance "the noble cause to restore the freedom of the Greeks" in Asia Minor by fighting the Persians wherever they could be found, but the truth was simpler. The Spartan government was desperately short of ready cash and was compelled to hire out a king and some of its meager band of Equals to raise revenue. The embarrassment was palpable.

When Agesilaus arrived in Egypt the pharaoh's top commanders paid him a courtesy visit. He was an international celebrity and they were amazed by what they found. Plutarch describes the scene:

> Everyone crowded round to catch a glimpse of him. The spectacle proved to be nothing brilliant, just a pathetic old man of slight build, wrapped in a coarse, shabby cloak, and lying on some grass by the sea. People began to laugh and jeer at him.

The long career of Agesilaus—more than forty-one years on the throne—has a tragic dimension. Although he was a man of some ability, he saw the world as if he suffered from tunnel vision. He allowed his values to be distorted by a hot-tempered fidelity to his homeland. Whatever was in his country's interest, narrowly defined, was right, and whatever was not was wrong.

He refused to accept, for example, that the illegal seizure of the

Theban citadel had been counterproductive. His long-standing prejudice against the Thebans encouraged them to military reforms and so
contributed to the disaster of Leuctra. He never accepted the loss of
Messenia and demotion from the status of a great power.

At the height of his success he believed himself destined to lead an
invasion of the Persian Empire and so avenge the criminal aggression
of Darius and Xerxes. He represented Sparta in its days of unparalleled
authority, but he lived long enough to see it reduced to a maddened
impotence.

Relations with the Egyptians were complicated and unsatisfactory.
But Agesilaus had to swallow his pride and fulfill his contract. In 360, a
rival pharaoh, to whom he had switched his loyalties, let him go. He
was given a fine formal leave-taking—and the sum of 250 talents.

Agesilaus never made it home. Since it was winter, he had his fleet
hug the shore. At a deserted spot on the Libyan coast, called the Harbor of Menelaus, he died. As a rule the bodies of Spartans who lost
their lives abroad were buried where they fell, but kings were brought
home. The custom was to steep their corpses in honey, but on this occasion none could be found. So his comrades embalmed their leader in
wax.

As he approached his end, Agesilaus gave instructions, according to
Plutarch, to his staff that they should not commission any image of his
person: "If I have accomplished any glorious act, that will be my memorial. If I have not, not all the statues in the world—the products of
vulgar, worthless men—will make any difference."

Into which category, one wonders, did the calamitous king place
himself?

As its power diminished, Athens became the ancient equivalent of a
university town, where wealthy young men just out of their teens could
finish their education.

Sophists had usually been itinerant, but from the end of the fifth
century some of them settled down and founded higher education es-

tablishments, especially in Athens. Groups of teachers, students, and researchers came together in one place for a common purpose. They arrived from all parts of the Greek world and Athens was soon more than one *polis* among many, but a genuinely Panhellenic center. At last the dream of Pericles was coming true—culturally if not politically.

For most of these establishments the basic offer to the student, as Plato put into the mouth of Protagoras, was to promote "sound judgment in his personal life, showing him how best to manage his household, and in public life to make the most effective contribution in action and speech."

The first to open his school in Athens shortly after 399 was Antisthenes, a devotee of Socrates (although he placed more emphasis on the written word than Socrates and expected those attending his classes to take notes). Then a few years later came Isocrates' establishment, many of whose students came from abroad. One of his favorites was the then young and promising Timotheus.

Plato (a nickname perhaps meaning broad-browed, his given name being Aristocles) was by far the most able of the disciples of Socrates. He had a bad time of things during the early postwar years. He was born about 429 to a distinguished and wealthy upper-class family and could have expected a career in public affairs. Critias, leader of the Thirty, was an uncle of his as was one of his colleagues in power, Charmides. The violence of the regime disillusioned him with politics and "it soon showed the preceding government to have been an age of gold." The revived democracy was scarcely an improvement, for it put Socrates to death.

The grief-stricken Plato and other disciples retreated to Megara. He spent the next twelve years traveling—first, to Cyrene in North Africa, then to southern Italy and Sicily where he met followers of the sixth-century polymath and mystic Pythagoras. He visited the court of Dionysius, tyrant of Syracuse, but disliked its pleasure-seeking atmosphere. (He made two more visits to the city in the vain hope of training his son and successor to be a virtuous ruler.)

In 387, Plato bought a small estate next to the Academy, a public park and gymnasium just outside the city. Here he opened a school of philosophy and mathematics of which he remained the head until his death in 347. Unlike most of his competitors he banned the teaching of rhetoric, the art of making the worse seem the better cause.

Plato wrote about twenty-five philosophical dialogues, all of which survive (the authenticity of a few has been questioned). He does not appear in any of them himself and he never announces his own Platonic doctrines. This detachment sends an important message to the inquirer after truth: he should never accept any philosophical proposition without testing it. Knowledge can only be won through intellectual struggle.

However, some overriding themes do emerge in Plato's work. Values are absolute and virtue is essential to an individual's life. True knowledge, what Socrates in the dialogues calls wisdom, enables whoever has it to see that sense impressions are illusory and to understand their ideal or perfect "forms" (see page 323). These forms are actual entities, but can only be grasped by abstract reflection and inquiry, not by experience. Wrongdoing stems from ignorance; those who truly know what is good will inevitably do good. In *On the State,* Plato, no democrat, describes an ideal state governed by wise guardians or philosopher-kings.

The historical Socrates used his technique of question and answer, the *elenchus,* or dialectic, to test definitions of, say, love or justice. However, the technique has a weakness in that it tends to show what these things are not, not what they are. In Plato's later dialogues "his" Socrates plays a lesser role or fades away altogether. Positive theories or teachings are put forward (for instance, a belief in reincarnation, so that new knowledge is really an act of remembering what we had known before we were born) and we may guess that what we read derives from the disciple rather than the master.

Plato was an inspiration to his contemporaries (including to that well-known intellectual King Philip of Macedon, who paid him memorial honors when he died) and has remained so to the present day. A leading British thinker of the twentieth century wrote: "The safest general characterization of the European philosophical tradition is that it consists of a series of footnotes to Plato."

One of Plato's best students was a seventeen-year-old lad called Aristotle, a native of Chalcidice. He was the son of the court physician to the king of Macedon and may well have been, or become, a citizen of the kingdom. He enrolled at the Academy in 367 and was quickly recognized as an outstanding student. It seems that while respecting Plato he was not slow to criticize him. Plato was reported to have said of him: "Aristotle kicked against me as a colt kicks against his mother."

Aristotle remained at the Academy until Plato's death and at about that time left Athens, probably because of his association with the unpopular Macedonians. He settled for a while with fellow-philosophers in a small city-state in the Troad under the protection of Hermeias, an intellectually inclined tyrant who had studied at the Academy under Plato. Aristotle married his niece and adopted daughter.

Hermeias conspired with Philip of Macedon and rose against the Great King, but was tricked into attending a meeting with the Persian general commissioned to quash the revolt. Sent in chains to Susa, he was tortured, mutilated, and impaled. He died saying: "I have done nothing unworthy of philosophy."

The sad end of this aspirational despot throws light on the seriousness with which educated Greeks pursued intellectual inquiry. Philosophy was a new discipline that transformed the world, ferreted out the secrets of the universe, and solved the mystery of life. How could any rational human being resist its allure?

Aristotle retreated to the greater safety of Mytilene on the island of Lesbos and wrote an ode in Hermeias's memory. Then after a few years he was summoned to Macedon to tutor Philip's teenaged son, Alexander. In 335 he returned to Athens and started teaching at the gymnasium in the Lyceum, a grove sacred to Apollo Lyceus ("belonging to a wolf"). Apparently he lectured to his students in the morning and the public at large in the evening. The venue was a covered walk or *peripatos* and from this came the name given to his style of philosophy—peripatetic.

Aristotle disagreed with Plato in that he favored observation over abstract speculation. In his pioneering *History of Animals* he sought to catalogue, describe, and explain the biological world. He included in it human beings, both their physical characteristics and, in other books, their social and political arrangements.

He was extraordinarily productive and four hundred works were attributed to him, of which about one fifth have survived. They fall into three categories. These comprise, first, polished popular books of philosophy for a general readership, often in dialogue form, which have all been lost; collections of historical and scientific data, often assembled in partnership with research assistants, such as lists of victors at the Olympic and Pythian games, records of theatrical productions at Athens, and analyses of some 158 Greek states, of which only a study of the Athenian constitution survives; and, finally, philosophical and scientific texts, frequently in the form of lecture notes that were not intended for publication and are mostly extant.

These texts cover rhetoric (again in opposition to Plato, he included this in the curriculum of his school at the Lyceum); a group of works (what we call the *Organon*) on logic and the science of reasoning; metaphysics (he disagreed with Plato's doctrine of the forms, believing them to be immanent in objects and without an external reality); natural science, ethics, and politics; dramatic and literary theory (the *Poetics,* in two books, the second of which is lost).

Aristotle's influence in the Middle Ages in almost every field of inquiry was absolute; his work on logic retained its validity until the development of mathematical logic in the nineteenth century.

The schools of Athens were the city's main cultural achievement in the fourth century.

While the Greeks were indulging in their customary internecine feuds, the young Philip returned to his native Macedon from being a hostage in Thebes. His two elder brothers died violently, one by assassination and the other in battle, and in 359 he assumed the regency of his younger brother's son, Amyntas IV, then a child of less than ten years.

There was no reason to suppose the monarchy's traditional pattern of murderous incompetence was to be broken or that Philip would fare any better than his predecessors on their slippery throne, but he turned out to be bright, determined, and ruthless.

The kingdom was lucky to have him, for enemies were circling. The Illyrians in the west were planning an invasion; the Paeonians were launching raids across the northern frontier; the Thracians in the east were plotting to replace Philip with a pretender to the throne; and, as always, the Athenians were anxious to strengthen their position in Chalcidice and were promoting a pretender of their own.

Philip was a master of the art of divide-and-rule. By a mixture of crafty statecraft and military force he confronted, outwitted, and finally defeated in the field each of his foes one by one. In 356, once his people had gotten his measure, they elected him king in his own right. He took the cruel precaution of hunting down and (eventually) liquidating three stepbrothers on the grounds that they were potential rivals for the throne, although he kept his prepubertal predecessor at court and treated him kindly. He was pitiless, but, if he felt unthreatened, not bloodthirsty.

Now that he had secured the kingdom and calmed the untamed barons of Upper Macedonia, he gave Lower Macedonia access to the sea by taking control of the *poleis* of the Thermaic Gulf. This brought him into conflict with Athens, which wanted nothing to impede the free flow of maritime traffic from the Black Sea to Piraeus along the Greek and Thracian coastline, but one by one the great independent city-states of the region—among them, Methone—fell to the king or came over to his side, as Olynthus did. Athens had lost Amphipolis to the Spartan commander Brasidas in 422, and ever afterwards yearned to get it back. But Philip won it by a typical combination of force and deceit.

He picked a quarrel with its government and laid the city under siege. When it applied to the Athenians for help, he promised to hand it over to them in exchange for Pydna on the Thermaic Gulf, a member of the Athenian League. But once he had taken Amphipolis in 357, he kept it for himself. To add insult to injury, he proceeded to capture Pydna too. To reduce the influence of Athens in the region, he made advances to the Chalcidian League, which was a potential threat to Macedonian interests and uncertain which side to favor.

The Athenians declared war on Philip, but were powerless to do much about it, for their hands were full at the time with the War of the Allies. In any case, the treasury was bare and they did not have the money to send a major expeditionary force to prize Philip's ill-gotten gains from his grasp. Nevertheless, hostilities dribbled on for a number of years.

Philip was now the most successful and popular monarch Macedonia had ever seen. All that he lacked was a reliable income to pay for his soldiers. He looked towards Thrace and, seizing a pretext for intervention, marched east and in 356 founded the city of Philippi inland from the island of Thasos. It was no accident that it lay in the neighborhood of highly profitable gold mines. Philip expropriated them and they contributed to his treasury the huge annual sum of 1,000 talents. He now had his own copious counterpart to the silver mines at Laurium.

Never satisfied, the Macedonian king looked for fresh conquests. By now, if not before, he guessed at the dizzying prospect of uniting Hellas under his leadership. As a first step, he accepted an invitation to intervene in northern Greece on behalf of Thessaly's feudal barons against the tyrants of Pherae. They were horse lovers like the Macedonians and found him a congenial ally, so perhaps as early as 352 they elected him as their Archon, or commander-in-chief for life.

There were two parts to the Macedonian constitution—the warrior king and an assembly of soldier citizens. For most of the time the former ruled absolutely and embodied the state; he owned all the land, commanded the army, was the supreme court of appeal and, as high priest, presided over daily sacrifices that ensured the well-being of the realm. However, the assembly was the king-maker. It elected the monarch by acclamation (it also presided over trials for treason). The men wore full armor and clashed their spears against their shields to show their approval.

Philip knew that this approval could be withdrawn and that continuing popularity depended on success in battle. He was interested in power and not its trappings; he never described himself as king in any official document. People called him Philip and he wore no royal insignia.

He was a man of great personal charm and had a dry sense of humor. He often deployed these qualities to mislead. He lied to and tricked his opponents with a smile on his face.

Philip preferred diplomacy to war, although he adopted an original style. A polygamist, he married seven times and never divorced any of his wives. The motive for these unions was invariably reason of state. Lust seems to have played a part, never love. As one ancient commentator neatly observed, he "made war by marriage." His third bride was the hawk-eyed and ferocious Olympias, a princess of Epirus (as well as wedding her, Philip is also reported to have seduced her brother, a good-looking boy). In 356, she gave him a son and heir, Alexander, to the promotion of whose interests she devoted the rest of her monomaniacal life.

Philip's other main negotiating technique was bribery. No city was impregnable, he liked to say, if it had a postern gate big enough to admit a donkey laden with gold.

When diplomacy failed, Philip unhesitatingly resorted to war. He was brave in battle, as his scars attested, and set a powerful example to his men. His idea of war owed something to the individual heroism of Homeric heroes. At the siege of Methone, a *polis* on the coast of the Thermaic Gulf, he was inspecting his lines when a defender on the ramparts shot an arrow that struck his right eye and blinded him. Despite this dangerous wound, he remained in active command and when the city sued for peace some days later he generously gave them easy terms. Other injuries left a hand and a leg permanently damaged and a shattered collarbone.

Personal courage, though, was not enough to ensure victory. Inspired by Epaminondas and Pelopidas, Philip introduced sweeping military reforms. He professionalized the army by introducing regular pay, providing armor at his expense, and establishing a system of promotion. He made his soldiers carry their own armor, weapons, and food, so reducing the need for a cumbersome baggage train. They were no longer seasonal peasant farmers, but full-time career soldiers.

Philip was inspired by the primal phalanx in Homer's *Iliad*. The Greeks confront the Trojans in battle with

an impenetrable hedge of spears and sloping shields, buckler to buckler, helmet to helmet, man to man. So close were the ranks that when they moved their heads the glittering peaks of their plumed helmets met and the spears overlapped as they swung them forward in their sturdy hands.

But Philip was also an innovator. He took the concept of the phalanx to its logical conclusion. He introduced an extraordinarily long pike, the *sarissa*. This was between fourteen and eighteen feet in length and had to be held in both hands. It was carried upright and, when approaching the enemy, the first five ranks of the phalanx lowered their *sarissas*, creating the effect of a super-sized porcupine, and charged. The shield-wall of the ordinary Greek phalanx found itself facing a spear-wall. Old-fashioned hoplites were unable to reach enemy combatants and fight them hand-to-hand with their short swords.

Philip deployed his new-look phalanx in close association with his heavy cavalry. Like Epaminondas, he ordered the latter to attack at the beginning of a battle rather than waiting for the infantry to engage. While the phalanx pinned down the enemy's center, the cavalry, riding in wedgelike squadrons, did their best, slashing and stabbing, to disrupt the opposite line and, above all, to ride against its flanks or rear.

Greek armies did not have the technology to capture walled towns with any ease, and when they fell it was usually because of treachery. In about 350 Philip established an engineering corps. Its commander designed new siege machines, such as a covered battering ram, and seems to have invented the torsion catapult, whose missiles had a greater range and speed of travel than the traditional mechanically drawn catapult.

Macedonian kings gathered around them an elite force, the Companions, who were friends and advisers at home and led the cavalry in the field. They functioned as royal bodyguards. Philip expanded their number to eight hundred and personally chose each one of them.

With his new supplies of gold Philip could afford to add mercenaries to his native Macedonian troops. These men were necessarily loyal to him alone and, as well as strengthening his military capacity, they made it more difficult for his own citizens to apply political pressure on him.

On campaign, discipline was fierce and training relentless. On one occasion the king dismissed an officer for taking a hot bath in camp and another was flogged when he broke ranks for a drink. But if we are to trust the fourth-century historian Theopompus, many were hell-raisers off-duty.

According to him, they were addicted to drink, with a shocking propensity for unmixed wine, the ancient equivalent of spirits, and for gambling. There was worse to come.

Some of them used to shave and depilate their bodies, although they were men, while others made love to their companions, although they were bearded [in other words, they were adult homosexuals in our modern sense, something Greeks found distasteful]. They habitually took two or three rent boys about with them, and themselves provided the same service for others. It would be perfectly fair to call them courtesans rather than courtiers, escorts rather than bodyguards.

Even if some of this is exaggerated, we know that Philip admired the Theban Sacred Band and we may infer that he encouraged sexualized male bonding among his special forces as a method for managing morale.

This was not a boy with obvious potential. He was delicate and underdeveloped. He had been skinny and sickly ever since he was a child. He had a weak voice and found it difficult to pronounce the letter "r." His manner seems to have been effeminate, for other boys nicknamed him Battalus, after a well-known and very effeminate flute player. (As an adult, he was accused of frequenting workingmen's taverns in drag and was criticized for his alleged homosexuality: but he also married and had three children. We do not know where the truth lies.)

Born in 385, the infant was called Demosthenes after his father, who was a successful businessman and owned a factory that manufactured swords and cutlery; he also produced couches. Unfortunately, he died when his son was only seven years old. Relatives who were appointed as guardians in his will so mismanaged the estate that when Demosthenes reached his majority at eighteen there was hardly any of it left to inherit.

He was in his teens when he heard a leading statesman of the day, Callistratus, speak at a trial and was so impressed that he chose oratory as his future vocation. He gave up his other studies, enrolled with teachers of rhetoric, and read textbooks on public speaking.

The law courts in the fourth century were busier than ever and litigation thrived. There were careers, and money, to be made. The provision of legal advice and the writing and delivery of speeches on behalf of accusers and defendants was professionalized. There were honorable advocates and real criminals to pursue, but enemies with grudges, business rivals, politicians flooded the courts with false or frivolous charges. There was no public prosecution service, although a state official could raise an action if it concerned the community as a whole. Any citizen was allowed to bring a preosecution, and a class of habitual litigants came into being, nicknamed *sycophants* (literally, one who brings figs to light by shaking the tree; whence our word for a fawner or flatterer). Ostensibly, they worked in the public interest, but in fact for financial gain. They blackmailed innocent citizens by threatening them with court proceedings. In some cases, the state paid for convictions. It was this murky world that Demosthenes aspired to enter.

The young orator underwent a strict training regime. If we are to believe the stories told about him, he spent every waking hour practicing declamation and acquired a full-length mirror to monitor his performance. He liked to go down to the sea at Phaleron where he shouted above the sound of the waves and, as he was short-winded, he hired an actor to teach him how to deliver long sentences in a single breath. He corrected his indistinct articulation by reciting speeches with pebbles in his mouth and developed his vocal strength by speaking at the same time as walking uphill.

Despite all his hard work, Demosthenes' maiden speech was a disaster. He was heckled and laughed at. However, he spent three years suing his former guardians for negligence and fraud, during which time he learned to perfect his craft. Eventually he won the action, but probably recovered only a little of his lost family fortune. However, his reputation grew and he earned a good living as a popular writer of courtroom speeches. Through sheer willpower, he had realized his dream.

His attention turned to politics and he gave speech after speech to the *ecclesia* in which, like a dog with a bone, he obsessively worried at the threat from the north. He soon became Philip of Macedon's most feared and hated critic.

Phocis was one of the smallest states in Greece, but it contained within its boundaries the international center and oracle of Delphi. The oracle was guaranteed its independence by a committee of neighboring powers, called the Amphictyonic Council, which had the authority to punish any state's sacrilegious acts. Phocis had been forced unwillingly to join the Boeotian alliance after the Battle of Leuctra, but now that the power of Thebes was fading and Epaminondas had lost his life at Mantinea, it began to act independently.

The Thebans took offense and accused Phocis of failing to pay the oracle a fine for sacrilege; apparently it had been tilling land in the plain below Delphi that was sacred to the god's sacrificial animals. They were met with defiance, a refusal to hand over an obol, and a quotation from the *Iliad* to justify an ancient claim to the land in question.

Here were the origins of what the Greeks came to call a Sacred War. Phocis had many enemies on the Amphictyonic Council—the Thessalians, the Locrians, and, worst of all of course, the Thebans. If it did not act now it would be under their thumb for the foreseeable future. Unlike the Athenians and King Philip, it had no silver or gold mines. However, in Delphi it possessed something almost as good—the treasuries where Greek states stored their silver and gold gifts to Apollo. In 356 the Phocians seized Delphi and "borrowed" these possessions of the god and used them to pay for an army of mercenaries. They even dug beneath the floor of the temple of Apollo itself on a rumor of secret treasure, only to be disappointed.

They raided the treasury of the long-ago king of Lydia, Croesus, rich with gold and silver artifacts and ingots. All this was melted down into coins worth 4,000 gold talents. Croesus's silver offerings were also recast as ready money—totaling 6,000 silver talents.

Over the coming years vast sums were extracted from the treasuries of Delphi and the Phocians enjoyed a brief heyday of military glory. In their opinion Delphi was not only an international institution, it was a national possession. Rather as the Athenians had made use of the precious metals in their temples when the Peloponnesian War was going badly for them, they believed they were justified in exploiting the riches of Delphi. At least to begin with, they had every intention of repaying what they saw as loans. However, after a while their indebtedness grew so large that repayment in full would take many years. From borrowers they insensibly mutated into thieves.

Sparta, which also owed the god a steep fine for capturing the citadel of Thebes during a time of peace (see page 399), and Athens discreetly supported Phocis, largely because any enemy of the Thebans was a friend of theirs.

The Macedonian king was drawn into the affair when the Phocian general Onomarchus marched into Thessaly to help Pherae, which complained of Philip's rough treatment of them. He was defeated by Onomarchus and withdrew to Macedon. He was used to winning his battles and growled: "I am retreating like the ram, to butt harder."

He told the truth. In 353 or 352 he returned and expelled the Phocians from Thessaly. In a plain by the sea where a crocus field was planted, he drove their army into the waves. One third of it was destroyed. A friendly Athenian fleet helped pick up survivors. Onomarchus was carried out to sea on his horse and drowned. Philip insulted his corpse by displaying it on a cross.

Philip prepared to march south and rescue Apollo and his shrine at Delphi from the temple-robbing Phocians. Athens, ever anxious about Macedon's seemingly irresistible rise, moved fast. Eubulus, usually an advocate of parsimony and peace, sent a large force to guard the pass at Thermopylae and so halted the king in his tracks. He withdrew and went campaigning instead in Thrace, where he threatened the interests of Athens in the Chersonese. All the while he awaited a new opportunity to deal with Phocis.

The next stage in the growth of Macedonia was the annexation of the peninsula of Chalcidice. Olynthus proved to be an unreliable ally and harbored a claimant to Philip's throne (one of his stepbrothers, see page 426). Fearful of Philip's intentions they entered into an alliance with Athens. In 348 this was enough to persuade the king to intervene and place the city under siege. He distracted Athens by fomenting trouble in Euboea and, by the time a relief force of two thousand Athenian hoplites and a cavalry squadron arrived, Olynthus had fallen. It is presumed that the unlucky pretender was caught and killed.

Philip always punished disloyalty; he razed the city to the ground and sent its surviving inhabitants to Macedon where they were put to work as slaves in the mines or the fields.

The *ecclesia* was furious and feelings against Philip ran high, but Athens was broke. It needed peace. So too did the king, for, now that he had gotten his way over Chalcidice, he had another project in mind. The Thebans had invited him to march south on behalf of the Amphictyonic Council and crush the Phocians. This was very tempting, for victory would make Macedon the dominant power in mainland Greece. Before embarking on this new military adventure, though, he needed to clear his desk.

In 346 peace negotiations were opened. Demosthenes joined a delegation to Philip whom they met in Pella, Macedon's capital. The encounter appears to have been a disaster, if we can trust the lip-smacking account of Aeschines, a fellow-envoy and no friend of his. Apparently when his turn came to address the king, Demosthenes succumbed to stage fright. He forgot his lines and suddenly stopped speaking. Philip behaved very well, encouraging the orator to take heart and try again, but the speech had to be abandoned.

A treaty was agreed on the terms that all parties should retain the territories of which they were in possession at the time. The allies of Macedon and Athens were included in the pact—with the major exception of Phocis, which had now emptied the treasuries of Delphi and was no longer the serious military threat it had been. Philip hoped that the treaty would lead to a friendly and active partnership with Athens, but Demosthenes made sure that anti-Macedonian sentiment was reignited.

Philip had no special grievance against Phocis, but its sacrilege gave him an ideal means of strengthening his political position by intervening in central Greece. His army was allowed through the pass at Thermopylae, thanks to a treacherous Phocian general. To the general surprise the government of Phocis surrendered to Philip without demur or delay, and some suspected the king to have eased his way with gold. Members of the Amphictyonic Council were grateful for the fall of Phocis and argued that the maximum legal penalty for the sacrilege to the god should be imposed; that is, all Phocians should be thrown from the top of some high cliffs.

Philip, who was appointed chairman of Delphi's Pythian Games, a high honor, persuaded the council to adopt a more lenient approach. Phocis lost its seat on the council and its two votes were given to Macedon. It was no longer allowed to consult the oracle at Delphi. It was required to repay the money value of the stolen treasures in annual installments.

As usual, though, it was ordinary people who suffered the ravages of war. Demosthenes recalled traveling through a devastated landscape:

When we recently made our way to Delphi, we could not help but see everything—houses razed, fortifications demolished, countryside empty of adult men, a handful of women and children, miserable old people. No one could find words to describe the trouble [the Phocians] now have.

The winner of these proceedings was, without a doubt, Philip. He was now a member of an ancient and respected Panhellenic institution and had a foothold in the polity of mainland Greece. Of great practical value, his army's boots were firmly on the ground. Nobody could say any longer that he was not a Greek, as he had always claimed he was.

The people of Athens were a grave disappointment to Demosthenes. In the first of a series of great speeches he delivered against the threat that Philip posed to the Hellenic world, he compared their lack of spirit to a boxer who covers where he has been hit rather than aggressively counterattacks.

You wage war on Philip in exactly the way a barbarian boxes. When struck, he always grabs that spot; hit him on the other side and there go his hands. He neither knows nor cares how to parry a blow or how to watch his adversary. So if you hear of Philip in the Chersonese you send a relief force there; if at Thermopylae, you vote one there. If he is somewhere else, you still run around to keep up with him.

If the Athenians were less than eager to take the war to Philip, he was not looking for a fight with them. He greatly respected the city, which was the cultural and intellectual center of the Greek world. While he knew how to drink deep with his Companions, he liked to associate on equal terms with Athenian philosophers and writers. In 343 he chose Aristotle, Plato's onetime student, to be tutor to his teenaged son Alexander, whom he wanted to grow up into a fully fledged Hellene. The boy studied literature and philosophy, just as if he were a young Athenian.

Many Greeks approved of King Philip. A reader of the speeches of Demosthenes might gain the impression that all Hellas hated and feared him. Nothing could be further from the truth. It was not only intellectuals like Isocrates who, in the grand manner, saw in Philip a long overdue pacifier of Greece's poisonous *poleis*. Small states in the Peloponnese felt threatened by an angry Sparta desperate to restore her power over the peninsula. The weakness of Thebes and its inability to protect them as it had in the days of Epaminondas meant that Philip's arrival was a godsend. In many quarters the Macedonian king was genuinely welcome.

This was a curious phenomenon—a popular enemy whom most people did not wish to fight, an aggressor who admired the civilization he wished to vanquish. And yet the logic of events brought about a renewal of hostilities.

Demosthenes organized a deep Athenian sulk. At his prompting, the city made an implied protest against Macedonia's membership of the Amphictyonic League by deciding not to attend the Pythian Games, but backed down after Philip sent a polite but firm ultimatum. Having marched the *demos* up the hill, the orator was forced embarrassingly to march it down again by conceding that it would be folly "to go to war for the shadow at Delphi."

As time passed, though, anti-Macedonian propaganda had its effect. The public mood swung decisively against the peace. Its leading Athenian negotiator was charged with treason and fled the city. He was condemned to death in absentia for contempt of court. In 343 Demosthenes then impeached Aeschines, his great oratorical rival and supporter of the treaty with Philip. The defendant needed all his skills as a public speaker to obtain an acquittal.

The king lost patience with a state that was ostensibly his friend and ally, and seems to have financed a failed attempt to fire the dockyards of Piraeus. He probably wanted to neutralize the still powerful Athenian fleet before proceeding with his next great enterprise—the permanent and final conquest of Thrace. After a ten months' campaign in 342 and 341 he was victorious. He doubled the size of his kingdom and extended the Macedonian frontier to the edge of the Chersonese.

Athens rightly regarded this as a threat to the uninterrupted passage of the grain imports on which its population depended. It deployed to the region a few ships and some mercenaries, who unwisely broke the terms of the peace by raiding a recognized ally of Philip. This prompted an angry note from the king.

The Athenians were obviously in the wrong, but Demosthenes was having none of it. He delivered a speech in which he claimed that it was the Macedonian king who had broken the peace.

Now there was no doubt in anybody's mind that Philip was looking for any opportunity to increase the power of Macedon. His presence at the Chersonese was indeed dangerous and he was being provocative when he encouraged *poleis* on the island of Euboea to set up oligarchies with Macedonian support.

However, although the Athenian fleet ruled the Aegean waves, Philip's military superiority by land was there for all to see. Macedonia was wealthy and populous. In the long run, relatively impoverished and un-military as it had become, Athens could not hope to compete with the new great power. Its interest lay in the friendly and active alliance that Philip sought. Indeed he proposed that the treaty between Macedon and Athens should be enlarged to become a common peace for all who wished to join in it.

Demosthenes believed, though, that the king's chief aim was not to enter into a partnership with Athens, but to bring about its ruin. Ha-tred outweighed reason in the orator's mind. There was no doubting his sincerity. He resisted bribery from Macedon, although, writes Plu-tarch, he was "overwhelmed by Persian gold, which poured from Susa and Ecbatana in a torrent." Demosthenes gave the *demos* sincere but very bad advice.

Athenian efforts to mount a common Hellenic front against the king were beginning to show signs of success. At home the *ecclesia* lev-ied taxes, and monies from the Festivals Fund were diverted to prepa-rations for war. The Great King, fearful of Philip's invasion plans, agreed to offer his support. In 340 two allies of Macedon in the north-east, Perinthus and the well-fortified *polis* of Byzantium, changed sides. Philip laid both of them under siege, but even his new torsion catapult failed to dent their defenses.

In compensation, Philip scored a victory at sea. His small fleet at-tacked and captured an Athenian grain convoy of 230 vessels near the mouth of the Propontis, the contents of which were sold for the enor-mous sum of 700 talents. All those belonging to Athenians, some 180 ships, were destroyed.

The king marched home through Thrace where he conducted a brief campaign and picked up a serious thigh wound. He limped for the rest of his life, but he had secured Thrace and could safely (and with a certain regret) turn his attention to dealing with Greece.

Philip's aggressions in the Chersonese were a serious threat to Ath-ens. The loss of the convoy was the last straw. The *ecclesia* declared war on Macedon and the marble column on which the terms of the peace were inscribed was formally shattered. The policy of Demosthenes had triumphed and he was voted a gold crown in gratitude for his services to the state.

Once again a dispute in the Amphictyony gave Philip the opportunity he needed.

After the battle of Plataea in the previous century, the Athenians dedicated at Delphi a set of gold shields with an inscription reading "From the spoils of Persians and Thebans who fought together against the Greeks." Recently they refurbished and re-presented the trophy. The Thebans had always found this reference to their long-ago alliance with Xerxes to be offensive and this new display opened an old wound.

In the spring of 339, whether prompted by Thebes or of their own volition, the people of Amphissa, a town in nearby Locris, reported Athens to the Amphictyonic Council on grounds of sacrilege. This was because the work on the trophy had been done while Phocis had been illegally and impiously in control of Delphi and Apollo's oracle. The point was correct but technical. Athens was threatened with a fine of fifty talents.

The orator Aeschines was a member of the Athenian delegation to the council and he brilliantly turned the tables on the Amphissans. It turned out that they had committed a far worse sacrilege, for they were cultivating sacred land in the plain below and had even put up buildings on it. If true, this was a serious offense. The claim was investigated and confirmed.

How are we to explain Aeschines' inspired guess? The ancient sources do not say, but we may surmise that, over the years, adherence to rules had been lax; everyone knew this, but turned a blind eye.

In any case, nothing more was said about the complaint against Athens, and Amphissa was instructed to remove the buildings and quit the land. Doubtless hoping for support from Thebes (which never came), the delegates refused.

At an emergency meeting Philip was appointed commander of the

Amphictyonic army with a view to dealing with the Amphissans. Although Aeschines had cleverly evaded the charge of sacrilege, it was at the very high price of allowing Philip to intervene once again in mainland Greek affairs.

What nobody knew at the time was that the king had finally given up on Athens and its Greek allies. He had offered the hand of friendship, he felt, and been spurned. The only alternative was war. The king understood that the sharpest weapons in a general's armory were deception and surprise. He awaited his moment.

Few people were much troubled by the prospect of a new Sacred War and nothing much was done about it, largely because Philip was still recovering from his Thracian wound. But in the autumn of 339 he marched down into Greece, ostensibly to fulfill his commission from the Amphictyonic Council. But then, ignoring Amphissa, he suddenly turned east and captured the town of Elateia by surprise, a key point on the road to Thebes and Attica. The news, which came at night, stunned the Athenians. An emergency meeting of the *ecclesia* took place soon after dawn. Plutarch catches the atmosphere:

> Nobody dared to mount the speakers' platform, nobody knew what ought to be said, the assembly was dumbfounded and appeared completely at a loss.

The herald asked: "Who wishes to speak?" No one came forward. He repeated the question again and again to a silent assembly. Then Demosthenes stepped up to the platform and took charge of the situation. He announced a "struggle for freedom." The *ecclesia* approved a proposal for an alliance with the Thebans.

Demosthenes headed a delegation to win over the old enemy. When they arrived in Thebes they found envoys from Philip already there. After an impassioned debate, the Thebans agreed to join forces with Athens against the Macedonians. This was despite the fact that they were in Philip's debt for quashing Phocis. However, they knew they had little choice, for if he conquered Athens they would stand alone and be too weak to resist whatever he demanded. They could only safely be his friend if Athens was his enemy.

The Thebans drove a hard bargain. Athens was to pay two thirds of the costs of the war and to accept a Theban commander-in-chief of land forces. Athens was also to recognize Theban supremacy in Boeotia.

The new allies defended the passes that led into Boeotia and Attica, and winter passed without incident. The ancient historians are silent about this interval, but it appears that at the eleventh hour Philip was still anxious to avert war if he could and may have offered negotiations. If so, he was rebuffed. Demosthenes was awarded a second gold crown. When the summer of 338 came, Philip moved. He forced one of the defended passes, and the coalition retreated to a fallback position on the plain of Chaeronea, a town in Boeotia.

The Macedonians followed and at dawn on August 4, 338, battle commenced. The two armies were more or less equal in numbers, with 30,000 infantry on each side. Philip's 2,000 cavalry were outnumbered by the coalition's 3,800. But there was a real difference. The Macedonians were well trained and experienced; the citizen soldiers of Athens and Thebes had scarcely wielded a spear in anger in the previous two decades.

The opposing lines of battle stretched for about two miles between rising ground below the citadel of Chaeronea and a river skirted by marshland. Philip led his elite infantry, the *hypaspists,* on his right wing with a gentle incline behind him. His son Alexander, now eighteen years old but already a seasoned soldier, commanded the cavalry on the left.

The Athenian hoplites formed up against Philip; various Greek allies stood in the center and the Boeotians on the right. The Sacred Band were placed on the far edge next to the boggy ground.

Philip's line was echeloned back at an angle from his position. His

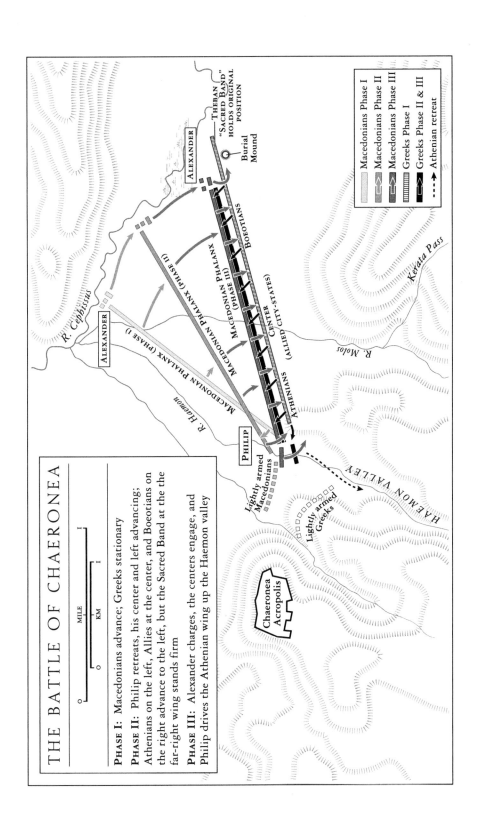

THE BATTLE OF CHAERONEA

PHASE I: Macedonians advance; Greeks stationary

PHASE II: Philip retreats, his center and left advancing; Athenians on the left, Allies at the center, and Boeotians on the right advance to the left, but the Sacred Band at the the far-right wing stands firm

PHASE III: Alexander charges, the centers engage, and Philip drives the Athenian wing up the Haemon valley

plan was for the troops under his direct command to make contact with the inexperienced Athenian phalanx. They would then slowly retire in good order up the slope behind them to their right, tempting the Athenians to follow.

This was a trap. The Greeks would almost insensibly shift across to fill the opening the Athenians left as they advanced. The Greek line would be stretched thin and eventually a gap would emerge through which the Macedonian cavalry would be able to gallop.

The trick worked. As Philip's right wing pulled back at an angle towards Chaeronea, his left moved forward as if the line were rotating on a pivot. As the Athenians moved after Philip, the Greek line thinned out as predicted, except for the Sacred Band at the other end of the battlefield, by the river, which obeyed orders and did not move. As a result a space soon appeared to their left. Alexander saw his chance and thundered through it with the Macedonian horse. The Sacred Band were surrounded. They fought on and most of them died where they stood.

Meanwhile, the Athenians ran overenthusiastically after Philip's *hypaspists*. Their commander shouted: "Let's drive them back to Macedon!" As they scrambled up the slope they lost formation. Philip gave his men the order to countercharge. The stunned Athenians scattered. They were pursued into the foothills. One thousand men died and two thousand were captured.

The rest of them escaped, including Demosthenes. He was no general and had taken his place in the ranks of hoplites, but as the tide of battle swung towards the Macedonians, he took to his heels "in the most shameful fashion" (writes Plutarch). His cloak caught on a bramble bush behind him and he shouted in a panic: "Take me alive." It was a cruel irony that the inscription on his shield read "Good luck."

Two stories are told of Philip's reaction to his victory. As they reflect aspects of his contradictory personality they could both be true. After the battle the king presided over a celebratory banquet at which he drank deep of unmixed wine. After the meal he roamed around the battlefield with some companions. They looked at the bodies of the dead and jeered at them. The king took a childish pleasure in repeating the preambles to the bills laid before the *ecclesia* on the Pnyx, beating time to the rhythm—"Demosthenes, son of Demosthenes, of Paeonia, proposes."

An Athenian prisoner of war, a leading politician called Demades, reproved Philip, in a reference to two characters in the *Iliad*—the Mycenaean king who led the Greeks at Troy, and an ugly and abusive soldier with a foul tongue. He said: "Fortune has cast you as Agamemnon. Aren't you ashamed to act the part of Thersites?" To his credit Philip sobered up instantly.

It must have been on the same occasion that the king came across the corpses of members of the Sacred Band and, perhaps recalling those whom he had known as a hostage in Thebes, he burst into tears. He said: "Perish any man who suspects that these men either did or suffered anything shameful." They were then buried in a mass grave where they had fallen. Philip ordered the statue of a lion to be erected to mark the spot.

The lion still stands guard and, nearby, modern archaeologists found and excavated the Thebans' grave. Lying in seven orderly rows were 254 skeletons, sad relics of the brigade of lovers.

As usual, Philip was kind to Athens. This was not only a matter of sentiment, but also because the city could still cause him a good deal of trouble. It disposed of a large and powerful fleet and even his new torsion catapults would hardly leave a dent on its high stone walls. It was essential that Greece's leading *polis* was settled and peaceful before the king launched his invasion of Persia, plans for which were in active preparation.

Alexander escorted the Athenian dead back to the city and passed on an offer to return prisoners of war without charge. The maritime league was finally dissolved, although a number of islands, including

Samos and Delos, were allowed to remain under Athenian control. In theory, Athens was still free and unregulated, if only at home and not abroad (by contrast Thebes was obliged to accept a Macedonian garrison and to replace its democracy with an oligarchy).

The city showed its gratitude, but grudgingly. The *ecclesia* erected a statue of Philip on a horse and granted him and Alexander the citizenship of Athens, but it also conferred the franchise on Theban refugees. It chose Demosthenes, of all people, to deliver the funeral oration over the war dead. Philip overlooked the snubs.

Great changes are not always felt or observed at the time. Chaeronea was decisive in that it brought to an end the independence of the *poleis*. Macedon had shown itself to be the region's superpower and they were too weak, even when united, to oppose it. Small self-governing cities continued to exist, of course, but they were now tamed members of a larger union.

The dream of Isocrates had finally come to pass, but not according to his plan. He had imagined a free coming together of the Greeks and a genuinely collective decision to send another army to sack another Troy. He was accustomed to democratic politics and in his eyes a combination imposed by force was not at all the same thing.

In the autumn of 338, at the time of the annual burying of the war dead, the old man, now in his late nineties, starved himself to death.

In winter or spring 337 delegates from all Greek states were summoned to a conference in Corinth, at which Philip announced a Common Peace. He would guarantee it with military force if necessary and a grand committee of the signatories would supervise it. Everywhere pro-Macedonian politicians were swept to power. For those tired of endless bickering and small pointless wars this was a welcome new world. Only the Spartans, impotent and embittered, refused to join in. It was a self-defeating gesture, for Philip accepted an invitation to march down into the Peloponnese where he readjusted borders to their disadvantage.

The move was very well received. The Greek historian Polybius wrote that the leaders who induced

> Philip to enter the Peloponnese and humble the Spartans, allowed all its inhabitants to draw breath and think of freedom, and to recover the territory and cities of which the Spartans in their prosperity had deprived the Messenians, Megalopolitans, Tegeans, and Argives. In this way they unquestionably increased the power of their own states.

Later in the year at the committee's second meeting, Philip announced his intention to punish the Medes and Persians for their desecration of Greek sanctuaries one and a half centuries previously and to free the Greeks of Asia Minor. For all his triumphant campaigns and the gold mines in Thrace, Philip was overdrawn by 500 talents. It was not just for glory that he intended to invade Persia, but also to refill his treasury.

The expedition would be an appropriate project with which to activate Philip's new league of nations. How much real appetite there was for such a distant and dangerous enterprise is uncertain, but many young hoplites throughout Hellas were unemployed. They had all heard of Xenophon's adventures in barbarian lands and were thrilled by the prospect of following in his footsteps.

The king sent to the oracle at Delphi, asking for Apollo's approval of his plan to "liberate the Greek cities" in Ionia. The Pythia gave him a characteristically ambiguous or at least gnomic response. "The bull has been garlanded. Everything has been done. The priest is here to conduct the sacrifice."

Philip was a little puzzled, but he accepted the oracle as a promise of victory.

At this point the spinners intervened and cut the thread of a human life.

A family quarrel broke out at the court in Pella, the causes of which are poorly understood. Apparently Philip repudiated Olympias on grounds of adultery and fostered rumors that his glamorous young heir was illegitimate. Late in 338, he announced his marriage to an attractive young woman from an aristocratic clan in Lower Macedonia.

Hard words were exchanged at the wedding feast. Everyone drank too much. The new bride's uncle, an important general called Attalus who was high in favor, gave a speech in which he called on Macedonians to beg the gods that the union between Philip and his latest wife would produce a legitimate heir to the throne.

This was too much for the twenty-year-old prince, who was among the guests. He shouted at Attalus: "You scum, are you saying I'm a bastard, then?" and hurled a cup at him. The infuriated king staggered to his feet and drew his sword, intent on cutting down his son. Drink and his lame leg made him trip and he fell headlong to the ground.

Alexander said contemptuously: "Here's the man who is planning to cross from Europe to Asia. He can't even make it across from one couch to another!" He stormed out. He took his mother away to her native Epirus and withdrew to the comparative safety of untamed Illyria.

What was going on? We do not know, but we can safely reject the ancients' notion that Philip's behavior was down to sexual infatuation. The king was too much of a realist to upset all his political calculations for a pretty face. The most likely explanation is that, rightly or wrongly, he suspected his son and Olympias to be plotting his overthrow. There could be no other justification for the complete disruption of his dynastic plans on the eve of his expedition to Persia.

If the king was hoping for a new heir he was disappointed, for his bride gave birth to a daughter. He would be foolish if he left his kingdom without a successor, even if only a symbolic one, an infant. An advance guard had already crossed into Asia and there was no time to dally. He was obliged to recall and reinstate Alexander, albeit not to his old position of trust, and to reassert his legitimacy. Relations between the two men were icy.

However, in June 336 Philip had every reason to be pleased with life. The preparations for Persia were going well. The Great King and all his sons were poisoned by his grand vizier, a eunuch called Bagoas, who chose a cousin to succeed him as Darius III. The new ruler was his own man and immediately forced the kingmaker to down a dose of his own medicine. But although he was determined and capable, he was inexperienced.

Philip's new queen at last produced a son. The balance of power at court changed again now that there was an alternative to Alexander, albeit a baby. The happy event coincided with lavish celebrations to mark the dynastic marriage of his daughter by Olympias to Alexander, king of Epirus—Olympias's brother (and so her uncle) and Philip's onetime flame.

Everyone who was anyone in all Hellas was present. Athens showed that it had already mastered the arts of deference and flattery. It was one of many cities that gave the king a gold crown, and it announced that it would hand over any plotter against the king who sought asylum in the city. Religious ceremonies in honor of the gods were conducted, music competitions held, and sumptuous meals provided for the guests. Large crowds flocked to the festivities.

A star actor sang arias at a state banquet and on the following morning at the theater at Aegae, the old capital, splendid games were scheduled. Spectators took their seats while it was still dark and at sunrise a magnificent procession entered, headed by statues of the twelve Olympians and accompanied by one of Philip, "suitable for a god."

Finally, the king came in wearing a white cloak. He had dispensed with the royal bodyguard, for he wanted to show that he was no despot who needed protection from his people. The Greeks had chosen him as their leader and he was guarded by their goodwill.

A young man jumped forward with a sword, which he drove into the king's side. Philip died at once and Pausanias, for that was the assassin's name, ran off. Unfortunately for him, he tripped on the root of a vine and three young Macedonians, all of them close to Alexander, caught up with Pausanias and killed him. This meant that he could not be interrogated and tell his tale.

Later, the story went the rounds that Pausanias was one of Philip's discarded lovers; when he complained about his treatment, he was gang-raped on Attalus's orders. On this account the motive for the deed was revenge.

There may have been another explanation for what happened. The crown prince's political position and that of his mother were precarious. Motive and opportunity point to their involvement. If we can believe the reports that have come down to us, Pausanias was a friend of Alexander and had previously asked for his advice about the rape. Also, Olympias's behavior after the event was suggestive. Pausanias's body was hung on a cross and she placed a gold crown on its head. When it was taken down she arranged for its cremation.

The tale had a moral that every intelligent seeker after truth was wise to heed. When asking for the god's advice at Delphi, he should never interpret an ambiguous answer to his advantage. Philip should have remembered the story of Croesus of Lydia.

It was not the Great King who was the garlanded bull. The king of Macedon himself was the sacrificial victim to be offered up to the gods.

The king's great opponent, Demosthenes, also died a violent death, but by his own hand.

The orator received the news of Philip's assassination with delight: he appeared in public dressed in a magnificent costume and with a wreath on his head. He persuaded the *boulē* to vote a crown for Pausanias. He was certain that the Macedonian hegemony was finished.

Nothing was further from the truth. Alexander succeeded his father and made it clear that he meant to keep Greece under his thumb. He turned out to be a field commander of genius. In 335 Thebes revolted, but in a lightning expedition he captured the city and razed it to the ground as "a terrible warning." The atrocity shocked all good Hellenes. They never forgave him, but they gave up any thought of resistance.

Demosthenes kept a low profile, although he was implicated in a massive financial scandal that led to his exile. When Alexander invaded the Persian Empire, the orator wrote letters to Persian generals in which he encouraged them to defeat Alexander. In public, though, he was silent on political matters. More than ten years passed, during which the invincible young king scored victory after victory over the Persians and became Great King himself.

Then in 323 Alexander, worn out from wounds and drink, unexpectedly succumbed after a few days of fever. When the news arrived in Athens, Demades advised the *ecclesia* not to believe a word of it. "If Alexander has really died, the stench of his corpse would have filled the world long before now."

A new anti-Macedonian Hellenic League instantly formed itself. It was headed by Athens. Demosthenes was recalled and arrived at Piraeus to cheering crowds. It was like the return of Alcibiades, he remarked complacently, "but with greater honor." The attempt to regain liberty was a last, failed roll of the dice. The Macedonian fleet was victorious at sea and Antipater, who had been Alexander's deputy in Macedon, quashed the revolt by land. He led his army towards Athens and the city swiftly surrendered.

Alexander had shared his father's soft spot for Athens, but Antipater was no sentimentalist. He was determined that Athens would never give him trouble again. So he insisted that the Athenian fleet should not be rebuilt. He installed a garrison in Piraeus and replaced the full democracy with a restricted franchise. He demanded the surrender of Demosthenes and other anti-Macedonian politicians. They fled from Attica.

Wherever he went Demosthenes knew he was too famous to escape notice, and he did not travel far. He made for the tiny, hilly, and densely wooded island of Calauria (today's Poros) in the Saronic Gulf. It is about thirty-six miles from Piraeus. On a hill overlooking the main town stood a temple of Poseidon, famous for offering sanctuary to men on the run, and here the orator found refuge. Its ruins can still be seen.

It took only a few days for his whereabouts to be discovered. A Macedonian officer called Archias, accompanied by some soldiers, arrived at the temple at the head of a military detachment. His orders from Antipater were to hunt down all the Athenian opposition politicians and send them to him for execution. A former actor, he was good at his work and was nicknamed the exile-catcher.

Demosthenes emerged from the shrine to talk with Archias, who assured him that he would not be harshly treated. He was not taken in. "I was never convinced by your acting when you were on stage," the orator said, "and I am not convinced by your advice now." When Archias threatened to remove him by force, local people prevented him.

The orator went back inside the temple. He picked up his writing tablets, put to his mouth a pen made from a reed, and bit it, his custom when thinking what he was going to write. After a time, he covered his head with a cloak and lay down.

Some Macedonian soldiers gathered at the temple door and jeered at him for being afraid to take his own life. In fact, the pen contained a poison that he sucked up. Once it began to take effect Demosthenes uncovered himself. To avoid polluting the shrine by his death, he asked to be helped outside. As he passed the altar, he collapsed and died. He was sixty-two.

Demosthenes was a man out of his time. He would have flourished in the fifth century when Athenian citizens were energetic, ambitious, and ready to fight for the leadership of Greece. The Peloponnesian War had cut back the city's population and the loss of empire had reduced its wealth. It could still muster a powerful fleet, but could not afford a lengthy war.

A brilliant orator whose speeches uphold the cause of freedom, Demosthenes dominated the *ecclesia,* but his foreign policy was based on a false premise—that he was a latter-day Pericles. Against the evidence, he believed that Athens was still a first-rate power.

Among his fellow-Greeks he was a contentious and divisive figure.

A narrow nationalist, he did not have an answer to the real question of the day—how the Greeks could unite to counter the rise of an aggressive power, whose resources far outstripped those of the multitude of mini-states that made up Hellas. It had done so triumphantly but briefly during the Persian Wars, but the trick could not be repeated in an unheroic age and another solution had to be found.

Opponents of Demosthenes, such as his great rival Aeschines, were also patriots—despite his best efforts to subvert their reputations for honesty and loyalty. They advocated genuine cooperation with Macedon under the umbrella of a Common Peace. This was a superior alternative to the abrasive and inflexible approach of Demosthenes and his war party. It was much more likely than confrontation to maintain Athenian independence and influence in the world.

It was a bitter truth, but Demosthenes was politically responsible for Chaeronea and the loss, permanent as it turned out, of freedom. One cannot imagine a greater failure of policy. But the orator was unrepentant. Even if Athenian efforts were doomed, it had still been right to resist Philip. In a speech in 330, he claimed:

No, you were not wrong, men of Athens, you were not wrong, when you accepted the risks of war for the redemption and the liberties of mankind. I swear it by our forefathers who bore the brunt of battle at Marathon, who stood in the phalanx line at Plataea, who strove in the sea-fights of Salamis and Artemisium, and by all the brave men who lie in our public cemeteries.

This was little more than nostalgia. There was to be no return to the great days of old.

23

Afterword—"A God-forsaken Hole"

Alexander of Macedon took being Greek very seriously. After all, he was the new Achilles whose Companions were latter-day successors of the mythic warrior's trusty Myrmidons. He merged metaphor and fact.

Xerxes had seen his invasion of Greece as payback for the Trojan War, and the young Macedonian returned the compliment. Almost the first thing Alexander did, after crossing the Hellespont from Europe into Asia in 334, was to leave his army for a few days and ride to the ruins of Troy.

All that remained of the ancient city was a large tumulus and a tumbledown village with a gimcrack little temple. Tourists were shown a collection of bogus relics. Like the Persian king before him, Alexander sacrificed to Athena, Troy's tutelary goddess. He received some gold wreaths from a committee of local Greeks and sacrificed at the (so-called) tombs of the Greek heroes Ajax and Achilles.

The king and Hephaestion, his best friend since his school days and probably lover, laid wreaths on the tomb of Achilles and *his* best friend or lover Patroclus, whose celebrated relationship lay at the heart of Homer's epic the *Iliad*. Then, bizarrely, they stripped off, oiled themselves (as Greek athletes routinely did), and ran a race around the tombs.

Alexander made an offering of his own armor and took in exchange a shield and panoply, purportedly preserved from the Trojan War and hanging on the temple walls (at his first victory against the Persians at the river Granicus in May 334 he dressed up in them and had them carried before him in later battles).

Alexander continued to play the role of Achilles during the campaign in Asia. When driving south towards Egypt, the Persian official in charge of the great city and port of Gaza refused to bow to the king even in defeat. Alexander tied him to his chariot and dragged him, still alive, around the city, just as Achilles had done with the corpse of Hector in the *Iliad*.

The years he spent as a pupil of Aristotle under whom he studied ethics and politics made a powerful impression on the young prince. He was devoted to philosophy and, when king, funded leading thinkers of the day. He was also excited by his tutor's researches in the sciences and brought with him to Persia a team of architects, geographers, botanists, astronomers, mathematicians, and zoologists.

Alexander was an enthusiastic reader. His personal copy of the *Iliad* that he kept in Darius's confiscated casket was annotated by Aristotle in his own hand. When campaigning deep in the interiors of Asia, he asked for books to be sent to him from Greece—histories and poetry anthologies and many of the tragedies of Aeschylus, Sophocles, and Euripides.

Alexander fell out with Aristotle when the philosopher published his teaching notes. These should have remained confidential, the king wrote, as distinct from the books he wrote for the general reader. He complained: "What advantage shall I have over other men if these theories in which you have trained me are to be made common property?" This was a misunderstanding, the philosopher replied. His technical work was not a secret, but was simply inaccessible to the public at large. The royal student's advantage remained.

Alexander was one of the world's greatest commanders. In a string of astonishing victories he defeated the Great King Darius III and took over the empire, becoming Great King himself. But his most lasting achievement, cultural rather than military, was to diffuse the Greek language and civilization throughout the lands of the Persian Empire. He founded numerous cities, many of which, and most especially Alexandria in the Nile Delta, promoted the arts and sciences. In effect, he Hellenized most of the known world. Here lay the future.

Alexander's brief but incident-packed career is another story, but together with that of his father, Philip, it added a full stop to the achievements of three very different types of warring state, whose interweavings have been one of this book's themes—Athens, Sparta, and the Persian Empire. They competed with one another, and each rose and fell in turn within the space of three centuries, leaving the stage empty for the Macedonians.

Sparta was the most brittle and least appealing of them. Militaristic and introverted, its viability depended on the enslavement of its neighbors. What impressed contemporaries in the ancient world was its self-discipline. Its constitution promoted *eunomia,* or good order, obedience to good laws, stability. The average Spartiate, or Equal, saw himself not so much as an individual but as an undifferentiated member of a unified citizen body. The demands of the collective always trumped personal concerns.

The life of imagination and the arts was firmly discouraged and so was agricultural labor and economic activity, which was the responsibility of a servile class, the *helots.* As in totalitarian societies of the modern era, every aspect of an Equal's private and public life was carefully monitored and controlled.

Spartan society was designed to produce military efficiency. This it did with considerable success. Its citizen hoplites were famous for courage, discipline, and technical competence. They did not expect to lose battles and very seldom did. Unfortunately, inequalities in landholding led to a slow decline in their number. The outside world scarcely noticed this development, which was masked by a cloak of invincibility. As already noted, 8,000 Equals in 480 dwindled to only about 1,500 at the time of the Battle of Leuctra in 371.

This defeat exposed Sparta's reputation as a confidence trick. It never recovered from the blow.

The failure of Persian aggression in the fifth century had a benign consequence, in that it instilled into Greeks throughout the Eastern Mediterranean a strong sense of their identity and, so they believed, their superiority. They were proud members simultaneously of Hellas as a whole and of their small but vociferous city-states.

By contrast Persians and their subjects were barbarous and could not even speak intelligibly. Generations of European scholars and students have tended to underrate the achievements of the Achaemenid Empire and seen its history through a Hellenic lens. This is understandable, for the Persians left behind virtually no narrative account of events.

But their empire was a considerable achievement. For the first time it brought together lands from the Indus to the Balkans, from Central Asia to Upper Egypt under a political and military administration. Improved communications (in particular the Royal Road), strong regional governors, and an efficient bureaucracy held the sprawling, feudal empire together. Although the Great King held absolute powers, he did not impose himself on his subjects. "Through a wise and salutary neglect," as Edmund Burke said in another context, he left old ways, local religious and cultural customs untouched. In return for the payment of taxes and levies of men for the army, he provided peace and stability. Provinces prospered. Astutely, the Macedonian invaders took over most of the institutions of the empire they vanquished and governed it in the same tolerant manner.

Greeks like Xenophon admired the empire, despite the fact that his Persian adventures exposed its military weakness and helped give it a misleading reputation for effeminacy and decadence. If we set on one side an elite force like the Immortals, much of the Persian army was a multitudinous if not very militant militia, which was no match for highly professional Greek mercenaries. Great Kings were happy to recruit hoplites to stiffen their hordes.

Athens grew to greatness against a background of favorable economic conditions and unfavorable foreign threats. From the eighth century onwards, Greeks sent merchants sailing around the Mediterranean, opening them up to diverse cultural influences. Population growth led to the establishment of overseas colonies. International trade became essential for Athens when the number of its citizens required more food than its farmers were able to supply, and the city was forced to rely on grain imports from the Black Sea.

The historical record shows that after the establishment of democracy a booming Athens was suffused with energy and creativity. It seems likely that there was a causal connection. The system of direct democracy not only demanded, enforced even, popular participation and communal religious observance, but offered individual citizens an opportunity, perhaps unique in history, to mold their political destiny at first hand.

The fact that the *polis* was small (although not as small as Plato and Aristotle would have liked) enhanced the felt excitement of the process. The individual and the collective were interlinked and mutually magnified. The Athenian was free, but the state could also be pitiless towards him in return, as (in their different ways) the careers of Socrates, Alcibiades, and others go to show.

Love of liberty was a value of cardinal importance, which the democracy fed and watered. It was the foundation for rational inquiry and free artistic expression. It also inspired (positively) the Greeks' ferocious resistance to the Persians and (negatively) their own internecine quarrels.

Small wonder that this fertile soil produced a flowering of extraordinary personalities, and great art and thought. The Hellenic city-states took advantage of a briefly opened window of opportunity. They were too small and weak to survive for very long when surrounded by stronger and larger neighbors.

However, for the time that the fates allowed, Athens made the most of her chances.

After Alexander's death in 323, his empire quickly broke apart into the great kingdoms of the Hellenistic age—Macedon, Egypt, the imperial heartland in Asia, and in fourth place, Pergamum.

Athens was reduced to being a walk-on political actor inside the Macedonian sphere of influence. The place became rather dilapidated; the Long Walls between Athens and Piraeus collapsed and were not rebuilt. The city would never again be a full and free democracy with universal adult male suffrage. It would never again dominate the seas with its fleets, although from time to time trade picked up and Piraeus remained a major international port. The city's unique selling point was as a center for higher education, specializing in rhetoric and philosophy. For centuries young Greeks and, later, Romans spent a year or so in Athens completing their education.

Athens had no alternative but to rest on its laurels. In fact, "laurels" were all that it had: with its temples, its colonnades, its colossal statues of Athena, and its open-air murals, it was a memorial of its own glorious past, a historical theme park packed with tourists.

The city faced competition. Under the Ptolemies, the Macedonian pharaohs, Alexandria became a sophisticated and deluxe metropolis. The state-sponsored museum was an academic center for poetry, scholarship, and the sciences. Its vast library sought to collect every Greek book ever written.

So the idea of Greece shifted from the antiquated mainland *poleis* to the modern Hellenistic kingdoms of the Middle East. Then in the second century these were absentmindedly conquered by the Roman Republic. In 87 Athens, implicated in an uprising against Rome, was besieged and sacked by the Roman general Sulla. A generation later, the city chose the wrong side in Rome's civil war. Julius Caesar, the victor, pardoned it, remarking drily: "How often will the glory of your ancestors save you from self-destruction?"

Good question. Under various Roman emperors, among them Augustus and Hadrian, grand new public buildings were commissioned. In the latter's reign, the temple of Olympian Zeus, enormous but incomplete since the time of Pisistratus, was finished at last in A.D. 132.

A century later Athens was sacked again. It never recovered. Many of its major buildings lay in ruins. The population dwindled. The city became little more than the Acropolis. Successive Gothic invasions washed over it. Weeds grew in the pavements of the Parthenon. A resident Christian archbishop in the late twelfth century described Athens as "a God-forsaken hole." He wrote a friend:

> You cannot look upon Athens without weeping. It is not just that she has lost her ancient glory: that was taken from her long ago. But now she has lost the very form, appearance and character of a city. Everywhere you see walls stripped and demolished, houses razed to the ground, their sites ploughed under.

As Byzantium gave way to the Ottoman Empire, Athens was a small impoverished community. The Parthenon became a mosque and sheep, donkeys, and camels grazed in the *agora*. In the seventeenth century, in a war between Venetians and the Turks, the temple was used as an arsenal and was blown up by enemy fire.

In the nineteenth century Lord Elgin removed marble masterpieces from what was left of the Parthenon. The Greeks fought for and, with European help, won their independence. Romantic poets made Hellenic liberty their cause. Shelley said: "We are all Greeks." Lord Byron joined the insurgents and died on campaign of a violent fever and incompetent doctors in 1824.

In 1834 the victorious revolutionaries chose Athens as their capital. For the first time in two millennia, the violet-crowned city was free.

GLOSSARY

Achaemenid Empire: the Persian Empire.

Acropolis: citadel, the highest part of a *polis*.

agogē: the Spartan education and training system.

agora: marketplace, the center of the public affairs of a *polis,* and of commercial and retail activities.

Amphictyonic League: association of twelve states in central Greece charged with the upkeep and management of the oracle at Delphi.

Archon: one of nine high government officials, who served for one year. The Eponymous Archon was so-called because he gave his name to the year, which unlike our calendar was not numbered.

Areopagus: hill in Athens; council of former Archons.

aretē: excellence of every kind, moral virtue.

barbarian: non-Greek speaker

Boeotarch: chief official of the Boeotian League.

boulē: state council; in Athens it managed the day-to-day operations of the democracy and prepared the agenda for the *ecclesia.*

bouleuterion: meeting place for the *boulē*, city hall.

cella: chamber in a Greek temple.

Cerameicus: a district of Athens inside and outside the city walls, also a public cemetery.

chiliarch: commander of a thousand men.

choregos: a wealthy citizen who paid for and produced dramatic or musical events.

cleruchy: a small colony of Athenian citizens. Unlike ordinary colonies *cleruchies* retained their Athenian citizenship. Their numbers ranged from 250 to 4,000 settlers.

Companions: members of the elite cavalry of Macedon, royal bodyguards.

Crypteia: a secret police in Sparta.

demos: the people; in Athens the totality of male citizens. A local ward or deme.

Dionysia: annual festival in honor of Dionysus at which plays were performed. Great Dionysia, March/April, and Lenaea or Rural Dionysia, December/January.

drachma: silver coin, equivalent to a day's pay in the late fifth century.

ecclesia: the general assembly; in Athens it met frequently and made all the important political decisions.

emporion: a trading post.

ephebos, or *ephebe:* an adolescent male seventeen or eighteen years old.

ephors: five *ephors* were elected annually, the executive arm of the Spartan state.

Equal: an adult Spartan citizen. Also Spartiate.

erastes: a male lover.

eromenos: a male beloved.

eunomia: good order.

eupatridae: noblemen.

Euxine Sea: literally the Hospitable Sea (meaning the opposite); today's Black Sea.

gerousia: council of elders at Sparta.

gymnasium: exercise ground.

harmost: a Spartan military governor.

heliaea: supreme court of Athens.

Hellenotamiae: finance officers at the Delian League.

helot: a serf from Laconia and Messenia, subjugated by Sparta.

Herm: bust of Hermes on a stone column with genitalia.

hetaira: a high-class prostitute (literally, a companion).

hippeis: cavalry.

hoplite: heavy-armed infantry soldier.

Lacedaemon: Sparta, the capital city.

Laconia: the territory of Sparta.

liturgy: subsidy by wealthy citizens of public activity, including arts events or the cost of warships.

medize: to collaborate with the Persians.

metic: a resident alien at Athens, without civic rights. Usually a manufacturer or merchant.

metropolis: mother city of a colony.

mothax: son of a Spartiate and a *helot* woman, or a Spartiate who could not afford the *syssitia* fee.

oba (plural *obai*): a Spartan village or small settlement.

obol: coin worth one sixth of a drachma.

oligarchy: rule of the few in a *polis*.

ostracism: a referendum on exiling a leading Athenian for ten years.

ostracon: broken piece of pottery.

paedogogus: a slave responsible for a child's upbringing and for taking him to school.

palaestra: a wrestling ground and school.

Panathenaea: major Athenian festival in honor of Athena.

pankration: all-out sport combining boxing and wrestling.

parthenos: a virgin, umarried girl, and young woman.

peltast: lightly armed soldier.

pentacosiomedimni: wealthiest class of Athenian citizen.

peplos: ankle-length woolen robe or shawl worn by women.

perioeci: free residents of Laconia without voting rights.

phalanx: a formation of hoplites, many ranks deep.

phratry: club of Athenian citizens with religious/state functions—e.g., naming and registering a newborn boy (literally brotherhood).

Pnyx: meeting place of the Athenian *ecclesia*.

polemarch: a war leader, one of the Athenian Archons.

polis (plural *poleis*): Greek city-state.

polites: citizen of a *polis*.

Prytaneum: the state headquarters, with a community hearth and an eternal flame. Office of the senior members of the *boulē* of Athens.

Pythia: the priestess at Delphi.

satrap: provincial governor in the Persian Empire.

seisachtheia: a shaking off of burdens (Solon's reforms).

sophist: an intellectual and teacher of young men in rhetoric.

Spartiate: the name for an adult Spartan citizen. Also an Equal.

stele: inscribed stone slab, often a gravestone or decree.

stoa: a covered colonnade.

strategos: a general (one of ten elected annually by the *ecclesia* in Athens).

symposium: a drinking party, usually in aristocratic circles.

synoecism: the union of several towns as a unitary state.

syssitia: a Spartiate's military mess.

thetes: members of the lowest economic class in Athens.

The Thirty: oligarchs who governed Athens from 404 to 403.

Tholos: the headquarters of the Prytaneum in the *agora.*

timē: honor, personal status.

trireme: warship with three banks of oars on either side.

trittys: a regional division of Attica.

tyrant: sole ruler who took power unconstitutionally, *turannos.*

zeugitai: third tier of Solon's social classes, rich enough to own a hoplite's armor and weapons.

TIME LINE

B.C.

c. 3000	Minoan civilization in Crete begins.
c. 2000–1300	Hittites flourish in Asia Minor.
c. 1400	Palaces at Cnossos and Phaestus destroyed. Decline of Cretan power.
c. 1600–1200	Mycenae flourishes.
1287	Battle of Kadesh. Decline of Egyptian and Hittite power.
1230–1150	Breakdown of settled conditions.
c. 1200	Overthrow of Hittite Empire.
c. 1180	Myceneans sack Troy, according to tradition.
c. 1150	Mycenaean settlements destroyed.
c. 1100	"Dorians" settle in the Peloponnese.
c. 1050–950	"Ionians" and others colonize Asia Minor. Athens plays leading role. Beginning of Iron Age in Greece.
c. 850–730	Athens becomes a leading cultural center in Greece.
776	First Olympiad.
c. 750–700	Invention of Greek alphabet. Homer composes the *Iliad* and *Odyssey*.
c. 735–650	Foundation of Greek colonies across the Mediterranean.
730–10	Sparta conquers Messenia.
c. 700	Hesiod flourishes. Midas king of Phrygia.
c. 700–650	Invention of hoplite warfare.
683/2	First annual Archon at Athens reported.

650–600	Age of lawgivers in Greece.
	Rise of tyrannies in Corinth, Megara, and Sicyon; and in Ionia.
c. 632	Cylon attempts tyranny at Athens.
	Alcmaeonids exiled from Athens.
c. 620/1	Dracon legislates at Athens.
c. 624–546	Thales flourishes.
c. 620	Sparta suppresses Messenian revolt.
c. 600	Sappho and Alcaeus flourish on Lesbos.
	Periander tyrant of Corinth.
595	Earliest Greek coins minted at Aegina.
595–86	First Sacred War for control of Delphi.
594/93	Solon Archon. *Seisachtheia.*
566	Inauguration of the Great Panathenaea.
561/60	Pisistratus, tyrant of Athens, first time.
560–50	War of Sparta with Tegea.
560–46	Croesus king of Lydia.
559	Cyrus king of Persia.
c. 559–56	Miltiades senior, tyrant in Thracian Chersonese.
557/6 or 556/5	Pisistratus expelled.
550	Cyrus conquers Media.
550/49	Second tyranny of Pisistratus. Expelled again.
548	Temple of Apollo in Delphi burns down. The Alcmaeonids partly fund its rebuilding.
547 (?)	Cyrus conquers Lydia. Fall of Croesus.
546/5	Persia conquers the Greeks of Asia Minor.
545–40	Cyrus pushes into Central Asia.
540/39	Third tyranny of Pisistratus.
538	Cyrus captures Babylon.
530	Cyrus dies.
528/7	Pisistratus dies, succeeded by sons Hippias and Hipparchus.
525	Cambyses, Cyrus's successor, invades Egypt.
522	Fall of Polycrates, tyrant of Samos.
	Cambyses dies. Darius assassinates his successor and becomes king of Persia.

521	Darius seizes power in Persia.
520	Cleomenes king of Sparta.
519	Athens at war with Thebes over Plataea.
514	Harmodius and Aristogeiton assassinate Hipparchus.
c. 512	Darius conquers Thrace.
510	Expulsion of Hipparchus from Athens.
508/7	Cleomenes of Sparta invades Attica, besieged in Acropolis.
506	Peloponnesian army invades Attica. Athenians defeat Boeotians, Chalcidians, and acquire the Chalcidian plain. They also acquire Oropus.
503/2	Reforms of Cleisthenes begin at Athens.
501	System of ten *strategoi* established.
499–93	Ionian cities revolt from Persia.
493	Themistocles Archon.
c. 492	Persia subdues Thrace and Macedonia. Trial of Miltiades.
491	Envoys of Darius tour Greek states demanding fire and water; those who visit Athens are executed.
490	Persia launches a punitive expedition against Greece. Battle of Marathon.
487	First known ostracism. War of Athens against Aegina.
487/6	Archons appointed by lot. *Strategoi* supersede the polemarch.
486/5	Egypt revolts from Persia.
485	Darius dies, succeeded by Xerxes.
484/3	Egyptian revolt suppressed. Xerxes prepares for invasion of Greece.
483	Persians cut canal through Mount Athos.
483/2	New vein of silver found at the Laurium mine.
482	Ostracism of Aristides. Athenian fleet enlarged.
481	Conference at Sparta; Greek states plan resistance to Persian invasion. Athens concludes peace with Aegina.

480	Xerxes enters Greece. August: Battles of Artemisium and Thermopylae. September: Battle of Salamis. Xerxes flees to Persia.
479	Second evacuation of Athens. Battle of Plataea. Battle of Mycale. Persia loses Sestos and the Hellespont.
478/6	Walls rebuilt at Athens.
478	Pausanias liberates Cyprus, captures Byzantium. Delian League against Persia founded.
477	Themistocles fortifies Piraeus.
476–73	Victories of Cimon.
472	*The Persians* of Aeschylus.
472 or 470	Ostracism of Themistocles; goes to Argos.
471	Pausanias expelled from Byzantium.
c. 471	Death of Pausanias, flight of Themistocles.
470	Cimon brings back the "bones of Theseus."
469	Naxos revolts from Delian League. Themistocles flees to Corcyra, then to King Admetus.
468	Themistocles arrives in Persia. Cimon's first expedition against the *helots*.
466	Battle of the Eurymedon.
465	Revolt of Thasos from Delian League. Assassination of Xerxes. Artaxerxes I succeeds.
c. 464	Earthquake at Sparta. *Helots* revolt.
463	Siege of Ithome. Sparta rejects Athenian allies. Surrender of Thasos.
463–61	Reforms of Ephialtes at Athens; Areopagus loses its powers.
462–60	Pericles influential at Athens.
462	Athenians and Egyptians defeat Persians.
461	Ostracism of Cimon. Athenian alliance with Argos and Thessaly.
460	Assassination of Ephialtes. Intermittent hostilities between Athens and the Peloponnesians start (the First Peloponnesian War).

459	Athens wins Megara.
	Final defeat of the *helots*.
	Athens at war with Aegina.
458	*Oresteia* of Aeschylus.
	Athens builds Long Walls.
	Athenian expedition to Egypt.
	Themistocles dies.
	Athens conquers Aegina.
457	Athens conquers Boeotia.
	Archonship opened to *zeugitai*.
454	Egyptian expedition ends in disaster.
	Delian League treasury moved to Athens.
	Long Walls completed.
451	Five years' truce between Athens and the Peloponnesians.
	Return of Cimon.
	Citizenship law of Pericles.
449	Cimon dies in Cyprus.
449	Peace of Callias with Persia.
447	Building of Parthenon begins.
	Athens loses Boeotia.
	Battle of Coronea.
447/6	Euboean revolt suppressed. Athens loses Megara.
445	Thirty Years Peace between Athens and the Peloponnesians.
443	Ostracism of Thucydides, son of Melesias.
441	Euripides' first victory at the City Dionysia.
	Antigone by Sophocles.
440/39	Revolts of Samos and Byzantium. Sophocles a *strategos*.
436	Foundation of Amphipolis.
436/5	Disorder at Epidamnus.
c. 435	Pericles' expedition to Black Sea.
435	Spring: Corcyra wins sea battle against Corinth.
433	Athenian alliance with Corcyra.
432	Revolt of Potidaea.
	"Megarian Decree" at Athens.
431	Peloponnesian War begins.
	First Peloponnesian invasion of Attica.

430–26	Plague at Athens.
429	Pericles dies.
	Siege of Plataea.
428	Revolt of Mytilene.
427	Mytilene surrenders. Debate at Athens on Mytilene.
	Athenian fleet visits Sicily.
426	Plataea surrenders.
	Civil war in Corcyra.
	Demosthenes in northwest (Aetolia).
425	Occupation of Pylos in the Peloponnese. Spartans captured.
	Truce between Athens and Sparta.
	Invasions of Attica cease.
	The Acharnians by Aristophanes.
424	Brasidas in Thrace.
423	Peace negotiations; one-year armistice.
422	Armistice expires.
	Deaths of Brasidas and Cleon outside Amphipolis.
421	*Peace* by Aristophanes.
	Peace of Nicias.
	Fifty-year alliance between Athens and Sparta; breaks down after a year.
417	Ostracism of Hyperbolus.
	Conquest of Melos. Athenian "war crime."
415	*The Trojan Women* by Euripides.
	Sicilian Expedition.
	Alcibiades recalled, defects to Sparta.
413	Sicilian Expedition ends in complete disaster.
412	Athenian allies revolt.
	Alcibiades leaves Sparta.
411	June to September: Council of Four Hundred.
	Army and fleet at Samos remain loyal to the democracy.
	Alcibiades rehabilitated, commands fleet. Athenian victories.
	Lysistrata by Aristophanes.
	Thesmophoriazusae by Aristophanes.
410	Battle of Cyzicus.

	Full democracy restored at Athens.
407	Alcibiades at Athens.
406	Athenian defeat at Notium; Alcibiades withdraws.
	Athenian victory at Arginusae; trial of the generals.
	Euripides dies in Macedon.
405	*The Frogs* by Aristophanes; in 404 *The Frogs* is restaged in revised version.
	Battle of Aegospotami.
405/4	Blockade of Athens.
	Death of Darius II, accession of Artaxerxes II.
404 Spring:	Athens surrenders. Long Walls pulled down.
Summer:	Rule of the Thirty.
	Death of Alcibiades.
	Death of Theramenes.
403	Spartan garrison at Athens.
September:	The Thirty overthrown, democracy restored.
401	Cyrus's attempt on the Persian throne; killed at Cunaxa.
399	Trial and execution of Socrates.
398	Agesilaus becomes Spartan king.
397	Conon commands Persian fleet.
396–94	Agesilaus campaigns against Persia.
c. 396	Antisthenes opens school.
395/4	Anti-Spartan alliance of Athens, Thebes, and others.
395–87	Corinthian War.
395	Work starts on rebuilding Long Walls.
394	Conon defeats Spartan fleet at Cnidus.
	Battle of Coronea.
393	Conon in Athens.
c. 390	Isocrates opens school.
389	Death of Thrasybulus.
387/6	Peace of Antalcidas, the "King's Peace," between Persia and Greek states.
387	Plato opens Academy.
386	Old tragedies revived at Dionysia.
c. 385	Aristophanes dies.
	Artaxerxes at war in Egypt.

384–79	Plato's *Symposium*.
382	Spartans seize citadel of Thebes.
379/8	Spartans expelled from Theban citadel.
378	Raid of Sphodrias.
378/7 Spring:	Second Athenian League founded. Renewal of Athenian power. Athens declares war on Sparta after acquittal of Sphodrias. Agesilaus invades Boeotia. Mausolus satrap of Caria.
After 377	Plato's *Republic*.
375	Jason of Pherae becomes ruler of Thessaly.
374	Peace between Athens and Sparta.
374/3	Peace broken.
371	Thebes, led by Epaminondas, defeats Sparta at Leuctra. End of Sparta as a great power.
370	Jason of Pherae assassinated.
370–61	Theban invasions of the Peloponnese. Foundation of Messene.
368	Foundation of Megalopolis.
367	Aristotle joins the Academy.
362	Epaminondas killed in victory at Mantinea.
361	Agesilaus in Egypt.
360	Death of Agesilaus.
359	Philip II rules in Macedon.
357/6	Philip and Athens at war. Athens at war with league allies (Social War).
356	Sacred War begins.
355/4	Athens concedes defeat in Social War.
351	First of series of speeches by Demosthenes against Philip (Philippics).
348	Philip captures Olynthus.
346	Peace between Philip and Athens. Philip defeats Phocis and ends Sacred War. Open letter by Isocrates to Philip.
345–43	Persia regains Egypt.

343	Aristotle tutor to Alexander.
342/1	Philip conquers Thrace.
338	Philip marches down into Greece.
	Philip defeats Thebes and Athens at Chaeronea.
	End of Greek independence.
336	Philip assassinated, Alexander succeeds him.
	Alexander's first descent on Greece, elected general of the Greeks.
335	Alexander's second descent into Greece.
	Destruction of Thebes.
334	Alexander leaves for the Persian Empire.
c. 331	Foundation of Alexandria.
331	Alexander wins decisive battle at Gaugamela, assumes the Persian throne.
323	Alexander dies.
322	Greeks revolt (Lamian War), are defeated. Demosthenes kills himself.
286	Athens rebels against Macedon.
146	Roman conquest of Greece.
86	Sulla sacks Athens.

A.D.

c. 120–35	Hadrian restores and rebuilds Athens.
1687	Venetians blow up Parthenon.
1801	Lord Elgin removes carvings from Parthenon.
1821–33	Greek War of Independence.
1834	Athens becomes capital of Greece.

ACKNOWLEDGMENTS

My warmest thanks go to Roddy Ashworth for his advice throughout and assistance with research. I am greatly indebted to my editor at Penguin Random House, Will Murphy, and to my literary agent, Christopher Sinclair-Stevenson, for their guidance and enthusiasm. Grateful thanks are also due to Mika Kasuga, assistant editor at Penguin Random House, for her support. As in the past, Professor Robert Cape of Austin College, Texas, has very kindly read a draft and given me useful comments and suggestions. Professor Sulochana Asirvatham, associate professor of classics and humanities, Montclair State University, has also offered helpful advice. Any errors, of course, must be laid at my door.

SOURCES

The sources for the story of Athens vary in quality and many of them survive only as fragments or as quotations in other books. What we have is mainly related to Athenian affairs, and relatively little is known about the rest of Greece.

Two very great writers dominate the field. The first of these is Herodotus (c. 484–25) from Halicarnassus in Asia Minor, in the eyes of the ancient world the "father of history." The word "history" derives from the Greek term for investigation and his book is the product of his inquiries as he traveled around the Eastern Mediterranean. He describes the various peoples in the region and sets the scene for a comprehensive narrative of the two Persian invasions of Greece in the early fifth century.

Herodotus is essentially a storyteller and he will cheerfully give space to a good yarn whether or not it is plausible. He wrote an epic in prose and the towering figure of Homer lies behind his literary enterprise; he too was concerned with a titanic struggle between Hellenes and an oriental power.

Herodotus describes what he has seen for himself and what he has been told in conversations with apparently well-informed individuals. He is open-minded about different cultures, although he does not always understand the real meaning of what he is describing. However, he recognized the importance of disinterested research and tried to give an accurate record of events. He wrote a generation after the Persian Wars, and so will have been able to gather information from those who took part or at least their close descendants.

If Herodotus is not an altogether reliable guide to what happened, he gives a completely truthful picture of how an intelligent Greek might see the world around him.

By contrast, his contemporary Thucydides (c. 500–c. 399), an Athenian aristocrat, chose another conflict as his subject, the Peloponnesian War between Athens and Sparta. He believed that this war, closely studied, would be an example to future generations. His history was to be "a possession for all time" and not something "written for display, to make an immediate impression" (in other words, like Herodotus).

He was determined to report events as accurately as possible and took trouble to interview those who took part in them. He is quite exceptionally impartial, exact, responsible, and trustworthy—so much so that he leaves little room for scholarly interpretation. We are obliged to accept what he says (where available, other sources almost invariably confirm his narrative). An innovative feature was his reporting of public speeches given by military and political leaders. While keeping as close as possible to what was said, he wrote what he believed the situation required. Readers must bear this in mind when they encounter quotations from speeches in this book—for instance, the great funeral address of Pericles at the beginning of the Peloponnesian War.

After a brief summary of early Greek history, Thucydides reports on the rise of the Athenian Empire between 479 and 435. He then covers in detail the first ten years of the war, the Peace of Nicias, the renewal of hostilities, and the disastrous Sicilian Expedition. He takes the story to 411 and breaks off in mid-sentence (presumably overtaken by illness or death).

A number of historians wrote continuations of Thucydides, none of which has survived except for the *Hellenica* of Xenophon. The book has a certain freshness and directness, but what does not interest the author is ignored. He is heavily biased in favor of Sparta and cannot even bring himself to mention the name of Epaminondas, architect of the Theban victory of Leuctra. He omits some incidents altogether, but was an eyewitness of some scenes in his book which he describes well.

Xenophon's *Anabasis* is an exciting narrative of the author's days as a mercenary in the service of Cyrus the Younger. He was a friend of the Spartan king Agesilaus, and wrote a eulogy of him. He produced numerous other works, including dialogues featuring Socrates and essays on horsemanship, hunting, and home economics. His *Education of Cyrus* is a curious mixture of romance and documentary.

The main continuous narrative source for the period is the *Historical Library* of Diodorus Siculus, a Sicilian who flourished in the middle of the first century B.C. This "universal history" is an assembly of summaries of other historians. His coverage of the years 480 to 302 has survived in toto. He is invaluable, but only as trustworthy as the source he happens to be using at the time.

Behind Diodorus and the rest stand the shadowy figures of historians and chroniclers, all of whose books have vanished but who appear indirectly in the writings of their successors or in late epitomes (Theopompus, for instance, or Pompeius Trogus).

The trouble with all these ancient authors is that they concentrate more or less exclusively on military and political affairs. The dismal science of economics had not been invented, nor the more cheerful one of sociology. Little is said of the lives of women or slaves. To gain an idea of everyday life we have to scavenge passing references in all kinds of surviving text.

The biographies and essays of the Greek author Plutarch (c. A.D. 46–120) are not history, strictly speaking, but are gold mines of historical data and offer fascinating insights into the personalities of Athenian and a few other leaders.

Literary masterpieces illumine moral attitudes—Homer, above all, and the epic farmer Hesiod, the Athenian tragedians Aeschylus, Sophocles, and Euripides, the comic author Aristophanes, and a range of other poets, often represented only by fragments. Speeches by orators and pamphlets, especially dated to the fourth century, are useful political and social documents, but have to be interpreted with caution. The many works of Plato and Aristotle allow us to track the intellectual development not only of Athens, but of Greece as a whole. Two studies of the Athenian constitution were misattributed to Aristotle (probably written by a pupil) and Xenophon, but offer a mass of detail about the democratic process.

Archaeologists have added greatly to our knowledge. Nearly two hundred Athenian state decrees between 478 and 336 and several hundred other administrative documents (for example, building accounts for the Parthenon and records of religious cult activities) have been unearthed, usually inscribed on stone. Ostracism potsherds have been found on which the names of candidates for exile are scratched. Ceramic vessels of great artistry display every kind of interpersonal activity.

For readers who want direct access to the main original materials, the Loeb Classical Library offers the original Greek (or Latin) with translations on the facing page. Modern translations of most of the main texts can be found in Penguin Classics.

Most of the translations are mine. A few are by other hands, usually poetry, of which the most important is E. V. Rieu's translation of Homer's *Iliad* in Penguin Classics. It is my favorite version and for all its flaws it captures the spirit of its great original.

The endnotes that follow identify quotations and particularly important, telling, or controversial scholarly developments. The main sources for each chapter are mentioned, but no further details are given of the authority for specific incidents.

BIBLIOGRAPHY

SELECTED MODERN STUDIES

Barnes, Jonathan. *Early Greek Philosophy*. London: Penguin Classics, 2002.

Behistun (Bisitun) Inscription, trans. Herbert Cushing Tolman, Vanderbilt University, Nashville, Tennessee, 1908.

Bicknell, Peter J. "Axiochus Alkibiadou, Aspasia and Aspasios." *L'Antiquité Classique,* T 52 (1982), pp. 240–50.

Bloch, Enid. "Hemlock Poisoning and the Death of Socrates: Did Plato Tell the Truth?" Issue 1, *Journal of the International Plato Society,* University of Notre Dame, 2001.

Burkert, Walter. *Greek Religion*. Oxford: Blackwell, 1985.

Burn, A. R. *Persia and the Greeks,* 2nd ed., D. M. Lewis, Postscript. London: Duckworth, 1984.

Bury, J. B. *A History of Greece to the Death of Alexander the Great,* 3rd. ed., rev. by R. Meiggs. London: Macmillan, 1951. Still the best narrative history of the period.

Cambridge Ancient History, Vol. 2, part 1, to Vol. 6. Various editors. Cambridge: Cambridge University Press, 1971–1994.

Camp, John M. *The Archaeology of Athens*. New Haven: Yale University Press, 2001.

Cohn-Haft, L. "Divorce in Ancient Athens." *Journal of Hellenic Studies,* Vol. 115, pp. 1–14, 1995, London.

Connolly, Peter, and Hazel Dodge. *The Ancient City: Life in Classical Athens and Rome*. Oxford: Oxford University Press, 1998.

Crowther, N. B. "Male 'Beauty' Contests in Greece: The Euandria and Euexia." *L'Antiquité Classique,* Vol. 54, 1985, Brussels, Ghent, Liège, and Louvain.

Curtis, John, and Nigel Tallis. *Forgotten Empire: The World of Ancient Persia*. London: British Museum Press, 2005.

Daiva Inscription XPh, Archaeological Museum, Tehran.

Davies, J. K., *Democracy and Classical Greece,* Fontana History of the Ancient World. Fontana: 1993.

Diels, Hermann. *Die Fragmente der Vorsokratiker.* Berlin, 1903, 6th ed., rev. by Walther Kranz. Berlin: Weidmann, 1952 (the editions after the 6th are mainly reprints with little or no change).

Dillon, Matthew, and Linda Garland. *Ancient Greece: Social and Historical Documents from Archaic Times to the Death of Alexander the Great,* 2nd ed. Abingdon: Routledge, 2000.

Fornara, Charles W. *Archaic Times to the End of the Peloponnesian War (Translated Documents of Greece and Rome),* 2nd ed. Cambridge: Cambridge University Press, 1983.

Forrest, W. G. *A History of Sparta, 950–192 B.C.* London: Hutchinson, 1968.

Forsdyke, Sara. *Exile, Ostracism, and Democracy: The Politics of Expulsion in Ancient Greece.* Princeton: Princeton University Press, 2005.

French, A. *The Growth of the Athenian Economy.* London: Routledge and Kegan Paul, 1964.

Garland, Robert. *Daily Life of the Ancient Greeks.* Westport, Conn: Greenwood Press, 1998.

Goldhill, Simon. "The Great Dionysia and Civic Ideology," eds. John J. Winkler and Froma I. Zeitlin. *Nothing to Do with Dionysos? Athenian Drama in Its Social Context.* Princeton: Princeton University Press, 1990.

Green, Peter. *Alexander of Macedon.* Harmondsworth: Penguin, 1974.

———. *The Greco-Persian Wars.* Berkeley: University of California Press, 1996.

Hall, Edith. *Greek Tragedy: Suffering Under the Sun.* Oxford: Oxford University Press, 2010.

Hallock, R. T. *Persepolis Fortifications Tablets.* Oriental Institute Publications 92, Chicago, 1969.

Hammond, N. G. L. *History of Greece.* Oxford: Oxford University Press, 1959.

Honor, Hugh, and John Fleming. *A World History of Art,* 7th ed. London: Lawrence King, 2009.

Hornblower, Simon, and Antony Spawforth. *Oxford Classical Dictionary*, 3rd ed. rev. Oxford: Oxford University Press, 2003.

Jacoby, F. *Die Fragmente der griechischen Historiker.* Leiden 1923–64 (for Jacoby online, see Brill.com).

Kagan, Donald. *The Peloponnesian War.* New York: Viking Penguin, 2003.

———. *Pericles of Athens and the Birth of Democracy.* Guild Publishing by arrangement with Secker and Warburg, Suffolk, UK, 1990.

Littman, Robert J. "The Loves of Alcibiades." *Transactions and Proceedings of the American Philological Association,* Vol. 101, 1970, Johns Hopkins University.

Meiggs, R., and D. M. Lewis. *A Selection of Greek Historical Inscriptions: To the End of the Fifth Century B.C.,* 2nd ed. Oxford: Oxford University Press, 1988.

Migeotte, L., trans. Janet Lloyd. *The Economy of the Greek Cities, from the Archaic Period to the Early Roman Empire.* Berkeley: University of California Press, 2009.

Morrison, J. S., J. F. Coates, and N. B. Rankov. *The Athenian Trireme: The History and Reconstruction of an Ancient Greek Warship.* Cambridge: Cambridge University Press, 2000.

Murray, Oswyn. *Early Greece, Fontana History of the Ancient World,* 2nd ed. London: Fontana, 1993.

Overbeck, J., ed. *Die antiken Schriftquellen zur Geschichte der bildenden Künste bei den Griechen.* Leipzig, 1868.

Princeton Encyclopedia of Classical Sites. R. Stillwell and others. Princeton: Princeton University Press, 1976.

Pritchard, James B., ed. *Ancient Near Eastern Texts,* 3rd ed. rev. Princeton: Princeton University Press, 1969.

Raubitschek, A. E. "The Case Against Alcibiades (Andocides IV)." *Transactions and Proceedings of the American Philological Association,* Vol. 79, 1948, pp. 191–210, Johns Hopkins University.

Rhodes, P. J., and Robin Osborne. *Greek Historical Inscriptions, 404–323 B.C.* Oxford: Oxford University Press, 2003.

Rubel, Alexander. *Fear and Loathing in Ancient Athens: Religion and Politics During the Peloponnesian War.* London: Routledge, 2000.

Scott, Michael. *Delphi: A History of the Center of the Ancient World.* Princeton: Princeton University Press, 2014.

Sellars, John. "Simon the Shoemaker and the Problem of Socrates." *Classical Philology,* Vol. 98, pp. 207–16 (July 2003), University of Chicago Press.

Sommerstein, Alan H., and David Barrett, trans. Aristophanes, *The Birds and Other Plays.* London: Penguin Classics, 2003.

Strauss, Barry S. *Athens After the Peloponnesian War: Class, Faction and Policy, 403–386 B.C.* London: Croom Helm, 1986.

———. "Thrasybulus and Conon: A Rivalry in Athens in the 390s B.C." *The American Journal of Philology,* Vol. 105, No. 1 (Spring 1984), pp. 37–48, Johns Hopkins University.

Swaddling, Judith. *The Ancient Olympic Games.* London: British Museum, 1980, 2011.

Tod, Marcus Niebuhr, ed. *A Selection of Greek Historical Inscriptions.* Oxford: Oxford University Press, 1948.

Waterfield, Robin. *Athens: A History from Ancient Ideal to Modern City.* London: Macmillan, 2004.

Waters, Matt. *Ancient Persia: A Concise History of the Achaemenid Empire, 550–330 B.C.* Cambridge: Cambridge University Press, 2014.

Worthington, Ian. *By the Spear: Philip II, Alexander the Great and the Rise and Fall of the Macedonian Empire.* Oxford: Oxford University Press, 2014.

———. *Demosthenes of Athens and the Fall of Classical Greece.* Oxford: Oxford University Press, 2013.

NOTES

Ancient Sources, Abbreviations

Aelian, *Varia Historia*	Ael
Aelius Aristides, *Sacred Tales* (*Hieroi Logoi*)	Ael Ar
Aeschines, *Orations*	Aes
Aeschylus *Agamemnon*	Aesch Ag
Aeschylus, *Choephori* (*Libation Bearers*)	Aesch Cho
Aeschylus, *Eumenides* (*Kindly Ones*)	Aesch Eu
Aeschylus, *Oresteia*	Aesch Orest
Aeschylus, *Persae*	Aesch Pers
Aesop, *Fables*	Perry Index
American School of Classical Studies Digital Collections	ASCSA
Andocides, *Against Alcibiades I*	Ando Alc
Andocides, *On the Mysteries*	Ando Myst
Apollodorus, *Epitome*	Apo
Appian, *Civil War*	App
Aristophanes, *The Acharnians*	Ar Ach
Aristophanes, *The Clouds*	Ar Clo
Aristophanes, *The Frogs*	Ar Frogs
Aristophanes, *The Knights* (or *The Cavalrymen*)	Ar Kni
Aristophanes, *Lysistrata*	Ar Lys
Aristophanes, *Peace*	Ar Pe
Aristotle, *The Athenian Constitution*	Arist Con

Aristotle, *Metaphysics*	Arist Met
Aristotle, *Nicomachean Ethics*	Arist Ethics
Aristotle, *Poetics*	Arist Po
Aristotle, *Politics*	Arist Pol
Aristotle, *Rhetoric*	Arist Rhet
Arrian, *Anabasis of Alexander*	Arr
Athenaeus, *Deipnosophistae*	Ath
Clemens Alexandrius, Paedogogus	Clem Alex Paed
Cornelius Nepos, *Miltiades*	Nep Milt
Curtius Rufus, Quintus, *Histories of Alexander the Great*	Curt
Cyrus Cylinder, trans. Irving Finkel, British Museum	Cyr Cyl
Demosthenes, *Against Neaira*	Dem Neaira
Demosthenes, *On the Crown*	Dem Steph
Demosthenes, *On the Peace*	Dem Peace
Die Fragmenter der Vorsokratiker (*Fragments of the Presocratics*), ed. H. A. Diels, Berlin, 1903, 6th ed., rev. by Walther Kranz, Weidmann, Berlin 1952	DK
Dio Chrysostom, *Discourses*	Dio Chrys
Diodorus Siculus, *Historical Library* (NB trans. Peter Green, with Introduction and Commentary, Diodorus Siculus, Books 11–12:37:1, *Greek History 480–431 B.C.: The Alternative Version,* University of Texas Press, Austin, 2006)	Diod
Diogenes Laertius, *Lives of Eminent Philosophers*	Diog Laer
Dionysius of Halicarnassus, *On the Composition of Words*	Dion Comp
Empiricus, Sextus, *Contra Mathematicos*	Sex Emp
Euripides, *Ion*	Eur Ion
Euripides, *Trojan Women*	Eur Troj

Eusebius, *Praeparatio Evangelica*	Eus
Fouilles de Delphes, *École française* *d'Athènes, 1902–*	Delphes
Die Fragmente der Griechischen *Historiker,* Weidmann, Berlin, 1923ff	FGrH
Greek Anthology	Gr Anth
Greek Historical Inscriptions, *404–323 B.C.,* ed. P. J. Rhodes and Robin Osborne, Oxford 2007	GHI
Herodotus, *The Histories*	Herod
Hesiod, *Theogony*	Hes Theo
Hesiod, *Works and Days*	Hes Works
Homer, *Iliad*	Hom Il
Homer, *Odyssey*	Hom Ody
Inscriptiones Graecae, Berlin-Brandenburgische Akademie der Wissenschaften, 1825–	IG
Isocrates	Isoc
Isocrates, *Letters*	Isoc Letters
Justin, *Epitome of the Philippic History* *of Pompeius Trogus*	Just
Lucian	Luc
Lycurgus, *Against Leocrates*	Lyc
Lysias	Lys
Nepos, Cornelius, *De Excellentibus* *Ducibus Vitae Exterarum Gentium* *(On Eminent Foreign Leaders),* Miltiades	Nep Milt
Nepos, Cornelius, *De Excellentibus* *Ducibus Vitae Exterarum Gentium* *(On Eminent Foreign Leaders),* Alcibiades, Conon, Iphicrates	Nep Alc, Con, Iph
Parian Marble	Par
Pausanias, *Periegesis Hellados* *(Description of Greece)*	Paus
Philochorus, *Atthis*	Phil Atthis
Pindar, *Odes*	Pind

Plato, *Alcibiades 1*	Plato Alc 1
Plato, *Apology*	Plato Apol
Plato, *Charmides*	Plato Charm
Plato, *Critias*	Plato Crit
Plato, *Epistles*	Plato Ep
Plato, *Euthyphro*	Plato Euth
Plato, *Gorgias*	Plato Gorg
[Plato], spurious *Hipparchus*	[Plato] Hipp
Plato, *Laws*	Plato Laws
Plato, *Menexenus*	Plato Men
Plato, *Phaedo*	Plato Phaedo
Plato, *Phaedrus*	Plato Phaed
Plato, *Protagoras*	Plato Prot
Plato, *Symposium*	Plato Symp
Plutarch, *Amatorius*	Plut Amat
Plutarch, *Life of Agesilaus*	Plut Age
Plutarch, *Life of Agis*	Plut Agi
Plutarch, *Life of Alcibiades*	Plut Alc
Plutarch, *Life of Aristides*	Plut Arist
Plutarch, *Life of Artaxerxes*	Plut Art
Plutarch, *Life of Camillus*	Plut Cam
Plutarch, *Life of Cimon*	Plut Cim
Plutarch, *Life of Demosthenes*	Plut Dem
Plutarch, *Life of Lycurgus*	Plut Lyc
Plutarch, *Life of Nicias*	Plut Nic
Plutarch, *Life of Pelopidas*	Plut Pel
Plutarch, *Life of Pericles*	Plut Per
Plutarch, *Life of Phocion*	Plut Phoc
Plutarch, *Life of Themistocles*	Plut Them
Plutarch, *Life of Theseus*	Plut Thes
Plutarch, *Lives of the Ten Orators*	Plut Ten Or
Plutarch, *Moralia*	Plut Mor
Plutarch, *Precepts*	Plut Pre
Plutarch, *Sayings of the Spartans*	Plut Sayings Spartans

Poetae Comici Graeci, ed. Rudolf Kassel and Stephan Schröder, Verlag Walter de Gruyter, Berlin and New York, 1839– — PCG

Polyaenus, *Strategemata* — Pol

Polybius, *Histories* — Polyb

Pseudo-Lucian, *Erotes* — Luc

Simonides, *Epigrams* — Sim Ep

Sophocles, *Antigone* — Soph Ant

Themistius, *Orations* — Themist

Thucydides, *History of the Peloponnesian War* — Thuc

Tyrtaeus, *Fragments* — Tyrt Frag

Tztetzes, John, *Chiliades* — Tzet

Xenophon, *Anabasis* — Xen Ana

Xenophon, *Constitution of Sparta* — Xen Lac

[Xenophon], *Constitution of the Athenians* — Xen Con

Xenophon, *Hellenica* — Xen Hell

Xenophon, *Memorabilia* — Xen Mem

Xenophon, *Oeconomicus* — Xen Oec

Xenophon, *On Taxation (de Vectigalibus)* — Xen Vect

Xenophon, *Revenues (Poroi)* — Xen Por

Zenobius, *Proverbs* — Zen

INTRODUCTION

xxiii *He took a copy with him* Plut Alex 26 1–2 5.

xxiv *even a woman* See Samuel Butler, *Authoress of the Odyssey*, 1897.

xxv *"His descent was like nightfall"* Hom Il 1 47–53.

xxvi *"unquenchable laughter"* Hom Ody Il 1 599.
"an obstinate old sinner" Ibid., 8 360f.

xxvii *"Put me on earth again"* For this famous episode, see Hom Il 11 465–540.

xxviii *"Let your motto be, I lead"* Il., 6 207–8.
"donkey who gets the better" Ibid., 11 558ff.
"the daring of a fly" Ibid., 17 570–72.
"Weighed down by his helmet" Ibid., 8 306–8.
"bright eyes" Ibid., 16 645.

1. NATIONAL HERO

The main source throughout is Plutarch's "biography" of Theseus.

4 *"the eldest land of Ionia"* Arist Con 5 2.

5 *"the Athenians from their splendid"* Hom Il 2 546–51. If these lines were not interpolated later by some Athenian patriot.

6 *"looked for her high and low"* Plut Thes 8 2–3.

7 *"nicknamed the Sow"* Ibid., 9 1.

"nice-looking" Paus 1 19 1.

8 *collectors of human tribute arrived* I follow the most common version of the famous story of Theseus and the Minotaur. There are variants (see Plut Thes 16–17).

9 *Their queen, Hippolyta* These are the Theseus and Hippolyta in Shakespeare's *A Midsummer Night's Dream*.

down into the underworld Apol E 1 24.

10 *"conceived a wonderful and far-reaching plan"* Plut Thes, 24 1.

11 *"founded a commonwealth"* Ibid., 25 1.

12 *"They are innovators"* Thuc 1 70 2.

2. A STATE OF WAR

Plutarch's life of Lycurgus is the main source, supported by his *Moralia* and Xenophon's *Constitution of Sparta*. Swaddling was used for the ancient Olympic Games.

13 *The Spartan boy was terrified* This story is told in Plutarch's *Moralia* 234a.

14 *"not so high as to be a landmark"* Paus 3 17 1.

There would be an impression Thuc 1 10 2.

"These are our walls!" Plut Mor 210c 29.

a young Spartan was brought up For the section on the upbringing of boys, see Plut Lyc 16 1–18 and Xen Lac 2 1–4.

"of no advantage" Plut Lyc 16 2.

15 *"obey orders"* Ibid., 16 6.

"any boy who is caught" Ibid., 17 4

16 *fearsome rite of passage* Xen Lac 2 9. Pausanias, writing much later, in the

first century A.D., describes a practice of scourging boys so that their blood stains the altar of Artemis Orthia (Pau 3 16 7–11). We are not sure whether this is the same ritual to which Xenophon refers—or perhaps some corrupted version of it laid on for Roman tourists.

"All this education" Xen Lac 2 7.

"The Spartan youths drink" Ath 432f. The poet was Critias of Athens (c. 460–403 B.C.).

17 *Three choirs would perform* Plut Lyc 21 2.

"For a good man to die" Tyrt Poem 10.

"Knowing how to take orders" Plut Mor 212c.

about fifteen The exact number is uncertain.

18 *"Come back with your shield"* Plut Mor 241f. Literally and laconically or "Either with this or on this," "this" being a shield and the command "come back" being understood.

Women in ancient Greece For the section on Spartan women, see mainly Plut Lyc 14–15 and Xen Lac 1 3–10.

19 *forbidden makeup* Clem Alex Paed 2 11.

"and they did not carry on" Plut Lyc 15 5.

"would fill her with noble sperm" Ibid., 15 7.

20 *"I, Cynisca, victorious"* Gr Anth 13 16.

21 *"man-taming,"* Plut Ages 1 2.

22 *"like frogs around a pond"* Plato Phaed 109b.

23 *"we captured Messene"* Tyrt Frag 5 = 4D.

24 *"The Lord of the Silver Bow"* Diod 7 12 6.

"Just like donkeys" Tyrt Frag 6.

"ballast for the ship of state" Plut Lyc 5 7.

25 *"In the daytime they scattered"* Ibid., 28 2–3.

helots were invited to volunteer names Thuc 4 80, Plut Lyc 28 3.

3. The Persian Mule

For the description of Delphi, see Pausanias and Scott. The story of Croesus is told by Herodotus. He is one of the main sources for this chapter together with various Persian inscriptions (itemized below) and Curtis and Tallis.

28 *"The highroad to Delphi"* Paus 1 55 5.

29 "know yourself" Ibid., 10 24 1; Plato Prot 343b and Charm 164d–165a.

34 *"The parapets of the first circle"* Her 1 98 5–6.

34 *"King Ishtumegu"* Nabonidus Chronicle, in Pritchard, p. 305.

35 *Croesus wanted to be sure that Delphi* The stories about Croesus, oracles, and the end of his reign are best taken with a pinch of salt. But they do illustrate the importance of Delphi and how the oracle pervaded Hellenic life.

"hard-shelled tortoise" Her 1 47 2 3.

"Croesus king of the Lydians" Ibid., 1 53 2.

36 *"Wait till a mule"* Ibid., 1 55 2.

never heard of a mule ruling a kingdom In much the same way, Macbeth had never heard of a wood marching about.

37 *"Cyrus, king of Persia"* Nabonidus Chronicle, in Pritchard, p. 305.

38 *Thales of Miletus* Bertrand Russell claimed that "Western philosophy begins with Thales." See Bertrand Russell, *A History of Western Philosophy* (New York: Simon & Schuster, 1945).

argued that the Ionians should unite Her 1 170 3.

"for the Spartans will not tolerate it." Her 1 152 2.

"without fighting or battle" and *"Their faces shone"* Cyrus Cylinder 17 and 18, https://www.britishmuseum.org/research/collection_online/collection _object_details.aspx?objectId-327188&partId-1.aspx.

39 *"perpetual seed of kingship"* For this phrase and the following quotation, Cyrus Cylinder 20–22.

His enraged mother The story is told in Her 1 214 4. There is another version of Cyrus's death that has him survive for three days after having been wounded.

40 *"O man, I am Cyrus"* Strabo 15 3 7.

"Nothing prevents these couriers" Her 8 98.

"the distance from Sardis" Her 5 54 2.

41 *"1:5 [?] quarts of flour supplied"* Persepolis Fortifications Tablets 1285, in Hallock, p. 365.

network of provincial governors This paragraph supposes that Xenophon's account is correct in the *Cyropaedia,* a romanticized biography of the young Cyrus—see Cyr 2 1.

"not to meddle with anything else" Xen Oec 4 9.

42 *a government inspector* This paragraph is based on Xen Cyr 8 6 4.

"I have enabled all the lands" Cyrus Cylinder 36.

"It is no more than fair" Xen Cyr 8 6.

43 *Babylonian deity, Marduk* Cyrus Cylinder 23.

According to Isaiah Isaiah 45 1, 41 4.

As in Zoroastrianism Scholars still sharply disagree about whether the Achaemenids were followers of Zoroaster.

"the man who has respect for that law" Daiva 46–56.

44 *scabbard of Cambyses' sword* Her 3 64 3.

"died his own death" Behistun 1 11.

"When Cambyses slew Bardiya" Ibid., 1 10.

impersonated Bardiya It is possible, some scholars argue, that a substitution ritual was held. According to this, in times of bad omens, a substitute king was temporarily installed, to protect the real king, who went into hiding and reemerged when the omens improved. However, if that is what happened, the fate of the real Bardiya is unexplained. See Waters, p. 75.

"The people feared him" Behistun, 1 13.

45 *"Phraortes, seized, was led to me"* Ibid., 2.13.

46 *"man is by nature"* Arist Pol 1253a2.

"outlaw, without a tribe or a hearth" Ibid. Iliad 9 63.

A city should not be not too small For this paragraph, see ibid., 1326b2 and 1326b11, and Plato Laws 5 737e, 738a.

". . . a little polis *living in good order"* Dio Chrys Disc 36 13.

47 *"It is a disgrace"* Her 5 49 2.

"These ships turned out" Ibid., 5 97 3.

49 *"I understand"* and *"You have levied"* GHI no. 12 = 35F.

4. THE SHAKING-OFF

For the Cylon episode, see Thucydides 1 126 3–12. The main sources are Plutarch's life of Solon and Aristotle's *Constitution of Athens,* 5–12.

53 *"Man's life is a day!"* Pind Pythian 8 95–98. I use Maurice Bowra's version of Pindar's Odes, Penguin Classics, 1982.

54 *"confidence of the people"* Arist Pol 1305a 22–24.

"greatest festival of Zeus" Thuc 1 126 5.

55 *the old temple of Athena* This shrine was destroyed by the Persians in 480. Its successor is the Parthenon, but it was not completed until 438.

56 *"In no way can [he] pray to Zeus"* Hom Il 6 267f.

57 *the Hellenic population* The study of population in the ancient world is a form of higher guesswork. One guiding factor is the number of graves discovered from different periods, but population size is only one explanation of rises and falls. However, there is a scholarly consensus that the population grew at this time even if we cannot say by how much.

"Wealth has mixed up the race" Theog 1 183–90.

58 *"This city is still a city"* Ibid., 1 53–58.

"The poor were enslaved to the rich" Arist Con 2 2.

59 *"The tyrant is set up"* Arist Pol 5 1310b.

Apparently, the death penalty Plut Sol 17 1.

"wrote his laws in blood" Ibid., 17 3. Scholarly opinion is divided on Dracon. Some have asked whether he existed at all. According to Ath Pol 4, he produced a constitution based on the franchise of hoplites, but this is doubted. Most agree that he produced a legal code.

"someone unjustly plundering him" Ins Graec 1³104.

60 *claimed descent from Codrus* For the story of Codrus, Tzet 4–5, 170–99.

financial difficulties This paragraph follows Plut Sol 2 1.

61 *"I am not prepared"* Sol Frag 13.

"owns much silver" Ibid., 24.

"I know, and the pain" Arist Con 5 2.

elected Eponymous Archon, in 594/93 B.C. Dates are uncertain at this time in Athenian history. Some argue for 592/1, and others for twenty years further on. 594/3 seems the likeliest. The sheer quantity of Solon's reforms makes one wonder whether he was allowed to serve for more than one year.

62 *a wolf at bay encircled* Arist Con 12 4.

63 *"Many evil men are rich"* Plut Sol 3 2.

"I have given the masses" Arist Con 12 1.

four economic groups Ibid., 7 3.

64 *the principle of randomness* There are divided opinions about Solon's introduction of sortition for the Archons. Arist Con 8 1 is likely to be right, even if contradicted by Arist Pol 2 1273b–1274a, 3 1281b. Presumably the innovation was repealed by the tyranny; if so, it was reintroduced in 487/6.

65 *a citizen who held back* Plut Sol 20 1.

67 *the lawgiver lost an eye* Ibid., 16 1.

"And if I spared my homeland" Ibid., 14 5.

"I grow old, forever learning" Ibid., 31 3.

lost island of Atlantis Plato Tim 24e–25a, Crit 113a–121c.

"It so accurately fits" Plut Sol 27 1.

69 *"A man to whom I would pay a fortune"* Her 86 4.

"Cyrus learned through interpreters" Ibid., 1 86 6.

"on the knees of the gods" Hom Il 17 514 and elsewhere.

70 *"Have you enacted"* Plut 15 2.

5. FRIEND OF THE POOR

The main sources are Plutarch's life of Solon, Herodotus, and Aristotle's *Constitution of Athens*, 13–17.

72 *"I have come as a herald"* Plut Sol 8 1–3.

"Let us go to Salamis" Diog Laert 1 47.

73 *"Ajax brought twelve warships"* Hom Il 2 557. If the interpolation took place, it has survived in the canonical text, although eyebrows have been raised.

this is not implausible Modern scholars have doubted the story.

"with a boy in the lovely flower of youth" Solon F25, Plut Amat 751b.

74 *"Aren't you pregnant yet?"* Plut Amat 768f.

Achilles is presented as the erastes In other accounts, Patroclus is the *erastes,* and Achilles the *eromenos.*

"And you rejected my holy reverence" Ath 13 601A–B.

in neighboring Boeotia, man and boy Xen Con Spart 2:12.

"Here a man solemnly" IG I³ 1399.

75 *"There is a certain pleasure"* Theog 1345–48.

76 *"I swear by Apollo of Delphi"* Insc Graec XII.3 543.

"Barbax dances well" Ibid., 537.

"great friend of the poor" Plut Sol 29 2.

the aged Solon arrived The historicity of Solon's late appearances has been challenged. There seems to be no solid reason for doubting them.

"You listen to the words of a crafty man" Diod 9 20 3.

77 *"Men of Athens"* Her 1 60 5.

78 *"the silliest idea I have ever heard of"* Ibid., 60 3–5.

79 *"These were people"* Ibid., 1 62 1.

bee-loud Mount Hymettus Hymettus honey is still available in shops today.

"The net has been cast" Her., 1 62 4.

6. CHARIOTEERS OF THE SOUL

The sources for this chapter include Aristotle's *Athenian Constitution* and Herodotus. For the *agora,* see Camp, pp. 32–37. For Harmodius and Aristogeiton, see principally Thucydides 6 56–59 and *Athenian Constitution* 18.

82 *the famous agora of Athens* There may have been an earlier marketplace somewhere else in the city, but if so it has not been found.

83 *"humane, mild and forgiving"* and *"more like a citizen than like a tyrant"* Arist Con 16 2. The policy of Pisistratus recalls that of Augustus, Rome's first emperor, who preserved the forms and offices of the Roman Republic while in fact exercising autocratic power as an open secret. One wonders whether he learned from Pisistratus's example.

He left the constitution and institutions Her 1 59 5.

"Onetorides" IS I³1031a.

84 *step-uncle of the Miltiades* For the account of Miltiades and the Chersonese, see Her 6 35–36.

85 *centuries before the building was completed* The Roman emperor Hadrian brought the project to fruition in the second century A.D.

A hymn to Apollo The quotations come from Hom Hymn Ap 146f and 51–61.

86 *he alone of all the poets* Lyc Leo 102.

87 *"A reminder from Hipparchus"* For both reminders, [Plato] Hipp 229a–b.

men of very different character Arist Con 18 1.

88 *Hipparchus was younger and flightier* Some ancient opinion made Hipparchus the elder of the brothers, but it is more likely that Hippias was.

He sent a state warship For this sentence, see [Plato] Hipp 228c.

"Young man with the girlish looks" Anac 360–63.

"Any man is good" Plato Prot 344e–345a.

"hissless hymn" Bury, p. 204.

Aristogeiton was losing his patience The story of Harmodius and Aristogeiton is told in Arist Con 18, Thuc 6 53–59, and Her 5:55–57.

89 *one of their fellow-conspirators* Much the same thing happened before the assassination of Julius Caesar, when Brutus and Cassius saw a friendly senator chat with the dictator immediately after wishing them and their "project" well.

"died no easy death" Thuc 6 57 4.

91 *"Fine warriors and from good families' "* Arist Con 19 2–3.

The initial contractors failed See Scott, p. 100.

"like eyebrows on a smiling face" Eur Ion 185ff.

92 *"more beautiful than the plan"* Her 5 62 3.

"First of all free Athens" Ibid., 63 1.

Cleomenes was a man For the career of King Cleomenes, see Herodotus books 5 and 6 *passim*.

93 *A pillar was set up* Thuc 6 55 1–2.

94 *"high principles and intelligence"* Ibid., 6 54 5.

"was still governed by the laws" Ibid., 6 54 5–6.

"Athens, which had been great" Her 5 66 1.

7. INVENTING DEMOCRACY

Aristotle's *Athenian Constitution,* 20–22, is a major source for this chapter. Also Herodotus for the main narrative of events.

95 *"A bright light shone"* IG I^3 502.

So reads the inscription The inscription survives, but the statues are gone.

"Darling Harmodius" Ath 695b, Skolion 894 PMG.

97 *"Spartan stranger, go back"* Her 5 72 3.

revolutionary nature of his analysis The career of Cleisthenes bears a curious similarity to that of Soviet president Mikhail Gorbachev, who initiated what he intended to be reforms but were in fact a revolution; and who disappeared from the political scene as soon as his work was done.

Cleisthenes invented democracy One of the great challenges facing the scholar is the paucity of information in the literary sources about most Greek city-states: we are well informed about the constitutional arrangements of Athens and Sparta and to a lesser extent Thebes, but of few others. It may well be that some other unknown reformer brought democracy to his *polis* before its introduction in Athens.

"enlisted the people" Her 5 66 2.

99 *"Let each man come to close quarters"* Tyrt poem 11.

100 *ten life-size bronze statues* See Camp, pp. 157–59.

102 *Pnyx* Ibid., pp. 46–47, 264–65.
"the poor have more power" Arist Pol 1317b.

103 *Bouleuterion* Camp, pp. 44, 127.

104 *Another innovation of Cleisthenes was ostracism* It is uncertain whether this was a project of Cleisthenes or a later development, but the former is probable. What is known is that the first ostracism took place in 487.
"humble and cut back" Plut Arist 7 2.

106 *"archaic rationality"* Murray, p. 279.
"everyone is governed" Arist Pol 1317b.

107 *"Now Athens grew more powerful"* Her 5 78 1.
"This potsherd says" Murray, p. 286.

8. EASTERN RAIDERS

The main source for the Persian raids on Eretria and Athens is Herodotus. He is cited here *passim*.

111 *The young man was tired out* For the story of Pheidippides, see Her 6 105–6.
It was August 5, 490 There is an argument. Some scholars believe that the month of Marathon was September. I prefer August. See Green, *Greco,* p. 31.
Mount Parthenium Paus 8 54 7.

112 *a hallucination caused by exhaustion* Green, *Greco,* p. 31.
"Pheidippides, kindly ask" Paus 6 105 2.
Then nine tents, called "sunshades" Ath 4 141.

113 *"Men of Sparta, the Athenians"* Her 6 106.
"Sir, remember the Athenians" Ibid., 5 105 1–2.

114 *preventing the sale of Ukrainian grain* Green, *Greco,* p. 25.

"After bridging the fish-rich Bosphorus" Her 4 88.

116 *Cleomenes went to Aegina* Ibid., 6 75–84 for the last days of Cleomenes.

117 *"started to mutilate himself"* Ibid., 6 75 2–3.

Marathon was a good place See Green, *Greco,* pp. 30–31, Burn, pp. 242–43, and Wikipedia "Marathon."

118 *In early August 490* The traditional date is September 12. But the battle may have been fought a month earlier, if, as is possible, the Athenian calendar was one month behind that of the Spartan; also, the timing depends on the exact dates of the Spartan festival.

the people were enslaved Her 6 119 1–4.

an army of some 25,000 men Army and navy numbers in Hellenic wars were usually absurdly exaggerated in the ancient sources. Modern approximations are seldom more than good guesses, but they are all we have to go on. It is sometimes possible to judge maxima, based on logistical needs in relation to the terrain crossed by armies.

During daylight hours The Persians would hardly have made the short crossing from Euboea by night. I assume they landed at Marathon around midday and spent the afternoon disembarking. The fire signal had to await darkness for it to be seen and surely identified.

where there was an abundant spring Today's Kato Souli.

120 *The most battle-hardened of these commanders was Miltiades* For the career of Miltiades, see *passim* Her 6 between 39 and 136; and Nep Milt.

121 *appointed by lot* Her 6 109 2.

his fellow-commanders agreed Ibid., 6 110.

122 *"provide themselves with rations"* Arist Rhet 1411a10, Schol to Dem 19 303, and Paus 7 15 7.

The hoplite army entered the plain of Marathon The course of the battle of Marathon is uncertain and different opinions are held. Broadly I follow Burn and Green, *Greco.*

123 *"bronze men"* Her 2 152 3.

As Herodotus points out, the clan Ibid., 6 123–24.

"The cavalry has gone" I follow the reconstruction in Green, *Greco,* p. 35. Hammond in *Cambridge Ancient History* 4, p. 511, suggests that the Persian cavalry were for some reason late coming back from pasturage and so not available for the battle. But they could have turned up at any moment. I prefer the proposition that most of the cavalry had been loaded onto the ships and were definitively gone.

124 *"having got the upper hand"* Her 6 113 2.

125 *the services of Pheidippides* A late source identifies him, and has him col-

lapse and die after running the twenty-five or so miles from Marathon to Athens (Lucian in his *True History*). We do not need to believe this legend. But it was from this story that today's marathon race is derived.

126 *the defeat was of little or no strategic consequence* A poem by Robert Graves, "The Persian Version," sums it up neatly. Its opening lines read: "Truth-loving Persians do not dwell upon/The trivial skirmish fought near Marathon."

"those who died in the cause" IG 11² 1006 line 26.

given them a proper burial Paus 1 32 4.

a German visitor Camp, p. 47.

"to Apollo first fruits" Meiggs and Lewis, 19L.

Miltiades is given pride of place Nep Milt 6.

127 *"are coming to grips with the barbarians"* Paus 1 15 4.

"The entrance to this cave" Ibid., 1 32 7.

The cave has been rediscovered in modern times Eran Lupu, "The Sacred Law from the Cave of Pan at Marathon," *Zeitschrift für Papyrologie und Epigraphik,* Bd. 137 (2001), pp. 119–24, Bonn.

128 *"I am goat-footed Pan"* Simonides Ep 5 (Planudean Anthology).

9. Fox as Hedgehog

Herodotus tells the famous story of the Persian invasion, with help from Diodorus Siculus and Plutarch's lives of Themistocles and Aristides.

129 *a walk along the beach* Plut Them 2 6. Ancient stories about the early years of famous people seek to please. Plutarch's accounts of the childhood and youth of Themistocles are not especially flattering and, even if fictional or "written up," give a sharp and convincing picture of his complicated character.

"man of no particular mark" Ibid., 1 1.

"impetuous, naturally quick-witted" Ibid., 2 1.

130 *"pleasing accomplishments"* Ibid., 2 2.

"The wildest colts" Ibid., 2 5.

131 *portrait of the man in stone* An apparently accurate Roman copy of a Greek original portrait Herm was discovered in Ostia in 1939.

"was wrapped up in his own thoughts" Plut Them 3–4.

132 *"make war on the islands"* Nep Milt 7.

"make them all rich" Her 6 132.

133 *he should oil his body* Plut Them 3 4.

"The announcement of these orders" Her 7 1 1–3.

134 *"This is the stone statue"* *Cambridge Ancient History* 4, p. 263. National Museum of Iran.

"What is right, that is my desire" DNb 8b (11–5).

The small boy crawled The account here of the mines at Laurium is drawn from Green, *Greco,* pp. 53–55, and French, p. 78. Tunnels have been excavated by archaeologists. Child labor is deduced from their size.

135 *"since time immemorial"* Xen Vect 4 2.

"The fox knows many things" Zenobius 5 68.

137 *the seat of government should be moved* Thuc 1 93 7.

"deprived the Athenians of the spear" Plato Laws 4 706. Also Plut Them 4 3.

"fountain of silver" Aesch Pers 238.

138 *two hundred triremes* Her 7 144. Plut Them 4 2 and Arist Ath Pol 22 7 say "one hundred," but the higher figure was reached by the time of the Persian invasion.

The trireme ("triple-rower") For more on this warship, see Morrison, Coates, and Rankov.

glorified racing eight W. W. Tarn, *Hellenistic Military and Naval Developments* (Cambridge: Cambridge University Press, 1930), p. 124.

139 *a daily rate of one drachma* This seems to have been the going wage at the end of the fifth century.

140 *He made a point of refusing* The two anecdotes in this paragraph can be found in Plut Arist 4 1–2.

Stesilaus of the island of Ceos Ibid., 2 2–3.

141 *the weapon of ostracism* Arist Ath Pol 22.

142 *treasure trove of more than eleven thousand* ostraca Burn, p. 605.

"'Athens, the mighty city!'" Pindar Pyth 7 1–5 and 15.

an illiterate farm worker Plut Arist 7 5–6.

10. INVASION

Herodotus is the primary source, with support from Plutarch's lives of Themistocles and Aristides; also from Diodorus Siculus.

144 *a magnificent plane tree* Her 7 31 and Ael 2 14.

gardening before dinner Xen Oec 4 20–25.

145 *"Europe is a very beautiful place"* Her 7 5 3.

146 *generous donor to the Achaemenid cause* Ibid., 7 38–39.

The procession of men Ibid., 40–41 and 83.

the Immortals This is the term Herodotus gives. He may have confused the Persian for "companion" with that for "immortal." There is no reason to disbelieve the recruitment policy given.

147 *absurdly inflated numbers* I rely on the discussion at Green, *Greco,* pp. 58–61, which itself is indebted to Burn, pp. 326–32.

Xerxes assembled 1,700,000 For Herodotus's calculations, see Her, 7 184–87.

eunuchs, female cooks, concubines Her 7 187 1.

"What body of water" Ibid., 7 21.

148 *So far as the fleet was concerned* Ibid., 7 89–99.

149 *unhinged rage* Ibid., 7 35.

legendary young Leander He still lives in Christopher Marlowe's poem *Hero and Leander.*

review of his land and sea forces Her 7 44–49.

Xerxes congratulated himself Ibid., 7 45–53 for the conversation between the Great King and his uncle.

150 *"You are doomed. Why sit around?"* Ibid., 7 140 1–3.

151 *"Zeus the all-seeing"* and *"O divine Salamis"* Ibid., 7 141 3. It is unclear whether there were two separate trips to Delphi to consult the oracle and if there were whether they took place in 481 or 480. I opt for one trip and 481, and believe that the debate in the *ecclesia* about evacuating Attica was held in 480. But these are best guesses.

153 *heavier and less maneuverable* Ibid., 8 10 and 60a.

"The greatest of all his achievements" Plut Them 6 3.

155 *"They considered the survival of Hellas"* Her 8 3 1.

Eurybiades was in charge Ibid., 8 2, Diod 11 12 4.

The sacred snake Her 8 41 2–3.

156 *"The god [Apollo] had spoken"* Bury, p. 246.

157 *"After their deliberations about the oracle"* Her, 7 144 3.

"guarding the possessions of the gods'" and *"starting tomorrow"* Meiggs and Lewis, p. 23. In 1959 an inscription purporting to be the Decree of Themistocles was discovered at Troezen. It was inscribed in the third or possibly late fourth centuries B.C. and some scholars think it is an untrustworthy fake. More probably it is a pulling together of authentic decisions taken in 480 and announced by the *ecclesia.*

Dogs howled Ael Ar 46 p. 257 DK.

158 *his hound plunged* Plut Them 10 6.

"what the city now needed" Plut Cim 5 2–3.

a few obstinate old men Paus 1 18 2.

159 *"So tell me," Xerxes asked him* For this conversation, see Her 7 103–4. If it is fictional, we may suppose that it broadly expresses Persian attitudes.

11. "The Acts of Idiots"

Again, the classic stories of the battles of Artemisium and Thermopylae are mainly as told by Herodotus 7 175-8 1–21 and 7 200–233. Diodorus Siculus supports.

160 *strange smell* See Green, *Greco,* p. 114.
hot, sulfurous springs Her 7 176.
"The bluest water" Paus 4 35 9.

161 *"man much concerned with his courage"* Diod 11 4 2.
a force of four thousand men I follow Burn, pp. 378–79, in his interpretation of Herodotus's numbers.

162 *sunken ship* The shipwreck may have been Roman—perhaps carrying loot from the sack of Corinth in 146 B.C. The statue dates from about 460 B.C.

163 *lost "at the lowest estimate"* Her 7 190.
stripped naked for exercise Ibid., 7 208 2.
"The truth, namely" Ibid., 7 209 1.

164 *"Hand over your weapons!"* Plut Sayings Spartans Leonidas 11.

165 *"Have a quick breakfast"* Ibid., 8 2, Diod 11 9 4.
"Many of the barbarians fell" Her 7 223 3–224 1.

166 *Eurybiades lost his nerve* Ibid., 8 4.

169 *fight on purpose like cowards* Her 8 222.

170 *"They learned from their own achievements"* Plut Them 8 1–2.

12. "O Divine Salamis"

Herodotus is the main source; also Plutarch's lives of Aristides and Themistocles. For the battles of Salamis and Plataea, I rely on Burn and Green, *Greco.*

171 *oracle at Delphi* Her 8 27–39, Diod 11 14.

172 *The news was received* Her 8 99 1.

173 *Xerxes paid it a personal visit* Ibid., 8 67–69.
"The Greeks will not be able to hold out" Ibid., 8 68 2.

174 *A very similar debate, in reverse* For the discussions that follow, ibid., 8 49–50, 56–63.
"If you do not remain here" Ibid., 8 62 1.

175 *A day passed* The passage of time is unclear in the sources and some modern scholars argue that as many as three weeks of inactivity followed the Persians' arrival before the Battle of Salamis was fought.
"I have been sent" Her 8 75 2–3.

177 *The narrows of Salamis describe a semicircle* There is scholarly disagreement

on where various place-names should be located. The ancient sources are confused about the course of the battle. My reconstruction is indebted to Burn and Green, *Greco,* but its basic narrative follows N. G. L. Hammond in *Cambridge Ancient History,* 5 pp. 569–88, although I do not agree with him that Psyttaleia is Saint George island but, rather, today's Lipsokoutali.

a golden parasol Plut Them 16 2.

179 *"Then from the Hellene ships"* Aesch Pers 386–400.

180 *plucky Artemisia* Her 8 87–88.

181 *"My men have become women"* Ibid., 8 88 3.
"The Hellenes seized" Aesch Pers 424–26.
the Phoenician contingent See Burn, pp. 467–68.

183 *the sacred chariot* Her 8 115 4.

184 *oath of fidelity* See Burn, p. 512ff. Diod 11 29 1–2, Tod 2 204 lines 21–51. The exact wording may not have come down to us, but the event is authentic. It is known as the Oath of Plataea.

185 *Modern archaeologists* For an account of the destruction of Athens, see Camp, pp. 57–58.

186 *"It was worth seeing"* Her 9 25 1.

187 *omens stayed resolutely unfavorable* Plut Arist 17 6–18 2. Some modern scholars believe that Pausanias manipulated the sacrifices to ensure that the Greeks, or at least the Spartans, attacked at just the right moment. But Greeks took their religion very seriously and barefaced trickery of this kind in public is unlikely.

188 *Hellenic losses amounted to a modest 1,360* According to Plut Arist 19 4. A plausible number.

189 *"spread out through the whole camp"* Her 9 80 1–2.
"That is an act" Ibid., 9 79 1–2.
"What a fool Mardonius was" Ibid., 9 82 3.
with his 110 ships One source says that the fleet now numbered 250 ships. If so it could be that the Athenians sent their triremes to join the allies at Delos after the Spartans had begun their march to Plataea.

190 *"to deliver the Ionians from slavery"* Ibid., 9 90 2.
"remember freedom first and foremost" Ibid., 9 98 3.
a chain of beacons This after all is how the news of the fall of Troy is conveyed in Aeschylus's drama *Agamemnon,* first performed in Athens in 458.

191 *the unarmed Samians and other Ionians* Diod 11 36 4–5.
a state of shock Ibid., 11 36 7.

192 *"The Athenian people"* Thuc 1 89 3.

193 *"attached the city to the Piraeus"* Plut Them 19 3.

    "I will not rebuild" Lyc 81. Some modern scholars do not accept this citation as historical, but it is certain that the Athenians did not rebuild the temples and shrines for a generation after the Persian Wars.

13. LEAGUE OF NATIONS

The literary sources dwindle with the creation of the Athenian Empire. Herodotus has finished, Thucydides takes over with his abrupt summary of the next half century, the so-called Pentakontaetia. Plutarch's life of Cimon helps, as do a growing number of administrative inscriptions. An explosion in the number of these inscriptions throws light on the workings of the Athenian democracy.

197 *"Go tell the Spartans"* Her 7 228 2.

198 *the head and torso of a Greek warrior* The excavation was conducted in 1920 by the British Archaeological School.

    "Did not forget their courage" Dillon and Garland, 11:48 (Simonides Elegy 11).

    Serpent Column Meiggs and Lewis 27. The Roman emperor Constantine took the column from Delphi and installed it in the courtyard of the Hagia Sophia at Constantinople. It was later moved to the Hippodrome, now a public square, where, albeit damaged, it survives to the present day.

    "If the greatest part of virtue" Sim Ep 8.

199 *a statue of himself* A good Roman copy has been found at Ostia.

200 *"can't stand Themistocles"* Plut Them 21 2–3.

    Themistocles felt for himself the ingratitude Successful war leaders are often discarded by ungrateful democracies—for example, Lloyd George and Winston Churchill.

    various scratched opinions Forsdyke, p. 155.

    Pausanias, the victor of Plataea His downfall and death are recounted in Thuc 1 128–34.

201 *killed a Byzantine woman* Plut Cim 6 4–5.

203 *Themistocles became entangled* The story of his escape to Persia and death are told in greater detail in Plut Them 24–32 and Thuc 1 136–38.

    "secret hoards" Thuc 1 137 3.

    his father had been assassinated This is my interpretation of the odd account in Arist Pol 1311b36. For a different version, see Diod 11 69.

204 *"For the past you owe me a good turn"* Thuc 1 137 4.

205 *"A man who showed the most unmistakable signs of genius"* Ibid., 1 138 3.

206 *"there you look down"* Plut Them 32 5.

207 *"to stay at home"* Plut Cim 11 2.

"the quality which makes a real general" and *"suited a money-box"* Plut Arist 24 4.

208 *"the Athenian people are thought to act"* Xen Con 1 16.

209 *"He earned himself a bad name"* Plut Cim 4 3–4.

210 *"Plain and unadorned"* Ibid., 4 4.

he transformed . . . the Academy Ibid., 13 8.

a handsome colonnade For this paragraph see Camp, pp. 68–69. The Stoa and four of its paintings were seen six hundred years later by Pausanias.

"He was not such a scoundrel" Plut Cim 15 3.

the chief reasons for these defections Thuc 1 99 1.

211 *"This was the first time"* Ibid., 1 98 4.

212 *"not a single Persian soldier"* Plut Cim 12 1.

Cimon sailed out For the battle of the Eurymedon, see Diod 11 60 5–6.

213 *"These men lost the splendour"* Sim Ep 46.

Theseus, the national hero of Athens For the story of the discovery of Theseus's bones, Plut Thes 36 1–4 and Plut Cim 8 3–6.

214 *"no sense of shame"* Thuc 1 5 1.

215 *"And now he lies buried"* Plut Thes 36 2.

14. THE FALLING-OUT

The main sources are Thucydides and Plutarch's lives of Pericles and Cimon, with help from Diodorus Siculus and, regarding constitutional reforms, *Athenian Constitution*. See Barnes for pre-Socratic philosophers discussed below.

216 *a series of tremendous earthquakes* We have no firm dates and scholars place the earthquakes at different times during the decade. I follow *Cambridge Ancient History* 5, p. 108.

Some young men and boys Plut Cim 16 5.

twenty thousand deaths according to one source Diod 11 63 1.

"all the ephebes" Plut Cim 16 4–5.

217 *"when Pericleidas the Spartan came here"* Ar Lys 1137–40.

"put Sparta's interests" Plut Cim 16 8.

persuaded the assembly to send out an expeditionary force It is possible that there were two Athenian expeditions—ibid., 16 8.

four thousand hoplites Ar Lys 1143.

"grew afraid of the enterprise" Thuc 1 102 3.

218 *"I am not, like some Athenians"* Plut Cim 14 3.

"On a slight pretext" Ibid., 17 3.

219 *"Let Cimon take his sister"* Unpublished: see *Oxford Classical Dictionary* under Cimon.

the lost leader was soon forgiven Plut Cim 17 5.

he was lucky to have survived The account given here of Pericles' education is indebted to Garland, pp. 58, 61–63, 102–4, 172.

221 *"played the role of masseur"* Plut Per 4 1.

"His was a tongue" Ibid., 4 3. Timon of Phlius was the commentator.

222 *"About the gods"* DK80b4.

"man is the measure" DK80b1.

an eclipse of the sun Per 35 1–2.

223 *self-preservation and ambition* Ibid., 7 3.

224 *"Elpinice, you are too old"* Ibid., 10 5.

225 *Ephialtes was kidnapped one night and murdered* Diod 11 77 6.

a certain Aristodicus Plut Per 10 7.

"poisonous accusation" Ibid., 10 6.

a citizenship law Arist Con 26 3.

226 *two obols a day* Some say it was one obol a day.

227 *up to twenty thousand citizens . . . were in receipt* Hammond, p. 301. Arist Con 24 3.

"The poor, the men of the people" Xen Con 1 4. This document was probably written in the 420s and so too early for Xenophon. Its author has received the modern nickname of the Old Oligarch.

"everywhere on earth" Ibid., 1 5.

228 *A broken inscription survives* Fornara, p. 78.

230 *many Athenians escaped* For the Egyptian expedition, Thuc 1 104, 109–10.

232 *"From the time when the sea"* Sim Ep 45 1–4.

Peace of Callias Some dispute that the peace was ever agreed, but see Isoc Pan 117–18 and Plut Cim 13 4–5.

234 *a Panhellenic congress* Plut Per 17.

15. The Kindly Ones

Aeschylus's *Oresteia* is the main source (I am indebted to Philip Vellacott's translation, Penguin Classics, London, 1959). Also Connolly and Dodge's *The Ancient City* and Garland's *Daily Life of the Ancient Greeks*. See Hall as well as Goldhill for a full account of Greek tragedy.

235 *A watchman stands on the roof* This opening section derives from Aesch Ag 1–39.

237 *"tragedy, then, is an action"* Arist Poet 3 4–8, 3 13 21–25, 28–30.

238 *performed only once* In the fourth century the quality of new tragedies declined in step with a loss of political energy in the Athenian polity. Revivals of the classics became popular.

239 *Athens spent more on theater* Plut Pre 349a.

as many as 1,500 persons were involved Garland, p. 182.

"Lysicrates, son of Lysitheides" Camp, p. 147.

241 "slices from the great banquet" Ath 8 347e.

"ships and ropes rotted" Aesch Ag 194–95.

"harness of necessity" Ibid., 218.

he that's coming must be provided for Lady Macbeth in Macbeth, 1 5 71–72.

242 "As our guest, call this your home" Aesch Cho 707.

"Oh misery!" Ibid., 691.

"How shall I escape my father's curse" Ibid., 925.

243 "The old is trampled by the new!" Aesch Eum 778–79.

"Share my home with me" Ibid., 833.

"provoke bloodshed" Ibid., 856–63.

244 During the opening ceremony See Goldhill, pp. 101–2.

the names of men Ibid., p. 104.

245 "Since this is how matters have turned out" Aesch Eum, 481–88.

"Never let civil war, which eats men" Ibid., 979–84.

246 "ancient children" Ibid., 1034.

16. "Crowned with Violets"

Plutarch's life of Pericles, Diodorus Siculus, and Thucydides are the main sources. Also Garland, Camp, and the findings of archaeologists.

247 "On one street" Plut Per 7 4.

248 "harmonised with his way of life" Plut Per 8 1.

"that eyesore" and "war rushing down" Ibid., 8 5.

249 nicknamed the Olympian Ibid., 8 2–3.

"the Athenians were under no obligation" Ibid., 12 3.

A decree was passed in 448 Some scholars believe the bill was passed into law in the 430s or 426/5, but I follow mainstream opinion.

250 "In this way he relieved" Plut Per, 11 5.

"the size of the Athenian forces" Ibid., 20 1.

251 the guilty polis was the island of Samos The Samian revolt is described in Thuc 1 115 1–117 3 and Plut Per 24 1–28 6.

the building of an aqueduct The aqueduct can still be seen and is now part of a UNESCO World Heritage Site, the Pythagoreion.

253 Plutarch mentions a report Plut Per 281–83.

within an inch of depriving Athens Thuc 8 76 4.

"as if the spring had been taken" Arist Rhet 1365a 34.

A sentry runs to the ruler This section describes the plot of Sophocles' tragedy Antigone. I am indebted to the translation by E. F. Watling, Penguin Classics, Harmondsworth, 1947.

254 *"Wonders are many on the earth"* Soph Ant 332ff.

255 *"And yet you dared to contravene it?"* Ibid., 449–55.

    the beautiful Aspasia The section on Aspasia is indebted to Bicknell, who argues that Axiochus, the father of Aspasia, was the same man as the father-in-law of the elder Alcibiades, and so grandfather of Axiochus, son of the elder Alcibiades.

256 *"From her comes all the race"* Hes Theo 590–95. The translation is by Dorothea Wender, Penguin Classics, Harmondsworth, 1972.

257 *met her lover at a funeral* Lys 1 8.

    "your duty is to stay indoors" Xen Oec 7 36.

258 *"Perhaps I should say a few words"* Thuc 2 45 2.

    "We have hetairae*"* Dem Neaira 122.

259 *Plato has Socrates hint* Plato Alc 1 118d-e.

    "To find our Zeus a Hera" Plut Per 24 6. I am grateful to the late Ian Scott-Kilvert for his translation of this verse.

    madam of a brothel Ibid., 24 3.

    procured free-born Athenian women Ibid., 32 1.

260 *"great art and power"* Ibid., 24 1.

    "Yesterday I heard Aspasia" Plato Men 236b.

261 *"regarding his beauty"* Plut Alc 1 3.

262 *Once as a small boy* Ibid., 2 2–3. Childhood tales about the famous are rightly distrusted. But this incident of the knucklebones has the ring of truth and casts anticipatory and accurate light on the character of the adult Alcibiades.

    "Leave the flute to the Thebans" Ibid., 2 5.

    "Alcibiades, you bite like a woman" Ibid., 2 2.

    "If he's dead" Ibid., 2 3.

    "I'm trying to work out" Diod 12 38 3 and Plut Alc 7 2.

    Socrates took Alcibiades under his wing For Socrates' relations with Alcibiades, see Plut Alc 6.

263 *the time of the Great Panathenaea* For this festival, see Burkert, pp. 232–33, Connolly and Dodge, pp. 80–87.

265 *not to rebuild* Diod 11 29 3.

    Athena Promachus The statue had a long life. After one thousand years on the Acropolis, it was removed to Constantinople, capital of the Eastern Roman Empire. It was eventually destroyed in A.D. 1203 by a superstitious and frightened mob that believed the goddess was beckoning to an army of crusaders who were threatening the city.

266 *"The Greeks must be outraged"* Plut Per 12 2.

"entertaining the people" Ibid., 11 4.

Pheidias was placed in overall charge Ibid., 13 4.

"The materials to be used" Ibid., 12 6–7.

267 *"To Praxias, resident at Melite"* Overbeck, p. 860.

268 *because of the dry atmosphere* Pau 5 11 10.

all kinds of trophy Fornara 141.

269 *"eight and a half boxes"* IG I³ 343–46, 350–59.

a new monumental entrance The Brandenburg Gate in Berlin copies the central portion of the Propylaea.

tended by a priestess IG I³ 35 9–10.

in honor of Hephaestus Miscalled for many centuries the Theseum, after Theseus, the mythical founder-king of Athens.

temple of Poseidon Among the names that vandals carved on the temple at Sunium we find that of Lord Byron.

270 *The exact total expenditure* The financial estimates in this section derive from Davies, pp. 94–99.

"Mighty indeed are the marks" Thuc 2 41 4.

271 *"Brightly shining"* Pind Fragments 76.

17. THE PRISONERS ON THE ISLAND

Thucydides (books 2 to 5) comes into his own in this chapter, and is the main and very reliable source of the first half of the Peloponnesian War. Also Plutarch's lives of Pericles and Nicias, the comical take on topical events of Aristophanes, and Diodorus Siculus.

275 *"for the violence of his character"* Thuc 3 36 6.

276 *"more than anyone else he corrupted"* Arist Con 28 3.

a series of prosecutions The details and indeed the dates of these cases are uncertain, but it does appear that an attempt was made to weaken Pericles.

one of the sculptors working for Pheidias Plut Per 31 2–5 and Paus 5 15 1.

Pheidias's workshop Princeton Encyclopedia of Classical Sites, p. 648.

They attacked Aspasia Plut Per 32 1.

277 *"anyone who did not believe in the gods"* Ibid., 32 1.

the scientist Anaxagoras There are different stories. See Plut Per 32 1–2 and Diog Laer 2 3 12–13. I propose a probable version.

"succeeded in placing the empire" Thuc 1 118 2.

278 *"for sundry purposes"* Plut Per 23 1.

279 *"If they bide their time"* Thuc 2 65 7.

Epidamnus was a place of no importance See Peter R. Prifti, "Hellenic Colonies in Ancient Albania," *Archaeology,* Archaeological Institute of America, vol. 39, no. 4 (July/August 1986), pp. 26–31. Later, Epidamnus was the setting for the Roman author Plautus's comedy *Menaechmi*, the inspiration for Shakespeare's *The Comedy of Errors.*

the greatest military conflagration Thucydides rather over-egged his cake when he claimed that the war between Athens and Sparta was the greatest disturbance in the history of Greece—"indeed I might almost say or mankind" (1 1 2). It was his history that has made history, rather than the event itself.

280 *the headland of Actium* A more famous sea battle was fought at Actium in 31 B.C. when Octavian and Agrippa defeated Antony and Cleopatra.

283 *"Before anything could happen to him"* Ar Pe 606–14.
they sent to Delphi Thuc 1 118 3.
"We have done nothing" Ibid., 1 76 2.

284 *"Others may have a lot of money"* Ibid., 1 86 3.
"Most Athenians still lived in the country" Ibid., 2 16 1.

285 *"You will get no glory"* Ibid., 3 59 1.
about sixty thousand heavy infantry into Attica Plut Per 33 4.

286 *"a general discussion resulted"* Thuc 2 22 1.
On a winter's day every year This section is indebted to Thuc 2 33–46.
oration in praise of the fallen We do not know how close Thucydides' version is to what Pericles actually said. But they cannot have been far apart. One of Thucydides' devices is to give historical personages speeches that raised relevant issues even if these had not in reality been mentioned by the speaker himself. However, Pericles' Funeral Speech was so important a text and so many people, probably including Thucydides himself, would remember having heard it that the historian must have taken care not to stray far from the statesman's own words.

287 *"When it is a question"* Thuc 2 37 1–2.
"We are lovers of beauty" Ibid., 2 40 1.
"I declare that our city" Ibid., 2 41 12.
"Think of the greatness of Athens" Ibid., 2 43 1.
"Perfectly healthy men" Ibid., 2 49 1–4.

288 *suddenly began to have burning feelings* Ibid., 2 49 2–3.
"Nothing did the Athenians so much harm" Ibid., 3 87 2.
"It was the one thing I didn't predict" Ibid., 2 64 1.

289 *Aristotle wrote in his study* Arist Po 16 29ff.
"Beyond all telling" Soph Oed 179ff.
"War with the Dorians" Thuc 2 54 2.

290 *He became depressed* Plut Per 37 1.

"*as is the way with crowds*" Ibid., 2 65 4.

"*Your empire*" Thuc 2 63 2.

291 "*Being powerful because of his rank*" Ibid., 2 65 8–11.

293 "*War is a stern master*" Ibid., 3 82 2.

294 "*persuaded about fifty of them*" Ibid., 3 81 2–3.

"*kill themselves by thrusting into their throats*" Ibid., 4 48 3.

"*In theory the crime was*" Ibid., 3 81 4–5.

295 "*Reckless aggression was now regarded*" Ibid., 3 82 4–5.

296 "*right to act as it saw fit*" Ibid., 3 28 1.

"*the most violent of its citizens*" Ibid., 3 36 6.

297 "*By giving way to your feelings*" Ibid., 3 37 2.

"*The right way to deal with free people*" Ibid., 3 46 6.

298 "*Mytilene had had a narrow escape*" Ibid., 3 49 4.

all the adult males of Scione Ibid., 5 32 1.

Perhaps to remind the world I am obliged to Kagan, *Peloponnesian,* p. 203, for the suggestion.

"*A starving wolf*" Perry Index 346.

299 "*a living piece of property*" Arist Pol 1253b23.

anonymous author Modern scholars have named him the Old Oligarch.

"*allowed to take the greatest liberties*" Xen Con 1 10.

"*get a house, a bought woman*" Hes Works 405f.

300 *An auction sale list* IG 1³ 421, col. 1.

"*it is contrary to nature*" Arist Pol 1253bl4.

301 *a magnificent natural harbor* Today's Navarino Bay.

"*make what use he liked*" Thuc 4 2 4.

304 "*I'll shout down*" Ar Kni 358.

"*He's the best of citizens*" Plut Nic 4 6.

"*If only our generals were real men*" Thuc 4 27 1.

305 *Some captured shields were sent back* ASCSA Agora Object B 62.

They were still on show in the second century Pau 1 15 4.

"*Nothing that had happened*" Thuc 4 40 1.

306 "*For everyone that's here*" Ari Kni—Sommerstein, p. 73.

two thousand able and troublesome helots Thuc 4 80 3–4.

"*He quietly observed the movements*" Plat Symp 221b. This quotation is taken from Plato's *Symposium,* which makes no claim to historical accuracy, but rather to imaginative verisimilitude. The anecdote, well known in the retelling and easily checked by contemporaries, is surely true.

rode alongside Socrates Plut Alc 7 4.

18. The Man Who Knew Nothing

Plato's *Symposium,* cited *passim,* is a main source (usually, but not always in the translation of Walter Hamilton, Penguin Books, Harmondsworth, England, 1951), and secondarily Xenophon's *Symposium* and *Memorabilia.*

310 *"Kissing Agathon"* Gr Anth 5 78.

311 *"As you sip your wine"* Cited in Garland, p. 94. I am indebted to Professor Garland for information about food and drink in ancient Greece.

313 *"Let us entertain ourselves today"* Plato Symp 177D.

314 *"used all their eight limbs"* Ibid., 190A.
     "They will walk upright" Ibid., 190D.
     "love is simply the name" Ibid., 192E.

315 *"I am walking on air"* Ar Clo 225.
     "The Clouds are the only goddesses" Ibid., 365–67.

317 *"Both Homer and Hesiod"* Xenophanes, DK 22 B 12.
     "permanent entity was water" Arist Met 1 983b.
     "applied themselves to mathematics" Ibid., 1 985b.

318 *"You cannot step"* Fragment DK 22 B 12, quoted in Arius Didymus apud Eusebius, Preparatio Evangelica 15:20:2.
     "The barley drink" DK 22 B 125, quoted in Theophrastus On Vertigo 9.
     "The bit I understand is excellent" Diog Laer 2 5 22.
     "is generated from fire" Ibid., 9 1 8.
     Socrates, as he really was It is hard to know what Socrates was like and what he believed. Plato and Xenophon, our two sources, give inconsistent accounts, which probably reflect how their very different personalities interacted with Socrates, rather than factual disagreements. Plato's early dialogues probably throw the brightest light on their "cool, distant, reticent and ironic" (*Oxford Classical Dictionary,* p. 1419) subject.

319 *"The unexamined life is not worth living"* Plato Apol 38a.

320 *One day Socrates came across him* Diog Laer 2 6 48.
     "Socrates was always in the public eye" Xen Mem 1 1 10.
     a shoemaker called Simon Sellars, pp. 207ff.

321 *Unlike Gorgias, who claimed to know everything* Plat Gorg 447d.

322 *"is the perpetual possession"* Plato Symp 206A.
     "bringing forth such notions" Ibid., 210c.
     "By gazing upon the vast ocean" Ibid., 210d.
     "a beauty whose nature is marvelous" Ibid., 211a–b.

323 *Men have been kept as captives* Plato Rep 514a–520a for the allegory of the cave.

324 *wore his hair long* Ath 12 534C.

"Good evening gentlemen" Plato Symp 212e–213b.

"If I compliment anyone but him" Ibid., 214d.

"mass of imperfections" Ibid., 216a.

19. DOWNFALL

Thucydides (books 6 and 7) remains the main source for the war, supplemented by Diodorus Siculus. Towards the end he hands over the baton to Xenophon's much less adequate *Hellenica*. Plutarch also continues the life stories of Alcibiades and Nicias.

326 *At dawn on a fine June day* The description of the fleet's departure is taken from Thuc 6 30–32 and Diod 13 3.

327 *"This expedition . . . was by far and away"* Thuc 6 31 2.

"Now we can wank and sing" Ar Pe 289–90.

328 *"The Spartans have not kept their oaths"* Sommerstein, p. 230.

330 *a celebratory ode* Plut Alc 11 2.

"The Hellenes expected to see our city" Thuc 6 16 2 and 3.

He married well The story of Alcibiades' marriage and alleged plan to kill Callias is told in Ando Alc 4 13–15 and Plut Alc. Some argue that the Andocides speech is a forgery, but see Raubitschek. Even if it is spurious it contains truths. Such accounts, which place Alcibiades in a poor light, are not improbable and are consistent with what we know of his public career.

331 *A third-century poet wittily remarked* Bion, c. 325–c. 250. See Diog Laer 4 49.

Divorce seems to have been uncommon See Cohn-Haft.

Venus de Milo The statue is to be found today in the Louvre museum in Paris.

a debate between spokesmen Thuc 5 84–116.

"It is a necessary law of nature" Ibid., 5 105 2.

332 *"Dear, lifeless lips"* Eur Troj 1180–85. I use Philip Vellacott's translation, *Euripides, The Bacchae and Other Plays,* Penguin Classics, Harmondsworth, 1954.

an execrable poet Ar Frogs 86ff.

333 *"to conquer the whole of the island"* Thuc 6 6 1.

"Cleon in hyperbole" Bury, p. 459.

334 *"no great expectation"* Plut Alc 17 4. See also Plut Nic 13 6.

Scattered throughout Athens stood Herms Rubel, pp. 74–99.

335 *"exaggerated the whole thing"* Thuc 6 28 2.

336 *A contemporary who later admitted to having played a part* Ando Alc 16. The man was Andocides. His testimony must be treated with caution, for he

was defending himself years later in a courtroom speech. But there is little doubt that he is voicing here widespread fears. The real perpetrators of the defacement of the Herms and the mock Mysteries were never identified beyond doubt.

336 *Lamachus, an elderly man* Plut Alc 18 1.

337 *"Thessalus, the son of Cimon"* Ibid., 22 3.

338 *"six perfume bottles"* IG I³ 421h.
   "I'll show them that I am still alive" Plut Alc 22 2.
   "I will render you services" Ibid., 23 1.
   "when they saw him" Ibid., 23 3.

339 *resold into servitude at rock-bottom prices* Hell Ox 17 4.
   "Every single thing the city needed" Thuc 7 28 1–2.

340 *"kept on sitting around"* Plut Nic 14 4.
   "The Syracusans no longer thought" Thuc 6 103 3.

341 *"We thought we were the besiegers"* Ibid., 7 11 4.

342 *"The flash of armor"* Plut Nic 21 1–2.

343 *"After once being thrown"* Thuc 7 44 8.

344 *two and a half thousand Athenian infantry* Diod 13 11 3–5.
   "It is better for Athens" Thuc 7 47 4.

345 *Herodotus reports that Thales* Her 1 74 2.
   "rather over-inclined to divination" Thuc 7 50 4.
   "three times nine days" Ibid., 7 50 4.
   "was not unfavourable" Plut Nic 23 5.

346 *"To conquer the Athenians by land and by sea"* Thuc 7 56 2.

347 *"The two armies on the shore"* Ibid., 7 71 1 and 4.

349 *"forced to do everything"* Ibid., 7 87 2.

350 *people did not believe* Ibid., 8 1 1.

351 *"This was the greatest achievement"* Ibid., 7 87 5–6.

20. THE END OF DEMOCRACY?

Thucydides' history came to an abrupt end in 411 (presumably on his death). In his *Hellenica* Xenophon picks up where he leaves off and narrates events until 362. Diodorus is a not entirely reliable backup. *The Athenian Constitution* helps with constitutional developments. Plutarch's life of Alcibiades runs its course and is superseded by his life of Lysander.

353 *"Ships gone, Mindarus dead"* Xen Hell 1 1 23.

354 *"'Men of Athens'"* Diod 13 52 3ff. Xenophon does not mention this peace initiative, but there is no reason to doubt Diodorus.
   first reaction of the Athenians Thuc 8 1–2.

355 *"As is the way with democracies"* Ibid., 8 1 4.
    "new policy of justness" Hel Oxy Florence Fragments V2.
    always had a bad conscience Thuc 7 18 3.

356 *"the overthrow of the Athenians"* Ibid., 8 2 4.
    "enjoy great wealth" Diod 11 50 3.

357 *drenched in alcohol* Waters, p. 168.
    Pharnabazus and Tissaphernes These are Hellenized versions of the sa-
    traps' Persian names, Farnavaz and Cithrafarna.

358 *An early draft has survived* Thucydides writes of three treaties in rapid suc-
    cession (8 18, 8 37, and 8 58); it is much more likely that the first two
    were interim drafts. Persia's wish to take control of the Ionian *poleis* was
    explicit in the first text, but less obvious in the later ones.
    "All the territories and cities" Thuc 8 18.

359 *"said, in his mocking way"* Plut Alc 23 7–8. Stories about Alcibiades' sex
    life were legion and it is hard now to distinguish between fact and enter-
    taining fiction. But even if a given anecdote is unhistorical, the general
    direction of travel about his character is undeniable.

360 *"surrendered so completely"* Ibid., 24 5.
    he was homesick Ibid., 32 1.
    The Lioness on a Cheese-Grater Ar Lys 231–32. The meaning is obscure;
    perhaps the woman is crouching like a lioness over the man and by pel-
    vic movement to and fro imitating the motion of a grater. See "The Li-
    oness and the Cheesegrater," Cashman Kerr Prince. *Studi Italiani di*
    Filologia Classica, 4th series, 7:2 (2009): 149–75.

361 *"the splendour running in the blood"* Pind Nemea 3 40.

362 *"enacted by the* boulē *and the* demos*"* Ando Myst 96. The first recorded
    use of the phrase after the institution of the Five Thousand.

363 *"during the first period"* Thuc 8 97 2.

365 *"I will use a dagger"* Aes 2 76.

366 *"on the grounds that he was"* Xen Hell 1 4 20.

367 *to look for money and rations* So Plut Alc 35 3–4. But Diod 13 71 1 has
    Alcibiades sail to Clazomenae and Xen Hell 1 5 11 to help Thrasybulus
    at a siege of Phocaea. Money was the Athenians' greatest need and Al-
    cibiades had gone off on such expeditions before, so I follow Plutarch.
    an unthinking lowlife Plut Alc 35 4.

368 *the Athenians lost twenty-two ships* Hell Oxy 4 3.
    "who had won his confidence" Plut Alc 36 1–2.
    Alcibiades paid for some mercenaries Ibid., 36 3.
    "longs for him, but hates him" Ar Frogs 1425.

369 *"It is a sad day for the Greeks"* Xen Hell 1 6 7.

    a marble relief was commissioned of Hera The relief can be seen at the Acropolis Museum, Athens.

370 *"the greatest naval battle in history"* Diod 13 98 5.

    Socrates happened to be sitting Plato Apol 32b–c.

371 *discharge the vows to the gods* Diod 13 102 2.

    "the masses . . . from making peace" Arist Con 34 1. There is some doubt whether this episode should be attributed to Sparta's earlier peace offer after the Battle of Cyzicus.

372 *A horseman trotted* My account of Aegospotami draws on Xen Hell 2 1 22–29, Plut Alc 36 4–37 1–4, Nep Alc 8–9, and Diod 13 105–6.

    "they would incur the blame for any defeat" Diod 13 105 4.

373 *"We are the admirals now"* Xen Hell 2 1 26.

    thirty Athenian triremes set out I follow Diod 13 106, whose account is more plausible than that of Xen 2 1 27–28.

    "Lysander first asked him" Xen Hell 2 1 32.

    "A sound of wailing" Ibid., 2 2 3.

374 *"root and branch"* Paus 3 8 6.

375 *"They could not be sure of the loyalty"* Isoc 16 40.

    Critias had once boasted in a poem Plut Alc, 33 1.

    "Unless you cut off Alcibiades" Nep Alc 10.

376 *Plutarch reports that a* hetaira Plutarch reports the death of Alcibiades at Plut Alc 39. According to Ath 13 34, a monument was erected at the scene of his death and the emperor Hadrian had a statue of him placed on it. He also ordered yearly sacrifices in his honor.

21. Sparta's Turn

Xenophon's *Hellenica* is this chapter's main source, together with Plutarch's lives of Lysander and Agesilaus. The trial and death of Socrates are covered by Xenophon's and Plato's *Apologies,* also Plato's *Crito* and *Phaedo.*

380 *The city's economy had collapsed* The Greeks paid little attention to recording their economic history and modern scholars have to derive tentative generalizations from scrappy evidence. For the impact of the Peloponnesian War on Athens I am mainly indebted to Strauss, pp. 42–54. Many of the numbers I give in this section are at the right level of magnitude, but are necessarily estimates.

381 *the value of whose estate* Lys 19 45.

382 *"When I heard reports about Athens"* Isoc 17 4.

One afternoon in 404 Lysias For the persecution of Lysias and Polemarchus, as described here, see Lysias's own account given in a court speech towards the end of 403 against a member of the Thirty, Lys 12 3–17.

383 *"To Polemarchus, the Thirty"* Ibid., 12 17.

384 *a democracy, of all things, in Thessaly* Xen Hell 2 3 36.
"Some shrewd man first" Sex Emp 9 54 12–15.
Socrates was ordered Plato Apol 32c–d.
a respectable former military officer I follow W. James McCoy, "The Identity of Leon," *American Journal of Philology,* Summer 1975, pp. 187–99.
"If it's not crude of me" Plato Apol 32c–32d.

385 *"Here's to the lovely Critias!"* Xen Hell 2 3 56.

386 *"he had destroyed the power"* Delphes 3 1 50.

387 *an admiral at Aegospotami* For the account of Conon, the brief life by Cornelius Nepos is untrustworthy but helpful.

388 *Great King was content to allow the Ionians* Modern scholars suppose an agreement to this effect in 407, the Treaty of Boiotios.
the queen mother had other ideas The palace intrigues are reported in Plut Art 2–4 and Xen Ana 1 1 1–6.

389 *"And now it was midday"* Xen Ana 1 8 8–9.

390 *"Get out of the way! . . . Artaxerxes was wounded and unhorsed"* Plut Art 11 2–3.
imitate the nightingale's song Plut Age 21 4.

391 *"the person of the Great King"* Ibid., 15 1.

392 *"The Spartans . . . lost their supremacy"* Isoc 9 56.
"I don't know what effect my accusers" Plato Apol 17a. This section on the trial and death of Socrates is indebted to Robin Waterfield's introductory material to his and Hugh Tredinnick's translations in Xenophon, *Conversations of Socrates,* Penguin Classics, London, 1990.

393 *"This indictment and affidavit"* Diog Laer 2 5 40.
"a hooked nose" Plato Euth 2b.
whom Aristophanes attacked Ar fragments 117, 156 Kassel-Austin

395 *in a rather offhand manner* Xen Apol 1.
"Men of Athens, I respect you" Plato Apol 29d.

396 *When his wife complained* Diog Laer 2 5 35.
concoction of poison hemlock See Bloch, who argues that Plato's description of the effects of poisoning by poison hemlock is accurate.
" 'Really, my friends, what kind of behavior' " Plato Phaedo 117d–118a.

397 *a repentant demos* Diog Laer 2 5 43, Themist 20 239C.

398 *"King Artaxerxes believes it to be just"* Xen Hell 5 1 31.

 "in the most shameful and lawless way" Plut Age 23 1.

 "was not considered to be a man" Xen Hell 5 2 28.

399 *Gorgias, a one-man traveling university* See Plato Gorg.

 Plato has Socrates foretell Plato Phaed 278e–279a.

400 *"Who would desire a state of affairs"* Isoc 4 115–17.

 "And so far has our city distanced" Ibid., 4 50.

401 *"compel the Spartans"* IG 2² 43.

402 *membership rose to about seventy* Diod 15 30 2.

 It was the winter of 379 The conspiracy is described in detail in Xen Hell 5 4 2–12, Plut Pel 8–12, and Plut Moral *De genio Socratis* 25–34.

403 *a Spartan called Sphodrias* Sphodrias may have been bribed by the Thebans, a neat device for winning Athens over to their cause.

405 *He asked Epaminondas* Plut Age 28 1–2.

 an allied army of ten thousand hoplites Plut Pel 20 1.

 of about six thousand men Bury, p. 593.

407 *"It is now possible to take vengeance"* Xen Hell 6 4 19–20.

 "they ordered the women not to cry out" Ibid., 6 4 16.

408 *"Where are the Spartans now?"* Plut Sayings Spartans 23.

 a well-fortified capital city, Messene Paus 4 27 5–9.

409 *The bones of Aristomenes* Ibid., 4 32 3.

22. CHAERONEA—"FATAL TO LIBERTY"

Plutarch's lives of Demosthenes and Alexander the Great, speeches of Demosthenes and Aeschines, Diodorus Siculus, book 16, and Justin are the main sources.

410 *Chaeronea—"Fatal to Liberty"* John Milton, "To the Lady Margaret Ley," Sonnet 10, line 7.

 "I turned to Athens" Isoc 5 129.

411 *"is so intelligent a general"* Xen Hell 6 1 15.

 "foremost of our race" Isoc Letters 1 7.

 "Men of good counsel" Ibid., 9 14.

412 *"I have chosen to challenge you"* Isoc 5 128.

 "gardens of Midas" Herod 8 138 2.

413 *He would rather not accept favors* Arist Rhet 2 23 8.

414 *the usurper sent some distinguished hostages* Diod 16 2 2–3.

 the roving eye of Pelopidas Dio Chrys 49 5.

 Sacred Band, whose self-discipline Plut Amat 761b.

415 *helpless chicks in a nest* Xen Hell 7 5 10.

"In that case" Plut Mor 194c.

416 *"the people, discouraged by their experiences"* Aes 3 251.

major new building works Camp, pp. 144–60.

a young admirer had himself locked up Luc 15.

418 *"a complete end to war"* Xen Por 5 9.

419 *One of its best admirals was killed* Chabrias. He spent most of his career in the 380s and 370s before Leuctra fighting the Spartans.

the city had spent 1,000 talents Isoc 7 9.

420 *"the noble cause"* Plut Age 36 2.

"Everyone crowded round to catch a glimpse" Ibid., 36 4–5.

421 *"If I have accomplished any glorious act"* Plut Sayings Spartan Agesilaus.

422 *"sound judgment in his personal life"* Plato Prot 318e–319a.

"it soon showed the preceding government" Plato Ep 7 324b–d.

423 *opened a school of philosophy* The Academy remained in being until its destruction in war in the first century B.C. It was revived as a center for Neoplatonism in the fifth century A.D. and was finally closed down by the Byzantine emperor Justinian in A.D. 529.

who paid him memorial honors FGrH 115 F 294.

424 *"The safest general characterization"* Alfred North Whitehead, *Process and Reality* (New York: The Free Press, 1978), p. 39.

"Aristotle kicked against me" Diog Laer 5 1 2.

Hermeias conspired with Philip Dem 10 32.

"I have done nothing unworthy of philosophy" FGrH 124 F2.

an ode in Hermeias's memory Ath 15 51g.

425 *The schools of Athens* These achievements in higher education cemented the cultural dominance of Athens and more widely of Greece during the long centuries of the Roman Empire.

427 *he guessed at the dizzying prospect* Diod 16 1 5.

Archon or commander-in-chief for life I follow Green, *Alex,* p. 47; others place the appointment later in 344 or thereabouts.

428 *lied to and tricked* Just 8 3.

"made war by marriage" Athen 13 557b–e.

a good-looking boy Just 7 6.

No city was impregnable Green, *Alex,* p. 33.

shot an arrow that struck his right eye Just 7 6. In 1977 a richly furnished tomb was excavated at Vergina. The cremated remains of a bearded adult male were found, which were identified as those of Philip on the grounds that the right eye was seriously disfigured. More recently, this judgment has been contested.

429 *Other injuries* Dem 18 67.

 "an impenetrable hedge of spears" Homer Il 13 131ff.

430 *Philip established an engineering corps* Worthington, *Spear,* p. 37.

 taking a hot bath in camp Poly 4 2 1.

 "Some of them used to shave" Ath 6 206e–f.

431 *Philip admired the Theban Sacred Band* Plut Pel 18 5.

 nicknamed him Battalus Plutarch also suggests that in Attica the word was a slang term that signified "asshole." See Plut Dem 4.

432 *underwent a strict training regime* For Demosthenes' training, see Plut Ten Or 844d–f and Plut Dem 5.

433 *a quotation from the* Iliad Hom Il 2 517–19.

 what the Greeks came to call a Sacred War A "sacred war" was one connected in some way with the oracle at Delphi. There were three of them, this one being the third. The first two are not mentioned in this book.

 They even dug beneath the floor of the temple Diod 16 56 7.

 the treasury of the long-ago king of Lydia Ibid., 16 56 6.

434 *"I am retreating like the ram"* Pol 2 38 2.

 Onomarchus was carried out to sea Eus 8 14 33. There are different versions of Onomarchus's death. I prefer this one.

435 *Demosthenes succumbed to stage fright* Aes 2 34–35.

 A treaty was agreed It was called the Peace of Philocrates, after the Athenian lead negotiator.

436 *"When we recently made our way to Delphi"* Dem 19 65.

 "You wage war on Philip" Ibid., 4 40.

438 *"to go to war for the shadow at Delphi"* Dem Peace 5 25.

 He delivered a speech The Third Philippic. Philippic was the generic name given to a series of anti-Macedonian speeches made by Demosthenes.

439 *"overwhelmed by Persian gold"* Plut Dem 14 2.

 the marble column Phil Atthis FGrH 328 54.

440 *"From the spoils of Persians and Thebans"* Aes 3 116.

441 *"Nobody dared to mount"* Plut Dem 18 1.

 "Who wishes to speak?" Dem Steph 18 170.

442 *on August 4, 338, battle commenced* Plut Cam 19 5 states that the battle took place on 7 Metageitnion, for which August 4 is the most likely equivalent.

 The two armies were more or less equal Information on the Battle of Chaeronea is scarce and vague (see Diodorus, Polyaenus, and Plutarch). I follow Hammond's reconstruction, pp. 567–70. It is not at all clear what part if any the Greek cavalry played in the battle despite its numerical superiority.

444 *"Let's drive them back to Macedon!"* Pol 4 2 2.

"in the most shameful fashion" Plut Dem 20 2.

"Take me alive" Plut Mor 845f. Perhaps this story, if not invented by his enemies, has grown in the telling.

445 *"Demosthenes, son of Demosthenes"* Plut Dem 20 3.

"Fortune has cast you as Agamemnon" Diod 16 87 2.

"Perish any man who suspects" Plut Pel 18 5.

447 *"Philip to enter the Peloponnese"* Polyb 18 14 6–7.

"The bull has been garlanded" Diod 16 91 2.

448 *Philip repudiated Olympias* Justin 11 11 2.

"You scum, are you saying I am a bastard" Plut Alex 9 4–11 for this complete episode.

he suspected his son and Olympias In this account of the obscure dissensions at Philip's court I follow Green, *Alex,* p. 90ff.

kingdom without a successor There was another son, Philip Arridhaeus, but he had learning difficulties.

449 *lavish celebrations to mark the dynastic marriage* Green, *Alex,* pp. 102–10, for a detailed account of Philip's assassination.

"suitable for a god" Diod 16 92 5.

450 *Olympias's behavior after the event* Justin 9 7 1. This may be a distortion or, even, an invention.

a crown for Pausanias Plut Dem 22 1–2.

"a terrible warning" Arr 1 9 10.

451 *"If Alexander has really died"* Plut Phoc 22 5.

"but with greater honor" Plut Dem 27 5.

Wherever he went Demosthenes knew For the death of Demosthenes, see ibid., 29–30, and Plut Ten Or 846d–e 847a–b.

452 *"I was never convinced by your acting"* Plut Dem 29 2.

a contentious and divisive figure Polyb 18 14 1.

453 *"No, you were not wrong, men of Athens"* Dem 18 208.

23. AFTERWORD—"A GOD-FORSAKEN HOLE"

The main sources are Plutarch's life of Alexander and Waterfield's *Athens.*

454 *Xerxes had seen his invasion* Herod 7 42 2–43 2.

Almost the first thing Alexander did For the visit to Troy, the main account can be found at Arr 1 11 7–12 1. Also Plut Alex 15 4.

455 *Alexander tied him to his chariot* Curt 4 6 26–29.

just as Achilles had done Hom Il 22 395–404.

"What advantage shall I have over other men" Plut Alex 7 4.

457 *"Through a wise and salutary neglect"* Edmund Burke, *Speech on Conciliation with America* 1775.

459 *Athens was reduced* These impressionistic paragraphs describing the city's decline are indebted to Waterfield, pp. 279–314.

460 *"How often will the glory of your ancestors"* App 2 13 88.

"You cannot look upon Athens" Waterfield, p. 314. Michael of Chonae, Letters 8.

"We are all Greeks" Waterfield, p. 340.

Sources

478 *"a possession for all time"* Thuc 1 22.

INDEX

ANTHONY EVERITT, formerly a visiting professor in the visual and performing arts at Nottingham Trent University, has written extensively on European culture and is the author of *Cicero, Augustus, Hadrian and the Triumph of Rome,* and *The Rise of Rome.* He has served as secretary general of the Arts Council of Great Britain. Everitt lives near Colchester, England's first recorded town, founded by the Romans.